CAN EMERGING TECHNOLOGIES MAKE A DIFFERENCE IN DEVELOPMENT?

In this innovative and entirely original text, which has been thoughtfully edited to insure coherence and readability across disciplines, scientists and practitioners from around the world provide evidence of the opportunities for, and the challenges of, developing collaborative approaches to bringing advanced and emerging technology to poor communities in developing countries in a responsible and sustainable manner. This volume will stimulate and satisfy readers seeking to engage in a rich and challenging discussion, integrating many strands of social thought and physical science. For those also seeking to creatively engage in the great challenges of our times for the benefit of struggling farmers, sick children, and people literally living in the dark around the world, may this volume also spark imagination, inspire commitment, and provoke collaborative problem solving.

Rachel A. Parker is a Research Staff Member at the IDA Science and Technology Policy Institute. She received her PhD in Sociology from the University of California, Santa Barbara where she worked with Richard Appelbaum at the NSF-funded Nanoscale Science and Engineering Center, Center for Nanotechnology in Society; her research focuses on issues relating to emerging technologies and globalization.

Richard P. Appelbaum is MacArthur Chair in Global & International Studies and Sociology at the University of California, Santa Barbara. He is co-PI at the NSF-funded Nanoscale Science and Engineering Center, Center for Nanotechnology in Society, where he directs the interdisciplinary research group on globalization and nanotechnology.

CAN EMERGING TECHNOLOGIES MAKE A DIFFERENCE IN DEVELOPMENT?

Edited by

RACHEL A. PARKER
IDA Science and Technology Policy Institute

RICHARD P. APPELBAUM
University of California, Santa Barbara

Routledge
Taylor & Francis Group

NEW YORK AND LONDON

First published 2012
by Routledge
711 Third Avenue, New York, NY 10017

Simultaneously published in the UK
by Routledge
2 Park Square, Milton Park, Abingdon, Oxon OX14 4RN

Routledge is an imprint of the Taylor & Francis Group, an informa business

Library of Congress Cataloging in Publication Data
    Can emerging technologies make a difference in development/edited
    by Rachel A. Parker, Richard P. Appelbaum.
        p. cm.
    1. Technological innovations—Economic aspects. 2. Economic
    development. 3. Regional economic disparities. I. Parker, Rachel A.
    II. Appelbaum, Richard P.
    HC79.T4C366 2011
    338'.064—dc23   2011030235

ISBN: 978–0–415–88432–7 (hbk)
ISBN: 978–0–415–88433–4 (pbk)
ISBN: 978–0–203–13568–6 (ebk)

Typeset in Minion by Swales & Willis Ltd, Exeter, Devon

Printed and bound in the United States of America on acid-free paper
by Walsworth Publishing Company, Marceline, MO.

SUSTAINABLE
FORESTRY
INITIATIVE

Certified Sourcing
www.sfiprogram.org
SFI-00555
The SFI label applies to the text stock.

This book is dedicated to Karen Shapiro and James Walsh, whose enthusiasm and support for this and all of our projects is—and always has been—paramount.

CONTENTS

CONTRIBUTORS

Richard P. Appelbaum is MacArthur Chair in Global & International Studies and Sociology at the University of California, Santa Barbara. He is co-PI at the NSF-funded Nanoscale Science and Engineering Center, Center for Nanotechnology in Society, where he directs the interdisciplinary research group on globalization and nanotechnology. His recent books include *Behind the Label: Inequality in the Los Angeles Garment Industry* (with Edna Bonacich); *Rules and Networks: The Legal Culture of Global Business Transactions* (co-edited with William L.F. Felstiner and Volkmar Gessner); and *Towards a Critical Globalization Studies* (co-edited with William I. Robinson).

Rajiv G. Aricat is a doctoral student in the Wee Kim Wee School of Communication & Information, Nanyang Technological University, Singapore. Prior to that Rajiv worked in the editorial departments of various media organizations and web portals in New Delhi. Rajiv's Master of Philosophy (MPhil) dissertation from Jawaharlal Nehru University, New Delhi (2004) attempted a post-structuralist reading of a literary text in Malayalam. He is a recipient of the graduate award offered by Singapore Internet Research Centre, Singapore, under the program "Strengthening ICTD Research Capacity in Asia." Under this project, he currently works among temporary migrant workers from South Asia in Singapore to investigate how ICTs help them acculturate to their new culture.

Arul Chib is an assistant professor at Nanyang Technological University, and is the assistant director of the Singapore Internet Research Center. He examines the impact of development campaigns delivered via a range of innovative information and communication technologies (ICTD). The theoretical deliberation explicates the mechanisms underlying the process of impact; while taking a critical and evidence-based perspective regarding sustainability and scalability of technological interventions, as a counter to prevailing positivistic views. He has contributed to the conceptual progress of the discipline by proposing theoretical frameworks of analysis, including the ICT for healthcare development model, and the Technology-Community-Management model. Dr. Chib pursues action-oriented research with marginalized communities in cross-cultural contexts, particularly in resource-constrained environments. He has examined the impact of mobile phone usage in healthcare by community-based workers in the remote Himalayan regions of India and Nepal, and in tsunami-ravaged Aceh, Indonesia. He is currently conducting fieldwork on technology usage within healthcare systems in the rural settings of Arua, Uganda, Uttaradit, Thailand, and Xi'an, China.

Susan Cozzens is Associate Dean for Research in the Ivan Allen College of liberal arts at the Georgia Institute of Technology in Atlanta, Georgia. She has been active in science and innovation policy for over 25 years. She has served the US National Science Foundation as a policy analyst and later Director of the Office of Policy Support and member of the senior leadership team. She has consulted widely within the United States and around the world on science and innovation policy issues. She is past editor of *Research Evaluation* and *Science, Technology, & Human Values*, and senior consulting editor for *Science and Public Policy*. She has published over 50 articles and book chapters and authored or edited four books. Her current research is on equity, equality, and development, with a focus on science and innovation policies in developing countries.

Carlos Henrique de Brito Cruz graduated in Electrical Engineering from Instituto Tecnológico da Aeronáutica (ITA, 1978), received an MSc degree in Physics (1980) and a DSc degree in Physics (1983), both from the "Gleb Wataghin" Physics Institute at the State University at Campinas (Unicamp). Brito Cruz has been the Vice-President of the Brazilian Physics Society (SBF). He served as a member of the International Advisory Committee of the Optical Society of America (OSA) and has served as the Director of the Physics Institute at Unicamp where he has also been the Dean of Research. From 1996 to 2002 he has served as the President of the Foundation for the Support of Research in the State of São Paulo, Fapesp. From 2002 to 2005 he was the Rector of The State University of Campinas, Unicamp. Since 2005 Brito Cruz is the President of the Technology and Competitiveness Council of the São Paulo Federation of Industry (FIESP). In 2010 he was a member of the 12-member special committee formed by the Inter Academy Council, at the request of the UN Secretary General, to review the procedures of the IPCC. Since 2005 he has served as the Scientific Director at the São Paulo Research Foundation, FAPESP, one of the main research funding agencies in Brazil, where he organized research programs in Bioenergy and Global Climate Change. Brito Cruz is a member of the Brazilian Academy of Sciences.

Guillermo Foladori is an anthropologist with a PhD in Economics. He has worked as a professor in universities in Mexico, Honduras, Nicaragua, Uruguay, and Brazil, and had been visiting fellow at the Consortium for Science Policy and Outcomes (USA) and at the Federal University of Paraná (Brazil); he is currently teaching at the Doctoral Program on Development Studies at the Autonomous University of Zacatecas, Mexico, where he coordinates, with Noela Invernizzi, the Latin American Nanotechnology and Society Network (ReLANS). He has also been adviser for international organizations and several NGOs. He has co-authored with Noela Invernizzi *Nanotecnologías Disruptivas* and *Nanotecnología, Agricultura y Alimentación*.

Antje Grobe is Member of the Board of the Switzerland based Risk Dialogue Foundation. For more than 15 years she has facilitated stakeholder dialogues and citizen participation exercises in Europe on behalf of governmental bodies, academia, industry and civil society organizations. At the Universities of St. Gallen (Switzerland) and Stuttgart

(Germany) she lectures on Dialogue Management and leads several research projects on risk assessment and risk perception with a main emphasis on nanotechnologies. She also serves as an expert for the European Commission and accompanies the German Government's NanoKommission.

Barbara Herr Harthorn is Associate Professor of Feminist Studies, Anthropology & Sociology and Director of the Nanoscale Science and Engineering Center: Center for Nanotechnology in Society at the University of California, Santa Barbara. In CNS-UCSB she leads an interdisciplinary group studying nanotechnology risk perception, and she heads a similar group in the NSF/EPA-funded UC Center for Environmental Implications of Nanotechnology at UCLA. Her background in medical and psychological anthropology and social psychology frames her work on gender, race, and inequality.

Thembela Hillie is a MIT Sloan Fellow in Innovation and Global Leadership class of 2012. He holds a PhD in Solid State Physics and has experience in semiconductor physics and surface science at the nanoscale, where his current projects include surface alloys, quantum dots, photo catalytic nano-composites and rare earth doped nano-phosphors. He has served on the South African Nanotechnology initiative (SANi) as Vice-Chairperson from September 2005 to 2008, and presently serves on the National Nanotechnology Advisor Board (NAB) which will oversee and guide the implementation process of the nanotechnology strategy for the ultimate realization of its objectives. He is a member of the World Economic Forum council on emerging technologies, and was a South African National Contact Point for nanotechnology in the India–Brazil–South Africa trilateral cooperation agreement and in South Korea bilateral agreement.

Mbhuti Hlophe is Senior Lecturer in Chemistry at the North-West University (Mafikeng Campus) in South Africa. He holds an MSc degree in Advanced Analytical Chemistry from the University of Bristol in the United Kingdom and a PhD from the North-West University. Dr. Hlophe conducts water research, and is particularly interested in water service provision in rural areas. He developed a nanomembrane process for the purification of brackish groundwater in a rural village in North West Province of South Africa and subsequently set up a pilot water purification plant which supplies about 1,000 school pupils and their teachers with potable water.

Can Huang is a research fellow at United Nations University-MERIT and Maastricht University, the Netherlands. He holds a PhD in Industrial Management from University of Aveiro, Portugal, an MS in Engineering and a BA in Economics from Renmin University of China, Beijing, China. His research interests include economics of innovation and intellectual property rights and science and technology policy analysis. He is the author of *China: Building an Innovative Economy*, and is a contributor to the recently published OECD Review of Innovation Policy China. He has been leading the efforts in UNU-MERIT for two EU FP7 projects on nanotechnology: ObservatoryNano and ICPCNanoNet.

Noela Invernizzi is an anthropologist, and holds a PhD in Science and Technology Policy. She currently works at the Education Faculty of the Federal University of Parana, Brazil. For several years she had researched the impacts of industrial innovation on workforce skills and employment conditions. Her current research addresses the social implications of nanotechnology for development in Latin America with a particular focus on labor, poverty and inequality issues. Together with Guillermo Foladori, she coordinates the Latin America Nanotechnology and Society Network (ReLANS).

Dave Irvine Halliday received his PhD from the University of Aberdeen, Scotland; he is currently LUTW University Professor at the University of Calgary, where he focuses on Solid State Lighting, Renewable Energy, Fiber Optic Sensors and Communications, and Biophotonics (1983–Present). He is co-founder of Light Up the World (1997), as well as Visionary Lighting & Energy (VLE) in Hyderabad, India (2009). His honors and awards include Saatchi and Saatchi Laureate (2003), Tech Museum Laureate (2002) and Rolex Laureate (2002), and the Meritorious Service Medal (MSM) from Canada (2005).

Mark X. Jacobs serves as Senior Mediator and Program Manager at Meridian Institute, a US-based non-profit organization that designs and facilitates collaborative processes that help diverse parties identify critical issues, build relationships and trust, construct innovative solutions, and implement durable decisions. His work focuses primarily on addressing challenges at the intersection of environment, agriculture, and energy. Prior to joining Meridian in 2008, he worked on environmental policy for more than ten years, as a consensus and coalition builder in faith communities, as an advocate and organizer, and as a university instructor. He has an MA in International Relations and a Graduate Certificate in Development Studies from Yale University, as well as a BA in Sociology from the University of California at Santa Cruz.

Scott M. Lacy is founder and Executive Director of African Sky, Inc., a non-profit organization that serves hard-working farm families in rural Mali, West Africa. He is also a professor of anthropology at Fairfield University in Connecticut. He has worked in rural Mali since 1994 when he developed a high-protein maize project as a Peace Corps volunteer. With research interests in food production, community-based development, rural poverty and hunger, and cross-cultural knowledge production, he collaborates with farmers, plant breeders, engineers, teachers, and others to apply anthropology as a tool for social transformation.

David Lewis is Professor of Social Policy and Development at the London School of Economics. A social anthropologist by training, he has worked on development theory and policy, specializing in development policy issues in South Asia, with a particular focus on Bangladesh, and on the roles of non-governmental organizations and civil society in development. He is co-author (with Katy Gardner) of *Anthropology, Development and the Postmodern Challenge*; *The Management of Non-Governmental Development Organizations*; and (co-authored with Nazneen Kanji)

Non-Governmental Organizations and Development, and *Bangladesh: Politics, Economy and Civil Society*. He has regularly carried out fieldwork in Bangladesh since 1986, and has served as a consultant to a wide range of governmental and non-governmental development organizations including the UK Department for International Development (DFID), the Swedish International Development Cooperation Agency (SIDA), the International Food Policy Research Institute (IFPRI), and Oxfam Great Britain.

Andrew D. Maynard is Director of the University of Michigan Risk Science Center, and is the Charles and Rita Gelman Risk Science Professor at the University of Michigan School of Public Health. He is a leading authority on the responsible development and use of emerging technologies, and on innovative approaches to addressing new risks. An author of over 100 scientific papers, reports, and articles, he appears frequently in print and on television and radio, and often uses web-based media to engage with a broad audience on science, technology, and society. His current interests include exploring how integrative approaches to risk can support sustainable development in an increasingly complex, interconnected, and resource-constrained world.

Moses Kizza Musaazi has a PhD from The Imperial College of Science, Technology and Medicine, University of London. His specializations are in the fields of Electrical Engineering (Control Systems and Power Systems) and Appropriate Technology. He is a Makerere University lecturer and carries out research and development in Appropriate Technologies (AT) and has developed several AT for the betterment of mankind, focusing especially on the poor; he serves as the Team Leader of the Presidential Initiative to Support Appropriate Technologies (PISAT). He is an Ashoka Fellow. He is MD of Technology for Tomorrow Ltd. He has had consultancies with UN Habitat and UNICEF to provide low-cost housing and safe water, Meridian Institute (funded by the Bill and Melinda Gates Foundation) to reduce post-harvest losses for peasant African farmers and financial support from the Ford and Rockefeller Foundations to improve learning environment by installing AT in schools.

Todd M. Osman became Executive Director of the Material Research Society in September 2008, an international organization of 16,000 materials researchers from academia, industry, and government and a recognized leader in promoting the advancement of interdisciplinary materials research to improve the quality of life. As Executive Director, he has promoted the creation of new programs to encourage materials solutions to critical societal needs, to advance STEM (Science, Technology, Engineering and Mathematics) education and to engage all demographics and geographic regions in the scientific enterprise. He received his BS, MS, and PhD degrees in Materials Science and Engineering from Case Western Reserve University and has authored over 25 articles on topics including commercial and social impact of nanomaterials, materials for nuclear power, computational materials science and engineering, product development and mechanical metallurgy.

Rachel A. Parker is a Research Staff Member at the IDA Science and Technology Policy Institute. She received her PhD in Sociology from the University of California, Santa

Barbara where she worked with Richard Appelbaum at the NSF-funded Nanoscale Science and Engineering Center, Center for Nanotechnology in Society; her research focuses on issues relating to emerging technologies and globalization. Her dissertation investigated nanotechnology policies in the United States and China; while at the CNS-UCSB, she also worked on issues related to equitable development of nanotechnologies. She now works on program evaluation and research capacity building. She has an MSc from the London School of Economics in the Management of Non-Governmental Organizations and a BA in Sociology from Brandeis University in Waltham, MA.

Rex Raimond is a Senior Mediator and Program Manager with Meridian Institute in Dillon, Colorado, where he designs, manages, and facilitates collaborative processes aimed at helping people and organizations make informed decisions and solve some of society's most complex problems. He has focused much of the past decade on issues regarding international development, agriculture, and innovation, serving as project co-director for the Innovations for Agricultural Value Chains in Africa project (funded by the Bill & Melinda Gates Foundation), and generating innovative post-harvest technology concepts to benefit smallholder farmers. He is currently exploring options for a system to facilitate the successful commercialization of post-harvest technologies in sub-Saharan Africa. He has also been involved with the International Dialogue on Responsible Nanotechnology Research and Development. Until his relocation to the United States, in 1999, Mr. Raimond practiced environmental law and land-use law in the Netherlands, and previously worked with the UNDP's Africa 2000 Network in Zimbabwe.

Ortwin Renn serves as full professor and Chair of Environmental Sociology and Technology Assessment at Stuttgart University (Germany), where he directs the Interdisciplinary Research Unit for Risk Governance and Sustainable Technology Development (ZIRN) at Stuttgart University and the non-profit company DIALOGIK, a research institute for the investigation of communication and participation processes in environmental policy-making. He has a doctoral degree in sociology and social psychology from the University of Cologne, and has had teaching and research positions at the Juelich Nuclear Research Center, Clark University (Worcester, USA), the Swiss Institute of Technology (Zurich) and the Center of Technology Assessment (Stuttgart). He has served as the Chair of the State Commission for Sustainable Development (German State of Baden-Württemberg). His research focuses primarily on risk governance, political participation, and technology assessment. He has published more than 30 books and 250 articles, most prominently the monograph *Risk Governance* (London: Earthscan, 2008).

Mihail C. Roco is Senior Advisor for Nanotechnology at the National Science Foundation and a key architect of the National Nanotechnology Initiative. Prior to joining the NSF he was Professor of Mechanical and Chemical Engineering at the University of Kentucky. He is the founding Chair of the US National Science and Technology Council's Subcommittee on Nanoscale Science, Engineering and Technology (NSET). His research is concerned with multiphase systems, visualization techniques, computer simulations, nanoparticles and nanosystems. He is credited with 13 patents, and has contributed over 200 archival articles and 20 books, including *Managing Nano-Bio-Info-Cognition Innovations, Mapping Nanotechnology Knowledge and Innovation: Global and Longitudinal Patent and Literature Analysis,* and *Nanotechnology Research Directions for Societal Needs in 2020.* He is editor-in-chief of the *Journal of Nanoparticle Research,* and has been a member of international research councils including the International Risk Governance Council in Geneva. He is a corresponding member of the Swiss Academy of Engineering Sciences, a Fellow of AIChE, Fellow of ASME, Fellow of the Institute of Physics, and Doctor Honoris Causa of the Polytechnic University Bucharest.

Jennifer Rogers is an Assistant Professor of Sociology at Long Island University, CW Post. She received her PhD in Sociology from the University of California, Santa Barbara (UCSB). Her areas of research include intersections of race, class, and gender, environment and technology, and globalization. Her dissertation analyzes maize in Mexico, free trade, bioengineering, gender, and indigenous cultures. As a postdoctoral scholar at the NSF-funded Nanoscale Science and Engineering Center, Center for Nanotechnology in Society, at UCSB from 2008 to 2010, she studied public perceptions of nanotechnology and gender.

Christine Shearer is currently a postdoctoral scholar at the NSF-funded Nanoscale Science and Engineering Center, Center for Nanotechnology in Society, at the University of California, Santa Barbara, where she received a PhD in Sociology. Her research involves science and technology policy issues, particularly nanotechnologies, energy, and climate change. She is author of the book *Kivalina: A Climate Change Story* (Haymarket, 2011).

Chen Wang currently serves as the Director of the National Center for Nanoscience and Technology (NCNST) of China. From 1994 to 1995, he was a professor in the Department of Physics, Central China Normal University. He joined the faculty of the Institute of Chemistry, Chinese Academy of Sciences, in 1995. Prior to joining the NCNST he was the Director of the Laboratory for Molecular Nanostructures and Nanotechnology at the Institute of Chemistry. He received his BSc from the University of Science and Technology of China (1986) and his PhD in Physics from the University of Virginia (1992). He is also an adjunct Professor in the Department of Chemistry at Peking University, Jilin University, and Central China Normal University. He has been a Visiting Scholar at the University of California, Berkeley (2002–3). He and his colleagues have worked on the applications of scanning probe microscopy in surface characterizations and fabrications. His recent studies revealed several novel effects in organic and biomolecular self-assembling. He has published over 200 peer-reviewed papers in international journals.

Amy Zader completed her PhD in the Department of Geography at the University of Colorado, Boulder. Her research investigates the cultural and environmental geography of China through the study of agro-food systems after conducting dissertation research on the production and consumption of high quality rice from

China's northeast region. Amy holds an MA in Human Ecology from College of the Atlantic in Bar Harbor, ME and a BA in Political Science and Environmental Studies from Allegheny College in Meadville, PA. She has served as an environmental education Peace Corps Volunteer in Sichuan, China and conducted master's research on China's environmental movement.

FOREWORD
Mark X. Jacobs and Rex Raimond

Rarely are technical advances adapted to address the daily challenges of poor people in developing countries: the farmer who cannot afford to send his daughter to school because his produce spoils on the way to market. The pregnant woman in a remote village without access to basic medical diagnostic tools. The child living in a sprawling urban shantytown drinking polluted water. The villager whose world shrinks when darkness falls because there is no electricity or fuel for light.

The world is not lacking capacity for technical innovation. Large-scale investments in science and technology by corporations and governments yield a constant stream of innovations. High-income populations around the world voraciously consume each new generation of products that provide greater speed, ease, and comfort in daily life. From ever faster and smaller communications and entertainment devices to capacity-enhancing pharmaceuticals and diagnostic tools for rare conditions, scientific discoveries and technical advances are adapted rapidly for products geared to high-income populations.

Securing an equitable and sustainable future demands rapid technological innovation in a wide range of sectors. Neither traditional production systems nor conventional industrial systems today are able to sustainably provide sufficient food, fiber, clean water, shelter, and health care for the current human population over the long term. And population is expected to continue to grow rapidly through mid-century. Delivering climate-friendly energy, sustainable high-yield agriculture, low-cost high quality health care, and universal access to clean water on a global scale are all vital for global security, sustainability, and equity, and all will require both technical advances and changes in social structures.

Advanced and emerging technologies—such as nanotechnology, biotechnology, and wireless communications—offer new and compelling opportunities to address longstanding and widespread development challenges, such as universal access to clean drinking water, early diagnosis and treatment of disease, delivery of electricity to remote areas, and sustainably increasing agricultural yields on marginal lands. Yet, the potential of these new technologies to improve conditions and increase opportunities for poor communities in developing countries may not be realized. Social, economic, political, and cultural barriers have prevented application and adaptation of technical advances to problems faced by poor communities. And, even when new technologies are appropriately adapted, poor people often lack access to them.

What is the potential for emerging and advanced technologies to improve the lives of struggling farmers in sub-Saharan Africa, children growing up in shantytowns in

South Asia, remote populations of tribal peoples in the Amazon basin? How might that potential be realized? What are the obstacles, and how can they be overcome?

In order to assess the potential and understand the obstacles, there are a number of critical questions that must be addressed. What, if anything, is different about emerging technologies, and how might that affect their adaptation for and distribution to poor communities? Which technologies might enable more control by poor communities, and which less? Which technologies might increase, or even potentially universalize, access to vital goods and services, and which might increase inequalities? Will the fact that some emerging economies—and some of the poorest developing countries—are investing in some of these emerging areas of science and technology and producing innovations improve the likelihood that they will be applied to benefit poor communities? What specific interventions may help secure benefits to poor communities?

In addition to ensuring broad access to the benefits of advanced technologies, exposure of poor communities to harm as a result of insufficiently tested technology must be prevented. For example, nanotechnology has some known new risks, while much is still unknown. Many governance systems, particularly in emerging economies, are not well set up to understand and manage such risks. What strategies might be employed to rapidly increase governance capacity? What is the role of the private sector, national governments, and international organizations?

Answering these questions—and identifying and pursuing opportunities to leverage emerging and advanced technology for the benefit of poor people in developing countries—requires collaboration across numerous disciplinary and cultural boundaries. Working across these boundaries means overcoming intellectual, institutional, and geographical obstacles.

This volume represents one effort to overcome these obstacles and cross these boundaries. The Center for Nanotechnology and Society at the University of California, Santa Barbara, in collaboration with the Woodrow Wilson International Center for Scholars and Meridian Institute, brought together over 80 individuals with diverse academic backgrounds and areas of technical expertise from both the South and North for three days of dialogue about how emerging and advanced technologies might benefit poor communities in developing countries.

Researchers and engineers in nanotechnology, biotechnology, and materials sciences came together with social scientists and specialists in development, governance and agriculture to discuss four critical sectors: agriculture, energy, health, and water. Through presentations and discussions, they sought to address such issues as:

- characteristics of emerging technologies that support their use to overcome development challenges and that cause concern in a development context;
- potential unintended consequences of the commercialization of products containing or based on emerging technologies in developing countries;
- drivers of development and commercialization of these technologies and the ways in which development objectives might become stronger drivers of technological development and delivery;

- linking research and development of new technologies to the needs of poor communities in developing countries;
- social and cultural concerns raised by use of emerging technologies in a developing country context, and how they might be addressed; and
- governance issues raised by use of emerging technologies in a developing country context (e.g. risk assessment, risk management, oversight, intellectual property) and the kinds of corporate, institutional, and public policies and practices needed to advance responsible and sustainable commercialization of these technologies.

In large plenary and small break-out sessions, social and physical scientists, academics, and practitioners shared perspectives and began to develop a common understanding of the issues and challenges involved in ensuring equitable access to the benefits of emerging technologies. Many participants noted that this event was their first opportunity for true dialogue among such diverse perspectives. (Indeed, too often, even when diverse groups of academics gather at a conference, they listen to one another's papers and presentations but meeting formats preclude a sustained discussion in which many points of view are shared, probed, challenged, and affirmed.) Such dialogue can be the foundation of collaborative problem-solving across the many intellectual, social, and cultural divides implicated in ensuring that advanced technologies benefit poor communities.

Participants cautioned that while some dynamics and challenges may be common to many circumstances, and it is important to understand and address macro patterns and challenges at a macro level, each combination of technology and social setting represents a unique situation. Differences observed by participants included:

- A wide range of government roles in advancing technology and directing its application among the United States, Europe, China, and Africa.
- Different approaches of communities, organizations, and policy-makers in making choices between addressing current needs with immediate solutions and investing resources in larger-scale community-wide solutions (e.g. providing lighting in remote villages with household-scale solar panels versus building a biomass-to-electricity plant to power the community).
- Varying attitudes towards the appropriate role of science and technology in addressing international development challenges in the context of differing social, cultural, and economic needs.
- Differences in risk tolerance and where to strike a balance between precautionary testing and promoting innovations.

In addition to observing differences across contexts and communities, some more universal values and issues were raised and discussed, including:

- The requirement to do no harm—to people, the environment, and existing areas of social and economic progress.

- How anticipatory thinking—consideration of potential scenarios of results of technologies when they are brought to scale—might be institutionalized.
- The need for grassroots discourses and participation to create an open dialogue, particularly where there are already existing power dynamics and imbalances.
- The need to consider both social and technological approaches when dealing with development related problems affecting poor communities to avoid simplistic "techno fixes."
- The need for "proof of concept" case examples to create a practical vehicle for a broad range of stakeholders to grapple with the potential contributions and detractions of applying emerging technologies to development challenges (e.g. applications to curb the spread of tropical diseases transferred by mosquitoes).
- How intellectual property can be protected to encourage innovation while making products widely accessible.

The identification of critical areas of difference and commonality was a valuable intellectual outcome of the meeting. In addition to intellectual outcomes, the organizers of the event sought to support networking and build a foundation for future collaboration among participants. The conversations held at the 2009 conference in Washington have already yielded increased understanding and relationship building among people who otherwise might not have had contact with one another. Participants expressed enthusiasm for continuing the dialogue with one another and for including many others in the discussion, in various settings. We are hopeful that the relationships established and the conversations that unfold will yield fruitful collaborations. Though leveraging technological advancement for the benefit of poor communities in developing countries requires confronting global economic and political forces, it only can be accomplished through the collaboration of specific individuals and the institutions they represent.

Two exciting models of collaboration across intellectual and social divides were described by participants. Hubs for innovation and design that facilitate interaction and promote collaboration among scientists, technical innovators, and practitioners to address social challenges have been established in some countries. Another example is the "Innovations for Agricultural Value Chains in Africa" project of the Meridian Institute, supported by the Bill & Melinda Gates Foundation, which took a range of technology, engineering, and design specialists from all over the world on a field trip to Africa to meet smallholder farmers and learn about the challenges they face in bringing their maize, cassava, and milk to market. While in the field, these specialists developed basic concepts for innovations to leverage both conventional and advanced technologies to address farmers' problems. Several of these concepts are now in the process of being developed and prototyped for commercial-scale production. Both of these models—bringing diverse specialists in developing countries together at centers for innovation to address well-understood problems, and bringing leading technical experts directly to the field to observe the challenges faced by poor communities—hold much promise for leveraging the extraordinary flow of technical innovations to benefit those who most need assistance in meeting their basic needs.

In this volume, scientists and practitioners from around the world provide evidence of the opportunities for, and the challenges of, developing collaborative approaches to bringing advanced and emerging technology to poor communities in developing countries in a responsible and sustainable manner. This volume will stimulate and satisfy readers seeking to engage a rich and challenging discussion, integrating many strands of social thought and physical science. For those also seeking to creatively engage the great challenges of our times for the benefit of struggling farmers, sick children, and people literally living in the dark around the world, may this volume also spark imagination, inspire commitment, and provoke collaborative problem-solving.

PREFACE

Rachel A. Parker and Richard P. Appelbaum

Emerging technologies offer solutions for some of the world's most critical challenges: developing novel sources of clean and inexpensive energy; increasing the supply of potable water by utilizing advanced filtration techniques; enhancing food security through the engineering of new crops and fertilizers; improving health by means of advanced methods for disease diagnosis and targeted drug delivery. The need for such technological advances are greatest in the global South, where the problems are most severe and the resources for dealing with them are scarce.

Nanotechnology, biotechnology, information and communication technologies are among the emerging technologies that have great potential, yet they are not without controversy. Will they deliver on their promise—or will potential drawbacks outweigh their proffered benefits? How should they be best provided—through large-scale government programs, or through grassroots efforts? Given that such technologies are being developed in a handful of countries in the global North, how can they be made available to communities in the global South in a way that involves authentic and effective collaboration among all parties involved: the scientists and engineers who developed the technologies, the companies and nongovernmental organizations that provide them, the potential adoptees, whether they be national governments, village councils, or civil society organizations? Most broadly, how can emerging technologies contribute to more equitable and sustainable development?

Addressing such issues is itself a challenge, since it requires bridging the gap—more often a chasm—between the social sciences on the one hand, and science and engineering on the other. Yet that is exactly what this volume seeks to accomplish. The contributions are the result of a conference, optimistically entitled *Emerging Technologies/Emerging Economies: Prospects for Equitable Development* that was hosted at the Woodrow Wilson International Center for Scholars in Washington, DC, in November 2009. Some 85 stakeholders came together from different communities that all too often fail to communicate with one another: social scientists from diverse disciplines, scientists and engineers, public officials, private sector entrepreneurs, and community activists. They came from the United States, Europe, and Japan; three of the largest emerging economies (China, India, and Brazil); and other African and Latin American countries. The conference was a joint effort between the University of California, Santa Barbara (the NSF-funded Center for Nanotechnology in Society, College of Engineering, Institute for Energy Efficiency, and Social Science Division), Rice University's Center for Biological and Environmental Nanotechnology, and the Wilson Center. It was structured so as to foster an open exchange of ideas and experiences between the research community and solution-oriented on-the-ground actors. Discussion and dialogue were facilitated by the Meridian Institute, an organization that specializes in North/South dialogue, with the goal of fostering discussions among participants that would continue in the future.

The primary aim of this volume is to broaden that discussion beyond any one set of stakeholders or community. Scholars, students, and activists interested in how best to use emerging technologies to foster more equitable and sustainable development will find in its chapters a variety of concrete approaches, as well differing (and sometimes conflicting) opinions on what is best. The chapters in this book have been written with the aim of broadening the dialogue across an increasingly diverse set of stakeholders in the social sciences, science and engineering, and non-profit communities. While some are authored by scientists and engineers, all are framed in the context of the social sciences. We have sought to provide a coherent framework, one that will prove useful for a wide range of courses focused on issues of globalization, global poverty, development, and the potential role of science and technology in the global South.

ACKNOWLEDGMENTS

This volume—and perhaps most importantly—the *Emerging Technologies/Emerging Economies* conference would not have been possible without the insight, and dedication of our colleagues and the staff at the University of California, Santa Barbara Center for Nanotechnology in Society who helped to shape and support both the conference agenda, and the completion of this manuscript. Special thanks to Bruce Bimber, Roy Smith, and, sadly, the late Bill Freudenberg who were all paramount to the success of these endeavors. Research assistance was provided along the way by Alexis Ostrowski, Meredith Conroy, Summer Gray, Erica Lively, Nastassja Lewinski, and Jesse Farrell. Additionally, a very special debt of gratitude beyond measure is due to Tom Kalil for the support he has provided to the CNS in general—but particularly—to this project.

At the Woodrow Wilson International Center for Scholars, special thanks are due to Julia Moore, who shepherded our fledgling project to the Project on Emerging Nanotechnologies before heading to her new role at Pew Research. Julia facilitated an introduction to Dave Rajeski, Kent Hughes, and importantly, to Jennifer Turner, who graciously agreed to host *Emerging Technolgies/Emerging Economies* in Washington, DC, November 4–6, 2009. Peter Marsters, as well as other Woodrow Wilson Center staff Todd Kuiken, Patrick Polischuk, and Danielle Altman are also owed our debt of gratitude for their efforts in making this project a success. Kerri Wright Platais and Ann Olsen from the Meridian Institute skillfully aided in the facilitation of the break-out groups along with Rex Raimond and Mark Jacobs, who contributed to this volume in ways far beyond the writing of the foreword.

We are extremely grateful for the faith—and most of all—patience of our editor at Routledge, Steve Rutter, in his encouragement of this volume. The additional assistance provided by Leah Babb-Rosenfeld also at Routledge and to Serena Leigh Krombach, Alan Anderson, and Peter Burks for helping with portions of this volume is also greatly appreciated. We would also like to thank the reviewers of the project: Cong Cao of the University of Nottingham; Dick Kawooya of University of Wisconsin, Milwaukee; Samuel Cohn of Texas A&M University; Laura Hosman of Illinois Institute of Technology; Jan Nederveen Pieterse of University of California, Santa Barbara; Franklin Goza of Bowling Green State University; Peter Chua of San Jose State University; and Sara Schoonmaker of University of Redlands.

Portions of this book are based in part upon work supported by the National Science Foundation under Cooperative Agreement No. 0531184. Any opinions, findings, and conclusions or recommendations expressed in this material are those of the authors and do not necessarily reflect the views of the National Science Foundation or the Center for Nanotechnology in Society.

1.
INTRODUCTION
The Promise and Perils of High-Tech Approaches to Development
Rachel A. Parker and Richard P. Appelbaum

During the next 30 years, the world's population is projected to increase by nearly half, to 9.5 billion people. Almost all of that increase will be in the world's poorest countries, countries that already suffer from a host of challenges and are poorly equipped to deal with them. The current period of rapid globalization, which began in the 1970s, has lifted hundreds of millions of people out of poverty; its effects have been highly unequally distributed. In 2005, the most recent date for which World Bank (2010) data are available, 1.4 billion people—more than a quarter of the population in the developing world—struggled to survive on less than $1.25 a day, the official World Bank poverty line. Global inequality has increased in recent decades—not only between countries, but within countries as well.

Existing approaches to fostering economic growth—based on the premise that a rising tide will lift all boats—are being challenged from all quarters. The United Nations, under the urging of Columbia University economist Jeffrey Sachs, has called for a commitment to ending global poverty in all its facets. The Millennium Development Project, which Sachs directed from 2002 to 2006, set eight broad Millennium Development Goals for 2015, the first one of which calls for the eradication of extreme hunger and poverty. Among the recommended ways to achieve these goals, high-income countries are urged to increase their "official development assistance" to poor countries from 0.25 percent of their GDP (in 2003) to 0.7 percent by 2015 (UN Millennium Project, 2005: 127).[1] Congress created the Millennium Challenge Corporation (MCC) in 2004 to spearhead this effort; as of 2011 it had allocated some $7.5 billion for various forms of poverty reduction in dozens of countries (MCC, 2011).

Former World Bank economist William Easterly (2007) strongly disagrees; he criticizes foreign aid as a modern version of the "White Man's Burden" (the provocative title of his popular book), almost always doomed to failure. As Easterly sees it (and his reasoning is backed up with econometric analysis as well as anecdotal evidence), most foreign assistance—whether bilateral or though international institutions—winds up funding ill-conceived projects at best, and, at worst, sustaining the power of kleptocratic dictators who siphon off most of the funds. In such diverse areas as malaria control, hunger and nutrition, soil fertility, and potable water, technical fixes have been recommended for Africa for at least 70 years—with little evidence of success, at least when administered in a top-down fashion (Easterly, 2009: Table 3). Such an approach as exemplified in the MDGs, according to Easterly, will only succeed in magnifying the errors of the past. He explains:

> Most importantly, what the history of technology tells us is that … top-down development programs simply don't work. In fact, the principal beneficiaries of Western largesse today—African autocrats and dysfunctional regimes—are themselves the main obstacles to development. If there's anything that "must be done" to spur future development, it's to create the conditions necessary to empower the ordinary individuals who will create new and unforeseen technologies out of old ones. There's a Thomas Edison born every minute. We just have to help them turn the lights on.
>
> (Easterly, 2010)

Dambisa Moyo (2009), a Zambian-born economist formerly with Goldman Sachs, goes even further, calling for the replacement of "dead aid" (the provocative title of her popular book) by private enterprise. Africa in particular has suffered grievously as a result of three-quarters of a century of foreign assistance; turn off the spigot, she controversially argues, suggesting that low- and middle-income countries welcome private investors, whose business acumen is more likely to produce results than government bureaucrats. Similarly, in her book exploring the impact of the entire aid system in Africa, Carol Lancaster questions the effectiveness of technical assistance in development, which she explains was resultant of structural adjustment programs. Lancaster explains that adjustment programs limited a government's potential expenditure on key services which, in effect, forced many African governments to become overly reliant on expatriate support to fill the gaps. Ultimately, she explains that

> technical assistance aimed at strengthening African institutions has over the past several decades been among the least effective of aid-funded interventions. But more troubling, it appears in some cases to have become counterproductive—too much aid has been combined with too little understanding of the institutional problems it was intended to address.
>
> (Lancaster, 1999: 59)

In contrast to Easterly, the Economic and Social Council of the United Nations' Commission on Science and Technology for Development states that "access to information and sharing and creation of knowledge contributes significantly to strengthening economic, social and cultural development, thus helping all countries to reach the internationally agreed development goals and objectives, including the Millennium Development Goals" (UNCTAD, 2008). Problems related to clean water, energy shortages, limited access to such basic health care as diagnostic and treatment technologies, and food insecurity continue to plague the developing world. As the 2015 deadline for reaching the Millennium Development Goals fast approaches, it is perhaps more important than ever to ask how technology can contribute to achieving more equitable—and responsible—development.

Between state-sponsored solutions and private enterprise lies civil society, which includes the ever-expanding world of nongovernmental organizations (NGOs) and private philanthropic organizations that play an increasingly important global role in international development. By some estimates there are as many as 100,000 NGOs operating internationally,[2] and millions more that are based in a single country. NGOs range in size from a few individuals concerned with a well-defined set of issues in a single community (e.g. building a well for refugees in a war-torn African country), to mega-organizations with large memberships and hundreds of millions of dollars (e.g. BRAC, a Bangladesh-based global NGO that specializes in microfinance and education, reports having a total staff of 94,000, along with more than eight million microfinance group members; see BRAC, 2010). Among philanthropic organizations, the Bill and Melinda Gates Foundation (2010) has become a major player in the fight against AIDS; its Global Health and Global Development Initiatives have funded nearly $17 billion in projects since 1994. Former US President William J. Clinton, through the Clinton Global Initiative (CGI, 2011a), has brought together world leaders, CEOs and foundation heads, NGO directors, and others who have made nearly 2,000 commitments (as of 2010) valued at $63 billion, which have—at least according to the CGI—"already improved the lives of nearly 300 million people in more than 170 countries." The Clinton Health Access Initiative (CHAI), for example, claims to have reached more than two million people with HIV/AIDS, "accelerating access to life-saving technologies; and helping governments build the capacity required for high-quality care and treatment programs" (CGI, 2011b)

Yet NGOs have also been criticized for replicating the same errors as bilateral foreign aid: which all too often involves well intentioned but ill-informed outsiders, whose plans for assistance are too often grounded in schoolbook knowledge (or, sometimes worse, the priorities of their funders), rather than in the lived experiences of their intended beneficiaries. Moreover, NGOs—like bilateral foreign aid—have been criticized for letting national governments off the hook; at best, it is argued, they provide a band-aid solution for problems that are most effectively addressed by business, government, or a partnership between the two.

The importance of pursuing a global, multi-stakeholder approach to addressing pressing environmental and development challenges is well recognized. The way forward, however, is somewhat less established. Technology transfer is often touted as the best means for increasing capacity both for creating and using new and existing technologies. This has all too often resulted, however, in unfair and unrealistic expectations being placed on late-industrializing countries in the global South. What is called for is a two-way exchange of ideas—about the science and engineering aspects of application-specific emerging technologies, the social relations within which such applications occur, and the ways in which innovations might better lead to equitable development outcomes. International North–South and South–South cooperation is essential, as the UNCTAD report suggests when it calls for "harnessing knowledge and technology for development" (UNCTAD, 2008).

There are a growing number of individuals and organizations working to achieve a more equitable and environmentally sustainable future. While the technical community, comprised mainly of scientists and engineers, is well equipped to suggest technological fixes for many development challenges, there is also a clear role to be played by others. These include social scientists with expertise in a given region of the world, civil society actors working on the ground, and, importantly, the local population who are the presumed beneficiaries. It is within this context that the *Emerging Technologies/ Emerging Economies* conference was organized for November 2009 with a concerted effort to bring together such a diversity of stakeholders as described here.

Recently there have been several efforts to stimulate or renew interest in science, technology, and innovation (STI)—led development in Washington and around the world. Within the United States, many of the efforts from the US Agency for International Development, US Department of State, and the Millennium Challenge Corporation for example can be seen as aligning with President Obama's message in his first address *On a New Beginning* in Cairo. In his speech, the President noted:

> On science and technology, we will launch a new fund to support technological development in Muslim-majority countries, and to help transfer ideas to the marketplace so they can create more jobs. We'll open centers of scientific excellence in Africa, the Middle East and Southeast Asia, and appoint new science envoys to collaborate on programs that develop new sources of energy, create green jobs, digitize records, clean water, grow new crops.
>
> (President Obama, June 4, 2009)

On subsequent international visits, such as the one to Indonesia, President Obama again pledged an increase in international collaboration in science and technology when he noted "we must build bridges between our people, because our future security and prosperity is shared. And that is exactly what we're doing—by increasing collaboration among our scientists and researchers, and by working together to foster entrepreneurship."[3] Bringing science, technology, and innovation back on to the international development agenda is not only occurring as a political phenomena, however, with many scholars increasingly acknowledging that innovation "could and should become a prime driver for health and economic development" (Singer *et al.*, 2008: 143). With a focus on capacity building, in their case study of three African countries (Ghana, Rwanda, and Tanzania), Singer and his colleagues emphasize what they term "convergence innovation" which they see as helping to mitigate against the burden of "missing links between science, business, and capital" (2008: 143), or put another way—filling crucial gaps across the health and life-sciences value chain.

It is important, however, that this dialogue rethink the historical role played by "technology transfer" as a linear route toward a fixed and predetermined endpoint: what might be considered Western-style modernization. There is also a need to think about new pathways through which to engage with technology and development that span disciplinary and geographic boundaries. Emerging and developing countries must find new ways forward toward more equitable and sustainable development, foreign technical assistance notwithstanding.

The present volume addressed these issues, focusing on the role of science, technology, and innovation (STI) in responsibly and equitably addressing some of the most vexing problems that plague the developing world and beyond. The technological optimism that informed much thinking (at least in the global North) about economic development during the 1960s and 1970s faded in ensuing decades, replaced by an emphasis on appropriate technology, empowerment, and sustainability. Unfortunately, there were far too few examples of successful projects that reflected these laudable values. To take another recent example of the re-emergence of STI in the development agenda, the UK Collaborative on Development Sciences—a consortium of more than a dozen UK funders, policy-makers, and scientists created by the British government—in 2010 issued a 400-page report, *Science and Innovation for Development*, that provided detailed case studies of the contribution of science to what the authors termed "appropriate innovation" around the world, keyed to the Millennium Development Goals (Conway and Waage, 2010). In his preface to the book, Calestous Juma of Harvard's Kennedy School, challenges "the international community to jettison traditional development approaches that focus on financial flows without attention to the role of science and innovation in economic transformation," reminding us that "development is a knowledge intensive activity that cannot be imposed from the outside. It is consistent with leading theories that define development as an expression of the endogenous capabilities of people" (xiv).

Technological solutions can involve business, governments, or civil society organizations; they can be broad brush or microscopic in scale; they can be top-down, or emerge more organically from those who are to benefit—even when the recipients lack formal education, much less scientific knowledge. It is our belief that emerging technologies hold great promise in providing innovative and low-cost solutions to problems of energy, potable water, health, and food security in emerging economies. Yet at the same time emerging technologies pose a large number of daunting challenges.

More than a decade ago, a bibliometric study of 150 countries, conducted by Caroline Wagner and her associates at RAND (Wagner *et al.*, 2001: viii), concluded that

> International collaboration is replacing other models as the preferred method of building scientific capacity in developing countries and it appears to be producing results. Researchers from scientifically advanced countries collaborating with developing country counterparts report that these activities are building international-level scientific capacity in those countries.

The RAND study (Wagner *et al.*, 2001: x) described this growth in international collaboration as "distributive" rather than a one-way flow from global North to South:

> While collaboration among developed and developing countries were once referred to as "North-South" or "donor-host" relationships, regional groupings or unequal partnerships no longer adequately describe global relationships in S&T. Distributed growth over the past 15 years in S&T investment and infrastructure has resulted in more and broader excellence in science.

Although "scientifically advanced" countries accounted for more than nine-tenths of global R&D spending, scientific capacity—defined as "the infrastructure, investment, institutional and regulatory framework, and personnel available to conduct scientific research and technological development"—was found in some 50 countries (Wagner *et al.*, 2001: x). The number of papers co-authored between scientifically advanced and "scientifically developing" countries was increasing (although a category of some 80 countries they identify as "scientifically lagging" remained left out). Many reasons were identified for driving the increase in collaboration: English as the common language of science, shared problems and issues, common economic priorities, the need for expertise, the presence of scientific infrastructure, and—significantly—the role of information and communications technologies (ICT).[4] These trends have only increased in the decade since the RAND study. Wagner (2008) has since offered evidence that a "new invisible college" has emerged, a set of global networks that is replacing the "big science" once the exclusive province of the global North. This, in turn, has created new opportunities for emerging economies to advance their own scientific development.

Increased collaboration notwithstanding, building scientific capacity in the global South is not always easily accomplished. There are vast differences between so-called emerging economies such as China, India, Brazil, Argentina, Mexico, and Chile—which already have fairly advanced scientific institutions—and the low-income countries of Latin America, Asia, and Africa, where scientific infrastructure is weak or entirely absent. Successful technology transfer typically involves innovative equipment (although often simpler existing technologies are preferable), laboratory training, and—perhaps most significantly—a degree of trust that can only come from extended periods of collaboration tied to local needs. As Harris (2004: 11) summarizes her experience, based on 15 years of collaborative epidemiological research in Central and South America, "'parachute science', in which investigators from developed countries merely collect samples, return home and publish papers, is of no real use to scientists and citizens in developing countries."

Nanotechnology: A Promising Emerging Technology for More Equitable Development?

Nanotechnology is an emerging technology that is said to hold great promise for solving many of the world's ills. It is defined by the US National Nanotechnology Initiative (NNI) as

> the development and application of materials, devices and systems with fundamentally new properties and functions because of their structures in the range of about 1 to 100 nanometers[5] ... In essence, nanodevices exist in a unique realm, where the properties of matter are governed by a complex combination of classic physics and quantum mechanics.
>
> (Renn and Roco, 2006: 1)

By 2011 the United States was spending $1.8 billion through the NNI, representing one of the largest government investments in technology since the Apollo program (McCray 2009: 60; McNeill *et al.*, 2007: 10). More than 60 other countries have followed suit, developing their own national nanotechnology programs. By 2008, global investment in nanotechnology had reached $17 billion, roughly equally divided between public and private spending (Shapira and Wang, 2010). Because nanotechnology is defined by scale, it is inherently interdisciplinary: chemists, physicists, biotechnologists, material scientists, and engineers find themselves collaborating, using common instruments and developing shared understandings (Renn and Roco, 2006: 1).

These interdisciplinary collaborations are also becoming highly internationalized—arguably more so than for any previous major technological advance. One bibliometric study (Shapira and Wang, 2010: 627) of some 92,500 nanotechnology articles published worldwide during the year-long period from August 2008 to July 2009 concluded that "despite the initial focus on national initiatives, patterns of nanotechnology funding and collaboration transcend country boundaries ... Importantly, the concentration of funds—whereby research sponsors support relatively fewer institutions—seems to yield lower-quality research." International collaboration, in other words, pays off.

Investment in nanotechnology is predicted to yield enormous commercial returns—by some estimates as high as several trillion dollars globally—although the largest returns are likely to be years in the future. The US National Science Foundation initially predicted that by 2015, some \$1 trillion worth of products globally would incorporate nanotechnology (Roco and Bainbridge, 2003; Roco, 2009). New products can mean additional workers; one NSF study estimated that some two million workers will be engaged directly in nanotechnology-related enterprises by 2015, with an additional five million in supporting jobs—mostly in the United States, Europe, and Japan (Roco, 2003).

Although nanoscale materials have thus far found their way into a limited range of consumer products,[6] the future promise is extensive. Examples include (Lane and Kalil, 2005; NNI, 2006):

- low-cost hybrid solar cells;
- targeted drug delivery, achieved by constructing nanoscale particles that "search and destroy" specific types of cancer cells, offering a non-invasive cure for cancer without the toxic side-effects of radiation and chemotherapy;
- "labs-on-a-chip," providing instant diagnosis of multiple diseases in remote field settings found in poor countries;
- ultra high-speed computing, providing data densities over 100 times that of today's highest-density commercial devices;
- nanoscale filtration with high efficiencies at low costs, providing a solution for air pollution and water contamination.

Nanotechnology would seem to hold great promise for emerging economies. One study (Singer *et al.*, 2005: Table 1; see also Salamanca-Buentello *et al.*, 2005) consulted a panel of 63 experts—60 of whom were from developing countries—to rank the ten nanotechnology applications they felt would be of greatest benefit to developing countries over the next decade. In order of ranking (from top to bottom), these were energy storage, production, and conversion; agricultural productivity enhancement; water treatment and remediation; disease diagnosis and screening; drug delivery systems; food processing and storage; air pollution and remediation; construction; health monitoring; and vector and pest detection. Whether or not "one can conclude that nano has the potential to become the flagship of the industrial production methods of the new millennium in developed as well as in the developing world" (Bürgi and Pradeep, 2006: 648), it seems clear that nanotechnology—as well as other emerging technologies—have the potential to play a pivotal role in fostering more equitable, sustainable development.

The Conference: Emerging Technologies/Emerging Economies

But how can this potential best be realized? In November 2009, we hosted an international conference to explore these issues, posing the question: how might emerging technologies best contribute to more equitable development in emerging economies? The conference, which was held at the Woodrow Wilson International Center for Scholars, was organized by the University of California at Santa Barbara's Center for Nanotechnology in Society (CNS), and funded by the US National Science Foundation, with supplemental funding from the UCSB College of Engineering, the Institute for Energy Efficiency, the UCSB Division of Social Sciences, and Rice University's Center for Biological and Environmental Nanotechnology.[7]

Participants came from the United States and Europe; China, India, and Brazil, the three largest emerging economies; and Mexico, South Africa, and Uganda, and included leading scientists and engineers, government and NGO activists, social scientists and business entrepreneurs. They came with a single purpose: to explore new pathways for technology-based solutions to problems related to energy scarcity, finite clean water sources, diminished availability of sustainable food resources, and pandemic diseases. Discussion, dialogue, and break-out sessions were facilitated by the Meridian Institute, an organization committed to increasing a more equitable North/South dialogue. An ongoing commitment has been made to foster solution-oriented discussions among participants that would continue in the future.

A central concern of the conference was how to best manage science and technology to assure that the benefits of technological advancement contribute to more equitable development. Aneesh Chopra, US Chief Technology Officer offered a challenge in his plenary address at the National Press Club, claiming that if we hope to harness science and technology to solve basic human needs, we must first "get the PhDs to listen to the people ... [thereby] tapping into the collective expertise all over the world." High-tech projects, in other words, are likely to fail if they do not grow out of the needs and understandings of the communities that are the presumed beneficiaries—the people who will assume responsibility for implementation long after the experts from the global North have returned home.

A central aim of the conference was to rethink such approaches to what is commonly thought of as collaboration and technology transfer in the service of sustainable development, between economically developed and emerging economies. To achieve this goal, the Meridian Institute, a not-for-profit organization which specializes in multi-stakeholder mediation through expert-led facilitation, helped to bring together individuals who may not typically have the opportunity to interact. In this capacity, the Meridian Institute helps these diverse groups to learn from each other to build mutual agreement and understanding of complex challenges. Meridian helped to moderate both the plenary sessions of the conference as well as small break-out group discussions between conference participants. The break-out sessions were designed to address questions related to the social aspects of using emerging technologies in emerging economies. There were two break-out sessions during the three days of the conference, alternating with plenary sessions in which papers were presented and discussed. During the break-out sessions conference participants reflected on technological "successes" and "failures" within development contexts, and raised issues related to the varying different roles of the public sector in fostering STI-led development efforts. Additional topics included the public and private organizational contexts of technological innovation and development applications, and the role of civil society within debates about new technologies.

Break-out sessions were divided into the four conference focal areas: energy/environment, water, food security, and health. Each break-out group discussion, led by a Meridian facilitator, typically included conference participants from different countries, academics from the social sciences and different fields of science and engineering, representatives of nongovernmental organizations, and participants from the private sector. Each group was charged with discussing the same set of topics:

1. Identify characteristics of emerging technologies that might enable them to address development challenges in the group's focal area, as well as cause some concerns in a development context.
2. Increase understanding of the ways in which development objectives might become stronger drivers of technological development and delivery.
3. Suggest specific activities to strengthen the linkage between research and development of new technology, and the needs of poor communities in developing countries.
4. Support networking, and build a foundation for future collaboration among participants.

In addition to these questions, break-out groups were provided with brief introductory remarks on STI-led development, and some examples of the types of nanotechnologies that might serve equitable development in the focal area under discussion. Each group had two note-takers (a social science graduate student and an engineering graduate student) who were charged with taking notes during the session and reporting back to the full conference during the following plenary.

A brief discussion of the break-out group deliberations helps to illustrate some of the cross-cutting challenges that surfaced throughout the conference.

Energy/Environment. The energy/environment break-out group focused initially on which technologies were likely to provide the greatest potential benefit in terms of meeting the needs of emerging economies. Some of the end use applications that were discussed included more efficient appliances, solid-state lighting (see Chapter 11), enhanced energy storage with lithium ion batteries, and nano-enabled solar panels. Discussion focused on both the benefits of the technology, as well as potential problems that might arise in its implementation. Among the topics discussed were impact on natural resources, the use of appropriate technologies, and the possibility that the introduction of nanotechnology or other emerging technologies might enable a country to "leapfrog"[8] over more traditional, sequential development trajectories. Reliability and sustainability was another major concern: it is one thing to introduce a new technology, but another thing to assure its basic maintenance. If a technological solution is too costly to repair or too complicated to use, its potential will not be realized.

One conclusion was that, at least ideally, a fundamental first step may be to build national capabilities, independent of foreign expertise, thereby breaking down the traditional North/South relationship of technology transfer. This led to a discussion of the importance of true partnership and collaboration. Government funding mechanisms in emerging economies and in advanced industrialized countries in addition to other higher education initiatives could provide one of most direct ways to help scholars from emerging economies gain access to top research instruments, equipment, and scholars, thereby building the national capacity for innovation.

Along similar lines, the discussion in the energy break-out group focused on the difference between technologies that will help people directly in their everyday lives, and those that, at a larger scale, may help a country develop in order to be able to participate in the global innovation system as innovators rather than consumers. For example, biofuels can often be produced sustainably by developing countries, drawing on their own agricultural resources, such as sugarcane in the case of Brazil, for example, which is then sold to other countries (see Chapter 12). This, in turn, often requires supportive government policies and programs. There was some debate over which approach was preferable: small-scale efforts such as providing LED lights to a village so students can study at night, or large-scale government-led efforts to introduce new technologies on a wide scale. With regard to the latter, it was noted (by a participant from China) that even large-scale efforts to provide sustainable energy need to move slowly; in China, where the most energy derived is from coal, the need to increase efficiency needs to be balanced with the economics of converting to more sustainable sources.

Finally, the group noted that there is an important distinction to be made related to the promise of nanotechnology in particular: the extent to which nano will likely address the needs of the poor in emerging economies, or instead, enhance the economic competitiveness of already advanced economies, thereby exacerbating global inequality. The group discussion concluded that both are possible, and that the outcome will depend on how technology transfer is managed.

Water. The break-out group focusing on water began with a consideration of who currently benefits from innovation—notably the global North (where innovations are most likely to occur). Inequities in the development and application of water technologies are therefore of central concern and must be addressed if the benefits are to be realized in emerging economies. The discussion then turned to water technologies that have the potential to provide cheaper and faster diagnosis of contaminants, remove chemical contaminants, aid in the disinfection or desalination of water, as well as other filtration technologies such as enhanced nano-scale membranes. While nanotechnology in particular may help to provide clean water, some major challenges were also discussed. Most fundamentally, access to clean water is often not regarded as a basic human right, a major barrier to the implementation of clean water solutions. In many developing countries private providers truck water into villages, at costs exceeding that paid by people in more economically developed places where water is piped directly into their homes. Even readily available existing water treatment technologies have yet to penetrate deeply into many emerging economies. One challenge is knowing the proper scale for proposed solutions: should they be at the level of individual house-holds, neighborhoods, or entire cities or regions? Basic questions have to do with the degree of centralization of clean water provision, as well as the degree to which the best approaches are high-tech or low-tech. The group generally agreed that a "one size fits all" approaches will not work; solutions must relate to the local needs.

In places where there is an extensive dry season, there are additional needs for water storage solutions in ways not typically addressed in more developed countries— for example, developing a coating that releases chlorine or other known disinfectants over extended periods of time. What is needed is a library of appropriate technologies to address the needs of particular situations. Such a database would need to consider such topics as geographic specifications, cultural constraints, weather, topography, and demographic characteristics. One area where the group felt there was the greatest need and potential lies with affordable and easy-to-use diagnostic testing for contami-nants. Currently, there are no simple, fast, easily available approaches for determining whether a water supply is safe or not. The benefits would go beyond public and/or personal awareness; diagnostic testing has clear implications for emergency response following natural disasters.

One final hurdle that the group addressed has to do with the current drivers of water technologies. If water is not perceived to be relevant to Western markets, who will be most likely to drive innovation in this area? In a few instances, there are start-up firms in the United States and elsewhere working on nano-enabled water technologies; however without the venture capital needed to scale these efforts up, it is unlikely that these will be made accessible to those communities most in need.

Food Security. The break-out group on food security began with an introduction of the emerging food- and agriculture-related nanotechnologies. The United States Department of Agriculture, for example, has been engaged in nanotechnology research since 2001, at which point a document was drafted addressing the relevance of nano-technology for food and agriculture, highlighting such advances as nano-enabled sen-sors capable of detecting plant and crop disease, or measuring pest and fertilizer levels. Nanotechnologies can also be used to ensure food safety, which—in addition to the obvious individual benefits—can thereby reduce economic loss due to food-borne ill-ness. It may also be possible to increase the macro and micronutrient levels of certain foods using nanotechnology in nutrient supplements, to enhance the delivery of nutri-ents to the body. Nano-enabled packaging offers the potential for increasing the shelf life of food that requires lengthy transport.

This group discussed the possible ways that nanotechnology could solve problems for rural communities in the United States and in developing countries. These include increased bioavailability for greater nutrition content in food, enhanced delivery of pesticide control, increased animal fertility and reproduction rates, greater protection against food-borne illness, and early detection of pathogens and disease. With food security issues as a global concern, one participant argued that research must be done to understand the scope of possibilities that surround nanotechnology for food security.

However, a number of critics raised issues against the technologically optimistic approach that nanotechnology would solve food security issues. A major concern about introducing technologies into agricultural production has to do with its possible social impact. One participant noted that it is important to consider the regional needs of the farmers as well as analyze how farmers can assist in technological development. By taking ownership of the technology and working with it in the fields, farmers can educate biologists and nanoscientists about the productivity and problems of engineered seed and pesticides. Another noted that while Brazilian research institutes are testing food products enhanced with nanotechnology, there is little public knowledge and awareness about what these products are and what potential risks they might involve. There is also little government regulation of nanotechnology in Brazil, just as in most of the world. As we have learned from the Green Revolution and the recent history of genetically modified (GM) seed production, the process of integrating technology into the food system is not easy. Moreover, corporations enforce intellectual property rights on their seeds, making it difficult and/or expensive for farmers to access the seeds regularly.

In addition to concerns about the livelihoods of the farmers, the introduction of new technologies into the production process causes fears and concerns for consumers. In developed Western societies, especially those in Europe, fear is strong over the consumption of food products made with GM technologies. This break-out session discussed the ways biotechnology was introduced too quickly into the food system. The introduction of GM food into the US food system came without much public education. Activist campaigns to educate the public came as a result of growing public awareness and a lack of informed consent about GM varieties, such as tomatoes produced with fish genes.

From a development perspective, the break-out group participants questioned how unique nanotechnology is from other past technologies such as biotechnology. Much of the conversation in the food security break-out group focused on the question of whether or not the introduction of novel nano-enabled food technologies would attract consumers or drive them away? Whether a technology is meeting the needs of a developing or emerging country community is an open question in many cases. Further complicating this discussion, the break-out group noted the added complexity of intellectual property rights. One participant observed that among nanotechnologists there is an emerging open source community with researchers from Rice University, who published 'recipes' with the potential to use basic household ingredients to remove arsenic from water (Lounsbury *et al.*, 2009). In their article "Toward Open Source Nano," researchers from Rice Universiy's Opensource Nanotechnology project acknowledged that a "growing disquiet regarding the historic openness of academic science and technology and the ability of the general public and marginalized people to access its insights to solve localized problems" (Lounsbury *et al.*, 2009: 53). On its website, the Opensource Nanotechnology project provides step-by-step instructions for removing arsenic from water by making nano magnetite crystals from readily available materials.[9] Since arsenic is responsible for poisoning a large number of people in the developing world, this serves to make nano and other emerging technologies more relevant to a wider audience.

With the Green Revolution and genetically modified organisms (GMOs) in mind, the group focused much of the conversation on lessons learned from past technologies, and questioned whether nanotechnology might be able to address problems in a new way. Without a deep-rooted understanding of lessons from the past, the cultural context, and a strong consideration of the needs as articulated by the intended beneficiaries, nano-enabled food technologies are not likely to add value.

Finally, public health was a central concern of this group's discussion: is the consumption of nano-enhanced food safe? What is known about the safety of nano-enhanced food packaging? What are the environmental impacts of nano-encapsulated pesticides? Ultimately, it may prove to be fundamentally important to develop a dialogue with farmers and others using nano-enabled products, engaging a wide variety of stakeholders in conversation. The group acknowledged that the governance of food-related nanotechnologies would have to be multi-faceted for local, regional, national, and international standards.

Health. The break-out group on health-related nanotechnologies focused initially on nanomedicines, which try to take advantage of the small size of materials to advance drug delivery systems and establish new therapies. Nano-enabled drugs will likely be used for highly specialized purposes: peptides for biopharmaceuticals, targeted and controlled drug delivery systems, sensors and chips that contain thousands of nanowires which are able to detect proteins and biomarkers at the site of tumors, gold nanoshells for dual imaging and cancer therapies. One of the participants in the health break-out group cautioned almost immediately that the discussion should be a humble one since there is considerable risk associated with grappling with such issues, particularly when the community that will be affected is not present to participate in the conversation. Similarly, another participant observed that many of the problems being discussed are social rather than medial or technological in nature. Related to this, the issue of distributional justice—who has access and who does not—is of central concern to the development of equitable health-related nanotechnologies. Questions over who will benefit from these technologies dominated the conversation.

The issue of appropriate technology was also a dominant component of the conversation, with one participant noting that the funding priorities in the United States does not necessarily reflect global needs. Again the issue was raised as to what or who is driving the advancement of nano and other emerging technologies and who is likely to benefit—beyond those who stand to profit from such technologies. In the health break-out group the idea of scientific competitiveness was raised in relation to the development objectives of a given country. While specific products may be identified, ultimately, social and economic inequalities will remain on a global level; an upfront focus on issues of equity is therefore of central importance in considering potential advances in nano-health applications.

Across all break-out groups, ramifications of these insights were explored, and one recurring debate concerned the scale of appropriate technology: should the emphasis be on small-scale projects that are grounded in local communities, in which outside experts act in the service of local needs? Or are massive, government-led projects better suited to serving the needs of large numbers of people? David Irvine Halliday, founder and CEO of the NGO Light Up the World (LUTW) and Professor in the Department of Electrical and Computer Engineering at the University of Calgary, showed how simple LED lighting makes it far easier for children to read and study after dark, even in remote rural areas. At the other extreme, a conference participant from China empha- sized that to solve the energy needs of hundreds of millions of people requires the kinds of large-scale government-led projects that China is pursuing, noting that "observable progress can be found in the Chinese government's dedicated efforts toward promot- ing nanotechnologies in environmental remediation, public health care, and sustaina- ble agricultural development." Rex Raimond and Mark Jacobs touch on these tensions, suggesting ways in which we might more effectively build bridges through interna- tional collaboration, as one possible mechanism to close the gap between the global North and South in their insightful Foreword to this book.

The Book: Emerging Technologies/Emerging Economies

Todd Osman, Executive Director of the Materials Research Society, opens the discus- sion by drawing on lessons from materials science in Chapter 2 to argue that the devel- opment of new materials has been a driving force in socioeconomic change throughout history, and will continue to be so: "society's response to today's challenges will be cata- lyzed by materials" in such areas as solar power, energy storage, nuclear power, clean fossil fuels, wind energy, solid-state lighting, water purification, and sea water desalini- zation. Osman sees a clear role for government support of high-quality science—but he also calls for an active role on the part of professional societies in encouraging interdis- ciplinary engagement, facilitating social entrepreneurship, building global networks, education, and promoting sustainability.

Can science and technology provide the magic bullet, a technological fix for a host of social problems? Not by themselves. For STI to be effective in supporting more equi- table development outcomes in emerging economies, a number of other factors must be present. Four principal themes emerged in the chapters that follow: the importance of full local participation in development projects, including those that are based on new technologies; the need to assess the impact of such project on jobs and economic growth, since such impacts may exacerbate—rather than reduce—existing inequalities; the appropriate role for state-led development; and the need to be sensitive to issues of risk (and risk governance) when adopting new and often untested technologies.

The Importance of Local Participation in Development Projects

Ultimately, the question is not whether emerging technologies are capable of provid- ing solutions (clearly in some cases they are), nor whether such technologies must be appropriate to the setting (the answer is obviously "yes"). One conclusion that follows from the chapters in this volume is that there must be a balance of outside expertise and indigenous knowledge—not only in the service of producing more equitable out-comes, but because local conditions—which are known only to locals—can be crucial in determining whether a project succeeds or fails. Whatever solutions are offered, they must involve authentic collaboration with those who will hopefully benefit.

David Lewis, Professor of Social Policy and Development at the London School of Economics, points out in Chapter 3 the importance of avoiding "technological amne-sia"—forgetting to learn from the lessons of the past. Jose Gomez-Marquez, Program Director of MIT's Innovations in International Health initiative, stressed in his com-ments at the conference the importance of developing "strong, long-run community partners, in particular a willingness to understand each other's opinions."

Are emerging economies likely to fully reap the benefits of emerging technolo-gies, even when they are introduced? In Chapter 4, Guillermo Foladori, Professor of Economic Anthropology at Mexico's Autonomous University of Zacatecas and Coor-dinator of the Latin America Nanotechnology and Society Network, points out that most research and development is concentrated in the global North, which enjoys a monopoly on patents, and is more likely to be aimed at the production of profitable middle-class consumer goods than applications that benefit the world's poor. The larger issue, in his view, is that at least in Latin America, advances in nanotechnology and other emerging technologies is market-driven, rather than the result of national planning aimed at producing more equitable outcomes. This raises the question: when are large-scale, state-run projects preferable to smaller ones that grow more organically out of purely local needs?

Susan Cozzens, Associate Dean for Research at Georgia Institute of Technology's Ivan Allen College, in Chapter 5 addresses this question with a comparative study of five technologies in eight countries. While she concludes that even though the introduction of new technologies increased labor productivity, in most cases there were no signifi-cant effects on the number of jobs. While some high-tech advances clearly created jobs (mobile phones through Grameen Bank being an oft-cited example), in many cases the highest-tech manufacturing remained in advanced industrial countries, while the more dangerous, low-wage jobs wound up in the global South (the production of carbon nanotubes, not studied by Cozzens, would be one example). For a country to benefit job- and business-wise from high technology, it needs to make what Cozzens terms a "technological transition": it must move up the value chain to develop more homegrown innovation and production. Governments can play a role here, not only in terms of sup-porting R&D, innovation, and commercialization by means of public investment and even procurement, but also in assuring that the benefits are widely shared, and the risks of new and largely unknown technologies are recognized, regulated, and mitigated.

The Appropriate Role for State-Directed Development

Where central or local governments are equipped to play a major role in addressing widespread needs, government-led innovation, R&D, and applications are clearly a via-ble option. Kalpana Sastry, Principal Scientist with India's National Academy of Agri-cultural Research Management, has argued that food insecurity—which plagues nearly

900 million people globally and will remain a major concern throughout the twenty-first century—requires "understanding, integrating and deploying new advancements in science and technology in agricultural production." In her view, nanotechnology is fast emerging as the new science and technology platform for the next wave of development and transformation of agri-food systems (Sastry *et al.*, 2009: 91).

As Chen Wang, Head of China's National Center for Nanoscience and Technology, and Can Huang, research fellow at the United Nations University-MERIT and Maastricht University, show in Chapter 6, China has invested vast sums in emerging technologies, including policies that call for "leapfrogging development" by emphasizing "indigenous innovation." Nanotechnology is one of four mega-science areas slated for public investment. In the area of water filtration, Chinese engineers are developing a variety of nanoscale approaches to filtration that, if successful, will remove virtually all water and soil contaminants, whether they are bacterial in origin stemming from organic wastes, or industrial effluences such as toxic metals. Nanoscale advances are also being made in the area of health, particularly in the area of disease diagnosis and targeted drug delivery. In Chapter 7, Jennifer Rogers, Assistant Professor of Sociology at Long Island University, and Amy Zader, Center for Humanities and the Arts Fellow at the University of Colorado, take an example from a previous emerging technology, the Green Revolution: while it may have increased crop yields in India, "some should have questioned whether the costs associated with it were worth the extra yields, including whether the yields were reaching the people of India, displacing local farmers, and ruining the soil for future crop yields." Today nanotechnology holds similar promise for increasing Indian rice yields; the same questions should be asked. Rogers and Zader also point out that China has also become the world's fourth-largest producer of genetically-modified crops, thanks to public investment in biotechnology.

Yet whenever a project based on some new technology is thought to hold promise, it must be developed in concert with the local populations to be affected: it has to reflect their lived realities, incorporating local knowledge and opinions in development programs and projects.[10] It is therefore necessary to build bridges between the scientific community and local populations, not only because the scientists and engineers need to tailor their projects to the needs of the locals, but also because the locals have their own knowledge from which the outside experts can learn. As Scott Lacy, Executive Director of African Sky and Professor of Anthropology at Fairfield University, argues with respect to Malian farming in Chapter 8, "While it may be noble to ask how each new wave of science-based technologies can be *applied* in communities facing extreme poverty, we might find the more effective and humane question to be how these technologies might be *created* or *developed* in communities facing extreme poverty." To answer this new question one must become a "hybrid scientist." Participatory plant breeding in Mali benefited from the farmers' recommendation that field-testing new seeds be done in marginal rather than ideal areas, because they understood that it was in marginal areas that the need was greatest (and that they could not afford to jeopardize their best land to the uncertainties of testing new strains).

Science, like seeds, can benefit from developing hybrid approaches—and a first step would be for scientists to rethink some of their basic roles and assumptions.

As Lacy reminds us, this requires balancing publishing with doing what is best in the field; trusting the experiences of the locals, even if it doesn't meet scientific canons of objectivity; and looking for simple solutions, rather than complex ones. In the chapters of this book there are various proposals for achieving such a hybrid approach: sending the experts to do their research or lab work in the field, for example, or creating hubs of innovation and design that network experts, practitioners, and locals around well-defined projects. What the various approaches have in common is that they all require the specialists to learn from local communities: what their needs are, what they see as viable solutions.

There are many times when low-tech, local solutions may be preferable to a high-tech fix, which, however promising on paper, lacks grounding and salience in the local culture. In Chapter 9, Moses Musaazi, Senior Lecturer at Uganda's Makerere University and Founder and Managing Director of the NGO Technology for Tomorrow, provides two examples he has developed in his native Uganda: interlocking stabilized soil block technology, which enables villagers to build stable homes and granaries employing a press that requires only manual labor, and affordable sanitary pads that are made from local papyrus and recycled paper waste. (A major benefit of the latter is that it enables girls to attend school during their menstrual cycle, which they otherwise would not have done in large part due to cultural norms and concerns.) Both of these involve simple "technologies" that are labor-intensive, requiring little training since they rely on local skills, and require no special equipment, testing, or even user manuals—a major problem where illiteracy is widespread.

All too often, only lip service is paid to the importance of participation. In South Africa, where nanotechnology holds promise for water filtration, it is not yet a viable approach—partly because of high costs, but also because rural consumers lack the required technical knowledge and skill. When they are invited to participate in decision-making around water-related issues, they are passive participants at best; while their engagement gives the appearance of local participation, their lack of knowledge effectively renders them voiceless. In Chapter 10, Thembela Hillie, from South Africa's National Centre for Nano-Structured Materials, and Mbhuti Hlophe, from South Africa's Northwest University Department of Chemistry, conclude from case studies in Kenya, Uganda, Tanzania, Nepal, India, Bangladesh, and the Philippines that "local communities, after exposure to information, need to be given a chance to explore ideas and make their own decisions; public awareness and community participation are critical aspects to sustainability and ownership of any development intervention rights."

As mentioned earlier, in some instances the small-scale approach of NGOs such as LUTW in partnership with local organizations, may prove highly effective. As Irvine Halliday points out in Chapter 11, the estimated 1.6 billion people who lack access to electricity are forced to use fuel-based sources for their lighting. Kerosene—one widely-used source—is expensive, inefficient, and unhealthy.[11] LUTW, working with local groups and industry leaders in some 50 countries, has installed more than 30,000 solid-state lighting systems. While LED lighting requires an energy source, its minimal requirements make it compatible with small, portable solar energy sources, ideal for villages that are far from existing grids. In Irvine Halliday's view, solid-state lighting "significantly improves living conditions of the poor, enhances their safety and health, improves literacy, protects the environment and creates opportunities for income generation and enterprise development." It does not require massive government investments; the cost of individual lighting is often manageable through microcredit loans.

Brazil's efforts to develop biofuel energy sources provide another example of successful large-scale approaches to sustainable development. As Carlos Henrique de Brito Cruz, Physics Professor at Brazil's University of Campinas and Scientific Director at the São Paulo Research Foundation, shows in Chapter 12, renewable energy now constitutes nearly half of Brazil's domestic energy supply, seven times the OECD average—thanks in part to government subsidies for producers and tax incentives for consumers. Much of Brazil's renewable energy comes from the use of sugar cane to produce ethanol, which—when planted in degraded pasture areas—also contributes to carbon sequestration. Brazil has succeeded in creating "an indigenous scientific and technological capability" in this area, where it has emerged as a world leader. Brito Cruz argues that if we look at sugar cane instead as an "energy cane," by 2050 the world could produce nearly a third of its energy requirements from this source.

The Impact on Labor and Economic Growth

Emerging technologies such as nanotechnology are potentially *disruptive technologies*

> that will make obsolete the current competitive technologies, once established and entrenched in economies around the world. The social and economic effects on the international and national levels are difficult to foresee, but an effort must be made at this critical juncture in order to reduce the possible negative or unwanted consequences that have historically accompanied such dramatic transformations.
>
> (Invernizzi and Foladori, 2005: 104)

Emerging technologies must be designed to provide equitable results. All too often, the benefits are enjoyed by those who need them the least, while the costs fall on those who are most vulnerable. Costs may include loss of jobs, when technological advances render labor-intensive jobs obsolete; the elimination of marginal farms, when patented seeds are introduced that require costly fertilizers; or increased exposure to toxicity. Especially in the developing world, where production is labor-intensive, innovative capital-intensive technologies may increase productivity at the expense of employment. In Chapter 13 Noela Invernizzi, Anthropology Professor at Brazil's Federal University of Parana, and Coordinator of the Latin America Nanotechnology and Society Network ReLANS, argues that at least in Brazil, where a large number of companies are already using nanomaterials in commercial products, there is some evidence that jobs will be lost because of nanomaterials' greater efficiency, ability to combine different functions (such as cleaning, washing, and ironing) into a single product, enhanced longevity, and changes in raw material requirements. At the very least, nanotechnology involves industrial restructuring, in which less competitive firms will fail and their workers will lose their jobs. In Chapter 14, Professor Arul Chib and his graduate student Rajiv

Aricat argue the importance of economic, personal, and social contexts in the adoption of mobile phones among migrant-laborers in Singapore. The advancement of Information and Communication Technologies (ICTs) in development have greatly enhanced international development efforts—instigating "leapfrog development" in a variety of forms. Chib and Aricat demonstrate that mobile phones help to ensure better communication and information channels for migrant workers in their case study both in terms of social personal and professional contexts.

Sensitivity to Issues of Risk and Risk Governance

As has happened in the past, when well-intentioned experts parachute into a rural village with little or no local knowledge, offering grandiose solutions rather more modest approaches to clearly understood problems, their projects are likely to fail. In Chapter 15, Andrew Maynard, Director of the University of Michigan's Risk Science Center, along with Antje Grobe of the Risk Dialogue Foundation and Ortwin Renn, Professor of Environmental Sociology and Technology Assessment at the University of Stuttgart, warn us that experts' "dreams of technology innovation" can easily backfire, and while failure always carries costs, those costs are far higher in the more fragile communities of emerging economies.

Among the challenges facing the use of emerging technologies are the risks that may result, risks that are likely to be unknown and therefore unregulated. Risks are a problem throughout the value chain: they occur to researchers in the laboratory, workers in the factory, distributors during transit, and users when the product is consumed.

Unknown risks carry with them two kinds of challenges. There is the potential danger of toxic exposure, with effects that may manifest years in the future. Or there is the opposite danger—unfounded fears that prevent the adoption of beneficial technologies. When it comes to the perception of risk, there seems to be a greater mistrust of government and business than there is of independent citizens' organizations—but in any case, it is important to involve the voices of those who might be exposed to risk in a process that encourages an open discussion. Once again, a hybrid approach is necessary, one in which the outside experts authentically value the native expertise that resides in the communities they hope to serve.

There is a larger challenge as well—the fact that risks and harms are most likely to fall on those who are most poorly equipped to deal with them.[12] As Barbara Harthorn, Professor of Feminist Studies and Principal Investigator at UCSB's Center for Nanotechnology in Society (CNS), Christine Shearer, CNS post-doc, and Jennifer Rogers note in Chapter 16, the "risk makers" are likely to be from the global North, while the "risk takers" are found in the global South. Mismanagement of the fruits of scientific expertise is always a concern, but the consequences today are larger than ever before, given the high degree of economic, political, and environmental interdependence that has resulted from globalization. Yet at the same time, as Andrew Maynard, Antje Grobe, and Ortwin Renn argue in the preceding chapter, there is increasing awareness of such interdependencies, contributing to greater appreciation of potential risks and a growing awareness that proactive approaches are required. Modern communication technology has made this possible. When it comes to problem solving, if two heads have traditionally been seen as better than one, in today's Internet-mediated world it is possible to put countless heads together: experts, funders, project managers, farmers in their fields.

Finally, in Chapter 17 Mihail Roco, Senior Advisor for Nanotechnology at the US National Science Foundation, offers a hopeful forecast for the role of science and technology in alleviating many of the social problems that trouble the world today. In his view, science and technology are not only developing exponentially; they are also integrating across disciplines as well. What is needed, he argues, is a system of global governance involving visionary long-term planning, meaningful partnerships among stakeholders, substantial public investment, and increased attention to risk. Roco offers a number of suggestions to achieve these goals, endorsing research findings (Salamanca-Buentello *et al.*, 2005) that suggest nanotechnology "can help eradicating poverty, improve maternal health and reduce child mortality, combat AIDS and malaria, and ensure environmental sustainability."

In his remarks on the closing panel of the conference, Chief Information Officer of Ashoka, Romanus Berg, quoted William Gibson from an interview on National Public Radio in which he famously remarked: "The future is already here, it is just unevenly distributed." *Emerging Technolgies/Emerging Economies* the conference—and now this volume—provide examples of how a diverse group of unlikely collaborators might come together to solve some of the most pressing challenges facing our planet.

2.
CREATING THE FUTURE
Materials, Innovation, and the Scientific Community
Todd M. Osman

> History consists of a series of accumulated imaginative inventions.
>
> (Voltaire)

Science, Innovation, and Society

Societal change and innovation feed one another. Historians such as Fernand Braudel have noted that during periods of social calm—when "society was content with its material surroundings and felt at ease"—there was no driving force for change and therefore little evidence of innovation (Braudel, 1981). Bursts of scientific advancement coincided instead with periods of societal "discontent," when socioeconomic factors catalyzed technological development. According to Arnold Pacey, technology has developed "in response to pressures, purposes, and practices of human society" such that "changes in the direction of technical progress occur whenever the values and objectives of society change" (Pacey, 1974).

"Green" energy technologies, environmental stewardship, and global access to clean water are critical challenges facing societies around the world. And science and technology are being called upon to solve them. But do we have sufficient societal discontent to spur innovation?

The awarding of the 2007 Nobel Peace Prize to the Intergovernmental Panel on Climate Change (IPCC) and Al Gore Jr. was a turning point in awakening public concern for the environment (Nobel Foundation, 2007). Popular media, such as *Scientific American*'s "Energy's Future: Beyond Carbon" special issue (2006) and CNN's "We Were Warned: Tomorrow's Oil Crisis" (November 20, 2006) helped to raise awareness, such that energy and environmental concerns are now ingrained in the public psyche.

Calls to action on the environment are now on a global scale. The United Nations Human Development Reports have identified crises beyond energy, giving "eight reasons for the world to act on water and sanitation" (2006). BBC News (Kirby, 2000), *National Geographic* (Mayell, 2003), and other media outlets have reported that one person in five around the world does not have access to safe drinking water. The investment community has also weighed in, with Goldman Sachs, the London School of Economics and Political Science, and the Guanghua School of Management (Peking University) warning of the global risk of water shortages in the coming century (Global Investment Conference, 2008; Evans-Pritchard, 2008).

Prior to a 2007 G8 Summit, national scientific advisors from 13 countries issued a joint statement calling for "G8+5 countries" to develop research roadmaps to address energy and climate protection (*Joint Science Academies*, May 2007). Similarly, the United States National Academy of Engineering convened global experts and solicited global input to create the Grand Challenges for Engineering, with economical solar energy, energy from nuclear fusion, and access to clean water topping the list (National Academy of Engineering, 2008). The Millennium Project called specifically on the scientific community to engage in the broader societal challenge of ending poverty, highlighting the critical contribution of science in providing clean water, sound infrastructure, and good health (Juma and Yee-Cheong, 2005).

Recently, economic factors have also aligned behind science. The faltering global economy has led governments to increase investments in basic research and innovation. The rising cost of energy, along with the rising tide of public opinion, has encouraged industry and venture capitalists to investigate alternative energy technologies.

We do not have history's dispassionate eye, but it does appear that we have entered another period of societal "discontent." Socioeconomic driving forces are pushing for innovation. So how, and with what, will science respond?

The Critical Role of Materials

Looking again to history, it is the discovery, or creation, of new materials that has spurred the technological innovations necessary to produce societal change. Consider the following historical events:

*c.*3000 BC   Bronze smelting, prevalent in Egypt and Mesopotamia, signals the heart of the Early Bronze Age and advancements in human tools and art.

*c.*1300 BC   Iron smelting and smithing ushers in the Iron Age in the Ancient Near East, enabling new tools and construction methods.

1755   The modern concrete-making process is invented, making modern construction possible.

1844   Vulcanization of rubber is invented, enabling modern transportation.

1856   The Bessemer Process is invented, enabling the widespread utilization of steel.

1936   p- and n-type silicon is discovered, which, as a precursor to the invention of the transistor, starts the "Silicon Age," leading to modern computing.

1991   Carbon nanotubes are discovered, re-igniting interest in Richard Feynman's dream of nanotechnology (1960), launching the nanomaterials enterprise.

The critical role of materials in socioeconomic change has not changed with the dawning of the twenty-first century. In fact, Moskowitz states that "since the 1980s, technological change and economic progress have grown more mutually interdependent with both closely shadowing new-materials developments" (Moskowitz, 2009).

As such, society's response to today's challenges will be catalyzed by materials. Following are examples of recent discoveries and ongoing research in materials that are leading to innovative solutions to energy and water challenges:

Solar Power: research into making solar cells more efficient and cost-effective will facilitate the widespread utilization of solar. First-generation single-crystalline silicon solar cells operate at 10 to 15 percent conversion efficiency. Cadmium telluride (CdTe) photovoltaics may reach 20 percent efficiency. Multijunction, thin layer films promise 40 percent efficiencies. Quantum-dot structures hold high promise, with efficiencies approaching theoretical limits. While less efficient, current research with organic photovoltaics may produce low-cost, flexible solar cells to meet many new applications (Arunchalam and Fleischer, 2008; Ginley *et al.*, 2008; Green, 2004).

Energy Storage: new methods for energy storage are needed for large-scale utilization of renewable energy technologies. This will require marked advancements in batteries and capacitors. New nanomaterials may hold the key for economically viable and environmentally sustainable systems that move beyond current storage limitations (Whittingham, 2008).

Nuclear Power: next generation fission-based nuclear power plants could meet the demand for increased energy supply with near-zero carbon-dioxide emissions. These reactors will have more severe service conditions (i.e. more corrosive environments, higher irradiation levels, and higher temperatures) than seen in the current fleet of nuclear reactors, necessitating the development and qualification of new materials systems. Materials research is also needed through the fuel cycle, most notably to enable stable waste repositories. Beyond fission, the long-term development of fusion reactors will only be possible with a whole new suite of materials technologies (Osman, 2008; Rav *et al.*, 2008).

Clean Fossil Fuels: approaches to reduce carbon-dioxide emissions from fossil fuels are being developed. "Clean coal" technologies are at the forefront. New corrosion-resistant materials are needed to withstand higher temperatures and pressures specified for these plants. Also, the sustainable employment of carbon sequestration (i.e. capture and removal of carbon from the environment) may well hinge upon economical development of basalt and clathrate technologies as well as new stress corrosion-resistant materials for pipelines carrying supercritical CO_2 to geological sites for storage (Arunchalam and Fleischer, 2008; Powell and Morreale, 2008).

Wind Energy: increased turbine size and the proposed increase in offshore wind farms create challenges for wind energy. Research is under way to develop new polymer resins and reinforcements to improve buckling and fatigue performance. New modeling and inspection methodologies are also needed to enable large-scale production and ensure the structural health of next-generation wind turbines (Hayman *et al.*, 2008).

Solid-State Lighting: lighting consumes one-fifth of the electricity produced globally. Light-emitting diodes (LEDs) offer the potential to reduce lighting energy consumption by up to 50 percent. Galluim nitride appears to be the short-term workhorse, but other wide-bandgap semiconductors, including zinc oxide and scandium nitride, and novel phosphors may dramatically increase efficiencies (Humphreys, 2008).

Water Purification: low-cost, widely available methods to remove pathogens, chemicals, and other contaminants are needed to address the global need for clean water. Researchers are studying nanoparticles that adsorb and mineralize organic pollutants and nanofibrous media that show promise for next-generation membranes and filters (Shannon and Semiant, 2008; Vainrot *et al.*, 2008; Kaur *et al.*, 2008).
Desalination of Sea Water: the membrane cost and high energy demands are limitations for most desalination plants (Avlonitis *et al.*, 2003). Novel polymeric materials and nanofibrous media may enable high flux, low pressure membranes, thus reducing energy demand (Vainrot *et al.*, 2008; Kaur *et al.*, 2008). New polymer synthesis methods may also reduce the cost to production membranes.

Technology Is Only Useful if It Is Used

Many such alternative energy and clean water innovations will be destined for developing economies and underdeveloped regions of the world. Beyond supplying energy and clean water, the hope is that these will increase global prosperity and aid in fighting poverty.

These are noble goals, but they will not be realized if we do not heed sage advice from the agricultural community:

> Dissemination pathways—how people learn about or obtain a technology—play a fundamental role in determining who adopts new technologies … Therefore, before deciding which (dissemination) methods are most appropriate, we must know about the local cultural and power relationships to understand how people interact and learn.
>
> (Meinzen-Dick *et al.*, 2004)

Fernand Braudel summarized it well, stating that "technology is only an instrument and man does not always know how to use it." A group of students from Iowa State University that recently traveled to Mali (Stockdale, 2009) advanced this notion further, advocating for "appropriate technologies." In short, innovations must be suitable for the environment, culture, and economy for which they are intended.

Societal change will not occur simply because socioeconomic conditions encourage scientific research, which then gives birth to alternative energy and clean water technologies. "Practical" sustainability must be built into the system. This means accounting for indigenous conditions, including material supply, available capital, local culture, and regional scientific acumen. After all, innovation will not effect change unless it is used and its benefits are sustained.

Charting a Path for the Future

The challenges are great, and the scientific community must respond. International governments must support high quality science, and science must find a voice in a variety of arenas, from classrooms to the halls of government. Professional scientific societies must play an active role in creating this new era of scientific community engagement. Here are five ways they can make this happen:

Promote the "Medici Effect"

In his book *The Medici Effect*, Frans Johansson builds the case for radical innovation, which occurs when "ideas from different industries and cultures meet and collide, ultimately igniting an explosion of extraordinary new innovations" (2004). "The world is flat," says Thomas Friedman (2005), so we must engage talent from around the globe. Furthermore, no one discipline can solve society's grand challenges. Chemistry cannot do it alone, nor can chemical engineering, physics, metallurgical engineering, biology, or any other science or engineering discipline. Only an interdisciplinary approach drawing on the world's talent will succeed.

Science must also engage other professions in a meaningful way. In short, the scientific community must play an active role in charting the course to the future. Professional scientific societies can:

- *Encourage interdisciplinary engagement.* Technical solutions to alternative energy, clean water and other societal concerns will best occur by leveraging the unique talents and insights of the broad scientific and engineering enterprise.
- *Represent the scientific community.* This will take many forms, ranging from educating legislators on the importance of science to being active participants in establishing sound, realistic expectations for intergovernmental projects.

Facilitate Social Entrepreneurship

Social entrepreneurship, that which uses entrepreneurial methods and enthusiasm to address societal needs, is a popular topic these days (Auerswald, 2009). Often, small enterprises and nongovernmental organizations (NGOs) are considered as primary driving forces for grand change. But why can't professional scientific societies create social value?

Most professional scientific societies are non-profit entities whose missions are often consistent with social entrepreneurship; for example, the mission of the Materials Research Society is to "advance interdisciplinary materials research to improve the quality of life." Many societies (the Materials Research Society included) and their individual members are already engaged, creating STEM (science, technology, engineering, mathematics) education resources, encouraging the technology implementation in developing countries, promoting environmental stewardship, and advancing clean water technologies.

With their existing infrastructure of talented scientists and global networks, professional scientific societies can play an important role in the larger "social enterprise"; as we have learned, no one entity—whether it is a professional discipline, a funding organization, a NGO, or an individual social entrepreneur—can do it alone.

Build Global Networks

Governments are increasingly investing in global science and education efforts (Bement, 2005). For example, international governments have helped to create a roadmap for

Generation IV Nuclear Reactors (2002), supported a high-speed network to connect researchers in Pakistan, the United States, and the European Union (NSF Press Release, October 28, 2008), and formed a European–South American partnership to evaluate climate change impacts on La Plata Basin (European Commission Project 212492, 2008).

These programs typically address global scientific needs by engaging scientific expertise from around the world. Sometimes, these investments are also meant to support regional scientific infrastructures, consistent with the United Nations declaration that investment in science and technology is "a powerful cure for fighting poverty" (Juma and Yee-Cheong, 2005; Millennium Project Task Force Press Release (a), January 17, 2005). Professional scientific societies can help by:

- *Heightening awareness of global needs.* Communication of global needs is important. It must include informing governments and the public about growing global needs as well as ensuring scientists are aware and engaged.
- *Disseminating information.* Researchers must know about opportunities in order to benefit from them. A simple, yet powerful, service of professional scientific societies is the dissemination of logistical information regarding programs supporting global research networks.
- *Assisting regional scientific infrastructures.* Scientists are the foundation for local scientific infrastructures. They need access to state-of-the art technical knowledge and connections to a global support network of peers. They need support for the creation of research laboratories, or, perhaps, suggestions for avoiding capital investment by establishing collaborations with researchers and laboratories elsewhere. These are core functions of professional scientific societies.

Educate the Next Generation

Education is a key factor for improving economic and social conditions (Millennium Project Task Force on Education and Gender Equity, 2005). Furthermore, a country's ability to adopt new technologies is directly related to the quality of its higher education system (Millennium Project Task Force Press Release (a), January 17, 2005). Professional scientific societies can partner with other social entrepreneurs and funding organizations to:

Replicate existing science education programs. The *Rising Above the Gathering Storm* (2007 and 2009) reports have increased interest in K-12 science education around the world. Professional scientific societies have already created a multitude of education resources; many of these could be translated to foreign languages and adapted to the cultures in developing countries.

Provide effective member outreach. University professors are members of professional scientific societies, as are many scientists engaged in informal science education. This expertise could be leveraged to reach children in developing countries. The "digital study hall" approach that supplies video lectures to rural India could be replicated elsewhere (Stanford Social Innovation Review, 2009). On-the-ground outreach can also be facilitated by support networks established to provide best practices, quality resources, and cultural training.

Practice Sustainability

Sustainability means many different things on many different levels. Professional scientific societies can address the various facets of sustainability by:

- *Promoting sustainable technologies.* Environmental stability has been identified as a "critical foundation to end poverty" (Millennium Project Task Force Press Release (b), January 17, 2005. Government officials are calling for "sustainable, green economy" (Benn, 2009), and engineers have been challenged to aid in "reconciling economic growth with the needs of the environment and society" (Richards, 1999).
- *Scientific societies must also promote scholarly research for "green materials."* For this research to be meaningful, however, scientific societies need to facilitate interactions with social ecologists, economists, and other professions to generate reasonable expectations and sound roadmaps and policies for innovation.
- *Implement Sustainable Programs.* There is an apt Chinese proverb: "Give people fish, and you feed them for a day. Teach them how to fish, and you feed them for a lifetime." Implementing new technologies relies on more than scientific developments and socioeconomic desire. A support network for science education, the pursuit of scholarly works, and the appropriate implementation of innovations must be present to ensure sustainability—these all need the participation of professional scientific societies.

Conclusion

Societal change is a complex enterprise, one that has historically relied heavily on materials, innovation, and the scientific community. The same is true today, as our critical challenges will require interdisciplinary technical solutions. They also demand collaboration. As the chapters in this volume indicate, the scientific community must partner with social scientists, governments, and others to realize the potential of innovations discussed in this chapter, most notably for alternative energy and clean water technologies. Professional scientific societies can play an important role in this process, by providing an infrastructure for scientific advancement, enabling social entrepreneurship, and promoting truly sustainable endeavors.

3.
RURAL DEVELOPMENT, TECHNOLOGY, AND "POLICY MEMORY"
Anthropological Reflections from Bangladesh on Technological Change
David Lewis

The relationship between technology and development has been a long and often controversial one. This chapter explores issues relating to technology and development policy from an anthropological perspective, and argues that the relationship can only be meaningful from the point of view of contributing to sustainable development if lessons are learned from past experience. It focuses on the context of Bangladesh, an archetypal developing country that has throughout its 40-year history routinely been affected by extensive poverty, environmental instability, and weak institutions. It was famously referred to as a "basket case" by one of Henry Kissinger's aides shortly after it seceded from Pakistan in 1971. Yet more recently, Bangladesh has come to be seen differently as a partial success story in relation to its subsequent progress linked to technological change (Lewis, 2011). First, the so-called "Green Revolution" in agriculture that took place from the 1980s onwards on the basis of new hybrid seed, irrigation and fertilizer technologies rapidly succeeded in transforming the country from one that many international donors saw as destined to endure chronic food shortages and regular famines, to one that since the 1990s has approached food-grain self-sufficiency. Second, Bangladesh has become strongly associated with the emerging new mobile phone technologies through the promotion of the well-known Grameen Bank and its Grameen Phone associate company. Although this technology was developed in Western countries, Grameen has pioneered its introduction in the developing country context and its local adaptation for development purposes. Grameen's capacity to identify and disseminate the technology across the country has helped to stimulate the rapid growth of cell phones as "platform technologies" that have been adapted to address a range of poverty-focused development challenges, from income generation to information scarcity.

Yet while Bangladesh exhibits many positive aspects of technology-led development in fields such as agriculture and communications, it has proved more problematic in relation to climate change and environment, where there are important concerns about the current state of technology, knowledge, and policy. As a deltaic riparian country, Bangladesh has long struggled to develop effective interventions to deal with the problem of flood control, but with mixed results. In recent years, this challenge has become more complex and urgent in the context of new concerns about the growing impacts of climate change on society and environment. This chapter therefore reflects broadly on the role of technology, and discusses some of the lessons that may be available to policy-makers in facing up to the new challenges of climate change.

While technology is often conceived simply as "hardware," we must also recognize that technology can also be more broadly conceptualized in terms of the ways that knowledge and production become organized, and also as the skills, practices, and approaches that are generated—locally or externally—to the solution of problems, and the ways such "problems" become specified and defined. The familiar development planning tools such as "logical frameworks" form part of these technologies, along with new types of "progressive" language which serve to indicate that development policy is "moving forward" (Cornwall and Brock, 2005). Technology transfer has therefore come to mean more than the provision of improved technical equipment for industrial production or agriculture, but also as the means to develop policy interventions that can promote, for example, the mitigation of environmental problems such as climate change. The aim in this chapter is therefore to reflect selectively on aspects of the development and technology relationship during the past three decades in Bangladesh on a range of relevant topics, culminating in the current preoccupations among development agencies and government on the new issue of climate change.

An anthropological approach to policy is taken in this chapter. This approach emphasizes the social dimensions of policy-making processes around technological choice, and of the impact of technology itself. As Wedel *et al.* (2005: 34) have argued:

> The anthropology of policy takes public policy itself as an object of analysis, rather than as the unquestioned premise of a research agenda ... its enabling discourses, mobilizing metaphors, and underlying ideologies and uses.

Central to the argument of this chapter is the idea that those involved in policy processes need to be constantly reminded of the past and the need to draw lessons from it, since policy tends to favor a "perpetual present" in which the default position of policy actors tends to be the state of policy amnesia in which key historical lessons remain constantly in danger of being forgotten (Lewis, 2009). This is not a problem restricted to the world of development policy. It is also part of what the anthropologist Paul Connerton in his book *How Modernity Forgets* (2009: 2) has termed "structural forgetting," a phenomenon of destroying the past that may be "specific to the culture of modernity" within many modern capitalist societies more widely.

Science, Technology, and Development

The modern development era began in an age of technological optimism after World War II. A concept of "technology transfer" was an integral part of the dominant idea that development was a process that could be stimulated by a process of economic modernization. Improved technological capability was seen as a crucial requirement for building industrialization and increasing food production in the developing world.

Within this paradigm, it was argued that new technologies, for example in agricultural production, could simply be passed from rich to "third world" countries where they would be adopted and contribute to Western-style capitalist development.

However, this dominant mainstream view of development as capitalist modernization soon became challenged by those who argued that the proposed "trickle down" benefits from technology-led modernization rarely reached the poorest people, and worse still, often contributed to widening inequalities between rich and poor. For the so-called dependency theorists, working primarily from the context of Latin America, a critical position was taken that argued that technology transfer was a veil for corporations who merely saw developing countries simply as new markets for consumer products aimed at elites and middle classes. It was a view critical of the activities of both government and private sector initiatives that attempted to provide predominantly "high technology" solutions to development problems that had little relevance to the poor. In this view, the West was actively "under-developing" the third world, through its unfavorable incorporation into world markets and increasingly technological dependence on Western capital.

At the same time, at the level of policy and practice, another "alternative development" perspective began to emerge centered around new ideas about "participation" and "local knowledge." As Sillitoe (2001: 4) pointed out:

> The dominant development paradigms until a decade or so ago were modernisation—the class transfer of technology model associated with the political right—and dependency—the Marxist informed model associated with the political left. They are both blind to local knowledge issues.

Such thinking began to generate a wide range of counter-hegemonic or "alternative" approaches to the role of technology and development. Many critics pointed to the prevalence of planned, top-down technology-based development projects that simply became "white elephants," with little use or value beyond the life of the intervention, and which failed to respond to local contexts and needs. Others argued the case for a new view of technology itself—the "appropriate" or "intermediate" technology movement called for a different, people-centered approach to technology, one that favored predominantly small-scale, "low technology" approaches to solving community development problems. It challenged the idea that technology was a "neutral factor" within public policy that could be subordinated in simple ways to policy objectives (Willoughby, 1990). This challenged the idea that new technology could simply be invented and diffused to the developing world. There was an increasing emphasis on the design and application of technology as "co-production" between researchers and end-users. Yet the promise of "appropriate technology," which had been a live issue since the 1970s, rarely delivered. It tended to offer technological solutions that were either too small-scale and local to achieve significant impacts, or were out of step with the aspirations of local people who viewed "appropriateness" differently—as implying a sub-standard technology that kept them away from the benefits of mainstream "progress."

At the end of the Cold War, market-led development received a new boost, but the "alternative development" paradigm continued and diversified through the 1990s. It became strongly associated with the work of nongovernmental organizations (NGOs), which were now being given a new centrality as creative and effective private development actors. However, while their new development ideas about "empowerment" and "sustainability" were slowly being assimilated—some would argue co-opted—by more mainstream interests within the development industry, the role of technology in development began to receive less attention. Both benevolent neglect and active opposition played a role in this decline. The international system of public sector agricultural research institutes that had driven the technological changes in agriculture was no longer favored by donors and governments who were by now increasingly enamored by the ideologies of privatization and good governance that characterized the new unfolding neo-liberal development paradigm. Meanwhile, many of the development NGOs were critical of the "Green Revolution" technology that many scientists had argued contributed significantly to increased food yields in Asia and elsewhere.

Critics such as Vandana Shiva (1991) associated the type of intensive farming that had increasingly been made possible by the new seed and water technologies both with environmental degradation of farmland and with an undesirable increased role of multinational corporations in third world agriculture. Political scientists also argued that in many areas where the technologies were introduced, they were simply captured by elites and contributed to the further impoverishment of the poorer classes in rural areas. When the "Green Revolution" was followed by the rise of the new genetically-modified seed research agenda that was begun by agribusiness corporations in the 1990s, this was too much for alternative development proponents and the rise of "civil society" resistance to GM among many development activists consequently led to the further marginalization of technology-based solutions to development.

Today, it appears many people in the development policy community may be edging back towards an era of "techno-optimism." The recent publication of Conway and Waage's 2010 book *Science and Innovation for Development* appeared to signal a renewal in belief in the idea that science and technology are central for development and poverty reduction, and that more priority should be given to the strengthening of national and regional scientific capacity. For example they cite the case of "new rices for Africa" developed by scientists at the Africa Rice Centre in collaboration with Chinese researchers, and insecticide-treated mosquito nets developed by scientists in France and the UK. Both have begun to be further adapted and taken forward into a range of poor country contexts by local researchers, development agencies, private sector actors, and NGOs. This new technological optimism leads Conway and Waage (2010: 22) to suggest that such examples

> show how scientists in developed and developing countries can together address and solve problems, bringing us closer to the achievement of the Millennium Development Goals (MDGs). They illustrate the value of global science innovation systems and the collaboration they foster in improving science for development.

In the rest of this chapter, I want to argue that if we are to once again turn to emerging technology as a central key to development and poverty reduction, there are important pitfalls to be avoided and lessons to be learned. The next sections offers a brief and highly selective review of the recent history of technology and development in Bangladesh, and attempts to draw out some critical issues.

Technology and Development in Bangladesh

There can be no doubt that technological change has made a positive difference in the field of rural development in Bangladesh. This progress has been driven by research and dissemination work among the public sector, the private sector, and the nongovernmental sectors. The following section reviews three brief examples.

First, the so-called "Green Revolution" has made an enormous impact in rural Bangladesh since it began to take root during the 1980s. The economy is still primarily agrarian, and the rural sector continues to employ about 60 percent of the labor force, with around one-quarter of the gross domestic product coming from agriculture, forestry, and fisheries. The main crop is rice, Bangladesh's staple food. There has been considerable progress made with increasing the productivity of rice production during recent decades through the research and adoption of a range of new technologies, including a range of high-yielding hybrid rice and wheat varieties, small-scale mechanized ploughing technologies and an expansion of ground-water irrigation through the use of shallow and deep tube-wells across the country.

Rice research has played a significant role. National research on traditional varieties of rice dates as far back as 1935, but this has been more recently supplemented by research on modern varieties (MVs) through the national level research center the Bangladesh Rice Research Institute (BRRI) with the support of the regional International Rice Research Centre (IRRI), part of the Consultative Group for International Agricultural Research (CGIAR) system. By 2003, a total of 41 new high-yielding varieties had been developed that are tailored to different ecological conditions and the major adopters have been smallholder farmers. Research indicates that there have been both direct adoption impacts in terms of raising farm incomes and indirect benefits in the form of greater involvement in non-farm activities and better market access. Overall, despite the greater costs involved in growing MV rice, this is outweighed by the resulting increase in production that makes the unit cost of production 12 percent lower than traditional varieties, and this also makes rice prices lower for consumers in rural and urban areas (Hossain *et al.*, 2006).

There has also been an important expansion of the third winter *boro* rice crop made possible by the expansion of tube-well irrigation. Government policy decisions that promoted the importation of Chinese diesel engines for small-scale irrigation played an important and still under-appreciated part in this green revolution (Biggs *et al.*, 2011). The increase in *boro* has been dramatic, rising from 2 percent of the cultivated land area in 1971 to around 15 percent by the start of the new millennium. There has also been substantial diversification by farmers into wheat and vegetable crops. As a result, according to Bradnock and Saunders (2002: 68), "in the face of all expectations over the last 30 years, agricultural productivity has more than kept pace with growing demand for food and agricultural products." Bangladesh has also seen a considerable amount of activity on the "appropriate technology" front as well. One noteworthy example was the "treadle pump," developed at the end of the 1970s by an NGO called Rangpur-Dinajpur Rural Services (RDRS). The idea was to produce a low-cost human-powered twin cylinder pump that could be used with a shallow tube-well made of bamboo or PVC plastic that would allow small farmers to access opportunities for improving farm productivity using irrigation, particularly for winter rice and vegetable crops. The well was developed by RDRS and marketed by the US small business organization International Development Enterprises (IDE). The pump could be installed at a cost of just US$20, and by the early 1990s around 65,000 were being sold each year (Farrington and Lewis, 1993). The FAO website reports that over 1.3 million had been sold by 2005 (www. fao.org/teca/content/bamboo-treadle-pump, accessed 8/11/2010). While impressive, the massive expansion of mechanized shallow tube-well irrigation during the 1990s nevertheless ensured that the treadle pump remained, relatively speaking, only a marginal technology in rural Bangladesh. It has doubtless brought benefits to some categories of small farmer in certain localities, but it never went mainstream. Although the cost of owning a mechanized irrigation pump was beyond the reach of poor farmers in rural Bangladesh, new forms of small-scale service provision transformed this large-scale or "lumpy" mainstream technology in rural areas in a way that many did not anticipate: it was relatively straightforward (as I found in my village-level fieldwork during the 1980s and 1990s) for small farmers to buy water regularly from pump owners, who were keen to maximize returns on an asset that had surplus capacity well beyond their own landholdings. There was a similar story in the case of mechanized tractor ploughing, where new forms of rural entrepreneurship around the sale of ploughing services to small cultivators began developing among technology owners (Lewis 1991, 1996). The subsequent expansion of irrigated rice farming that lifted Bangladesh from its "basket case" status was primarily the result of farmers adapting and using modern technologies in new, relevant, and unpredictable ways rather than responding to self-consciously designed "appropriate technologies" provided by NGOs or well-meaning outsiders.

Advanced "emerging" technologies have also impacted significantly on local communities in rural Bangladesh. The best-known is the contribution of Grameen's village-level phone initiative, which has been widely acclaimed on several levels. Grameen Telecom and Grameen Phone, linked to the Grameen Bank village-based microfinance organization established by Nobel Prize winner Prof M. Yunus, has innovated a rural development intervention that involves leasing cell phones at village level to poor borrowers as part of its expansion of rural telecom infrastructure. When assessed from both the perspective of the sellers of phone services (the telephone lessees/owners) and from that of the buyers of services (the local villagers who use phones to get access to local price information, or to phone migrant relatives) it has been found that phones bring economic benefits, according to Bayes (2001). By 2010, there were more than 400,000 so-called "telephone ladies" among the Grameen Bank's eight million borrowers, and Grameen Phone has more than 2.5 million phone subscribers among the broader population (Yunus, 2010). Bayes (2001) argues that this technology—originally developed in rich countries for a different set of priorities and purposes—has been pragmatically deployed in the development field. In a village setting, phones reduce transaction costs by making market price information more visible to small traders, generate services for poor people, and create new income streams for those able to sell phone services. He also argues that there is a "perceptible and positive effects on the empowerment and social status of phone-leasing women and their households" (p. 261) along with a set of noneconomic benefits that include improvements in law enforcement and better disaster response.

The Case of Floods and Climate Change: Reaching for Technology

Annual flooding is a central component of Bangladesh's agro-ecological system, since it replenishes the fertility of farmland, but abnormal floods have long impacted on communities with devastating results. There has been a long history of flood control efforts that have aimed, largely unsuccessfully, to try to mitigate these negative impacts. Such efforts have primarily centered on public engineering efforts to construct river embankments intended to prevent overflowing. The devastating 1922 floods that affected the northern part of Bengal resulted in a celebrated report by Calcutta Professor Prasanta C. Mahalanobis on the ineffectiveness of flood mitigation through building embankments. The rapid siltation that would result, he argued, would simply raise the river beds. However, when the Pakistan government, assisted by international donor funds, began a multimillion-dollar flood control Master Plan in 1964 that centred around the construction of precisely this infrastructure, Mahalanobis' advice had been largely forgotten, and the scheme met with limited results.

At the end of the 1980s, history was to repeat itself again with the Flood Action Plan (FAP), launched after the heavy floods of 1987 and 1988. A communiqué from the G-7 summit held in London in July 1989 (World Bank 1989: 23, quoted in Adnan 1991: 8) stated:

> Bangladesh ... is periodically devastated by catastrophic floods ... [There was] ... need for effective, coordinated action by the international community, in support of the Government of Bangladesh, in order to find solutions to this major problem which are technically, financially, economically, and technically sound.

Approved formally in May 1990, the proposed FAP included a total of 26 studies and pilot schemes, 11 "main" components and 15 "supportive" components. The aim was to construct tall embankments along both sides of Bangladesh's three main rivers, at an estimated cost of US$5–10 billion. This mega-project was to be one of the largest development projects ever undertaken. The French government joined with Japan, UNDP, and USAID to engage a wide range of foreign experts, including engineers and later social scientists, to devise flood prevention and control schemes.

These were the final years of General H.M. Ershad's unelected military government, which agreed a proposed US$5–10 billion mega-project with a multi-donor group without reference to any form of democratic process. FAP aimed to produce the ultimate technological solution to the flood problem primarily through engineered embankments, drawing particularly on experiences with flood control efforts in the Netherlands and in parts of the United States—contexts later found to differ in important ways from the Bengal delta region. Only after campaigning involving local activists, researchers, and international civil society was any attempt made to consult local people on a limited level. In some areas the plan was resisted by local communities, who resented the top-down imposition of new infrastructure and water governance rules that many felt would have limited relevance to their needs. FAP was eventually rejected because it was based on similar technical assumptions to those Mahalanobis and other experts had earlier discredited (Adnan, 2009). General Ershad was removed from power after a "people power" mass movement in 1990, and a new "caretaker government" launched a task force to investigate the plan's viability. By 1993, despite already having spent millions of dollars of aid money on a small amount of infrastructure and many hundreds of technical reports by consultants, the FAP idea had been shelved.

In retrospect, FAP failed because it demonstrated a classic set of interrelated problems relating to technology and development:

- *A top-down rather than collaborative approach*: FAP took shape in a strongly top-down way under World Bank leadership at a meeting far from Bangladesh, without consultation or participation from the country's citizens. When General Ershad's military government fell in late 1990, a new interim caretaker government took power and convened a task force on the Flood Action Plan in February 1991, which reported a range of concerns, including the fact that the plan had not been opened to public debate (Custers, 1993).
- *The privileging of powerful interests, not equity*: FAP's primarily technical emphasis on the construction of embankments and sluice gates paid little attention to the potential of "softer" people-centered solutions, and largely ignored past traditions of community management of floods. FAP also seemed blind to the political and administrative complexity of how such infrastructure could be effectively or equitably managed. Conflicts of interest emerged within and between government, donors and foreign consultants. International civil society opposition began to mobilize, such as the US International Rivers Network, and formed links with local groups.
- *The centrality of outside experts with little local or community-level expertise*: FAP over-relied on external donor expertise drawn from contexts such as lowland water management in the Netherlands and flood control in the US Mississippi, both of which were potentially out of step with Bangladesh's own distinctive ecology and society. Even at a technical level (leaving aside history, politics, and society), problems quickly became apparent. Little effort was made to engage with local or indigenous knowledge relating to this complex ecosystem.
- *An all-consuming, "mega-project" approach*: the establishment of the FAP quickly began to dominate development activities in Bangladesh. Hundreds of preliminary studies were commissioned to consider a wide range of water-related issues around

the country, engaging large numbers of local and expatriate researchers, consultants and administrators, and drawing them away from work on other equally important issues. Development in Bangladesh, it seemed, had now become subordinated to the central problem of flood control.

Together these problems created a flaw in the FAP approach in which insufficient attention was paid to the context in which the new technological solution to the flood "problem" was being advanced. Indeed, local people in rural areas have always tended to see the "problem" of floods differently to either local officials or outside experts. For many rural people, the flood plain is viewed as a wet-land environment that supports a complex indigenous farming system that includes cropping, livestock, and fisheries—all of which depend on normal annual flooding of the land. This holistic view is at odds with the specialized and "partitioned" knowledge of outsiders who favor a dry-land scenario for increasing agricultural production. In this view, water is to be managed through the operation of flood control infrastructure, and kept away from the fields during the monsoon season (Adnan, 2009: 107):

> this official view is at variance with the social and cultural perceptions of the floodplain dwellers, and largely ignores the views of concerned professional experts on agricultural and environmental issues … the dryland scenario may be regarded as the product of a technocratic culture in which scientific principles and skills are marshalled to address a narrowly defined "problem", without adequate concern for the wider picture.
>
> This led those policy-makers driving the FAP to "reach for" a set of technological solutions that would be neither effective in nor appropriate to the context of Bangladesh's society, ecology, and institutions.

Today, 20 years on, it is remarkable how few policy-makers and donors in Bangladesh seem to remember the FAP experience. One reason is the high turnover of expatriate development personnel and the resulting lack of institutional memory within the aid agencies. Within the development policy world, this high turnover of staff contributes to the tendency to forget through what Sogge (1996: 16) refers to as a "continuity of discontinuity," in which postings are short and people are regularly replaced every few years. Another is the ideology of managerialism that creates strong pressures for development policy to "focus forward" onto new challenges such as the Millennium Development Goals or climate change—creating very little incentive for aid personnel to focus on failed projects of the past. This is the world of the "perpetual present" in which development interventions are premised on the idea of doing things differently and better in the future, which leads to an ahistorical culture of policy (Lewis, 2009). If we turn now to the new preoccupation with climate change among agencies and government in Bangladesh, we see this process in action.

In 2007, the Fourth Assessment Report of the Inter-Governmental Panel on Climate Change (IPCC) predicted that average global temperatures could rise by around three degrees centigrade by the end of the current century and sea levels by 59 cm. This will likely result in increased flooding as Himalayan snow and glaciers melt, and more frequent and destructive extreme weather events occur. Increasing periods of heat-wave and more heavy rainfall are also being predicted. Against this backdrop, climate change has rapidly moved to the center of the policy agendas of many of the main development agencies working in Bangladesh. For example, USAID now characterizes Bangladesh as "the most vulnerable country to climate change impact," with rising global sea-levels that are already altering local ecosystems and adding to economic hardship among the population. There is an increasingly pessimistic diagnosis of Bangladesh's situation: as sea levels rise, land is lost from the coastal areas, and as the flow of river water down into the delta from the melting Himalayan glaciers increases, more land will then be lost through more rapid soil erosion.

The Bangladesh government responded quickly and was among the first to produce a National Adaptation Plan of Action (NAPA) in 2005, in a process that included a wide range of consultations. In September 2009, the government produced its *Climate Change Strategy and Action Plan* based on six "pillars for action": food security, social protection, and health; comprehensive disaster management; infrastructure, research, and knowledge management; mitigation and low carbon development; and capacity building and institutional strengthening (MoEF, 2009).

While climate change is clearly an important issue for Bangladesh, there are growing concerns about the ways responses are unfolding. International media coverage increasingly draws on what might be termed a "crisis narrative." A Reuters news agency article dated April 14, 2008 proclaimed that "Bangladesh faces climate refugee nightmare," as internally displaced "climate change refugees" are forced to leave coastal areas in search of more secure environments. Johann Hari (2008) in the *Independent* reported on increased problems of saline drinking water, plots that have become too damaged to grow crops, and coastal waters that have become too dangerous to fish. Connecting Bangladesh's situation with the need for rich countries to take action, he concluded with the apocalyptic message that "if we carry on as we are, Bangladesh will enter its endgame." While climate change constitutes a major crisis, the invention of new terms such as "climate refugee" sits uncomfortably with longer narratives of poverty in Bangladesh. It implies a recent climate-driven break with past behaviors, rather than the continuation of and adaptation within people's long-term survival strategies. As Hartmann (2010) points out, the term "climate refugee" in fact replays an earlier idea from the 1990s about "environmental refugees," which in turn recycles unhelpful colonial stereotypes of environmentally destructive peasants.

One result is that economic and political causes of environmental problems run the risk of being obscured and the demographic pressure for migration over-emphasized. Another is that the complexities of environmental science in this unstable river and coastal ecology become over-simplified (Bradnock and Saunders, 2002). Rivers have regularly changed course, and coastal areas are constantly being eroded. For example, while the large numbers of people who live on Bangladesh's shifting silt islands (known as 'chars') have learned to cope with the frequent movements and migrations necessary to maintain a livelihood in what has long been an insecure and inhospitable environment, it is only during the last few years with the onset of climate change discourse that such people have come to be labelled "climate change refugees" by donors and nongovernmental organizations (NGOs). There is a danger that a "crisis discourse" of climate change is beginning to obscure other deep-rooted causes of insecurity, and the policy efforts to address these problems, such as the long-term issue of flooding in vulnerable areas due to poor water management policies, or the growth of salinity primarily caused by the expansion of commercial shrimp farming.

The need to migrate as a result of Bangladesh's unstable ecology is therefore not new, but has always characterized the prevailing harsh livelihoods of communities living in vulnerable areas. These livelihoods were fragile long before climate change issues registered with today's policy-makers. At the same time, a wide range of long-term government and NGO development initiatives—such as income generation, credit provision, community organization, land rights strengthening and infrastructure building—have been attempting to engage with such problems for many years, often with some success. The potential dangers are similar to those experienced during FAP: an over-emphasis on technological solutions and top-down interventions, the lack of value given to indigenous knowledge and local perspectives, and an over-simplification of the present that risks obscuring the potential value of lessons from the past. There is already growing resistance among some civil society actors to what is being perceived as a new top-down climate change discourse, reminiscent to that experienced during the FAP era. For example, a new $60 million World Bank adaptation loan for a planned Pilot Project on Climate Resilience (PPCR), that will include the building of coastal embankments, is at time of writing being met with increasing protests from NGOs and other groups.

Conclusion

This chapter has briefly considered the problem of "policy memory" in relation to broad issues of technology and development. This idea refers to a set of tendencies within development policy communities to over-focus on current and future priorities at the expense of opportunities to learn from past policy histories. This is particularly apparent among today's national and international policy-makers as they begin to mobilize to tackle climate change issues in Bangladesh. The largely unsuccessful efforts at promoting large-scale flood control technologies in the form of the FAP almost two decades ago may offer some potentially useful lessons and pointers, yet this policy history is largely absent from current debates. It is striking how far such episodes in earlier policy histories are only poorly remembered, or even sometimes entirely forgotten, within the "perpetual present" of policy-making discourses (Lewis, 2009).

Policy lessons and insights in relation to technology may therefore become lost to a form of "technological amnesia," and this raises important challenges for the new discussions of emerging technologies. If people were to revisit the FAP, they might find for example that there are many important lessons that would be potentially useful in relation to the rush to "mainstream" climate change within development policy in Bangladesh. In retrospect, the FAP can be seen as a case study of the ways development experts tend to conceive of problems in excessively "technical" ways and attempt impose top-down solutions, in preference to engaging locally with the people who live with their problems on a daily basis.

Why does this happen? An anthropology of policy approach draws attention to both the "mobilizing metaphor" of environmental crisis, which has a long history dating back to the colonial era, and the "underpinning ideology" of current policy-making, which is the neoliberal one of managerialism. The first is the recurring yet unhelpful power of the "crisis narrative" of environmental catastrophe, which as we have seen is comparable in many ways to that crisis narrative of flooding during the late 1980s, and to earlier colonial narratives of environmental refugees. The second is the power of managerialism, the ideology that now permeates the organized worlds of development as never before (Roberts *et al.*, 2005). This tends to discourage engagement with past and present ideas, through an unrelenting emphasis on novelty and change. One example of this is the way a strongly "imagined narrative" of development is maintained by the use of constantly changing development "buzzwords" such as empowerment, participation, and poverty reduction (Cornwall and Brock, 2005). As a consequence, the worlds of development practice become decontextualized, and an ahistorical approach is privileged. Such neologisms contribute to the removal of the development present from its deeper historical reference points, and ultimately has a depoliticizing effect by building forms of superficial consensus that distract from the need to address underlying issues of politics and power.

4.
ACHIEVING EQUITABLE OUTCOMES THROUGH EMERGING TECHNOLOGIES
A Social Empowerment Approach
Guillermo Foladori

Developed countries have invested considerably in nanotechnologies, and many developing countries are now putting public funding toward research and development. In Latin America, Brazil leads the way, followed by Mexico and Argentina, but many other countries in the region have active nanotechnology research centers (Foladori and Invernizzi, 2008). Nanotechnology development in many Latin American countries follows is market-driven rather than following state policies, an approach which suffers from two deficiencies: first, given the uncertainties of returns on this emerging technology, investment in nanotechnology has generally been limited; and second, this is a far different path than one aimed at satisfying the most pressing social needs.

Can nanotechnology be an instrument to boost the development of countries? This is an important question, and the answer depends on how we define *development*, bearing in mind that technological development in itself can lead to economic growth—which is one way of defining development—but it is not necessarily a guarantee of development, if we understand development to mean less inequality and poverty and a higher standard of living for people at large.

To answer the question, I examined the different discourses on the roles that nanotechnology and science and technology (S&T) policy play in development in Latin America. I found that nanotechnology development in Latin America follows the trajectory of the market, which is a far different path than that toward satisfying the most pressing social needs. In this chapter I review how these discourses work in favor of the market, and suggest alternate ways to craft and implement nanotechnology policy for the best social ends.

The Discourse of Nanotechnology Policy

Existing S&T policies in Latin America and proposals for research and development coming from universities and other organizations consider that nanotechnology can offer: (1) a road to increasing international competitiveness; (2) cheap and efficient technologies in key fields to satisfy social needs such as drinking water, energy, and medicine; and/or (3) a path to development if financial support and a regulatory framework are in place to ensure an even distribution of the benefits. These three concepts are not necessarily contradictory; in fact, they often complement one another.

International Competitiveness

Many official documents refer to the drive to compete on an international scale. The National Nanotechnology Initiative of the United States, for example, justifies the allocation of federal funds for nanotechnology research in order to maintain international competitiveness: "Federal support of the nanotechnology is necessary to enable the United States to take advantage of this strategic technology and remain competitive in the global marketplace well into the future" (NS&TC, 2000: 21).

The Brazilian Work Group for Nanosciences and Nanotechnology, which prepared the first document voicing support for nanotechnology research, also justifies public support for nanotechnology to ensure competitiveness:

> The aim of this program is to create and develop new products and processes in nanotechnology, implementing them in order to increase national industrial competitiveness and to train workers to take advantage of the economic, technological and scientific opportunities of nanotechnology.
>
> (GT, 2003: 8)

We find the same rationale in the decree that created the Argentinean Nanotechnology Foundation in 2005:

> a program to encourage, lay the foundations for and promote the development of human and technical infrastructure in Argentina so that, through its own and related activities, conditions can be established that allow the country to compete at the international level in the application and development of micro and nanotechnologies that increase the earned value of products for internal consumption and export.
>
> (Decreto Presidencial 380/2005)

In Mexico, nanotechnology appears as a strategy in the *Special Science and Technology Program 2001–2006*. A few years later, in the *Special Science and Technology Program 2008–2012*, the importance of nanotechnology, along with other fields, was justified as follows:

> The S&T sector establishes as fundamental the development in this field of quality education and the strengthening of basic and applied science, technological development and innovation to help improve the overall standard of living in our society and achieve greater competitiveness.
>
> (CONACYT, 2008: 25)

Unlike the other documents, the Mexican statement shows a clear intention to work toward improved standards of living, although competitiveness is a recurring theme. However, the announcement of the creation of the Nanoscience and Nanotechnology Network in 2009 reads: "Research into nanotechnology can afford our country the necessary innovation to create hi-tech companies to increase our level of competitiveness and create well-paying jobs" (CONACYT, n.d.).

These examples illustrate a kind of mechanical reasoning in which increased competitiveness will ensure improved living conditions, but this does not bear out. On the contrary, the wealth that comes from increased competitiveness is generally not distributed equitably, so competitiveness leads in fact to widespread inequality, as it did in Mexico from 1985 to 1995 (Delgado Wise and Invernizzi, 2002).

Efficient Technologies for Immediate Needs

The second rationale for nanotechnology development is that it can satisfy immediate needs. With this goal, the Task Force on Science and Technology and Innovation of the United Nations Millennium Project recommends directing nanotechnology development toward strategic sectors such as drinking water, medicine, and energy.

> The use of nanotechnology applications for water treatment and remediation; energy storage, production, and conversion; disease diagnosis and screening; drug delivery systems; health monitoring; air pollution and remediation; food processing and storage; vector and pest detection and control; and agricultural productivity enhancement will help developing countries meet five of the [Millennium Development] Goals.
>
> (Juma and Yee-Cheong, 2005: 70)

In the same vein, the editorial "Tackling Global Poverty" written by the Council of Science Editors for the second issue of *Nature Nanotechnology* (2007, 2: 661), proposes that nanotechnology development in specific areas such as water and medicine will be a significant step in ameliorating the life of the poor.

This seems to connect nanotechnology more directly with the end product and with consumers. However, there is no direct connection. Productive investments are ruled by the rate of profit, not by the needs of the poor. The market marginalizes many important fields that could benefit from R&D; countless diseases around the world are neglected for this reason (Trouiller *et al.*, 2001; Zumla, 2002). The millions of people living in poverty without access to clean drinking water are unlikely to pay enough for water-purification technology to make its production worthwhile to a manufacturer in search of profit.

Focus on Developing Countries

Finally, we also see in the discourse of nanotechnology proposals an agenda to bring in financing and international collaboration in R&D specifically to benefit "developing" countries. In one proposal, the nanotechnology work group at the University of Toronto Joint Center for Bioethics (Salamanca-Buentello *et al.*, 2005) made direct reference to development, identifying five of the eight Millennium Development Goals that could benefit from the nanotechnology revolution, and proposing a path for financial support: "To expand on this idea, we propose an initiative, called 'Addressing Global Challenges Using Nanotechnology,' to accelerate the use of nanotechnology to address critical sustainable development challenges" (Salamanca-Buentello *et al.*, 2005: 0383). The Meridian Institute suggests this alternative is already being achieved by some governments through their development assistance programs:

> Few governments have effectively connected their nanotechnology programs with their official development assistance (ODA) programs. Given the stated commitment by many aid-giving governments to helping achieve the Millennium Development Goals, a reasonable proportion of their ODA should surely go toward developing and transferring technologies that could be of help.
>
> (Meridian Institute, 2005: 12)

This type of proposal is a step in the right direction, but it is a small step. It does not identify the social forces that are responsible for continued inequality and poverty, nor does it identify the social forces that could push for efforts to solve the structural problems of development.

Despite considerable differences among the three positions promoting nanotechnology, they all share a technical approach to problems of development. In these discourses, development is conceived as a way of obtaining goods or better distribution of goods. Less development equals fewer amounts of goods. This reduction of development to a problem of distribution of stuff is what makes the approach a technical one. It does not question the social relations that cause inequality or lack of goods. It does not elaborate on the way that market relations reproduce inequity and constitute a barrier for accessing those goods.

Rather than express a desire to alter the market forces that push for inequality and poverty, they rely on the market to overcome inequality. Trust in the market is most evident in the first approach, which proposes nanotechnology as a route to international competitiveness. This is a dead-end path, because a competitive advantage can only be obtained at the expense of others' losing positions, thus creating inequity. The second approach recognizes that competitiveness is not enough, and encourages nanotechnology development in those sectors where the most urgent social needs can be satisfied; but it is also a technical approach because it does not examine the multiple barriers that market relations pose for capital to invest in those economic sectors. The third approach understands that a specific financial package needs to be implemented. But it is still a technical approach because it does not elaborate on the social forces that can push forward such kind of initiative or be twisted by market forces.

What Have Nanotechnologies Shown in Their First Decade of Development?

First, R&D for nanotechnologies in their first decade on the market has been rapidly concentrated in rich countries. According to Científica Consultants, specialists in nanotechnology, the eight largest players in the field in terms of public investment in 2008 were the European Union (if viewed as a single unit comprising 25 countries), Russia, China, the United States, Japan, South Korea, India, and Taiwan. The only developing countries in this list are China and India, both of which have a very large GDP (Científica, 2008: 36). Nanotechnologies require a large amount of capital, which accounts for why R&D is concentrated in more developed countries.

Another indicator of concentration of wealth in nanotechnologies is the monopoly on patents. According to data compiled by the Organización de Estados Iberoamericanos para la Educación, la Ciencia y la Cultura (OEI) in 2009, between 2000 and 2007 and from the World Intellectual Property Organization data, around 42 percent of patents are in the hands of ten large corporations such as Bayer, Philips, and 3M, in addition to some economically powerful American universities such as the University of California and the Massachusetts Institute of Technology (OEI, 2009). If we look at the countries where patents are concentrated, the situation is even clearer, with the United States holding over 60 percent of patents.

Yet another indicator is the concentration of nanotechnological raw materials. According to the exhaustive records of Nanowerk, almost 50 percent of the companies that supply nanotechnological materials are located in the United States (146 out of a total of 305 as of March 2009; Nanowerk Database, n.d.). The concentration of nano-technology R&D in wealthy developed countries, which is intrinsically linked to the market economy, does not hold out many possibilities for developing countries.

Second, nanotechnologies have been developed primarily for the production of luxury goods. The Woodrow Wilson International Center for Scholars, in Washington DC, publishes a study that has been carried out since 2005 to identify products with nanocomponents that are already on the market (over 1,000 in 2009). This inventory shows the degree of progress of nanotechnology to meet the needs of the consumer. The results show that the vast majority of products are luxury items (WWICS, 2009; Foladori and Invernizzi, 2006). Of course, market trends tend to favor sectors with high purchasing power, which is a far cry from combating inequality and poverty.

Third, concerns that have arisen over the potential risks of nanotechnology to health and the environment, and over their impact in the workplace, have not stemmed from the companies that are researching and producing nanoparticles and nanostruc-tures, nor have they stemmed from the governments that provide public funding for R&D in nanotechnology. Rather, the concerns that have been voiced have come from NGOs and trade unions (Foladori, 2009). As a result, the incorporation of regulation issues in the public agendas of Europe and the United States has occurred only recently and in the wake of declarations issued by international coalitions that include dozens of NGOs and trade unions (ETC group, 2003; ACTU, 2005; FoE—Australia, 2006; UITA, 2006–7; ICTA, 2007; ETUC, 2008). This illustrates the social forces in play, and which social forces can aid the responsible development of nanotechnologies.

What Should a Social Focus for the Development of Nanotechnologies Take into Account?

In Latin America, nearly all the funding for R&D in nanotechnology is public (Invernizzi, 2010). In some countries, such as Brazil, Argentina, Mexico, and Chile, there are funds specifically earmarked for nanotechnology. In other countries, nano-technology researchers have to compete with other fields for funding. Nevertheless, in all cases the norm is that financing should be short term and should be primarily provided to centers of excellence. These funds are normally awarded following a public contest and are for periods lasting from one to three years (Foladori and Invernizzi, 2008). This process of short-term funding is based on the reasoning that once governments kick-start the project, private companies will begin to invest in nanotechnology R&D in the longer term, and they will employ the knowledge gained in marketable products.

The reality that private companies are actually reluctant to invest in nanotechnology R&D is a far cry from these good intentions. Nanotechnologies do not enter a known market in which there are production chains and mechanisms that provide access to credits and an already functioning market. Instead, these new products are often disruptive in that they carry out multiple functions and are not exactly the same as products that already exist. They have to create new chains, from the purchase of raw materials to processes for incorporating nanoparticles and nanostructures into existing end products. There is no historical reference, which makes it difficult for private companies to invest in R&D and production under these conditions of uncertainty.

Furthermore, there are problems concerning consumer attitudes when it comes to unknown products. There is an ongoing international debate over the potential toxic effects of nanoproducts on human health and the environment.[1] Nevertheless, the public institutions that are responsible for propelling nanotechnology in Latin America, instead of taking the initiative to encourage R&D on toxicity and the environment, attempt to hide the possible negative effects in order to avoid market barriers and remain competitive. This is clear in the guidelines for nanotechnology funds, which include almost no mention of potential risks (Invernizzi, 2010). Therefore, the final stage of getting an end product to the consumer is built on quicksand, and this is something that private enterprise is not inclined to undertake.

Governments that promote disruptive technologies such as nanotechnologies must consider three interlinked levels and offer long-term funding: R&D, the production of products with nanocomponents and consumer access to these products.

Although funding for R&D in Latin America is public, there is no policy for long-term financing for strategic areas. Nor is there, in many countries, any serious consideration of which areas are strategic and which have scientific and technical knowledge and infrastructure for research and production in addition to mechanisms for reaching the consumer. This means it is possible that the direction the process takes will end up being determined by the market; and the pre-existing alliances and agreements among multinational companies and research institutes in developed countries will end up taking R&D increasingly in the direction required by the world market rather than towards satisfying the endogenous needs of countries.

The second level is the production of products with nanocomponents. Although they have been shrinking since the 1980s, Latin American countries have public sectors for material production, mostly for drinking water, energy, health, and transport. These could very well be used by public companies and integrated into R&D and boost the production of nanotechnologies to meet the urgent needs of the country. These sectors also have mechanisms for end products to reach the consumer (third level) without having to go through the market or depend on subsidies. A project of this nature would organically integrate R&D with production and consumption.

However, to carry out a project of this nature it is necessary to consider which social sectors would propel this type of proposal. The worldwide experience of a decade of development of nanotechnologies and the way they have developed in Latin America would appear to suggest that neither the business community nor the public sector would be interested in undertaking this task. This type of project could only be conducted by trade unions or NGOs interested in improving the living conditions of the people as a whole and providing guarantee for consumers.

Conclusions

With the advent of nanotechnologies, human society is experiencing a technological experiment on a worldwide scale. These technologies promise to radically change research, productive processes and daily life. Both developed countries and many developing countries are investing public money in R&D for nanotechnologies. In Latin America, this is happening in Brazil, Mexico, Argentina, Chile, Colombia, and several other countries.

But the processes through which public institutions in Latin America support the development of nanotechnology are not satisfactory. They offer only minimum funding in the short term for R&D and call it innovation, expecting the private sector to do the rest: to continue research, produce goods, and get the goods to consumers. This is not how things really work when it comes to disruptive technologies. There is no experience with already established productive chains, nor is there any private financing or established markets. This means that it is likely that nanotechnology R&D in Latin America will end up being directed to satisfy the needs of academic and scientific alliances with institutions that lie outside the region, or with multinational corporations.

Alternatively, most Latin American countries still count on productive sectors in the hands of the state, and these could become involved with the R&D. There is also the possibility of reaching the neediest sectors directly, especially in areas where the public sector has a monopoly or a great deal of influence, which is the case when it comes to drinking water, energy, transport, and health. The problem is that for this to happen, other social forces would have to propel the R&D for nanotechnology. As has been shown worldwide as well as in Latin America, these forces are trade unions and NGOs that are directly interested in the efforts of S&T that aim to bring about a reduction in poverty and inequality. The path lies ahead. It remains to be trodden.

5.
EMERGING TECHNOLOGIES AND INEQUALITIES
Beyond the Technological Transition
Susan Cozzens[1]

The innovation systems approach to societal development includes a critique of the common focus on high technologies in the development process—complex technologies that require high levels of knowledge and skill to develop and operate. Even in affluent economies, directing resources exclusively to high technologies neglects the broader innovative processes undertaken by doing, using, and interacting. In developing economies, with fewer resources, too strong a focus on high technologies is unlikely to produce as much benefit as a more inclusive concept of innovation.

Emerging technologies—a subset of high technologies—are defined as those that are new, science-based, and of potentially broad impact (Cozzens *et al.*, 2010). They are a particular subset of high technologies, located at what some call the technological frontier. Affluent countries compete for leadership in emerging technologies like bio- and nanotechnologies, and some less affluent countries have in the past found significant opportunities in the wide open spaces of the technology emergence process. In the context of developing countries, the distinction between emerging and older technologies may be less clear, since learning often takes place at the border between the two when new developments build on accumulated know-how and research knowledge.

This chapter looks at five examples of emerging technologies from the viewpoint of several developing countries, with particular attention to their distributional consequences. None of the examples represents the kind of dramatic opportunities that get so much attention in the innovation studies literature—there are no Koreas, Taiwans, or Singapores here. Precisely because of this, these cases may be more representative of the dilemmas emerging technologies present for countries that are trying to achieve inclusive growth.

The chapter presents some of the results from a cross-national, cross-technology study of the distributional effects of emerging technologies. The five technologies studied were: genetically modified (GM) maize, mobile phones, open source software, plant tissue culture, and recombinant insulin. The eight countries included were: Argentina, Canada, Costa Rica, Germany, Jamaica, Malta, Mozambique, and the United States. Half are high-income and half are low- or middle-income countries. This chapter focuses on the results of the study in the four low- and middle-income countries.

Emerging technologies are a strategic research site for examining the interaction of inequalities between countries and inequalities within countries.[2] Conceptually, we defined emerging technologies in this project as new and research-based, with potential broad impact. Operationally, we studied the distributional consequences of selected biotechnologies and information and communication technologies (ICTs). Our goals were to:

1. describe the dynamics that link emerging technologies to patterns of inequality;
2. identify the roles of public interventions in those dynamics; and
3. develop a framework that policy actors can use prospectively to analyze the distributional valence of a specific new technology in a particular national context. Our central research question is how policy interventions affect distributional outcomes for the same technology under different national conditions.

Studying Emerging Technologies

Why study emerging technologies in this project? First, precisely because they are new, emerging technologies are the site of change and growth in both global and local economies. The networks of social and economic relations that support them are still young and malleable, but are projected to be more significant as time goes on. They would therefore represent a good place for public interventions towards equality, if such interventions were needed. Second, because emerging technologies are research-based, they are more likely to be sold at high prices (as firms try to recoup research and development costs) and to demand high levels of skills in the production process. Both these characteristics give emerging technologies a higher potential than older technologies for increasing inequalities.

Third, emerging technologies stand at the intersection of global and national distributive processes. The dominant pattern in emerging technologies has been that new technologies have been developed in North America, Europe, or North Asia (the "Triad" regions), then diffused to other parts of the world, either when a multinational firm decides to place a production facility there or when the technology becomes available for purchase. The benefits and costs that people experience in the creating, producing, and using countries as a result of this process vary greatly among countries and technologies, but the global pattern of inequality sometimes appears inevitable. Technology-creating countries always seem to be those starting the revolutions, and technology-using countries always seem to be trying to catch up, when we consider only this pattern.

To create a different pattern, however, many non-Triad countries invest in their local capabilities in emerging technologies, not only to provide better local capacity to absorb the technologies, but also as the basis for using the emerging technology to meet local needs and create local competitive advantage. Indeed, the Millennium Project task force on innovation (Juma and Lee, 2005) recommended that every developing country invest in "platform technology" areas, including biotechnology, ICTs, advanced materials, and nanotechnology. These investments might create a new re-distributional pattern with significant implications for the relationships between technologies and inequalities.

Our study has provided an opportunity to examine both of these patterns in action. We assumed that reality is more complex than either the "dominating North" or "optimistic South" views, and we set out to describe the actual distributional dynamics generated by emerging technologies in various national contexts.

Initial Concepts

The basic logic of the data gathering and analysis has been that *technological projects* affect *inequalities* in *valued items* through pathways that are technology-specific, mediated by *national conditions*, and shaped by *public interventions*. Before turning back to the specific technological projects the study is examining, let us pause over each of these other concepts.

The term *technology* above is shorthand for the concept of *technological projects*, that is, organized efforts of a group or institution. While private industry is the main source of technological projects, public institutions or civil society groups may also put them into motion. The study is based on the assumption that technological projects are always inherently distributional, and that the distributional aspects of individual projects and portfolios of projects are open to choice.

Inequality is the unequal distribution of something people value. This project has not only considered inequality in incomes, the focus of the economic literature on the topic, but also inequalities in the distribution of the benefits and costs of technological projects. We explicitly include both vertical inequalities (the rich-poor dimension) and horizontal inequalities (differences by gender, ethnicity, or other culturally defined factors).

In this project, we have focused on inequalities in three *valued items*, each generated through a different relationship to the emerging technology: business ownership and opportunities, employment, and benefits/costs. Since under our definition, emerging technologies are research-based, innovation plays a strong role in bringing them into being, when the other necessary forms of capital and organizational skill are present. This is the process of technology *creation*. New intellectual capital for one actor can destroy the value of the intellectual property of another as, for example, when synthetic fibers undermined natural fiber-based industries and devalued knowledge and skills many developing countries possessed. Conflicts over intellectual property are a common feature of the process of incorporating an emerging technology into a national context. We have therefore included examination of the distributional aspects of those issues in our study. The ownership of intellectual property has been treated in context as part of capital accumulation and business ownership.

Relatively few jobs are associated with the creation of technology, but many are generated when the technology goes into *production, marketing,* and *sales*. Competition among countries for manufacturing production jobs is fierce, and technology-creating countries do not always win. Jobs can be generated directly, through production or sales of the technology, indirectly through raising the productivity of another business, or indirectly as the wages of workers in the new or expanding industry are spent in the local economy (the multiplier effect). Production jobs in ICTs or pharmaceuticals can significantly affect small economies, as can successful commercial agriculture. However, the higher labor productivity of new production processes may mean that fewer jobs are generated through these processes than through other industries, and they may be accessible to a narrower segment of the population. Employment is thus a key variable we have tracked in our analysis.

Technologies are ultimately designed to deliver benefits in health, food, environment, etc., through use. These benefits are technology-specific, as are the costs that might be generated in a specific national context. For example, the benefit from insulin would be better control of blood sugar and improved quality of life for diabetics, but if the insulin is only available to affluent consumers, these benefits could increase health disparities. To receive benefits, people must have access to the technology, through private purchase or public procurement, so in each case study we have characterized *access* to the technology in question.

The distributional effects of technological projects are mediated through a variety of *national conditions*, which are seldom discussed in the literature on technological impacts. As a starting point in analyzing the effects of these conditions, we described our case study countries in terms of national income level, poverty, general human capital in the form of educational attainment and specialized training of the nation's citizens, and technological capability. The last is a complex concept, only imperfectly captured in the many current indicators and indexes related to it, and we looked for its presence beyond the indicators in our cases. These are the kinds of general factors that we expected to be associated with common patterns across technologies within countries.

Finally, our study characterized the policy instruments available to S&T decision-makers to influence distributional consequences. We refer to these generically as *public interventions*, because they constitute a mix of policies, programs, and other kinds of actions. These interventions may either act to shape the technological projects themselves, for example through inputs from public research programs or incentives to firms, or by affecting the kinds of national conditions listed in the last paragraph, for example through investments in education to build human capital. Likewise, the absence of public intervention can influence technological projects profoundly, for example, the inability to establish a regulatory environment that creates trust.

Our early consultations with policy audiences about the project[3] produced an initial list of candidate areas for public intervention, including:

- regulatory policies (e.g. biosafety regulations that affect whether small or large farmers are more likely to benefit from planting a new crop);
- ownership provisions, for example, loose or tight intellectual property protection;
- shaping employment options through labor regulations; targeting specific technologies for faster development through public research;

- public procurement policies that provide markets for particular technologies, for example, health service purchases of recombinant insulin; and
- policies that develop human capital through specific training or general educational opportunities.

Choice of Technologies

We chose to study these issues through case studies because of the complexity of the relationships we are studying and the importance of context. As a team, we are very familiar with the available quantitative indicators, and therefore skeptical that they are able to reflect the dynamics we want to study. Our qualitative approach allowed us to put quantitative information in context, and at the same time to describe and compare factors that could not be included in a statistical analysis (Figure 5.1).

We chose technologies for case studies in light of our exploration of the literature and the conceptual framework of the study. One criterion was newness: we ruled out much older information and communication technologies like telephones and computers. Another criterion was relevance across the range of countries in the study. We would gain much less insight studying technologies that were only relevant in affluent countries. We tried to respond to opportunities arising from our team's experience and connections, and we attempted to balance the set in terms of the technological projects of large corporations versus smaller challengers.

In the ICT area, we focused first on *mobile telephones*. They are nearly ubiquitous: we have been able to study the mobile phone business in every country included in the study. The specific inventions that go into each mobile handset have origins in a number of different countries, and production is done on a distributed global basis. Furthermore, this technology is still evolving, with the emergence of third generation (3G) standards that are outside mainstream use in most countries. There are a number of creative uses of the technology, including by female entrepreneurs ("mobile phone ladies") in poor communities receiving microfinance. Because telephone service is a public utility, we expected to see a variety of public interventions in our cases. Indeed our preliminary review of national ICT policies in Africa, Asia, and the OECD countries, based on 62 policy documents available in English, showed wide variation in

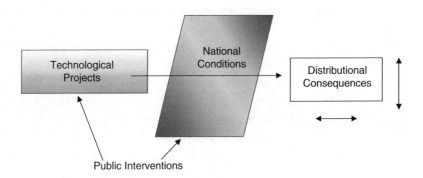

Figure 5.1 Initial model

approaches, with nearly one-third mentioning social inclusion or redistribution as one goal of the policy.[4]

To provide a counterbalance to the corporation-centered story of the mobile phone industry, we have also explored the open source software movement. Even in the poorest country of our group, Mozambique, it appeared that small businesses were growing up based on customization of open source software. The open source movement represents an alternative, democratized form of innovation (von Hippel, 2005), and has raised policy issues like the current debate on whether the European Union should use Linux exclusively as its operating system (Thurston, 2007).

In biotechnology, we divided our choice of cases into agricultural and health areas, which are quite distinct in industrial connections, production processes, and users. A good list exists of the genetically-modified crops in production worldwide and the countries that plant them (James, 2005). We were surprised to find that we could study a common genetically-modified crop planted in most of the countries of the study. Again, we chose a technology that has received less attention in the past. The literature on social impacts of GM crops has focused on soy and pesticide-ready cotton. GM maize, our case study technology, is in production in several countries in Europe as well as widely in the Americas and in South Africa.

There were, however, at the time we planned our study, only 21 countries in the world that were planting genetically-modified crops, including only one in Africa (James, 2005). To limit our study of agricultural biotechnology to these crops would have kept us from exploring why biotechnological capability is so high on the agendas of S&T policy-makers in a much broader set of countries. We therefore decided also to include case studies of the application of a much older biotechnology technique, plant tissue culture (PTC). Again, Mozambique provided a vivid example that helped us choose this example: while the technique is about 30 years old in the North, tissue culture of plants has only been possible in Mozambique in the past few years, through a new facility constructed with funds from the US Agency for International Development. Following through on the lesson learned from this story, we included analysis of several different locally important crops that were reproduced through tissue culture in the various countries in the study. The obvious candidate in Costa Rica was bananas, where almost all banana plants are grown in a laboratory, with 50 percent of the production by multinationals and the other 50 percent by 35 independent farmers. The focal crop across some other countries was potatoes, one of the fastest-growing food crops in the world.

Finally, we wanted a technology example from health biotechnology. Of the 256 biotechnology-based drugs approved by the US Food and Drug Administration at the time our study started,[5] only a few fell in areas where the World Health Organization has identified "essential medicines," important for developing countries.[6] A considerable and sometimes charged literature already exists on one such category, the drugs for HIV/AIDS (see for example Dodier, 2005; Homedes and Ugalde, 2006; Galvao, 2005; Baghadi, 2005). We chose a quieter case for our analysis. Recombinant insulin was the very first biotechnology-based drug approved by the US Food and Drug Administration (Walsh, 2005), and thus had the longest history of distributional consequences to trace.

It is an important drug, becoming more important by the year as the global epidemic of diabetes expands (World Health Organization, 2003). As with mobile phones, we were able to study the use of recombinant insulin in every country in the study. While it was developed first in the United States and one US firm still produces it, the largest producer is now Novo Nordisk, a Danish firm, which markets recombinant insulin in 179 countries. Social responsibility is a hallmark of Novo Nordisk, which is well known for working with nongovernmental organizations, and operates with a "triple bottom line," that is, financial, environmental, and social sustainability. The case thus gave us a chance to contrast business styles and philosophies.

Choice of Countries

Our partner project ResIST confined its efforts to three world regions, Europe, Africa, and Latin America/Caribbean, making the judgment that available resources did not permit the inclusion of Asia in its empirical studies, as important as developments there are. Resultar followed its lead in this. The ResIST researchers studied selected target technologies in their own countries, Germany, Malta, and Mozambique, and followed GM maize into the Czech Republic. The Resultar team complemented their efforts with a range of case studies in the Americas. In the end, the set included four "developed" countries and four "developing" ones, with a range of national income levels within each group (Table 5.1).

Methods

Our method is comparative case study. Each case is a technology-country pair, as indicated in Table 5.2. We have gathered information for each case represented there with XXs, using a common protocol, drawing information from published sources and interviews. We coded the reports on each case in NVivo, a qualitative analysis software tool, using a common set of categories: national conditions, technological project, public policy sphere (including public interventions), distributional consequences in business opportunities, employment, benefits and costs. Using this analysis, various team members have produced integrative chapters for each technology (synthesizing across the rows). Team members also identified policy implications within each of the national contexts (synthesizing down the columns).

Table 5.1 Countries

	Argentina	Canada	Costa Rica	Jamaica	United States	Germany	Malta	Mozambique
Population[1]	38.7m	32.3m	4.3m	2.7m	296.5m	82.5m	404,000	19.8m
GNI/capita[2]	$4,470	$32,600	$4,590	$3,480	$43,740	$34,580	$13,590	$310
Technological Achievement[3]	0.381	0.589	0.358		0.733	0.583	na	0.066

Notes
1 World Bank, World Development Indicators, data for 2005.
2 Gross National Income per capita, World Bank, World Development Indicators, data for 2005.
3 United Nations, Human Development Report 2001.

Table 5.2 Case Study Matrix

	AR	CA	CR	Ger	Jam	Mal	MZ	US
Mobile phones (8)	XX	XX	XX	XX	XX	XX	XX	XX
Open source (6)	XX	XX	XX	XX		XX	XX	XX
rDNA	XX	XX	XX	XX	XX	XX	XX	XX
Insulin (7)				EU				
GM maize	XX	XX	XX			XX		XX
(5)						CZ		
Tissue cultured crop (4)	XX	XX	XX		XX		XX	XX

Selected Results

One of the main lessons learned from the cases concerns diversity. On the one hand, the specific distributional consequences of the technologies are quite different and are clearly strongly influenced by all the factors displayed in the model: how the technological project was shaped by its champions; national conditions, in particular skills and poverty; and public interventions. On the other hand, the public interventions in each technology were relatively standard. And the overall distributional patterns followed some general patterns that we were able to see much more clearly from the comparison than we could have from individual cases.

In an earlier paper (Cozzens *et al.*, 2008), we discussed at length the lessons learned with regard to various parts of the model, so we only summarize here the main points of that analysis.

- The *technological project* was quite an important concept in the study. Each technology was shaped differently both by its champions and by the policy environment into which it was introduced. These differences profoundly affected both the business opportunities connected to the technologies and consumer access. For example, the introduction of competition in mobile phone markets stimulated the introduction of prepaid plans, which have had a huge impact on accessibility for low-income consumers.
- *National conditions* play a different role than we pictured when we started the project. Distributional consequences are not mediated by averages, like those given above for the case study countries, but rather by specific conditions for particular individuals or firms Some of the relevant conditions, however, are created by national governments, for example, an electricity infrastructure to underpin rural mobile networks. (If those conditions are specific to the technology, then we include them under "public interventions" rather than "national conditions.")
- *Public interventions,* a somewhat broader concept than public policies and programs but closely related, are key variables in our analysis. As the focus technologies were being commercialized or applied, we found five main categories of interventions in the cases: public procurement; public utility oversight; antitrust actions; health and safety regulations; and environmental protection.

The first three are mildly to strongly re-distributive, while the latter two affect access negatively because, while reducing overall risk and therefore overall costs to society, they raise costs for individual consumers, and sometimes for particular producers.

- With regard to the distribution of *business opportunities*, two factors were clearly significant. One was intellectual property protection. In some of our cases, multinational corporations held tight control of intellectual property around a new technology, limiting the opportunity for other firms to enter the market. A second constraint on business opportunity, however, is skill. If an environment does not have enough people at a high enough skill level to support or extend the technology, the ownership question is moot.

- Direct *employment effects* of the emerging technologies in our study were small, with the exception of the mobile phone service industry. In mobile phones, new jobs were created directly with the new form of service, but as landline subscriptions begin to drop, jobs will be lost in that part of the telephone business. For the other technologies, high-technology manufacturing jobs tended to stay in affluent countries (e.g. in recombinant insulin), and there was a modest shift from lower-skilled, more dangerous jobs to somewhat higher-skilled, less dangerous ones. Our study did not include any of the countries that experienced rapid growth in employment through electronics manufacturing—indicating that those experiences may be the exception rather than the rule.

- Considering the distribution of *benefits and costs* from the five technologies, we found a number of effects of public interventions (policies). Whether the product reached a particular consumer was usually due to a combination of action by the producing firm and the receiving government, along with specific conditions within a consuming firm or family. It was definitely not the case that the technology inevitably dropped in price until it reached a mass market; public interventions played a big role in shaping the market. What we are calling the "distributional boundary" for each technology is drawn by a combination of ownership structure, specialized skills, general educational levels, infrastructure—and price, which is itself often influenced by competitive conditions set by the state.

The Technological Transition

We are beginning to tie these various observations together with a new concept, a structural feature of the global economy that we call the *technological transition*.[7] One set of diffusion and adoption dynamics is characteristic above the transition point and another set below. Predictable shifts in dynamics therefore occur for any given technology at the point of transition. We suspect that the transition point is probably closely associated with the global absolute poverty line, but that point is still under investigation. Regardless of where the actual transition appears, it comes along with differences in income distributions such that below the transition point will appear a disproportionate number of women and members of disadvantaged religious and ethnic groups.

Above the transition point, champions can choose among luxury or mass markets for the products they create from the technological opportunity. Basic infrastructure can be taken for granted and champions must compete for the portion of a market created by the variety they offer. Technological choices involve relatively small shifts in costs in relation to income, and consumers have the resources and leisure to shop around.

Below the technological transition point, the product may be irrelevant (open source software for people without electricity, let alone computers) or downright dangerous (insulin in an urban slum, since the treatment itself can kill if the user does not have the right infrastructure to use it correctly). If the product reaches poor consumers at all, it is likely to be either lower quality (e.g. basic mobile service versus smartphones), in second-hand form (like the hand-me-down mobile phones common in Maputo), or broken down into small lots that cost more per unit (again, this point is illustrated by the higher rates per minute for prepaid versus contract mobile phone access). Poor consumers thus pay a larger share of their income to have access to the benefit, and the whole issue of benefits becomes more acute because the opportunity costs are relatively higher. The important questions then do not have to do with access per se, but rather with whether access might actually be counterproductive.

Developing Country Experiences

The preceding summary of results tracks the technologies across all eight countries in the study. How do these dynamics look from the viewpoint of the four middle- and low-income countries we studied? A few summary observations will have to stand in for the fuller analysis that will be available in the country chapters of the book we are preparing. Again, I draw here on the work my colleagues in Resultar and ResIST have reported.

First, while all the emerging technologies we studied did emerge in the North, scientists in developing countries were operating at the cutting edge in at least one case. An Argentinian scientist, Bernardo Houssay, won a Nobel Prize for his work on the relationship between diabetes and the pituitary (Gagliardino, 2000). Bovine insulin was also purified in Argentina within one year of its commercialization in the United States, and an Argentinian scientist established a production protocol and starting competing with other firms in the market shortly afterwards (Bisang *et al.*, 1986). But the US drug company Lilly moved in quickly and bought out the Argentine interest in the product, then produced it there for many years, close to a good supply of the bovine pancreas from which it was purified, which was a by-product of Argentina's active meat industry. Recombinant insulin disrupted this symbiotic business relationship by removing the need for the raw material.[8] The story is an even more familiar one today—large multinationals buying out the intellectual property of small firms in the South. In a much more recent example, another multinational in the insulin market, Novo Nordisk, acquired the Argentine firm Beta-Syntial in the 1990s. Such stories illustrate that the key to taking advantage of emerging technologies is not invention or discovery, but ownership and business opportunity.

Business opportunities. Across the four developing countries, there is significant variation in the extent to which local businesses grow up around the technologies. Argentina makes the strongest showing in this regard, with insulin production still happening there, partly based on the production facility left behind by Lilly but also supported by local biomedical expertise. Local seed companies coexist with huge Monsanto operations around genetically-modified crops, including in our case of maize. Outside the life sciences, however, the pattern breaks: mobile phones are entirely imported in Argentina and we found little business activity in open source software there, although some local universities and governments are pushing for the model.

In Costa Rica, a country with a similar level of wealth, local business was clearly helped by significant plant tissue culture operations, in a research facility supported by the banana industry as well as in several small firms.[9] But the plant tissue facilities were the only private business activity linked to our five technologies there. The puzzle in Costa Rica is why the significant local software industry, even aided by the efforts of some local social movements, does not generate any discernible open source business activity. In general across the countries, a local software industry is a necessary condition for open source businesses to emerge; but apparently it is not a sufficient one.

Another potential business opportunity that did not appear is plant tissue culture in Jamaica. There was an appropriate facility, used in a previous project with the European Union.[10] PTC does not need to be limited to bananas—planting materials for other local vegetatively propagated crops could be produced and sold. A few hundred miles away, in Florida, a thriving plant tissue culture industry thrives. "Why not in Jamaica?" we asked at the time of the study. Indeed, in the interim, a PTC company has begun there, the Christiana Potato Growers Association, propagating bananas as well as potatoes and other plants. It is still too new to know whether it will thrive.

In Mozambique, the technologies provide interesting support to livelihoods at the micro level (Brouwer, 2010). While mobile phone companies do not employ very many people, they do provide opportunities for hundreds of street vendors in Maputo to sell recharge cards on every corner. And tissue cultured planting materials prepared in a government laboratory and distributed by international aid organizations provide some help for subsistence farmers, many of them women, with perhaps some movement of the product involved into local markets.

In short, the variable experiences of our low- and middle-income countries show the business opportunities generated by emerging technologies depend crucially not only on the technical capabilities that already exist in a local environment, but also on some other set of complementary conditions that we were not able to identify.[11] Low technical capabilities keep the number of business opportunities low as well. Higher technical capabilities bring the possibility of more business opportunities, which innovation policies might be able to target.

Employment. As noted earlier, no major shifts in employment were visible in any of our case studies. The shift that seemed most likely was the substitution of recombinant for animal-based insulin that affected the production facility in Argentina; but local action prevented the plant from closing and a local market maintains it.[12] The contrast with the Asian Tigers, in which production of high-technology products has moved to developing countries, is striking and illustrates how limited those other experiences are and how hard it is to generalize from them to other developing countries.

Benefits and costs. All the technologies we studied were widely accessible in Argentina, Costa Rica, and Jamaica, with some rather specific holes in coverage. The wide availability of recombinant insulin was largely as a result of a combination health insurance and public health services, so where someone did not have access, it was because they were not covered—a situation that characterized a surprising 25 percent of Argentines. Many Jamaicans can afford to buy insulin from their own incomes, but the nearly 40 percent who work in the informal economy would have more trouble accessing insulin from the National Health Fund than others. Another hole in accessibility, this time of mobile phone handsets, was caused by the government telecommunications monopoly in Costa Rica, which managed to put a lot of obstacles in the way of acquiring the set—after which, service was cheap. With banana tissue culture material in Jamaica, small farmers in the past were not to be able to afford the materials, since they were not produced locally until recently. Larger farmers could import what they needed (pointing to a connection between business opportunity and access). Access to a basic level of the technology of course did not imply access to the best version that was available (the different versions of insulin illustrate), but mostly people living in middle-income countries are on the positive side of the distributional boundary.

The situation was different in Mozambique (Brito and Brouwer, 2010). Since there are only 20,000 computers in this country of 20 million, not many would have been able to benefit from open source software. Mobile phones are heavily concentrated among male users in Maputo, according to a telephone survey done by our Mozambican team. And for the estimated 80,000 diabetics in the country, only enough insulin for perhaps 50–100 people is imported. (Affluent Mozambicans in the south of the country can drive to South Africa and buy insulin over the counter in drug stores.) Doctors in Mozambique are reluctant to prescribe insulin to people in poor households who will not be able to maintain the necessary regimen. So ironically, while insulin is free through the public health service there, rich people are much more likely to benefit from that policy than poor ones. Likewise, ironically, prepaid phone plans make mobiles accessible to poor consumers, but they pay more per minute used.

None of these limitations is inevitable, as the story of the tissue-cultured orange flesh sweet potato plantings in Mozambique illustrates. When government and NGOs decide to work together to diffuse a useful technology, they can be successful, especially with a community-based multi-pronged approach involving education and subsidies. Our Mozambican colleagues recommend policies that incorporate these elements for other technologies as well.

To summarize, we can look at the information our cases provide across a continuum from innovation to production to use of the technology in question (Table 5.3). There is close to no innovation in the stories (with the exception of the very old example in Argentina). There is very little production except in the agricultural technologies: some plant tissue culture, some production surrounding GM maize seeds, but only a small FOSS effort in Costa Rica. Use, however, is widespread, except in GM maize, which is kept out of two of the four countries by regulation. Our cases thus provide

Table 5.3 Distribution of Creation, Production, and Use across Technologies

	Creation	*Production*	*Use*
GM maize	no	no	some
Open source software	no	some	yes
Mobile phones	no	no	yes
Recombinant insulin	no	no	yes
Plant tissue culture	no		yes

support for the claim, often made but not often supported with data, that developing countries need to "move up the value chain" to get the most benefits from technological change. Rather than just buying the products from abroad, the country would benefit more from local production, particularly if it is based on local innovation. These are steps that public policies can address.

Policy Options

Clearly, there is no one-size-fits-all set of recommendations that can be made based on our findings, even among these four "developing" countries. Across the developing countries, however, the cases do suggest some winning strategies along the pathway from innovation to production to use.

In order to generate business opportunities, a country's R&D capacity does make a difference. It is, however, a necessary but not sufficient condition. In order to turn R&D capacity into a commercial opportunity in a country with limited overall R&D capacity, the expertise must be concentrated in one or a few particular areas. National governments can certainly play a role in finding the areas to target and concentrating resources there to bring the capacity up to the level needed to break through. Progress can be made on both the production and consumption side at once, with proper planning.

In choosing areas for that kind of targeting, governments need to consider more than just whether someone can make money. In fact, policy can work on reducing inequalities in all three valued items at once, using business opportunity as a wedge. Some new products will lend themselves to local production and others will not. In crafting a technology strategy, the government should take the potential for production, sales, and service jobs into account. The characteristics of the national labor pool are very important in this regard, and governments can also implement training strategies targeted at the skills needed for industries emerging from local innovations.

Governments can also make sure that the targeted technologies provide benefits for the poor, not just wealth creation for current elites. I have described this kind of strategy setting elsewhere (Cozzens, 2010) as "adding a quality of life dimension" to a standard foresight analysis. South Africa is following an interesting strategy of this sort in its nanotechnology initiative.[13] This initiative has a traditional industry-oriented branch contributing to the competitive status of large-employment economic sectors including chemicals and mining. But it also includes a "social cluster" of projects that are specifically designed to address problems of health, energy, and water in poor communities, for example through low-cost diagnostic tools.

One of the strongest findings of our study, however, is that setting R&D agendas is only one policy tool for making technologies work better for the poor. Regulation, liberalization, and public procurement also played important roles in spreading the benefits of the technologies we studied. Governments should therefore include these policies in their technology strategies. First, it is helpful for governments to open up market competition for consumer goods, as was done in the mobile phone case in all our countries. Poor consumers probably benefited most from the resulting diversification of phones and plans. Second, governments can use their own purchasing power to help build local businesses. This is probably happening less in open source software in our four developing countries than we would have expected, perhaps because expertise within the relevant governments departments themselves is missing. A small targeted investment in that expertise might provide the conditions for a new business symbiosis in that area. Finally, public procurement must be used to provide access to technologies in basic needs areas. Health is clearly one of those, but the concept probably needs to be extended into other areas, including energy and water. Well-designed government programs to buy or subsidize technology used by poor households in areas like these can provide two benefits at once: improving quality of life and stimulating local business. Governments should also consider the unequal distribution of costs, at the very least by ruling out regressive pricing schemes in public utilities, such as the higher per unit costs paid by prepaid plan consumers of mobile phones.

I close with observations from our colleagues in Mozambique (Brito and Brouwer, 2010). Their country paper points out that emerging technologies do not have to diffuse passively into developing countries. National governments can choose to work on absorbing ones that make a difference locally *and* hold the potential for increasing the innovative capacity of the country. Such selections need to be surrounded by training, supported with facilities, and stimulated through community participation. If they are, however, then even emerging technologies can contribute to inclusive development.

6.
THE PROGRESS OF
NANOTECHNOLOGY IN CHINA
Chen Wang and Can Huang

The advances of nanoscience and nanotechnology (hereafter referred to as "nano-technology") in both developed and developing economies are closely associated with expectations that the technology can address various societal needs. Possible broad applications of nanotechnology in various areas, including health, energy, environment, and manufacturing, have aroused the keen interest of policy-makers, academics, and industrialists in China. The potential of the technology has been clearly reflected in the prioritizing of nanotechnology development in various science and technology programs at both national and local levels. However, given the current restraints in funding capability as well as existing infrastructures in China, we argue that exploring technological solutions to meet societal needs is essential for promoting nanotechnology development. Such solution is critical for public R&D investment to benefit society at large.

In this chapter, we review the Chinese national strategy to promote nanotechnology development in the last decade, introduce the major programs that fund nanotechnology R&D in the country and the new institutions that conduct it, and analyze Chinese progress in terms of scientific publications and patents. We reveal the contribution of international collaboration to the visibility of the research done in China and a few promising applications invented by Chinese scientists.

The Chinese National Strategy to Promote Nanotechnology

The first efforts to promote nanotechnology R&D in China in the 1980s were well received by Chinese scientists (Bai, 2001, 2005), and the Chinese Academy of Sciences (CAS), the National Natural Science Foundation, and the State Science and Technology Commission (the predecessor of the Chinese Ministry of Science and Technology) began to fund related research. In the 1990s, China hosted the 7th International Conference on Scanning Tunneling Microscopy (1993) and the 4th International Conference on Nanometer-Scale Science and Technology (1996), showcasing Chinese scientists' early participation in the field. From 1990 to 2002, nearly 1,000 projects were funded by the Ministry of Science and Technology (or the State Science and Technology Commission). Over the same period, the National Natural Science Foundation of China approved another 1,000 small-scale grants for projects related to nanotechnology.

Intensive R&D activities began in China in the early 2000s. In November 2000, the National Steering Committee for Nanoscience and Nanotechnology was established to oversee national policies and coordinate action. It involved all the stakeholders and R&D funding organizations in the country, making concerted policy action at the national level possible. The committee's director was China's minister of science and technology, with vice directors including vice ministers of science and technology, the vice president of the CAS, and the vice president of the National Natural Science Foundation. Officials from the Ministry of Education, the National Development and Reform Commission (a ministerial agency), and the Commission on Science, Technology and Industry for National Defense were also involved. The committee drafted the first Chinese national policy document intended to promote nanotechnology development, the National Nanotechnology Development Strategy (2001–10), an initiative reminiscent of similar strategies announced in other countries, such as the National Nanotechnology Initiative in the United States.

The National Nanotechnology Development Strategy (2001–10)—hereafter "the Strategy"—is composed of four parts. The first part, which introduces "opportunities and challenges," highlights the challenges that China faced in the coming era of nanotechnology. The second part, which covers "principles," proposes a set of tenets that nanotechnology development in China should follow. The third section of the Strategy focuses on five "targets" that nanotechnology R&D in China should achieve within ten years. The last part of the Strategy outlines concrete policy measures and suggestions.

The Strategy was the first comprehensive action plan designed to promote nanotechnology development in China. It emphasizes the importance of basic science and calls for strengthened financial support from the government. It prioritizes commercializing nanotechnology and appropriating intellectual properties from R&D activities. The Strategy argues that competent R&D personnel is a key to the success of nanotechnology development and highlights the need for training and retaining scientists in the field, which evinces a long-term view of policy-making. The Strategy maps out a blueprint for Chinese nanotechnology development in the following decade. Many principles and thoughts expressed in the document have had a far-reaching impact on Chinese progress in the field.

The National Mid- and Long-Term Science and Technology Development Plan for 2006–20 (hereafter the "Plan"), launched in March 2006, is another important policy document, comparable to the Strategy. The Plan is not a policy document specific to nanotechnology, but rather a comprehensive document supporting Chinese science and technology development more broadly over the following 15 years. The Plan, which sets a number of priorities, represents the ambitious goal of sustaining economic growth and social development through home-grown innovation and increased government-led R&D investments. In the Plan, nanotechnology is highlighted primarily within the section on basic science research, included as one of the four major scientific research areas (or "mega" projects) to receive substantial governmental funding. The Plan states that "nanotechnology is adopted by many countries as a strategic means of enhancing competitiveness and is one of the fields in which China can leapfrog technologically."

Public R&D Funding

Since the 1980s, China has established a series of funding programs that have set various priorities for supporting R&D activities in the country. The three main funding programs led by the Chinese Ministry of Science and Technology are the 973 Program, which supports basic science research; the 863 Program, which finances R&D in high technology, particularly in the high-tech industry; and the National Key Technology R&D Program, which funds technology development. The National Natural Science Foundation (hereafter "the Foundation"), which is independent of the Ministry of Science and Technology, is another important funding agency for basic science research. These programs, together with the funding managed by the Commission on Science, Technology and Industry for National Defense, are the main funding sources for nanotechnology R&D in China. Chunli Bai (2005), vice president of the Chinese Academy of Sciences, estimates that Chinese funding of nanotechnology development from 2001 to 2004 equaled about US$160 million. Such funding doubled every year between 1999 and 2002. From 1999 to 2001, Chinese scientists conducted nearly 550 research projects in nanotechnology.

The 973 Program and the 863 Program

The 973 Program began to intensively fund nanotechnology research after the late 1990s. In June 2008, the Ministry of Science and Technology published the 2008–10 budgets for all of the 897 projects funded by the 973 Program during fiscal year 2006–7. A rough estimation by the authors identified 84 projects (around 10 percent of the total projects) whose titles contained the word "nanometer." These 84 projects will receive funding in the amount of RMB303 million (US$44 million) during the 2008–10 period, accounting for 15 percent of the total funding from the 973 Program over that period.

The 863 Program supports R&D in nanotechnology under a "nanomaterial" rubric. Funding for the period of 2000–5 was estimated to have reached RMB200 million (US$29 million; *Economic Daily*, 2005). According to Huang *et al.* (2004), in 2004 the 863 Program budget was five times greater than that of the 973 Program; the 863 Program is expected to continue to be the larger supporter of nanotechnology R&D.

The National Natural Science Foundation

The Foundation began funding research on instrumentation development such as Scanning Probe Microscopy in late 1980s. The Foundation and the Ministry of Science & Technology (MOST) jointly established guidelines, policies, and blueprints for fundamental research in nanotechnology. The total budget of the Foundation in 2008 amounted to RMB6.3 billion (US$920 million). It was estimated that, between 1991 and 2000, the Foundation's funding to support nanotechnology R&D reached RMB920 million (US$134 million; *Economic Daily*, 2005), supporting nearly 1,000 projects. Such financial support was intensified between 2001 and 2003. In total, some 800 projects were funded by the Foundation between 2001 and 2003, with total budgets amounting to RMB196 million (US$29 million). In 2002, the Foundation included "nanotechnology basic science research" as one of several major research plans (or mega-projects).

From an international perspective, China's funding in basic nanotechnology research is competitive. According to Lux Research (2008), the US and Japanese governments invested US$1,816 million and US$1,060 million (by purchasing power parity or PPP), respectively, on nanotechnology R&D in the 2005–7 period. The Chinese government invested US$PPP893 million in the same period, which positions China in third place in the worldwide ranking (Figure 6.1). However, corporate funding in China amounted to only US$PPP348 million, which was only slightly more than one-third of government funding. Ranked by corporate funding, China was ranked fifth in the world after the United States (US$PPP2,362 million), Japan (US$PPP2,038 million), Germany (US$PPP467 million), and South Korea (US$PPP384 million). A different estimation by the European Commission (2005) showed that the Chinese government invested 83 million euros in 2004 on nanotechnology R&D, in comparison with the US government's 1.2 billion euros and the Japanese government's 750 million euros. China was thus ranked after the United States, Japan, Germany, France, South Korea, and the UK by amount of public investment in nanotechnology R&D in 2004.

New Institutions

The major undertakers of basic nanotechnology research in China are universities administrated by the Ministry of Education and research institutions affiliated with the CAS. In 2005, more than 50 Chinese universities and 20 research institutions in the Chinese Academy of Sciences across the country—a total of 3,000 researchers— were engaged in basic nanotechnology research (Bai, 2005). Table 6.1 lists the 30 most prolific departments and institutions in China. Nine of the 30 departments and institutions are located in Beijing, which has made that city the most important center

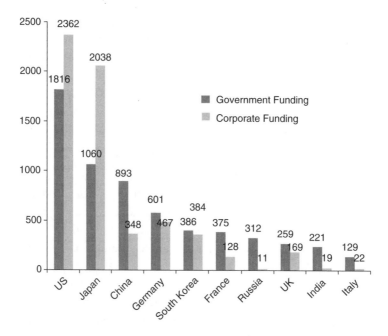

Figure 6.1 Estimated Government and Corporate Nanotechnology Funding, 2005–07 Period

Table 6.1 The 30 Most Prolific Departments or Institutions of China in Nanotechnology: 1998–2007

Rank	Number of Web of Science articles	University or Institution	Department	City and Province
1	2,360	Chinese Academy of Sciences	Institute of Chemistry	Beijing
2	1,713	Chinese Academy of Sciences	Institute of Physics	Beijing
3	1,668	Chinese Academy of Sciences	Graduate School	Beijing
4	1,485	Chinese Academy of Sciences	Changchun Institute of Applied Chemistry	Changchun, Jilin Province
5	1,472	Nanjing University	Department of Physics	Nanjing, Jiangsu Province
6	1,288	Chinese Academy of Sciences	Shanghai Institute of Ceramics	Shanghai
7	1,178	University of Science and Technology of China	Department of Chemistry	Hefei, Anhui Province
8	1,139	Jilin University	Department of Chemistry	Changchun, Jilin Province
9	1,075	Peking University	College of Chemistry and Molecular Engineering	Beijing
10	889	Tsinghua University	Department of Material Science and Engineering	Beijing
11	850	Tsinghua University	Department of Chemistry	Beijing
12	805	University of Science and Technology of China	Structure Research Laboratory	Hefei, Anhui Province
13	774	City University of Hong Kong	Department of Physics and Material Science	Hong Kong
14	722	Fudan University	Department of Chemistry	Shanghai
15	663	Chinese Academy of Sciences	Lanzhou Institute of Chemical Physics	Lanzhou, Gansu Province
16	583	Chinese Academy of Sciences	Institute of Solid State Physics	Hefei, Anhui Province
17	527	Wuhan University	Department of Chemistry	Wuhan, Hubei Province
18	489	Nankai University	Department of Chemistry	Tianjin
19	473	Peking University	Department of Physics	Beijing
20	473	Tsinghua University	Department of Physics	Beijing
21	465	Zhejiang University	Department of Material Science and Engineering	Hangzhou, Zhejiang Province
22	464	Zhejiang University	Department of Chemistry	Hangzhou, Zhejiang Province
23	404	Zhejiang University	State Key Laboratory of Silicon Material	Hangzhou, Zhejiang Province
24	397	Shandong University	State Key Laboratory of Crystal Material	Jinan, Shandong Province
25	365	China Center of Advanced Science and Technology World Laboratory		Beijing
26	341	University of Hong Kong	Department of Physics	Hong Kong
27	337	Chinese Academy of Sciences	Shanghai Institute of Technical Physics	Shanghai
28	327	Wuhan University	Department of Physics	Wuhan, Hubei Province
29	323	Zhejiang University	Department of Physics	Hangzhou, Zhejiang Province
30	322	University of Hong Kong	Department of Chemistry	Hong Kong

Source: MERIT Database of Worldwide Nanotechnology Scientific Publications. Authors' own calculation.

for nanotechnology research in the country. From 1998 to 2007, 261 departments or institutes in Chinese universities or the CAS produced more than 50 nanotechnology articles, with almost half produced by departments or institutes located in Beijing (22 percent), Shanghai (14 percent), and Hong Kong (10 percent; see Table 6.2 and Figure 6.2). These three cities are indeed the strongholds of basic nanotechnology research in the country.

Although Chinese nanotechnology R&D was certainly respectable in size, the research activities suffered from a lack of synergy. Competition among the various organizations for research funding made coordinated action—for example, co-purchasing large and expensive scientific instruments—rather difficult. In addition, successful commercialization of nanotechnology depends on strong linkages between industry and the academy, but universities and institutions that emphasized basic science research did not regard commercialization as their primary mission. To tackle these challenges, in the early 2000s policy-makers at the central and local government levels established more than 20 new institutions to specialize in nanotechnology. These new institutions, including the National Center for Nanoscience and Technology in

Table 6.2 The Location of Departments or Institutes Producing 50 Web of Science Nanotechnology Publications or More, 1998–2007

City Name	Abbreviation	Number of Departments and Institutes	Percent
Beijing	BJ	58	22.2%
Shanghai	SH	37	14.2%
Hong Kong	HK	26	10.0%
Hefei	HF	18	6.9%
Changchun	CC	14	5.4%
Nanjing	NJ	14	5.4%
Wuhan	WH	12	4.6%
Jinan	JN	9	3.4%
Shenyang	SY	8	3.1%
Changsha	CS	7	2.7%
Hangzhou	HZ	6	2.3%
Lanzhou	LZ	6	2.3%
Chengdu	CD	5	1.9%
Dalian	DL	5	1.9%
Guangzhou	GZ	5	1.9%
Tianjin	TJ	5	1.9%
Xiamen	XM	4	1.5%
Harbin	HB	3	1.1%
Xian	XA	3	1.1%
Fuzhou	FZ	3	1.1%
Kaifeng	KF	2	0.8%
Suzhou	SZ	2	0.8%
Baoding	BD	1	0.4%
Chongqing	CQ	1	0.4%
Liaocheng	LC	1	0.4%
Qingdao	QD	1	0.4%
Taiyuan	TY	1	0.4%
Urumqi	UQ	1	0.4%
Wuhu	WU	1	0.4%
Xiangtan	XT	1	0.4%
Zhengzhou	ZZ	1	0.4%
Total		261	100.0%

Source: MERIT Database of Worldwide Nanotechnology Scientific Publications. Authors' own calculation.

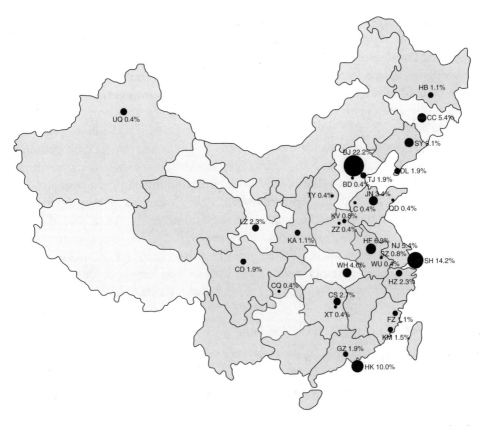

Figure 6.2 The Location of the Departments of Institutes Producing 50 Web of Science Nanotechnology Publications or More, 1998–2007

Beijing and the National Engineering Research Center for Nanotechnology in Shanghai, have trained a large number of young scholars and provided facilities for numerous research teams to carry out basic research in nanotechnology. They are now the major driving force for China's nanotechnology research.

The National Center for Nanoscience and Technology

The National Center for Nanoscience and Technology (hereafter "the Center") was co-established by the Chinese Academy of Sciences and the Ministry of Education in March 2003. The founding organizations of the Center were the Chinese Academy of Sciences, Peking University, and Tsinghua University, all of which are dominant players in nanoscience research in China, as shown in Table 6.1. The initial funding for the center, RMB250 million (US$37 million), was provided by the National Development and Reform Commission (a ministerial agency), the Ministry of Education and the Chinese Academy of Sciences (National Center for Nanoscience and Technology, 2009).

The Center aimed to gather the scattered resources from various research institutions affiliated with the Chinese Academy of Sciences, Peking University, and Tsinghua University and to strengthen cooperation among them. A vice president of the

Chinese Academy of Sciences was appointed as the first director of the Center, and the vice presidents of Peking University and Tsinghua University were two of the four vice directors. The Center subsidizes laboratories in the three institutions as part of a new network of laboratories. Half of the subsidy received by the collaborative laboratories must be used to support experiments done by researchers from other organizations, which assures the openness of the network.

One of the Center's most important accomplishments was the development of Chinese nanotechnology standards. The Center hosts the secretariat of the National Committee of Standards on Nanotechnology, which approves Chinese standards for nanotechnology. Assisted by the Center, the National Committee of Standards on Nanotechnology had developed 15 standards by 2007. The Center also submitted standards proposals to the International Origination of Standardization. In March 2009, the testing laboratory in the Center was accredited by the China National Accreditation Service for Conformity Assessment, as a result of which the testing and calibration reports issued by the Center are recognized not only within China but also in other countries that have signed mutual recognition arrangements with China.

The National Engineering Research Center for Nanotechnology

The National Engineering Research Center for Nanotechnology (hereafter "the Engineering Center") was established based on a limited corporation in Shanghai in October 2003. It is funded by an industry-academy consortium. In 2007, a project involved in the development of Ni-H batteries, carried out under the auspices of the Engineering Center, was successfully commercialized. The Engineering Center co-funded the Shanghai Wanhong Power and Energy Sources Co., Ltd., with the Shanghai Wanhong Industrial (Group) Investment Co., Ltd., the Shanghai Institute of Microsystem and Information Technology (a board member and founding organization of the Engineering Center), and the Shanghai Huge Development Co., Ltd., to commercialize the technology. The newly established company employed 150 staff members by 2009 and produced Ni-H batteries used in electric cars and bicycles and other industry sectors.

These two new institutions are diverse in their missions and activities. The National Center for Nanoscience and Technology in Beijing promotes cooperation, facilitates the sharing of facilities and equipment, and avoids duplicate investments between universities and institutions. It coordinates the development of nanotechnology standards in China, which provide a reference point on the basis of which governmental agencies can regulate products and markets related to nanotechnology. The National Center was also involved in the development of international nanotechnology standards, defending China's interests and participating in rule-setting for future industrial applications. It serves as a contact point for international academic collaboration and actively promotes exchanges with scientific communities outside China. Alternatively, the National Engineering Research Center for Nanotechnology in Shanghai strongly emphasizes industry-academy cooperation in commercializing nanotechnology. Representatives from several Shanghai-based venture capital companies and the Science Park sit on the board of the Engineering Center. The functions of these new institutions match up well with the fourth target set by the Strategy: that China should establish several key national laboratories and research centers in the field.

Scientific Publications and Patents

China's global rise in nanotechnology R&D has been phenomenal in the past decade. In 1998, there were merely 1,875 scientific publications out of China, compared with 9,468 in the United States and 4,423 in Japan.[1] By 2007, Chinese nanotechnology publications outnumbered those from Japan by a wide margin and occupied second place in the world in terms of number of publications, trailing only the United States. China's share in the world's nanotechnology publications went from 6 percent in 1998 to 19 percent in 2007. Figure 6.3 lists the number of nanotechnology publications produced by the world's ten most prolific countries over the 1998–2007 period. A calculation of the average annual growth rate in the number of articles by the ten most prolific countries reveals rapid growth in China, South Korea, and India. China's average annual growth rate of 27 percent each year between 1998 and 2007 is nothing short of extraordinary. In contrast, the other countries in the top ten, including the United States, Japan, Germany, France, the UK, Italy, and Russia achieved only 6 to 10 percent rates in annual growth.

China's progress is less impressive in patenting than in publishing. Counting the patent applications with the European Patent Office's nanotechnology classification Y01N in the PATSTAT database,[2] we find that Chinese patents accounted for only 0.88 percent of the world's total, in comparison with the US share of 34.2 percent and the Japanese share of 19.7 percent. Although China's share is very small, the number of patents filed by Chinese applicants grew rapidly, at an average rate of 36.8 percent per year, from 1998 through 2007 (Figure 6.4). Other than in South Korea, where the rate grew by an extraordinary 77.7 percent annually, patent applications in the rest of the top ten countries increased more slowly than in China. Some leading countries, such as Japan and France, have seen negative rates of growth in nanotechnology patents.

Indicators of scientific publications, patent applications, and public and corporate funding all reveal that China has been closing the gap with the leading countries in

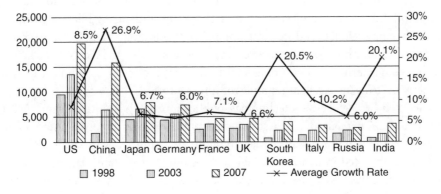

Figure 6.3 The World's Ten Most Prolific Countries in the Nanotechnology Field, 1998–2007

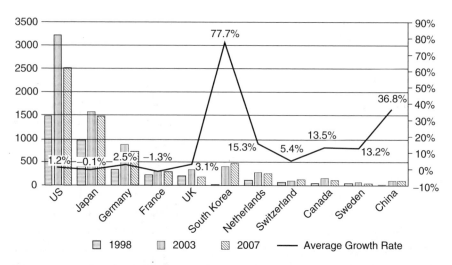

Figure 6.4 The Top Ten Countries and China (13th) in Terms of Nanotechnology Patent Applications, 1998–2007

this emerging technology field in the past decade and is becoming a major player in the world. Chinese scientists are contributing to the advancement of knowledge in the field, collaborating as well as competing in the global community. The progress made in China, particularly in the applied fields, should be deemed as a potentially important contribution to the sustainable development of this vastly populated country and the improvement of the quality of life of its citizens, which will in the end benefit the international community as well.

International Collaboration in Basic Science Research

The development of nanotechnology in China has benefited greatly from academic communications and exchanges between the Chinese and international scientific communities. Since 1990, China has organized tens of international and national conferences covering a wide range of topics in related fields. Nearly 1,500 participants from international and domestic institutions attended the recent conference ChinaNano 2009, and all recognized the value of promoting international collaboration such as setting up joint research projects and research groups, organizing bilateral symposiums, exchanging scholars and students, and so on. In addition, many Chinese scholars working in nanotechnology have overseas study or research experience. The collaborations between international groups as well as different groups inside China are highly productive, setting an excellent example for future efforts.

The Web of Science nanotechnology publication data show that from 1998 to 2007, about 17 percent of Chinese nanotechnology papers involved international collaboration. Figure 6.5 shows that the top 20 countries with which Chinese scholars collaborated in nanotechnology include the United States, Japan, Germany, Singapore, and the UK. Collaborative articles with scientists from the United States accounted for just over 5 percent of total Chinese nanotechnology publications in

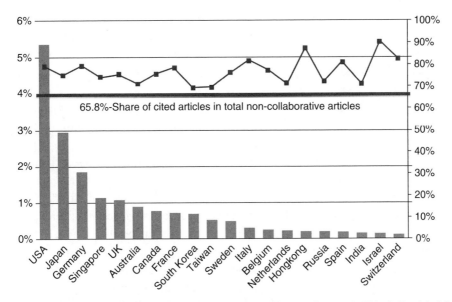

Figure 6.5 Comparison of the Shares of Cited Articles among Chinese Collaborative Articles and Non-Collaborative Articles, 1998–2007

the period of 1998–2007. The percentage of cited articles co-authored with scientists from these 20 countries is invariably higher than the percentage of cited Chinese non-collaborative articles, which clearly indicates that Chinese scientists have benefited from the "international collaboration dividend," as coined by Tyfield *et al.* (2009).

Nanotechnology Development to Meet Chinese Societal Needs

The research communities in China and the rest of the world are confronting common challenges in advancing nanotechnology. In the applied fields, China has its own priorities due to its national and societal needs, including increasing energy efficiency, developing low cost drugs and new treatment methods for fatal diseases, alleviating environmental pollution, and so on. Although promoting equitable development has not been an explicit goal listed in the Strategy which was launched ten years ago, as part of the national commitment to improve the quality of life of its 1.3 billion citizens, Chinese nanotechnology scientists have been making continuous efforts in providing the much needed knowledge and technical support to tackle the challenges and meet societal needs. Much of the technological progress demonstrated by Chinese scientists bears great potential. However, the technology is still in the early stages of development and has not yet been diffused at a large scale. Its impact on poverty reduction and equitable development in China has not been fully studied. However, we argue that it is critically important to develop feasible research approaches in order to ensure the future nanotechnology development in China will address these issues such as equitable development and poverty reduction along with industrial competitiveness and technological innovation in order to gain public support. Such approaches should provide a balanced consideration of fundamental research versus technological developments, and economic gains.

The multidisciplinarity of nanotechnology has led to a wide range of opportunities for technological innovations in various areas. Chinese academic communities have been called upon to join the effort of public agencies to provide careful assessment of the social impact of the emerging technologies, which has guided the research undertaken by both academia and industry. For example, a number of research groups across China have examined the biological effects of nanomaterials, focusing on fundamental characterization of the physical, chemical, and biological properties of a broad range of nanomaterials. The materials can be used in construction and therapeutic applications. Protocols of measuring such nanometer-scale objects, which will form the basis of future standards, are being investigated and developed. Chinese scientists have also carried out toxicology studies on nanomaterials. Such studies play a vital part in developing drug delivery agents using nanostructured materials. Efforts such as these must be substantially increased in order to address safety issues of common concern.

Nanotechnology research in China has recently focused on standardizations, safety evaluation of products containing nanocomponents, and protection of workspaces involving nanomaterial processing. These issues have attracted intensive attention and are important to ensure continued public support for nanotechnology development in China. As the result of earlier efforts, seven national standards were published in 2004, including four standards for nanoparticle products (nickel powder, zinc oxide, titanium dioxide, and calcium carbonate), and testing (gas adsorption method by BET and the granularity of nanopowder by XRD method). Currently more than 20 standards are being studied.

Environmental-related nanotechnology involves various nanomaterials and nanostructures and is being actively pursued by Chinese scholars, who are using various measurement techniques to analyze pollution and clean up local environments. Examples of such efforts include using nanomaterials for remediating water and soils contaminated by heavy metals and organic pollutants and repairing underwater ecology. Scientists in the Institute of Chemistry, CAS, have developed a printing process with dramatically reduced liquid pollutants. The nanostructured printing plates enable bypassing the photoreception and chemical developing process, eliminating the need for developing chemicals such as developers and fixers, as well as silver and aluminum, in this printing protocol. A crude estimate suggest that if 50 percent of China's printing capacity was adapted by this technology, China could expect an overall reduction of more than 30,000 tons of liquid pollution, 300 tons of silver, and tens of tons aluminum each year.

Effective strategies for disposing of heavy metal or organic-containing pollutants can be developed based on the very high surface area and adsorption affinity of nanomaterials. A number of laboratory studies have established that nanomaterials could transform harmful chemical pollutants into less toxic species and subsequently be removed from waste. Such methods have been demonstrated in treating waste water from printing manufactures and chlorate industry, for example, treating CrVI-Containing $Mg(OH)_2$ Nanowaste (Liu *et al.*, 2008). A pilot scale test has been demonstrated in a chlorate plant with processing capacity of multiple tons of CrVI containing supernatant liquid per day. This progress could help resolve the longstanding challenges in dealing with landfills in many Chinese suburbs containing heavy metal pollutants as the result of industrial sludge. In another successful example, groups from the Research Center for Eco-enviromental Sciences, CAS, developed nanostructured clays for treating the outburst of sprulina algae in Lake Tai, which posed a threat to the drinking water of the surrounding cities. Treatment with these clays achieved the recovery of underwater ecology in six month for large areas of the lake surface.

The invention of nanostructured dehydrogenation catalysts by investigators in Fujian Institute of Research of the Structure of Matter, CAS, has enabled the greatly improved purification efficiency of raw gas. This has reduced the load of noble metal while enhancing the selectivity of the hydrogenation process. This technology is critical for the establishment of a glycol plant with the production scale of 1.2 million tons per year.

Chinese scientists have been engaged in novel designs of nanostructures, such as microfluidic devices with nanoscale modifications, that could provide high efficiency, high throughput, and cost-effective venues for disease diagnosis, particularly infectious disease such HIV and hepatitis. Efforts have also been made to explore various nanoparticles for developing new drug delivery systems. A number of reports have shown that nanoparticles could be promising for treating cancer by penetrating into the depth of tumor tissue to enhance chemotherapy efficacy (Tang *et al.*, 2007). Another study shows that using metallofullerene molecules can effectively circumvent tumor resistance to cisplatin by reactivating endocytosis (Liang, 2010). These results, among many others, have shown that functionalized nanoparticles hold the potential to tackle challenges related to multidrug resistance often found in cancer treatments.

Motivated by the tremendous demands for energy supplies in the country, Chinese scientists have made concerted efforts in applying nanomaterials to develop new energy oriented applications. Various solar cells based on nanomaterials have been demonstrated, including dye sensitized solar cells, solar cells with silicon nanomaterials, organic solar cells, and so on. In addition, energy storage devices using nanostructures such as graphenes have been tested based on their superior charge storage properties. In the same time, nanostructured materials for energy-saving applications have also been intensively studied. Chinese scholars have developed nanocomposite materials for construction with improved heat insulation properties and novel coatings for glasses that can be responsive to environmental temperatures. Broad range activities in fundamental research, which aim at revealing mechanisms of energy conversion in nanostructures, are undertaken by the research groups across the country. For example, nanostructured photocatalysts have been reported in laboratory studies that could improve the efficiency of hydrogen production from water. It is noteworthy that technological demands for energy are diverse. Distinctively different materials and processing technologies are being used in portable devices, family- or community-level applications, and power grids.

Conclusion and Future Perspectives

In the past decade since China launched its national strategy to promote nanotechnology development, the country has invested an increasing amount of R&D to the field, produced a soaring number of scientific publications, established a number of new specialized institutions, and expanded its postgraduate programs in science and engineering to train nanotechnology scientists and engineers. The hope that China can pass through a window of opportunity to catch up and become a leading nation in the field has never been higher.

However, nanotechnology is still at an early stage of development in China and has not yet generated large-scale economic impacts. The next phase of research endeavors are expected to seek key technological breakthroughs that are mostly relevant to Chinese industries. The encouraging achievements in both fundamental research and industrial applications in the past decade have led to public awareness of the important potential of nanotechnology in China. Currently, promoting nanotechnology in China is not only motivated by pursuing academic excellence, but also addressing societal needs. The multidisciplinary nature of nanotechnology creates abundant opportunities for improving the quality of life of the general public through technological innovations. Promising applications have been demonstrated in China in the fields of environmental remediation, public health care, and sustainable agricultural development. We argue that it is crucial to include equitable development, poverty reduction and pollution alleviation and so on among industrial competitiveness and technological innovation as goals of nanotechnology development in China to ensure the technology development in future will benefit the Chinese citizens, communities, and society at large. We can envision that the Chinese nanotechnology scientists will continue to contribute to the quest for knowledge in the field and the solution of challenges in developing economies and international communities.

7.
FOOD SECURITY
From the Green Revolution to Nanotechnology
Jennifer Rogers and Amy Zader

Nanotechnology is forging a new frontier in agriculture and food production and could hold some promise for solving food security problems throughout the world. Recent research and development in agriculture and pesticides utilizes manufactured nano-particles and nanocapsules to enhance the efficiency of nutrients in vitamins and toxins in pesticides (Food and Water Europe, 2009). Vitamin producers are utilizing the small size of nanoparticles and the process of nanoencapsulation to increase bioavailability and absorption of nutrients (Schulz and Barclay, 2009). Also, nanotechnology is used to build better packaging to ship products, extend the shelf life of produce, and detect harmful bacteria before it reaches consumers' hands (Food and Water Europe, 2009). These developments represent new ways that technologies can enhance and strengthen the food system. The implementation of these technologies, or the prospects of imple-menting them, however, has not come without controversy (Friends of the Earth, 2008).

At the *Emerging Technologies, Emerging Economies* conference, the food security session focused on identifying the potential benefits of nanotechnology for food and agriculture production in emerging economies. Additionally, we discussed the potential questions, concerns, and future of such development. At this early stage in nanofood production, the group identified four main issues: (1) we should learn from previous and current endeavors to solve food security problems through technological R&D, such as genetic modification; (2) we must tackle the tough questions of intellectual property rights, such as open source possibilities for technological solutions; (3) we must consider the regionally specific needs of the community; and (4) we must weigh the benefits and risks carefully despite the lack of research on health and environmental risks from nanotechnology.

In this chapter we explore these main issues and highlight a few examples of nano-technology and genetic modification in recent agricultural development. According to a definition in a 2006 NanoForum report, *Nanotechnology in Agriculture and Food*, food is "nanofood" when nanoparticles, or nanotechnology techniques or tools, are used during cultivation, production, processing, or packaging (Joseph and Morrison, 2006). Much of the information we collected came from participants in the "Food Security" break-out sessions during the *Emerging Technologies/Economies* Conference. The ses-sions, covering two two-hour time blocks, included 13–15 participants from a wide array of professional, agricultural, development, activist, and academic backgrounds. While some participants were more versed in nanotechnology's food production capabilities, others expressed ideas that came from a background familiar with social issues related to technological innovation and agricultural development. A professional moderator guided discussion to focus on a set of questions concerning how nanotechnology is/can be used to address food security concerns in emerging economies. Given some of the promises and perils of the tense relationship between food security and agricultural technology outlined above, participants in our food security session addressed the following questions: if these technologies can solve problems and they are destined to shape the next generation of food and farming, who will own the technology? Will this come at a price? For whom? Is the enormous potential of nanotechnology to solve the world's hunger problems outweighed by the potential unknown risks from nanoparticles and nano-altered food, pesticides, and packaging?

We begin this chapter with background of the relationship between food security and agricultural technology. Since the advent of the Green Revolution, this relationship has been wrought with both high hopes and skepticism. Given this relationship, we then review the key concerns and hopeful benefits of the potential for nanotechnology and food security for developing countries. Additionally, because the group consistently revisited the history of technological solutions for food security concerns, we explore genetic modification as a lesson from which we can all learn. We provide two case studies—one in Mexico and one in China—that highlight the intricacies and difficulties of implementing GM technology in emerging economies as they relate to the four issues outlined above.

Background of Food Security and Agricultural Technology

Food security is a complex and complicated term. The general definition of food security refers to the ability of a population to feed itself. The term can be applied in a variety of ways and at different scales. For example, a nation such as China can implement food security policies that are aimed at ensuring Chinese grain production reaches the necessary production levels for self-sufficiency in grain production. At another scale, food security can refer to the ways that households in poverty can provide enough food to feed all members of the household. To many people, the term "food security" does not pose a problem in and of itself. Rather, the problem emerges when an identified population faces "food insecurity" and cannot access the necessary food to feed itself.

Due to widespread food insecurity and famine in the developing world, it has been the site of many efforts by scientists in developed countries to address the region's food security issues through advances in technology. The introduction of different kinds of technology into agricultural production has been controversial. For thousands of years, farmers experimented with different methods of production to find the most efficient systems. These methods included the introduction of various irrigation technologies, different cropping systems, and the use of organic fertilizers. However, technological advances to food production took a big leap in the 1960s with the introduction of Green Revolution technologies. At the forefront of these technologies was the introduction of high-yielding hybrid grain (wheat, corn, rice) seeds. Accompanying these seeds, farmers had to adopt specific irrigation and cropping techniques to ensure the growth of the seeds. Additionally, such large-scale agriculture made chemical fertilizers necessary. This technological package proved successful in increasing yields of grain produced.

While the introduction of the technological package showed higher yields in developing countries, it also caused widespread social, political, economic, and environmental problems. India is most often used as an example of how and why the Green Revolution failed. In the 1960s, India was a developing nation facing food security issues and welcomed the introduction of what was perceived to be modern, promising technologies. According to activist and author Vandana Shiva:

> The Green Revolution has been a failure. It has led to reduced genetic diversity, increased vulnerability to pests, soil erosion, water shortages, reduced soil fertility, micronutrient deficiencies, soil contamination, reduced availability of nutritious food crops for the local population, the displacement of vast numbers of small farmers from their land, rural impoverishment and increased tensions and conflicts. The beneficiaries have been the agrochemical industry, large petrochemical companies, manufacturers of agricultural machinery, dam builders and large landowners.
>
> (Shiva, 1991a: 57)

In general, the main lessons of the Green Revolution have been that the introduction of technologies to agricultural production needs to consider social and environmental conditions. Food security is a social problem as well as an economic one. No one questioned whether technology could increase yields, but some should have questioned whether the costs associated with it were worth the extra yields, including whether the yields were reaching the people of India, displacing local farmers, and ruining the soil for future crop yields.

Discussions of food security are often divided by technological optimists and those who are more critical or skeptical of the benefits technology can bring. As was the case with the Green Revolution, engineers and economists were in charge of implementing the technology and sought the most efficient and effective way to produce food. It was not until other effects were discovered, such as increased poverty for the poorer farmers and increased environmental degradation, that rural and development social scientists got involved in the implementation process. Although the Green Revolution successfully produced higher yields, it left unintended social and environmental consequences that social scientists noted, leading to a large body of work on development.

The next wave of research aimed at enhancing food production came in the 1980s when bioengineers began developing genetically modified seeds. Genetic engineering technology produces seeds by inserting genes from another species that enhance the seeds' resistance to pests, shelf life, and/or nutrition quality. Whereas hybrid seeds of the Green Revolution were bred over generations by taking the best characteristics of different seeds, genetic engineering inserted a gene to immediately create a new seed. However, both technologies promised to fix one problem with another technological solution.

78   J. Rogers and A. Zader

Genetically modified food has sparked public debate throughout the past decade and is easily more well known than the term "nanotechnology" in general. Recent news reports highlighted the ability of GM corn to lessen worm infestation in modified plant varieties and in nearby conventional seed fields (Charles, 2010). Additionally, news reports have shown images of "Frankenfish," genetically modified salmon that grow multiple sizes larger than conventional salmon (Jalonick, 2010). Scientists argue that larger salmon will result in a larger supply of food and protein, although because this is a novel innovation, evidence is limited. Less reported in the news are nanotechnology applications in food. However, in a 2008 report, Friends of the Earth found over 100 food and agricultural products containing nanoparticles. For example, *Nature Nanotechnology* recently reported findings that Michael Zimmerman and colleagues at the Swiss Federal Institute of Technology in Zurich were able to use nanotechnology to develop zinc and iron fortified food with increased bioavailability, but with no loss in flavor or change in color (Miller, 2010).

In contrast to GM technologies, public awareness about nanotechnology is low, as shown in a meta-analysis of public surveys from around the world (Satterfield *et al.*, 2009). An examination of public deliberations of nanotechnology shows some public concern, especially around unknown health and environmental risks, and social impacts (Pidgeon *et al.*, 2009). The UK's Nanodialogues (2006) were a series of four public deliberation experiments, where participants discussed nanotech applications such as nanotech for cleaning land and for cleaning water. The participants determined that the use of nanotechnology for land should not be applied until the long-term effects are studied and known, and the results made public (Stilgoe, 2007). With low public awareness about the emerging use of nanotechnology to address food security, public dialogue serves an important role in educating the public about the possibilities of nanotech and allows the public to address concerns about regulation, risk, and access.

The Promise of Nanotechnology for Food Security

As mentioned above, developing countries face a series of food security concerns that depend on region, climate, and economic situation. In general, these issues include pest control, crop yields, environmental limits, malnutrition, and availability of food (Sastry *et al.*, 2007). Therefore, to address these issues, research on nanotechnology for food and agriculture shows some promise for improvement of yields through genetic improvement of plants and animals (Kuzma, 2007; Scott, 2007), nanosensors for agriculture production and detection of pathogens, and nanoencapsulation for delivery of chemicals in pesticides and fertilizers. Each of these developments has the potential to radically change the communities in developing countries where families suffer from a lack of access to nutritious, safe food.

As R&D around nanotech in food and agriculture gains momentum, caution and careful examination of the needs, risks, and benefits that affect each decision to adopt these technological advancements based on past experiences is warranted. For example, as Vandana Shiva has clearly documented, a number of unforeseen side effects occurred with the haste under which Green Revolution technologies were implemented

(Shiva, 1991a, 1991b). With this understanding in mind, recent research has addressed potential applications for nanotechnology in Indian agriculture:

> Possible areas of nanotechnology with potential applications in Indian agriculture are: nanofertilizers for slow release and efficient use of water and fertilizers by plants; nano-cides—pesticides encapsulated in nanoparticles for controlled release, and nanoemulsions for greater efficiency; nanoparticles for soil conservation; delivery of nutrients and drugs for livestock and fisheries; nanobrushes and membranes for soil and water purification, cleaning of fishponds; and nanosensors for soil quality and for plant health monitoring, and for precision agriculture, controlled environment agriculture.
>
> (Sastry *et al.*, 2007)

Given both the hopes and promises of what nanotechnology can do for the future of food supply and the risks and fears the general public has expressed to GM food, it is important to understand the lessons of past technological success and failures. In other words, understanding what has happened previously in developing countries when technology was introduced will provide a better means to undertake risk analysis when new technology is adopted. In the following sections, we explore the recent histories of introducing GM seeds in rural communities.

Learning from Other Technologies: GM

The genetic engineering of plants is not a new phenomenon; however, the cellular manipulation of plant genes in laboratories (including biotechnology) is new and is an important element of the recent history of food production. More specifically, issues of food security addressed through technology highlight global inequalities between rich and poor, in terms of wealth and resources, and ownership of those resources. An analysis of the changing methods of genetic engineering and the move from valuing scientific, "Western" knowledge over indigenous traditional knowledge illuminates global inequalities between core and peripheral nations as well as power relations between transnational seed companies and indigenous peoples.

Cross-breeding and the discovery and use of medicinal plants have been used by indigenous peoples long before the biotechnology of today (Tauli-Corpuz, 2001). Therefore, it is important to recognize that the engineering of new seeds and plant life is not entirely born in laboratories and under microscopes, nor does it have inherent negative or dangerous consequences. However, we can contrast traditional farming and indigenous practices of cross-breeding to the biotechnology of today's agricultural scientists. Biotechnology is an "overarching term for a wide variety of new technologies, of which genetic engineering and the cloning of animals are only two of the best-known examples" (Tokar, 2001: 3). The technologies included under biotechnology all constitute some form of simulation and manipulation "of fundamental life processes at the cellular and molecular levels" (Tokar, 2001: 3). The changes at the cellular and molecular level are made in order to enhance particular physical or biochemical traits. This type of technology is fairly new, a product of science in the last half-century. Some forms of biotechnology are highly controversial,[1] especially reproductive, genetic, and cloning technologies.

One aspect of the biotechnology debate is the appropriation of indigenous knowl-edges and the patenting of indigenous materials, or bioprospecting. For example, the North American Free Trade Agreement (NAFTA) regulates the trade and consump-tion of materials and plants between Canada, the United States, and Mexico. Critics of NAFTA and Trade Related Intellectual Property Rights (TRIPs) claim that develop-ing countries are disproportionately affected by the trade agreements through piracy and the appropriation of indigenous resources. Much of the food crops and medicinal plants are taken from developing countries and emerging economies, such as Mexico. Beth Burrows discusses the criticism of the "bioprospecting" of raw materials:

> They [critics of biopiracy] observed that theft was twofold: first was the theft of knowledge of biological material and how to use it, and second was the theft of the material itself. Not-ing that no royalties had been paid for the use of this material, they called the unagreed to, unacknowledged appropriation of the material "biopiracy," and suggested that the World Trade Organization trade rules would likely be interpreted to make continuing theft of genetic material easier for the Industrial World.

> (2001: 240)

Indigenous people claim that seeds and plants (especially those domesticated over generations of seed saving, protection, and cross-breeding for diversity, weather con-ditions, and pest control) "were the result of millennia of study, selection, protection, conservation, development, and refinement by communities of Third World and indig-enous peoples," however, seed companies and scientists also now claim ownership over the same plants and seeds (Tokar, 2001: 241).

Corporations such as Monsanto, Novartis, Merck, Glaxo/Wellcome, and Pulsar, among others, are involved in the competitive pursuit of genetic material. These com-panies fall under the global "Life Industry" which is dominated by a small number of transnational corporations. "Life Industry" is a phrase commonly used by corporations that are interested in biotechnology and the patenting of biological organisms, seeds, and other forms of "life" (Shand, 2001). The patenting of biological organisms, such as seeds, places the control of "life" into the hands of companies that can charge for the use of their seeds. Therefore, the same farmers that once saved seeds for generations, now must purchase the same seeds from a company each year, especially with the increasingly com-mon use of engineered terminating seeds that are unable to reproduce fertile offspring.

Keeping with the theme of this volume as Emerging Technologies/Emerging Econ-omies, in the next section we highlight cases of genetically modified food in two large emerging economies where food security is and has been a concern: Mexico and China. Both of these countries have distinct regional or domestic needs and a national govern-ment that is negotiating its position in the international community. Because of wide-spread fear and distrust of GM seeds, both of these national governments face the needs of their domestic populations as well as consider their position in the international arena. Therefore, the implementation and regulation of GM seeds in these countries is a political process where the national state acts as intermediary. These two cases, drawn from our own PhD research (Rogers in Mexico, Zader in China), emphasize the difficult political decisions that need to be made to accommodate all parties and the importance of considering social implications.

Example #1: Corn in Mexico

For approximately 10,000 years, corn developed a reciprocal relationship with its human caretakers. Corn relies on humans to survive, and in turn, provides an unknown number of culinary, nutritional, and material (e.g. crafts, fuel, and religious) uses. Globally, it is the third largest crop by volume, just behind wheat and rice. Jolted by improvements in laboratories and the push for corn-based fuel (ethanol), corn entered a new phase in its development in the past 20–25 years. Throughout much of the world, corn is a staple crop, and in some countries such as Mexico, it is a part of indigenous religious practices (Esteva and Marielle, 2003). Part of corn's recent story and development is the shift from Mexican dominance in corn production to the United States as the leading producer and supplier of corn. Since the inception of NAFTA policies in 1994, Mexican corn farmers suffer from a lack of federal support and inability to find local and international markets to sell their harvest of indigenous corn varieties. Unable to compete with the inexpensive imported corn, which is subsidized by the US government and farmed using more productive technological tools, Mexican farmers are forced to find work through other means. In 2007, the demand for corn worldwide increased dramatically, prompting corn prices to rise, which led to Mexicans producing more subsistence corn. Because corn and tortillas are an essential part of the Mexican diet, a rise in the prices of these stable items potentially causes serious financial and hunger problems for Mexican families.[2] The story of corn in Mexico is a global food security story of the increasingly interconnected trajectory of food security, trade policies, and technological food/agriculture innovation.

In a highly publicized study by Quist and Chapala in 2001, genetically modified corn was discovered in southern Oaxaca, the second poorest state in Mexico (just above Chiapas) in areas were corn was first domesticated (Fitting, 2006; Cummings, 2002; Soleri *et al.*, 2006; Nadal, 2006). The discovery of GM maize in Oaxaca surprised seed companies and sparked an international debate over the findings and methods used by the researchers, in part because it was illegal to grow GM corn in Mexico at that time (Fitting, 2006).[3] GM maize is imported daily into Mexico for use as feed for animals and for human consumption. The imported GM corn is primarily imported from the United States and is generally less expensive than indigenous, local varieties. Rogers (2008) found that some farmers were growing GM corn because they understood it be an "improved" variety, however most farmers were not aware of transgenic or GM corn, and only a few expressed concern about the threat of GM corn to the diversity of indigenous varieties. With the first plots of GM corn officially planted within Mexico (given approval in October 2009), the potential implications for biodiversity, the autonomy of farmers, and land rights are escalated.

For most Mexican farmers, corn is now simply a subsistence crop, albeit an essential crop for daily sustenance. The influx of cheap, US corn has decreased the value of their indigenous corn and nearly erased their ability to profit from growing indigenous corn.

Rogers (2008) found that the combination of a loss of government subsidy programs, especially CONASUPO, and the influx of inexpensive, GM corn, pushed indigenous farmers to rely on corn as a subsistence-only crop, rather than a cash crop. Additionally, the changes to economic relationships and international agreements increased migration of family members to urban and border cities in search of income.

Example #2: GM Rice in China

For decades, rice breeding has been at the forefront of Chinese agricultural research efforts. In the 1960s and 1970s, China achieved international acclaim for successfully breeding high-yielding hybrid rice. Scientist Yuan Longping, the leading researcher behind this effort, became a national hero for succeeding at a task international rice breeders were not yet able to conquer. Yuan's discovery was significant in China for two reasons: (1) since the famine caused by the Great Leap Forward in the early 1960s, the Chinese state had struggled to produce enough grain to feed the nation; and (2) Yuan was able to make his discovery without external international help, thereby fulfilling the Mao era's obsession with maintaining self-sufficiency. The discovery and widespread use of hybrid rice seeds in China helped to alleviate China's food security needs at the national scale. Because China was inward-focused at the time, the development of this technology, which aimed to solve a specific national-scale problem, was heralded as a success that needed to be implemented. As we see below, the widespread introduction of GM rice in China has been more complicated.

Since political and economic reforms began in the late 1970s, the Chinese state has invested significantly in biotechnology. Currently, over 100 public sector institutions are involved in plant and agricultural biotechnology research (Huang *et al.*, 2002). China falls behind the United States, Canada, and Argentina as being the fourth-largest producer of GM crops. What makes China different is that much of the investment in biotechnology has been public, with money coming from the state, not private corporations. With its extensive potential for research in biotechnology, most of the GM crops currently grown in China are cotton, not food crops. Although Chinese researchers have spent significant time and energy developing GM rice, the process to grow it is slightly more complicated. Between 25 and 30 percent of China's total investments in the biotechnology sector lie in the development of GM rice. This figure places China in a stronger position than most multinational corporations regarding GM rice production potential (Keeley, 2006).

Chinese national pride embedded in both rice breeding and agricultural technology contributes to the central state's decision over whether (or when) to adopt and commercialize GM rice. Thus far, scientists have developed both insect and disease-resistant rice. In 2005 Jikun Huang and his colleagues published an economic assessment of pre-production trial sites of GM rice in *Science*, advocating the idea that GM rice will reduce hunger in the world (Huang *et al.*, 2005). Despite the push by Chinese scientists involved in research and development of GM rice, Chinese central state decision-makers have not yet approved GM rice. Reasons for the delayed approval vary: the Ministry of Agriculture biosafety office is not fully convinced of the Biosaftey Committee's recommendations, the state is concerned about losing the EU trade market, and concerned about the reaction of Chinese consumers to purchase GM food. In any case, the Chinese state's decision not to commercialize GM rice yet is very much a political decision involving more factors than a simple technical biosafety assessment (Keeley, 2006).

With the case of large emerging economies such as China and Mexico, the risks and benefits of emerging technologies need to be assessed. With the case of GM rice, China has shown its willingness (albeit stubbornly) to listen to what the rest of the world is doing. However, with China being a leading producer of nanotechnology (Parker *et al.*, 2009), it may decide to assess risks differently given its easy access to technologies. As one Chinese participant in our group noted, "the Chinese government is pushing technology to the extent that it becomes a religion; it is then controlled by the government to promote the government's agenda." Perhaps this participant's words are strong, but his meaning is clear; the Chinese government has a strong interest in its technological developments. Because it has invested so much time and money in research and development of nanotechnology, many fear the government will go ahead with its own agenda without proper risk evaluation. If the case of GM rice indicates anything, however, it is that for whatever reason, the state will put its own interests aside for fear of the global community.

Policy Recommendations/Suggestions

Nanotechnology promises to bring advancements to food production and distribution methods in order to solve some of the problems associated with food security. However, as the Green Revolution and the introduction of genetically modified seeds have shown, the food chain is a sensitive area in which to introduce new technologies. Not only are people involved in the food chain from production to consumption, but food provides biological subsistence for each of us. On the one hand, new technologies can be labor-saving and can enhance the shelf life and nutritional quality of food. On the other hand, some farmers may resist the introduction of new seeds and technologies, and consumers may also reject food that has been produced using various technologies where the effects may be unknown.

The main lessons of the Green Revolution involved the social and environmental impacts of new technologies at the production end of the food chain, while the main lessons of genetic modification involve seed ownership and the importance of creating a plan through which to introduce and explain the technology to the public. Moreover, lessons learned from the Green Revolution tend to focus on the ways that technology affects farmers, farming lifestyles, and agricultural environments in large developing countries, while lessons learned from genetically modified food tend to affect consumers and the broader public. As the case with GM corn in Mexico indicates, a combination of national policies and international trade has clearly affected the lives of indigenous Mexican farmers. As the case with GM rice in China shows, the Chinese state is executing precaution not only to look out for their farmers, but also in anticipation of what might happen to international trade. While policy at the national and international scales represent negotiation and commitment on the part of powerful state actors, it is important not to forget the farmers who are working on the ground in agricultural environments with these new technologies. Further, because technologies are used to grow food, consumers and the general public need to be involved in all decision-making processes.

As nanotechnology begins its ascent into the global food chain, it is important to understand the risks and benefits associated with it. Participants in our session identified three major topics that need to be addressed before nanotechnology can be fully introduced into the food system: public health, environmental impacts, and lack of public awareness. Just like GM foods, there are perceived risks and fears associated with consuming foods that have been produced using nanotechnology and concerns about nano-enhanced crops that may pollute the land, water, and soil. Considering these issues, and the crucial lack of food security, globally, the need for participatory approaches to agriculture-led development initiatives is not only timely, but necessary.

Considering the effects of the Green Revolution on India and the ways that the Mexican and Chinese governments have attempted to incorporate precaution into their agricultural policies, we believe there are a number of possible actions to mitigate against the potential harm of nano and other emerging agricultural technologies. Nanotechnology affects all aspects of the food chain; from production to consumption and even (especially) food packaging, nano particles are increasing integrated into modern food systems. While a number of NGOs are just starting to recognize the importance of raising awareness of technologies used in food production (Lee and Kigali, 2006), we believe that further public education can increase awareness of what technologies are being used and what potential impacts they might have. Furthermore, research and dialogue needs to continue to occur between farmers, scientists, governments, NGOs, and consumers.

Some possible actions to mitigate against the potential harm of nano and other emerging agricultural technologies may include:

1. Develop dialogue with farmers about specific needs, cultural practices, and the long-term feasibility of using nanotechnology in agriculture.
2. Understand the potential and perceived risks surrounding embodiment of nanotechnology in food because the risks are perceived to be higher in food products than food packaging, and also to understand animal health as it affects humans through the food chain.
3. Increase public education and the value of public information through traditional and non-traditional sources of media.
4. Continue research on the collaborations between government, civil society, scientists, consumers, and users in the implementation of development projects.

Further, governments, corporations, and scientists could better regulate and govern the integration of nano and other emerging technologies into the food system through:

1. A thorough examination of the lessons learned from regulation of bio and medical technology that has been integrated into pharmaceutical, health, and labor practices.

2. Regulations must be strictly enforced; lessons from the toxicology field have shown that self-regulation is not effective. Moreover, the nanotechnology industry is looking for rules and clarity to protect them from liability claims.
3. Consumers need to be able to trust the authority figure(s) who will uphold regulations, whether it is the government, scientists themselves, or industry. It is the responsibility of those who uphold regulations to effectively provide information to the public as well as opportunities for ongoing engagement and dialogue.

Conclusion

Above, we listed a set of recommendations and suggestions for integrating nano and other emerging technologies into the food system. These recommendations cover important issues that are necessary to examine when integrating new technologies into food systems.

In this chapter, we have provided the background on how technologies have been used in the past for food security purposes. While these cases indicate a number of instances where caution should be applied to technological implementation, they also tell stories and provide hope that communities can be more food secure if social and environmental concerns are addressed proactively, rather than reactively. Moreover, as we have kept with the theme of the volume, we have addressed the ways large developing nations have adopted policies based on the cautions and the fears of past attempts to integrate technological change and technologies into food systems.

Food is a support system of human life; we all need to subsist off of the calories we gain from the food we consume. Accompanying this fundamental need for food is a variety of issues. In poor, developing communities, issues surrounding food involve access to nutritious grains and other foods with enough vitamins and nutrients to survive. In developed communities, health issues caused by overconsumption are a major concern. In all contexts, the consumption of perceived toxins in food that appear at different stages of the food chain remains an issue, as does the pollution of the environment. However, it is mostly in developed economies with democratic systems of governance that people have full access to understand what toxins exist and how they affect the body.

We conclude this chapter with ongoing, unanswered questions raised through conversations in our session. In what ways does nanotechnology and food security produce feelings of hope and fear? In what ways does our session play a role in how nanotechnology is received, as a hope or a fear? Who is responsible for distributive justice and food security? Nanotechnology is just one more tool in our toolkit toward food security, but is it the best tool for food security?

8.
(NANO)TECHNOLOGY AND FOOD SECURITY
What Scientists Can Learn from Malian Farmers
Scott M. Lacy

The Numusala Quartier was where I first lived when I moved to Dissan, Mali as a Peace Corps volunteer. Village elders assigned me to Numusala, not because I am a blacksmith, but because I was a stranger. Historically Mande blacksmiths—besides having special-ized knowledge and skills critical to local food production and tool making—served as interpreters and liaisons between their communities and outsiders. As an unknown, untested stranger, the community placed me next door to the blacksmith's workshop on the edge of the village. It wasn't until years later that, as a rite of passage and accept-ance, the elders moved me out of Numusala and into the village center, Dugutigila.

I've worked in Mali for nearly two decades, but recent collaborations with US-based engineers remind me of my first days in the village. As an anthropologist among material scientists, mechanical engineers, and other technological geniuses, I feel like I am back in Numusala, learning a new language and culture while earning the trust and collaboration of a complex community. Several years ago I started working with the UC Santa Barbara chapter of Engineers Without Borders (EWB-USA). In the beginning I conducted interactive workshops with student engineers preparing for international service projects, but as I began to understand the immediate, high-impact potential that engineering brings to the "developing"/majority world, I started seeing my engi-neering collaborators as long-lost cousins of my Mali blacksmith friends.

Mali blacksmiths amaze those of us who don't make our own tools. These material alchemists, before your very eyes, transform natural elements into the tools and tech-nologies society needs to feed families. It was Malian blacksmiths, for example, who negotiated the widespread integration of the animal traction plow a half-century ago; now traction plows are ubiquitous throughout Mali, and blacksmiths keep them opera-tional. Whether we're talking about plowing or about screen-printing semi-conductors with nanoparticles of silicon ink, the kinship between engineers and blacksmiths is based on their specialized knowledge, which changes dramatically the way we live and work.

When an EWB-USA team first proposed a collaborative project with my Malian host community and my non-profit organization (www.africansky.org), I embraced the opportunity to unite a group of young engineers with their improbable counter-parts in Dissan. In an anthropologist's dream, I found myself betwixt a hoard of high priests, divided by their exclusive indoctrination into one of two rather powerful, tra-ditional knowledge systems: science, and what Malian blacksmiths and hunters call *knowledge-of-the-trees* (McNaughton, 1993).

Several years have passed since I first witnessed the promise and the transformative power of cross-cultural engineering, and now I cannot imagine my research, my teaching, my NGO, or even Mali without it. Collaboration across technocultural boundaries focuses my work within the nexus of science-based engineering and other "traditional" knowledge systems because I have seen this syncretic approach generate sustainable, locally salient solutions to alleviate suffering, and diminish inequality at home and abroad. Through anthropology I've become a bridge-builder for creative scientists and innovative local populations who together combat endemic poverty and hunger.

Becoming a Hybrid Scientist

Questions about the role of nanotechnology in "emerging economies" are no different from questions about the roles of previous exogenous technology as applied in the so-called developing world from pre-colonial eras through the present. From nanotech to plant genetics, the question of how we spread the latest scientific achievements to serve the poorest of the poor remains unanswered except for a few remarkable examples of rapidly adopted and adapted exogenous technologies such as cell phones and text messaging. One reason why generations of scientists have faced this same challenge stems from the way we frame our question. While it may be noble to ask how each new wave of science-based technologies can be *applied* in communities living in extreme poverty, we might find a more effective and humane question is how these technologies might be *created* or *developed* in communities facing extreme poverty. To answer this new question I became a hybrid scientist.

Coming from a country where barely 2 percent of the population is directly engaged in farming (USDA, 2010), and 73.7 percent of adults are overweight or clinically obese (NCHS, 2010), food security may not seem like one of the world's most pressing priorities, but living with small-scale farmers as a Peace Corps volunteer convinced me otherwise. When I first engaged with farmer and blacksmith friends to address critical development issues in the Dissan community, they channeled our mutual resources and energy on sorghum farming. With more experience in libraries than in the "developing" world, the enduring, well-documented inequalities (social, economic, and environmental) of the Green Revolution in Africa, Asia, and Latin America (Buttel *et al.*, 1985; Das, 2002; Kloppenburg, 1988; Lipton and Longhurst, 1989; Paddock, 1970; Shiva, 1991) fueled in me a youthful anti-science fervor. As a green anthropologist I theorized that Dissan farmers might best confront hunger and food insecurity by banning exogenous, science-based solutions. Even in the United States where technology-based innovations in agriculture brought unprecedented efficiency and higher yields, the grim history of the American family farm in the twentieth century cemented my cynicism of the efficacy and sustainability of high-tech agriculture for the masses, Africa and elsewhere (Barlett, 1993; Berry, 1986).

In the 1960s, local blacksmiths and innovative farmers championed the animal traction plow in rural communities, and Mali was a net-exporter of cereals (Lacy, 2004; Peterson, 2005). In the second half of the twentieth century, plant scientists, policy-makers, and many farmers embraced technology-based agricultural inputs (e.g. chemical inputs, modern/improved plant varieties) in hopes of increased yields; instead Mali's self-sufficiency as a nation of cereal growers withered. Furthermore, despite the introduction of science-based agricultural inputs and methods, cereal yields in Mali have remained constant since the 1960s (approximately 1,000 metric tons per hectare), in contrast to US cereal yields, which grew to nearly 7,000 metric tons per hectare in 2008 (see Figure 8.1).

There is no question that hybrid seed and an ever-growing knowledge of plant genetics (among other technologies) have increased yields and other desirable cereal traits—but for whom, and at what cost? Well-versed in inspirational "farmer-first" classics like Richard's *Indigenous Agricultural Revolution* (1985), I found it hard to see the glowing promise of techno-farming from the perspectives of hard-working Malian farmers gripped by extreme poverty and stagnant cereal yields. As a result, I spent almost a year collecting data to test the idea that the market-oriented, technology-infused food production helped only those farmers who could afford it most—families, communities, and nations who were already, relatively speaking, food secure.

I documented farmer knowledge and food production in Dissan with the intention to bring some "farmer science" to plant scientists who had struggled for decades applying scientific principles to bolster food security in the difficult economic and growing conditions in Mali. Through several years of ethnographic research living with poor family farmers in rural Mali, my vitriolic disdain for "science" was eroded by what only now appears as an obvious truth: neither scientists nor farmers hold a monopoly on ignorance, nor does either one of these parties independently possess solutions for a food-secure Mali. Determined to bridge the specialized and incomplete knowledge systems of Malian farmers and plant scientists, I set out upon a mission to make science-based agricultural research more responsive to the resources and needs of the poorest of the poor.

Leaving the Lab for the Village: Participatory Plant Breeding in Mali

As an anthropologist I was not a plant scientist, and I certainly wasn't a Malian sorghum farmer. That said, I studied and lived amongst both of these "exotic tribes" long enough to know that empirical evidence and history demonstrate that neither farmers

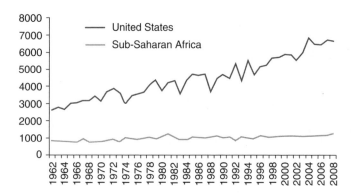

Figure 8.1 Cereal Yields in Metric Kilograms per Hectare, Sub-Saharan Africa versus United States, 1962–2008

nor scientists alone have the resources or knowledge to sustainably bolster food security in the poorest regions of the world with challenging and dynamic growing conditions. My hybrid-scientist days began when I identified a small band of plant breeders who were leaving the lab to conduct research with actual farmers in the farmers' household fields. This revolutionary group argued that the uniform, controlled conditions of the lab may make seed development replicable and scientifically sound, but these conditions produce crop varieties incapable of adapting to the diverse and challenging growing environments facing poor rural farmers in places like Mali (Ceccarelli and Grando, 2007). In other words, the conditions of the lab and the conditions found in the fields of family farmers are drastically different and perhaps in some ways incompatible. To make the products of science-based plant breeding more applicable to farmers and their fields, these pioneering plant scientists collaborated with farmers to develop crop varieties and seed that their rural collaborators would adopt—seed that is developed in and adapted to farmer's fields, not laboratory conditions.

In Mali where farmers were adopting less than 5 percent of the seed varieties produced through scientific plant breeding programs, I started collaborating with sorghum breeders, Eva Weltzien and Fred Rattunde, who were leading an effort to embolden regional plant breeding initiatives by bringing farmers deeper into the process of variety testing and research. Working at the Bamako station of the International Crops Research Institute for the Semiarid Tropics (ICRISAT) Weltzien and Rattunde's approach was in stark contrast to conventional breeding practices. Simply put, to develop a new variety of sorghum, a farmer or breeder crosses two different parent lines of sorghum. Then the resulting seed from offspring are planted to produce a next generation of plants and seed. Second generation plants manifest traits from their parent lines, but the results are anything but uniform. The abundant diversity of second generation plants create choices for the breeder; if, for example, the breeder desires a new sorghum variety that is tall, she will select seed from only the tallest of her second generation plants. The breeder repeats this process over multiple generations to develop new, progressively more uniform generations that, in this example, will produce higher percentages of tall plants. The process of developing a new variety by crossing two parent lines typically takes nine or more generations of seed selection to create seed that produces uniform plants with the breeder's desired traits.

Many highly desirable sorghum traits like increased drought tolerance are extraordinarily difficult to achieve, and as a result in conventional, science-based plant breeding programs farmers receive seed as "finished products" or uniform varieties. Scientists produce varieties, and farmers choose which varieties they want to grow in their household fields. Through their participatory plant breeding program, Weltzien and Rattunde brought farmers into the breeding process much earlier, to include their skills and household fields in seed selection and variety development. Instead of finding ways to make exogenous technology (in this case, seed) applicable to farmer's lives and fields, Weltzien and Rattunde found a way to develop technology with farmers where they live and where they farm (Weltzien and Hoffmann, 2005).

After observing Weltzien and Rattunde in their partner communities in 2000–1, I asked them for sorghum seed to conduct similar tests with Dissan farmers. In brief, I apprenticed with four master farmers in Dissan who each tested 23 varieties of sorghum seed provided by Weltzien. We followed Weltzien's protocol closely, and planted each variety in a single plot, each one five meters long with six planted rows of test seed. As directed, we planted these experimental plots square in the middle of each farmer's best sorghum field (optimal conditions). The results of these tests affirmed that developing new technologies collaboratively and in situ (in the target community/environment) can provide mutual benefits that serve science, as well as farmers living in extreme poverty. More specifically, this collaborative experiment produced two major outcomes: science gained critical information on farmers' values and methods for seed testing and sorghum variety choice, and local farmers identified and replicated several new sorghum varieties, one of which has greatly transformed local food production.

Benefits for Science

At the most fundamental level, "the scientist" benefited from this collaborative experiment because she found a way to create and disseminate the product of her scientific inquiry: the development and distribution of a sorghum variety that farmers adopted based on its strong performance in challenging local growing conditions. In addition, the scientist (Weltzien) and the social scientist (me) gained new insight into the values and practices of farmers relevant to the development and testing of new sorghum seed. After planting their official test plots in the center of their household sorghum fields (typically the most productive part of a field), participating farmers planted their surplus test seed in small secondary plots on the edge of their fields where soil fertility is least favorable. While scientists placed test their test plot in the center of the field in seek of higher soil fertility, farmers chose areas known for low productivity; given the delicate nature of their food system, planting the most productive part of their fields to unknown or untested seed is reckless. Collaborating farmers explained that they typically test new seed in the less fertile margins of their fields because seed that produces well in poor soil are worth a closer look; testing in the margins of their fields provides a way of distinguishing a new desirable variety from those that add little or nothing to existing (proven) local seed choices.

Following the variety tests, all participating farmers adopted several varieties for additional testing or production in future years. Their choices of some seed over others contributed to science-based agriculture by challenging two prevailing tenets of conventional plant breeding for marginal environments:

1. Participating farmers did not all adopt the same exact varieties. Conventional plant breeding programs typically work toward the development of a single effective variety to distribute within a specific region. The Dissan tests parallel variety tests elsewhere in Mali in that one type of sorghum doesn't please all types of farmers. Based on empirical evidence from variety testing and participatory plant breeding, conventional plant breeding may find increased success in marginal growing environments when they focus on developing variety portfolios rather than single "super" varieties (Lacy *et al.*, 2006).

2. While scientists and development workers in Mali struggled to encourage farmers to distribute new seed through market-oriented strategies (seed producer cooperatives and entrepreneurs), the simple tests in Dissan spread the products of scientific inquiry (seed) without exogenous assistance, nor any market mechanisms. Neighboring farmers and friends from other communities observed the Dissan variety tests, and then asked for seed. Since the original tests, Dissan farmers have gifted and traded out some of the seed they produced, and several of the test varieties have become popular local staples.

Benefits for Farmers

The farmer-led variety tests encouraged farmer "ownership" of their test plots and the resulting seed. Relative to conventional plant breeding programs, leaving the lab and developing varieties (i.e. technology) in farmers' fields gave participating farmers a greater measure of control over their livelihoods by expanding local variety portfolios with new sorghum choices that were evaluated in local fields. The increased biodiversity inherent in a larger portfolio of sorghum varieties can help Malian farmers efficiently adapt to the dynamics of their challenging growing conditions and climatic changes. Within one year, 17 different households adopted one or more of the 23 sorghum varieties grown by the four farmers who managed the test plots and served as diffusion agents for the resulting project seed.

The wide diffusion and regional farmer adoption of a variety named Bemba (Miksor 86-30-44) provides a specific example of the potential "embedded" impact of collaborative technology/seed development and local adaptation. Bemba expanded local sorghum variety portfolios by offering a seed choice that matures as fast as local three-month sorghum varieties while providing high yields comparable to local five-month varieties. Typically the yields of five-month varieties significantly outperform local three-month varieties presuming adequate or above average annual rainfall. In addition, a three-month sorghum variety requires significantly less weeding than five-month varieties, which frees household labor for other productive purposes and crops. Largely due to Bemba's extraordinary local performance during a remarkably difficult 2006 rainy season, five years after the first variety tests farmers disseminated (through gifting and trades for equal quantities of grain) this new variety to 20 households in Dissan, and to dozens more households in 12 surrounding communities. By the 2010 planting season, informal farmer seed gifting and exchange had cast Bemba seed to hundreds of households, some of them more than 300 kilometers away from Dissan.

Beyond the immediate benefits of the Dissan variety tests in terms of local and regional food security, another enduring contribution of this collaborative experiment is the emergence of dozens of essential new questions ripe for examination by farmers, scientists, anthropologists, policy-makers, and others. Two recent inquiries include the intellectual property rights of "collaborative seed" (Weltzien *et al.*, 2008) and the underlying social networks that influence and shape seed/technology diffusion in the developing world (Lacy, forthcoming). In short, the participatory variety tests in Mali accomplished a core principle of cross-cultural engineering: it fed science as much as it fed farming families.

Cross-Cultural Engineering: From Plant Breeding to Engineers Without Borders

As an anthropologist situated between scientists and impoverished farmers, the mutual and enduring benefits of the Bemba project taught me the value of anthropology as a means to bridge different ways of knowing our world for the purpose of achieving mutual, cross-cultural goals. This epiphany led me to consider all the other anthropological bridges I might build to jointly serve science and the poorest of the poor. Enter EWB. When the University of California-Santa Barbara chapter of EWB-USA invited me to help them navigate the cultural dimensions of their new project in Mali, I embraced the opportunity.

I organized the UC Santa Barbara chapter's first Mali excursion and took them straight to Dissan. I wanted the engineers to experience daily life in a hard-working farming community that, despite extreme poverty, was the most generous and creative community I have known. During our brief visit, the engineers learned that, like people all throughout the developing world, the people of Dissan were not passive victims waiting for exogenous experts and humanitarians to save them. In fact, the visitors learned that the people they came to help are actually teachers and partners who can help us save engineering and science. People may contest the idea that science and/or engineering need saving, but why is it that my obsolete iPod holds more songs that I could listen to, back-to-back, for a year, whereas 1.02 billion people in our world are undernourished—and that number is growing (FAO, 2009)? Why can't science address that problem before making my next iPod even sweeter? The answer is two-fold: priorities and perspectives; these areas are precisely where the world's poor and hungry can save science.

The Santa Barbara EWB team arrived in Dissan ready to talk and learn about jatropha (*Jatropha curcas*), a plant that grows like a weed throughout the southern half of Mali. Dozens of communities and fewer NGOs in Mali have organized jatropha projects to produce biofuel for operating community mills for grain and shea butter nuts (for example, see Mali Folklife Center, www.malifolkecenter.org). After their first porridge breakfast the EWB team met with Dissan elders to discuss the purpose of their visit, after which the community's youth association gave the team a village tour, which included a grand patch of wild jatropha. Encouraged by their first jatropha sighting the engineers walked back through the center of the village where they saw something that stopped them dead in their tracks.

There are some things that engineers simply find irresistible, and a broken machine torn apart into its component parts is just one of those things. On their return to the heart of the village the engineers found one of Dissan's two water pumps strewn about in pieces. While the elders showed enthusiasm for the EWB jatropha idea and project, the Dissan community had a far more pressing project in mind: maintaining adequate access to healthy drinking water. With minimal resources the village pump repair team was doing their best, but their aged pumps were breaking down at least once a month; the cost of repair materials and the eroding quality of the existing pumps were less manageable with each breakdown. Without preparation or delay, the EWB team took to analyzing the deconstructed pump. They picked up pieces, they consulted their faculty advisor, they asked questions of the pump repair team, and in fewer than ten minutes the engineers determined that the pump needed a new head and handle, but they also found that a simple preventative maintenance routine (namely, replacing bearings *before* they went bad) would delay for years the critical failure that manifested itself that day.

After a brief EWB huddle, a new project was born. Despite a year of preparing and researching the jatropha project, the team joyfully accepted the opportunity to adopt a completely different project, a project that directly addressed one of the most critical needs facing their Malian host community: technical and financial support for community-based pump repair and maintenance. Several days later the engineers invited four members of the pump repair team to return with them to Bamako, Mali's capital city, where together they organized an impromptu and informal conference with a pump supplies vendor and a Malian hydrologist. The myriad experts packed into the vendor's shop to share experiences and compare opinions to develop a simple preventative maintenance schedule and routine for the Dissan pumps. The EWB team used a good portion of their jatropha project funds to purchase a new pump head along with other supplies and tools, which the Dissan pump repair team has used for several years to keep their pump water flowing.

Since those first days with the Dissan team, their ad hoc pump repair and maintenance project has organically evolved to incorporate Peace Corps volunteers, a second EWB chapter, a handful of Malian communities, and African Sky (my Mali-based NGO). Most recently, the UC Santa Barbara and University of Arizona EWB chapters collaborated with African Sky and Dissan to organize and support two mobile pump repair teams that, since September 2010, are fixing pumps throughout Mali while simultaneously training local communities to do routine pump maintenance. Eventually the local community partners will learn the skills and acquire the resources to independently do pump repairs in their own villages and surrounding communities. In addition, the UC Santa Barbara chapter of EWB-USA has scaled out its operations in Mali to include additional project areas uncovered through their pump repair work: community water testing, and high-speed Internet access and computer network maintenance for a rather remote major high school.

While the jatropha project was and is an excellent idea supported by several successful Mali case studies, the UC Santa Barbara EWB team's first host village had needs and talents that were better aligned for a different initiative. As scientists and technical experts who want to work toward a better world, the ideas and discussions we have back home in our labs and classrooms are as great as our intentions, but they may not reflect the priorities and resources we find in the dynamic real world context in which our project host communities live and dream. If we truly want our work to make a difference in the world's poorest economies, we may need to cede what we can do for what we should do. The first step in such an effort is to develop a hybrid mode of science that meaningfully incorporates subjective ways of knowing, experiencing, and valuing our world.

Cross-Cultural (Nano)technology: Seeding a Hybrid Science

Nanotechnology, like any science-based, capital-intensive technology preceding it, has one of two potential outcomes in the developing world: it will either exacerbate or diminish economic, environmental, and social inequalities. As a hybrid science, cross-cultural (nano)technology begins with direct priority setting with stakeholders. It may be easy and exciting for us scientists to sit in seminar rooms and conference halls conceiving appropriate applications for nanotechnology in the developing world, but if these discussions are where we choose to launch this generational challenge, we may have already failed our international brothers and sisters, nearly half of whom live on less than $2.50 a day (World Bank, 2008).

I am not suggesting that scientists from resource-rich countries should refrain from imagining together ways that nanotechnology might improve lives and communities in countries like Mali. In fact, those kinds of discussions have already produced revolutionary technologies that are changing the way we think about energy and food production, health diagnostics, water and air purification, and many other contemporary challenges. Nevertheless, beyond our academic discussions and corporate-oriented R&D and patenting, nanotechnology needs voices and perspectives from emerging economies and the world's poorest citizens to diminish, rather than bolster, global inequalities (economic, technological, and otherwise).

Incorporating the poorest of the poor in priority setting for nanotechnology is a two-step process. Before talking with and listening to our community partners, we need to prepare for that discussion by first focusing inward. As the case studies on participatory plant breeding and EWB suggest, if we hope to make our work relevant to families living in extreme poverty, we cross-cultural engineers, material scientists, and anthropologists must rearticulate who we are and what we do. Specifically, we can evaluate our motivations and aspirations as scientists, we can redefine our concepts of the laboratory and objectivity, and we can evolve toward simplicity.

Evaluating Our Motivations and Aspirations as Scientists

As professionals in the scientific community our indoctrination process and quotidian work often obscure the core values and motivations that compel us into science-based careers. From the pressures of graduate school to professional publications, university and department service, and even daily email, we easily lose track of the bigger picture that inspired each one of us to dedicate our (professional) lives to science. When social scientists Bruno Latour and Steve Woolgar studied scientists as their chosen exotic tribe (1986), they observed the laboratory and the people who worked there. As cultural outsiders Latour and Woolgar conclude that the primary purpose of the laboratory is to produce papers. The observers see scientists and lab technicians reducing to writing ("inscription") everything they do, see, hear, say, and think. Ultimately, according to Latour and Woolgar, scientists dedicate their lives to producing "papers" to create "facts." This external point of view may be valid, but it fails to grasp the sociocultural significance of the act of producing papers and facts; somewhere within these laboratory cultures is an explanation for why people dedicate their lives to science.

When I speak to EWB audiences, I ask the attendees why they do what they do—that is, why they became engineers (or engineering students) in the first place. The answers I receive typically fall into one of a few categories. Most audience members explain that they are engineers or scientists because they are inextricably drawn to technology, building and creating, and/or practical and quantitative problem solving. In some cases the engineers also mention that they became applied scientists because they want their professional work to benefit humankind.

Scientists, including the EWB team, are an exceptional subculture in human societies. From ancient philosophers and early phenomenologists to the pioneers who collectively established what has become the scientific method, scientists believe that we humans have the capacity not only to understand the material world, but that we can harness that understanding in ways that promote learning and better living—however one may define that. Beyond producing papers and facts, scientists want to understand and change (or shape) the world. If aspiring cross-cultural engineers and scientists nourish this common aspiration they may be better prepared to balance professional obligations (i.e. producing papers and facts) with their energetic desire to practice science as a means to alleviate suffering and diminish inequality. The hybrid scientist, young and old, embraces the role of science as a creative tool for technological *and* social transformation.

Redefining Our Concepts of the Laboratory and Objectivity

Once we have accepted and made central our role as trailblazers for technological and social transformation, cross-cultural scientists must partially redefine two pillars of our empirical epistemology: the laboratory and objectivity. Why did our scientific ancestors create the sacred space we call the laboratory? Galileo, Newton, and countless others established the concept of the laboratory as an objective/neutral place for the production of replicable scientific knowledge. In reverence to empiricism, the laboratory boils down the physical universe into its constituent parts so we can observe each part in isolation. Then through replicating experiments we collectively eliminate potential errors and biases. Experimental reductionism allows scientists to rebuild our understanding of the universe piece by piece, atom by atom, nanoparticle by nanoparticle.

When we conduct experiments according to the scientific method, reductionism may help us to know and manipulate the elements that compose our universe, but this culturally specific perspective and the laboratory that produces it have their limits. A prime example takes us back to science-based plant breeding in Mali. Lab-oriented field stations allowed breeders to control growing conditions as they developed sorghum varieties. In one experiment, scientists produced a dwarf sorghum variety to redirect the plant's metabolism from growing three meters high to an increased capacity to produce grain; the biological trade-off was shorter plants for higher yields. When breeders took the seed from lab conditions to farmers' fields, farmers offered enthusiastic praise for the dwarf variety's remarkable fecundity. Nevertheless, most farmers chose not to adopt the variety; they explained that the short plants would attract cows and other pests that could more easily see, and thus destroy, any gains in sorghum yields. The engineered conditions of the lab or field station do not account for the "cow-factor" of a dwarf sorghum variety for Malian farmers. This episode along with successful variety testing in farmers' fields fueled the introduction of participatory plant breeding in Mali.

Participatory plant breeders sacrifice the controlled conditions of their laboratory (the field station) and conduct variety development and testing with farmers in farmers' actual fields with the hope that these less objective, variable, and imperfect conditions will produce plant varieties that farmers will actually adopt and grow. Both conventional plant breeding and participatory plant breeding are based on population genetics (i.e. a plant's phenotype is an expression of environment and genotype contributions, as well as their interaction), but participatory programs perform selection and testing of new germplasm in actual target environments (farmers' fields) instead of controlled, on-station lab environments. This decentralized approach to plant breeding improves farmer access and proximity to new varieties, but it also relies on farmers' work, knowledge, fields, and material resources. The significant and meaningful contributions of farmers to participatory breeding programs render farmers invaluable partners and contributors to a science that aims to help them feed their families. Similarly, if nanotechnology scientists and cross-cultural engineers aspire to create technologies that the poorest people in the world will adopt, we may need to expand our laboratories to include the actual living conditions and understudied resources of the poorest of the poor.

Evolving towards Simplicity

The third step in reimagining (nano)technology as a hybrid science capable of alleviating suffering and diminishing global inequalities requires would-be cross-cultural technologists to value the sophistication of simplicity. On a recent bus ride from a project site in Mali, I overheard several EWB students mulling over the idea of adopting the India Mark-II deep well hand pump as a "cool" design project for one of their graduate courses. The Mark-II pumps are ubiquitous in the developing world, and creating ways to improve the durability and/or ease of maintenance of these pumps would produce exponential benefits for countless impoverished communities that depend on these pumps for healthy drinking water. These students worked on a half-dozen pumps in communities throughout Mali, and they now understood viscerally the potential impact of a successful pump redesign. Nonetheless, following some initial excitement the students dismissed their idea because it was too simple.

In retrospect, I wish I had asked them to explain what they meant by the term simple. My favorite EWB faculty colleague would remind me: "simple solutions are a lot harder to develop than complex ones," because inventions typically evolve toward simplicity rather than being invented that way. An improved pump design is beyond the abilities of student engineers for the same reason that improving the bicycle is—both machines have evolved through so many talented hands that a novice engineer has an exceptionally difficult time finding ways to improve them. To further complicate matters, a successful pump design also requires ethnographic understanding and integration with diverse cross-cultural end-users. Ethnographic understanding is the result of long-term participant observation and field research. It is not produced in a controlled laboratory, and unlike engineers, faculty, and students in EWB, many of our scientific colleagues underestimate the invaluable contribution of rich, ethnographic knowledge in developing technologies for use in emerging economies and markets. On the surface level, a hand pump and its sociocultural context only *appear* simple. The hybrid scientists among us value sociocultural complexity no less than technological complexity.

As university-trained science professionals, we may feel compelled to produce and value complex systems because doing so requires enviable virtuosity. In fact, if one has dreams of winning a Nobel Prize for water filtration technologies, he or she would be wise to focus on carbon nanotubes or biopolymers rather than less-sensational sand-based filtration. But what if the Nobel committee consisted of family farmers who were living in extreme poverty? Might people like Professor Abul Hussam, who developed the inexpensive Sono arsenic filter for Bangladesh (using cast iron turnings, river sand, charcoal, brick chips and buckets) stand a chance to win one of the most revered international prizes in science? Similarly, how might the future of nanotechnology or science change if these same farmers sat on the editorial boards of our most respected journals, our tenure committees, or on National Science Foundation grant review panels? The answers to these improbable questions could help us imagine a hybrid science with the potential to not only dimininsh global suffering and inequality, but to bring forth new priorities and perspectives into the scientific community—priorities and perspectives that would align scientific achievement with the quality of life experienced by the half of our global family that lives on less than $2.50 a day.

Conclusion: Priorities, Perspectives, and Legacies

An ideal yet challenging place to begin imagining a hybrid science is nanotechnology. Nanotech is one of the most costly applications of contemporary science, and its potential benefits may be well worth the exorbitant time, resources, and money it requires. In 2008, the US federal government spent $1.5 billion dollars on nanotech research and development (PCAST, 2010: 25). Compare that with Mali's national education expenditure for the same year, which was $292 million, not including $169 million from external resources and donors (Pearce *et al.*, 2009). Science and engineering consume a lot of resources, and it is our responsibility to use them wisely, but that is not the sole reason for practicing science as a tool for social transformation and justice.

As new theories emerge by testing old ones, science is by definition a collaborative process. Just as pumps and bicycles have been shaped by countless, talented hands, all products of science emerge from a cross-generational legacy of technologists, scientific and otherwise. The debt of any science-based endeavor is nothing short of the pan-national history of all science and technology. Contemporary surveyors don't pay royalties for their use of calculations and surveying techniques as developed by Egyptians living 3,000 years ago, nor do engineers send a check to Italy every time they use Roman arches in a construction project. Drawing from the "open source" achievements of generations of technologists is the right of every scientist, but the most revered practitioners are the scientists who find innovative ways to pay back this consequential gift.

In our world of enduring social, economic, and environmental inequalities, scientists and engineers have a responsibility to re-imagine (nano)technology as a hybrid science capable of alleviating suffering and diminishing global inequalities.

But before we consider our cross-cultural (nano)technology as charitable work, we should remember that people living in poverty can make significant contributions to science and technology. A core principle of cross-cultural engineering in rural Mali is that it feeds science as much as it feeds farming families. Embedded participant observation in host communities like Dissan give the cross-cultural engineer a clearer perspective on problems that technologists should prioritize, and it identifies creative local collaborators. After welcome celebrations come to a close, daily life in rural Mali quickly distinguishes critical priorities like food production, access to clean water, firewood versus forests, and basic medical services. Local populations actively and creatively engage with these priorities, and so would any scientist who experiences more than a few days of life in one of these farming villages. Regardless of their target audience or client, all technologists must develop technology with an understanding of how and where it will be used. For cross-cultural technologists working in places like rural Mali, knowing one's target environment requires sharing and understanding daily life with poor farming communities. Without this perspective we will continue to reinforce global technological inequalities, and the promise of (nano)technology will be squandered on a twenty-first-century techno-colonization that will further exclude the poorest of the poor from ownership and participation in the benefits of contemporary science and technology.

9.
INNOVATIONS FOR DEVELOPMENT
The African Challenge
Moses Kizza Musaazi

Introduction

The numerous efforts to improve the lives of people living in developing countries by providing useful technologies are indeed commendable. Some well-meaning interventions can be clearly traced, and the millions of dollars spent for development can be accounted for in the form of positive impacts. In contrast, there are some technologies which are either not traced or have negligible impact on society. In some cases, unfortunately, the impact of a new technology can even be negative.

In this chapter the author discusses, through personal experience and the experience of others, the criteria that can make a technology successful in Africa by taking into account the living conditions, culture, and expectations of the intended users. Such technologies that satisfy these criteria are termed in this chapter "appropriate technologies." This chapter also argues that it should be possible to determine in advance whether a technology is likely to be "appropriate" or "inappropriate."

Essentially, when a technology is introduced, it should create an intended positive impact, be traceable, and be recognized as delivering "value for money." It should not only be sustainable, but should create a multiplier effect, promoting local skills among both users and those who learn to manufacture it for income. If it does not do so, it is deemed inappropriate. This chapter will address the key, but not always apparent, issues that would render a technology "appropriate or inappropriate."

Finally we will ask an even more difficult question: "How can we ensure that all emerging technologies are appropriate?"

Technological Needs of Developing African Countries

Nearly all technologies are introduced so as to address a particular need. It is often the case, however, that the intervention is shown years later to have failed to solve the shortcoming, or worse still, to have increased the problem or even created more problems. At this point, even though it is too late, people may finally ask a fundamental question: was there a real need at the outset, and if there was, were wrong assumptions made about addressing that need?

It is indeed true that developing African countries have a wide range of technological needs, ranging from basic tools to high-technology instruments. These needs fall under several familiar categories: water of sufficient quantity and quality, durable building materials, efficient farming methods, food security, health care, and quick and affordable communication devices.

To merely look at these needs from the outside may lead well-meaning people into misleading "solutions" which may have worked elsewhere but fail to take into account particular African conditions, which may range from climate to culture. Similarly, it is easy to neglect or ignore technological knowledge and skills that already exist in favor of new or imported ones. In addition, in producing a new technology, there is a tendency to disregard or devalue the use of human labor in favor of mechanization.

The following two examples are intended to provide insight into the qualities of "appropriate technologies."

1. The mobile phone, a high-technology product, has registered huge success in developing countries, despite the conditions of poverty and the high cost of the technology.
2. The solar cooker, a low-technology product, is highly functional and inexpensive, but is still struggling to gain a foothold in developing counties, even in those where solar energy is often available at no cost for 12 months a year.

Why is the mobile phone so much more successful than the solar cooker? The answer lies in understanding how highly the African people treasure communication with each other. The mobile phone answered the core need for people to communicate quickly and efficiently over long distances, which they could not do before the mobile phone arrived.

The solar cooker, on the other hand, offers a solution to the basic need to eat, but it does not automatically replace traditional cooking methods. So it may have to be re-designed to fit better into local cultures and to better demonstrate its inherent advantages.

Indigenous African Technology

It is tempting to believe that there is no indigenous technology in Africa or that, if it does exist, it is either insignificant, irrelevant, or inadequate. This assumption was inherited from colonial masters who tended to regard their own technologies as superior and wished to promote them in place of local technologies. Unfortunately, this bias has endured, and may even be growing worse, decades after the end of colonialism. Given this situation, it is appropriate to ask two questions:

1. Why does an African woman till the same land, with the same basic tools, from generation to generation?
2. Apart from survival instincts, are there some appropriate technologies that sustain the lives of the African people?

Clearly, if the land gave diminishing returns, the African woman could not sustain her family from generation to generation.

Scientists have recently learned that mountain gorillas, many of which are found in the Bwindi Impenetrable Forest of Uganda and Congo, administer medicine to themselves. More broadly, there exists a huge knowledge of medicinal practices among the African people which remains only partially exploited. Too often this wealth of knowledge is confused or deliberately mixed with African *juju*, or magical knowledge.

Poverty and Environment

Worldwide concern over protecting the environment needs to be understood alongside poverty, especially in Africa. Poverty is associated with high population growth, which cannot be sustained without overtaxing the environment. An example of poverty-driven behavior is the desire of a large poor family to turn a valuable wetland into farmland.

Poverty drives behaviors in ways that are not familiar to most people who live in developed countries. As a result, many interventions to help the poor people in Africa that seem reasonable "from the outside" have fallen far short of expectations.

For example, it sounds reasonable that a fisherman should avoid catching young fish or destroying the fish's breeding grounds. He is not only harming the ecosystems needed to support life, but he is also cutting off the source of his own livelihood. Several programs are attempting with little success to change these destructive behaviors.

The challenge is to find technologies that not only can help the poor, but will be accepted by them. We have learned that education and the provision of free or affordable family planning tools will not solve the problem of overpopulation. The only way to tackle this problem is by understanding why it happens and solving these fundamental causes.

Appropriate and Sustainable Technologies

Many technologies have been designed, developed, and marketed for African beneficiaries. Some of these still exist, but others have disappeared, along with their original reasons for being. Sustaining a product and its use remains the biggest challenge. It is most probable that sustainability is not achieved because a vital component has repeatedly been omitted from technology research and development: the needs and desires of the ultimate beneficiaries.

Let us return to the hypothetical example of such a technology: a simple and efficient cook stove for African women that is developed by an energy research center in a developed country. This stove brings with it many advantages, including low cost and reliability. However, it turns out that African women are slow to adopt this stove because of one critical condition: they are told that it has to be thoroughly cleaned every day, or its efficiency is greatly reduced. The African woman will then insist that the cook stove is impracticable; no busy woman, under the pressure of daily household chores, would have time to thoroughly clean the cook stove daily. The development center has focused on the engineering, but it has left out the vital component of the beneficiaries or end users themselves.

The success of any technologies or products will be assured only when the ultimate beneficiaries, together with intermediate players, are fully involved. The end users need not take part in the activities of the research laboratory, but their inputs on the design of the final product and the raw materials are vital. Increasing local adoption will promote the multiplier effect we seek, raising the likelihood of successful marketing.

There is no clear definition of an appropriate technology, but it is possible to list some of its characteristics. In most parts of Africa, the habits of reading and technology maintenance are very poorly developed. This cannot be attributed to illiteracy alone, but the author will not attempt to list the full set of reasons here. However, for a technology to be appropriate, it is imperative that it have the following characteristics:

1. It should be made out of as many local materials as possible.
2. Machinery should fabricated locally or adapted to local conditions.
3. The technology should be user-friendly, with clear and brief instructions and reliable operation.
4. It should require little maintenance, affordable parts, and repair that can be done locally.
5. Satisfaction among purchasers should promote a multiplier effect through increasing use and local skills development.
6. Local people should be able to make and/or sell the technology, promoting entrepreneurship.
7. The price should be affordable and comparable to existing practices.

Examples of Successful Appropriate Technologies

The author has been involved in research, development, and dissemination of appropriate technologies for the last 17 years. Described below are two examples of appropriate technologies he has developed.

Interlocking Stabilized Soil Blocks (ISSB)

The author developed a durable, inexpensive construction block by modifying an existing block press that was designed for the production of cement/compressed earth blocks. The new product, known as interlocking stabilized soil blocks (ISSB), are either straight (e.g. for building the straight walls of houses) or curved (e.g. for the curved walls of water tanks).

The ISSB technology offers several unique advantages. The press is 100 percent manual, providing new employment. The intention is to keep this manual system despite those who advocate a motorized system to reduce human involvement and increase production. The press is maintained by oiling the moving parts with used engine oil once or twice a week. Motorizing the press would require expensive fuel (electricity or gasoline), a skilled operator, and high maintenance and repair needs.

The press can be operated by just two people rather than the eight people recommended by the original innovators. The remaining workers can now be employed more productively in other sectors of construction.

Wide, deep interlocks are built into four of the six sides of each block. This feature ensures effective interlocks even if too much mortar is used or walls are dry-stacked. Construction accuracy, within a fraction of an inch, can hardly be expected in Africa where literacy levels are extremely low. The ISSB technology accommodates inaccuracies without compromising quality and strength.

Because of the interlocks, these blocks can be used to build large fluid containers, especially for water. This has resulted in skills training for rainwater harvesting and storage at the village level. The need to have water at each African homestead cannot be over-emphasized.

The blocks have also been used for other structures, such as granaries and round houses. Traditional wooden granaries were no longer practical because widespread deforestation reduced the supply of wood. The round houses, loved by many people as a cultural symbol, were being phased out because the mud or grass walls were vulnerable to fire and insect damage. The ISSB technology allows people to use this design once again.

The raw materials for ISSB technology are ordinary soil, or murram (laterite), which can be dug for free on site, and Portland cement. Until 2009, soil with high clay content was considered inappropriate for compressed earth blocks. But most of southern Sudan, for example, in immediate need of housing after years of internal wars, has clay-rich soil. In 2008 we blended grass with the local soil, and using the same standard 5 percent cement, we have produced some of the best ISSB to date.

ISSB technology offers many advantages over cement/compressed earth blocks. All the training required is gained through hands-on experience, rather than through classroom lectures or written instructions. Thus all persons, literate and illiterate alike, can be trained quickly and easily in about one day. Appropriate soil can be identified by finger feel, and does not require lab tests. Measurement of soil and cement is by batching, not by weighing. Soil is cleaned by hand, not sieved. Blocks are stacked for curing, and do not have to be wetted daily. The curing period is four hours rather than ten days. Training in the construction phase takes three days, not several weeks. The interlocks make construction easy and fast, and can be learned without any training in masonry.

Affordable Sanitary Pads

The primary motivation to provide poor schoolgirls with affordable sanitary pads was that most of them stayed away from school during their menstrual period, depriving them of three to five days of education per month. Providing them with imported sanitary pads was too expensive and unsustainable.

Provided with a grant from the Rockefeller Foundation, the author was able to develop an affordable sanitary pad, now trademarked MakaPads, to address this significant challenge. MakaPads are made from papyrus, a natural plant that is abundant along the rivers and swamps of Uganda, and blood-absorbing paper waste, which is donated by offices, universities, and commercial banks.

The positive impacts of MakaPads have surpassed the original aim of reducing absenteeism of schoolgirls. They also provide significant benefits to those who learn to make them, including refugees and people living with HIV/AIDS. Refugees no longer have to stretch out their hands to entrepreneurs for rations, and housewives in slums have turned out to be bread earners while not abdicating their family duties, since they are able to produce MakaPads at home. The ability of women to earn income in their homes has reduced domestic violence and brought a new and fresh breath of hope to the lives of those living with HIV/AIDS. These mothers are now better able to look after their children, many of whom are the products of rape during the two decades of war in northern Uganda.

To the extent possible, the author designed all the machinery for producing Maka-Pads as simple hand tools. The pads are locally fabricated by manual procedures, except for a few operations that use solar energy, and using the machinery requires minimum training and maintenance. The cost of the solar energy is minimal, and the work does not depend on access to an electrical grid.

Skills acquisition is simple, fast, and independent of literacy. Hence workers are trained on the job without an instruction manual or notes. The cottage-type production process is decentralized, so that women can work at their own speed, under their own local conditions. Consequently the individual level of commitment is high in response to both financial reward and flexibility of production times.

Conclusions

A global objective in the effort to reduce poverty is to identify emerging technologies that can solve central problems in emerging economies. Despite good intentions, however, it is not easy to identify or market a new technology, no matter how great its apparent value to the inventor. Successful creation of a new technology for a developing region depends not only on a sound technical concept, but also on deep understanding of those who will use, produce, or otherwise benefit from the technology. Even the best designed or best engineered products may have little impact if they do not satisfy local needs and customs.

In this chapter, the author has tried to identify some of the successes, challenges, and experiences of an African inventor/innovator as his innovations reach local and wider markets. While sustainability of emerging technologies is a continuing challenge, it can be enhanced by the involvement of end users and beneficiaries from the outset of the planning process.

A successful technology is one that creates a multiplier effect and becomes sustainable, requiring little or no external support as the product is understood, adopted, and provides increasing employment for people with little schooling, few resources, and limited mobility. To the immeasurable satisfaction of the innovator(s), a new technology may even yield unforeseen positive effects beyond those of the original aim—if one is successful in producing a product that is reproducible, affordable, and generally acceptable in the target culture.

10.
NANOTECHNOLOGY FOR POTABLE WATER AND GENERAL CONSUMPTION IN DEVELOPING COUNTRIES
Thembela Hillie and Mbhuti Hlophe

Water and Its Sources

Water is vital to sustain life in every organism, including human beings (World Health Organization, 2005). As a basic need for rich and poor alike, water takes on primary importance among public resources, one that we need to better understand and sustain.

Water accounts for about 70 percent of the surface of the earth, most of it in the salty oceans. The amount available as fresh water is relatively slight, and access is constrained by competing uses, most notably human consumption, industrial processes, and irrigation for agriculture. It has been predicted that about three billion people will not have access to adequate water supplies in 15 years, most of them inhabitants of the developing world. Therefore a basic and growing challenge is to better conserve and re-use the finite resources we must all share.

Surface Water

Surface water comprises the water in rivers, streams, lakes, wetlands, and the ocean. It is normally replenished through precipitation and lost through evaporation into the air and seepage into the ground. While the total amount of surface water on earth is estimated to be 326 million cubic miles, approximately 99 percent of it is stored in oceans, ice caps, and glaciers. Humans are left primarily with river water, which can be readily treated for economic use—but accounts for only about 1/10,000th of the total surface water. For this reason, water conservation is a global priority (DAI, 2011).

Groundwater

Groundwater is found among soil particles and in the fractures of geologic structures (historyofwaterfilters.com, n.d.; Philips, 2011), and is maintained through the transference of water from a surface water source. Unlike surface water, groundwater can be used in all the sectors of the economy, and accounts for a significant proportion of the fresh water available for drinking (historyofwaterfilters.com, n.d.; Philips, 2011). As populations increase, however, groundwater sources are often diminished by excessive withdrawals (Philips, 2011).

Water Pollution

Both surface water and groundwater are threatened by water pollution, which may be caused by two types of sources. A *point source* is a single place or site that directly introduces a pollutant into water. A *nonpoint source* is a process or activity that is responsible for the indirect introduction of a pollutant into a water source. Major causes of water pollution are summarized below.

Sewage

Sewage, including organic matter and animal and human excreta, is one of the most common causes of urban and rural water pollution. Sewage contains a wide range of microorganisms, some of which are pathogens, which cause waterborne diseases such as diarrhea, gastroenteritis, cholera, and typhoid. Sewage also contains nutrients such as nitrates and phosphates which stimulate the development of algal blooms, reducing water quality and ecological health (Krantz and Kifferstein, 2010).

Industry

Industries generally dispose of their waste effluents into water bodies. Such effluent contains a variety of substances, such as acids, bases, and dyes. These pollutants affect the pH of the water and contain toxic metals, such as lead, mercury, and cadmium, which are a health risk to humans. The effluent may also contains other chemicals, such as fluoride and ammonia, which render it unfit for drinking (Krantz and Kifferstein, 2010; Hlophe and Venter, 2009; Modise and Krieg, 2004).

Agriculture

Modern agriculture depends on the use of fertilizers and pesticides, which contain significant quantities of nitrate and phosphates. These nutrients are introduced into surface water as run-off from fertilized fields and percolate into groundwater through seepage. As water is constantly exchanged between surface and groundwater sources, so are its pollutants (historyofwaterfilters.com, n.d.) Besides causing eutrophication, nitrates and phosphates are also a health risk. Other agricultural contaminants may include arsenic and DDT.

Mining

Africa is endowed with a wide variety of mineral resources, which are extracted through both open-pit and underground mining. Tailings dams are often constructed to collect process effluent, and these dams sometimes overflow and discharge their effluent into surface or groundwater. Such tailings have high concentrations of salts and other pollutants (Hlophe, 2009).

Global Water Challenges

Water crises of several kinds currently confront the world. The challenges that affect people in developing and developed countries are different. The water crises in developing countries are essentially issues of inaccessibility, malnutrition, and waterborne diseases, such as diarrhea and cholera. In the developed world, a water delivery service could be hampered by either a wrong choice of appropriate technology or inadequate resources for treating the water. The challenges summarized below are most destructive in developing countries (Winpenny, 2003).

Poor Governance

Governance is the equitable distribution of water and must be overseen by legitimate representatives who are accountable to the public. It should ensure an efficient, transparent, and sustainable delivery of water supply and sanitation services for all. Decisions on water management should be coordinated at community, sub-national and national levels (UN, 2006).

Except for poor governance, there would be enough water for everyone on earth. The hard truth is that water is not equitably shared among communities, particularly in the developing world. Despite the fact that many people are now aware of their water rights, water management is still centralized and its institutions are plagued by corruption, fragmentation, marginalization, and low capacity. Good governance can be enhanced through proper remuneration of civil servants and improving accountability and transparency in management (UN, 2006). The worst governance systems are practiced in Africa where 40 percent of the population has inadequate access to water and sanitation (Winpenny, 2003).

Water Scarcity

Water scarcity applies to an area where water provision per person is less than 1,000 m³ per year. Some areas experience "absolute water scarcity," which describes an annual provision per person of less than 500 m³. Such scarcity can arise from either of two sources. First, an area may not have adequate water because of the physical lack of the water resource. Second, water may not be available or adequate because of poor governance systems and the accompanying waste and pollution. Some developing countries, home to about 1.2 billion people, do not have the infrastructure to extract water from surface and groundwater sources. It has been estimated that by 2025 about 30 percent of the world population will be affected by absolute water scarcity.[1]

Sanitation

According to the United Nations, a significant proportion (12 percent) of the world's population still relies on "unimproved sanitation," defecating in the open without access to toilets.[2] This poor sanitation, according to the World Health Organization (WHO), is directly responsible for about five million deaths annually from waterborne diseases. Of these, the WHO estimates that about 1.5 million are children (Krantz and Kifferstein, 2010).

Infrastructure

A crisis in water infrastructure is caused by urbanization, aging of structures, and poor governance, among other factors. The rapid rate of urbanization has outpaced the ability of governments to expand sewage and water infrastructure, particularly in developing countries (Krantz and Kifferstein, 2010). The United States and Australia have 100 times more water storage capacity per capita than Ethiopia. Pipe and reservoir leaks, pipe bursts, non-functional meters, and illegal connections to water supply contribute to an average 32 percent of non-revenue water (NRW) at certain municipalities in the North West Province of South Africa (Development Alternatives Inc., n.d.). The repair of the leaks and non-functional meters and better enforcement of connection laws could reduce the water demand by 15 percent. It is estimated that South Africa requires about $9 billion dollars to address the crisis in infrastructure (Sonjica, 2009).

Climate Change

It can take centuries for the Earth and its atmosphere and ecosystems to accommodate to changes in climate (South African Weather Service, n.d.). However, human activities during the past 200 years, especially the burning of fossil fuels and deforestation, have resulted in an altered and accelerated change in climate. The increased accumulation of so-called greenhouse gases results in the excessive absorption of radiation from the sun, which causes global warming, or an enhanced greenhouse effect. According to an international panel of climate experts, it is characterized by abnormal variations in the natural climate and may be accompanied by, among other factors, increase in temperature and sea level, changes in levels and patterns of precipitation, and changes in severity and frequency of extreme events, such as droughts and floods.[3] It is estimated that ongoing climate change could increase water scarcity by approximately 20 percent (Arriens, 2007). It is noteworthy that water stress and scarcity are projected to worsen in regions that are already dry.

Water and Development

Water is critical in sustaining livelihoods and plays a vital role in economic and social development. A comprehensive framework that strategically incorporates the social, economic, and environmental aspects of water is needed to promote sustainable development, especially in poor and water-deprived regions.

Water is also central to the eight Millennium Development Goals (MDGs) adopted by the United Nations in 2000.[4] The MDGs have 21 targets, each of which consists of assessment indicators by which it can be measured or evaluated (UN, n.d.). It has been observed that access to water and basic sanitation (Target 10) would facilitate the achievement of *all* the MDGs by the target date (2015). This remarkable statement bears up under close examination of the goals themselves. That is, water is needed for hunger reduction, universal education, empowerment of women, improved health, environmental sustainability, and global partnership for development. Water is the interconnecting thread among the MDGs, and the quality of life in poor countries can only be realized through stringent management of the water resource.

Progress towards the attainment of the MDGs, however, has not been uniform around the globe during the last decade. Significant progress has been made in reduction of absolute poverty, and 1.5 billion more people now have access to safe drinking water (UN, 2008) However, the rate at which the MDGs are being implemented in the developing world, particularly with respect to Target 10, is unsatisfactory. By 2015 there will still be about 700 million people who do not have access to safe drinking water and basic sanitation (Hlophe and Venter, 2009). Moreover, 2.5 million people will still not have access to improved sanitation (UN, 2008).

Nanotechnology-Based Water Treatments

Given the numerous threats to water security, including the many forms of pollution, development of more effective treatment technologies deserves the highest priority. These new technologies may offer better ways to remove salts and contaminants of all kinds. Conventional treatments, including a combination of coagulation, sedimentation, filtration, and disinfection, have been used with considerable success since the beginning of the twentieth century. Today, however, the field of nanotechnology has opened a new toolbox of capabilities for water treatment. The value of these tools, of course, will depend on the skills needed to use them most effectively, which vary significantly by country and region.

Nanotechnology-Based Water Treatment

Nanotechnology is the manipulation of matter at the nanoscale level, which is usually defined as 1 to 100 nanometers (billionths of a meter). Nanotechnology comprises, among other skills, the assembly of atoms and/or molecules to desired configurations and modification of existing structures. Nanostructured materials can be specifically designed for water treatment to remove undesired determinants (pollutants), such as toxic metals, pathogens, pesticides, insecticides, and dissolved salts.

Nanotechnology is now becoming an established technology in developed countries, where numerous commercial products have already reached the market. Some developing countries, such as India, Brazil, China, and South Africa, are also developing capacities in the field. Both developed and developing countries, however, are realizing the critical role that nanotechnology can play in the quest to provide safe drinking water and basic sanitation to all, particularly the developing world (chemicalprocessing.com, n.d.).

Nanotechnology has several advantages over conventional water treatment technologies. It can be used not only to remove microbial pollutants and particulates, but also dissolved salts. It can be used to produce alternative water supplies from hitherto unusable water sources, such as brackish water, seawater, and various wastewaters, including municipal and industrial effluents. Nanotechnology has a higher separation efficiency than conventional technologies, in particular for toxic metals, such as arsenic and mercury.

Some water treatment technologies already on the market or in advanced stages of development (Frost and Sullivan, 2006; Hillie and Hlophe, 2007; Grinshaw, 2009) may be grouped into the following categories.

Carbon Nanotubes (CNTs)

Carbon nanotubes, tiny, cylindrical tubes of carbon atoms, can be aligned into membranes that have the highest separation efficiency of all filtration methods. They can remove all types of pollutants from water with a separation efficiency comparable to that of conventional reverse osmosis, but at lower operating costs. Nanomesh carbon nanotubes can be assembled into a cylindrical water purification device called a "water stick" that can purify chemically or microbially contaminated water even as one drinks the water. This water stick is already being used by doctors in developing countries (World Water Day, 2007: Grinshaw, 2009).

Nanofiltration Membrane Devices

Nanofiltration (NF) membranes can be used to produce a range of water qualities, depending on the structures of their polymers. Hlophe and Venter (2009) treated brackish groundwater at a remote rural area (Madibogo village) in the North West Province of South Africa. The nanofiltration membranes proved to be very effective in the removal of contaminants, resulting in water that complied with World Health Organization (WHO) standards for drinking water. A pilot water treatment plant was subsequently set up in that village for the production of potable water for 1,000 pupils and their teachers at the primary school in which the pilot water treatment plant is located. The nanomembranes for this plant were supplied by a local company in Cape Town, South Africa, and they are manufactured by Filmtec in the United States. These nanomembranes are also commercially produced by Saehan Industries in Korea.

Nanoparticles can also be interspaced into the polymer matrix of a nanomembrane to form a composite membrane in which fouling is minimized. The separation efficiency of the composite membrane is comparable to that of conventional reverse osmosis treatment, but its operating costs are lower. Similarly, NF membranes that are derived from nanofibrous alumina have high separation efficiency and they essentially remove all (99.99 percent) viruses, bacteria, natural organic matter, DNA, and turbidity. They also remove essentially all (99.9 percent) dissolved salts, radioactive and heavy metals (Meridian Institute, 2006; Hillie and Hlophe, 2007; Grinshaw, 2009; Physorg, n.d.).

Nanoporous Ceramics, Clays, and Polymers

Nanoporous ceramics, clays, and polymers are used in environmental applications, such as drinking water purification, wastewater treatment, and site remediation. There are various types of nanoporous ceramics, clays, and polymers. The first one, nanoporous ceramic bio-media, are ceramic materials which consists of pores of a given size that hold aerobic bacteria able to convert organic pollutants and pathogens into non-toxic substances. The ceramic bio-media, commercially produced by MetaMaterial Partners in the United States, can also be functionalized to remove phosphates, microbes, and heavy metals, such as arsenic. Pathogenic microbes (bacteria and viruses) can also be removed by nanoporous ceramic membrane filters which are prepared from nanopowders. These have been applied in the treatment of wastewater from a milk factory in Algeria.

A second type of nanoporous ceramics, clays, and polymers can be used to remove virtually all (99.9 percent) heavy metal and radionuclide contaminants in water. This type depends on the fabrication of self-assembled monolayers on mesoporous supports (SAMMS). These SAMMS can also be functionalized for the removal of other specific pollutants.

The last type of nanoporous ceramics, clays, and polymers, cyclodextrin nanoporous polymers, are formed when starch is converted by a natural enzyme into rings of sugar molecules called cyclodextrins. Each ring, or "nanosponge," consists of six to ten molecules of cyclodextrin. These polymers can be injected directly into groundwater, where they can remove a wide spectrum of pollutants, such as benzene, polyaromatic hydrocarbons (PAHs), fluoride, nitrogenous pollutants, acetone, fertilizers, pesticides, and explosives. They have a higher removal efficiency than activated carbon or zeolites, and can be readily regenerated with methanol or ethanol for repeated use. They also have lower operating costs than reverse osmosis treatment. A pilot plant for water treatment has been established in South Africa (Meridian Institute, 2006; chemicalprocessing.com, n.d.; Grinshaw, 2009; Makoni, 2009).

Zeolites

Zeolites are adsorbents with crystalline structures that form nanopores. They are suitable for the removal of metal pollutants, including heavy metals such as arsenic and mercury. However, they have a low separation efficiency for organic pollutants. One of the strengths of this method is that the adsorbent can be easily regenerated with an acid solution. A particular nanozeolite has been commercialized for the removal of arsenic from water. In this application, the zeolite is packaged as a "tea bag" and introduced into the polluted water, attracting and removing the As ions (Meridian Institute, 2006; Grinshaw, 2009; Hillie *et al.*, 2006).

Nanocatalytic-Based Technologies

Nanocatalysts have greater catalytic activity in removing pollutants from water because of their greater surface area relative to the corresponding bulk material. They are indispensable for the degradation of organic pollutants, which are difficult and/or expensive to treat by conventional technologies. A type containing titanium (nanoscale titania [TiO_2] photocatalyst) decomposes virtually all organic pollutants when it is irradiated with ultraviolet radiation. It also adsorbs not only biological pollutants, but heavy metals as well. The shortcoming of the titanium photocatalyst method is the difficulty of its recovery after water treatment. A second type (nanoscale zero-valent iron, or NZVI), on the other hand, does not pose this problem, because its iron nanoparticles are readily recovered with a magnet (Meridian Institute, 2006; Grinshaw, 2009).

Researchers at the Center for Scientific and Industrial Research (CSIR) in Pretoria and the North-West University (Mafikeng Campus) in South Africa are investigating the disinfection and detoxification of microbially polluted water with titanium/silver nanocomposites. Their initial results have indicated a satisfactory killing efficiency of the nanocomposites. The study was prompted by the fact that chlorine gas and its compounds (the most widely used disinfectants), used in the disinfection of water, produce disinfection by-products in the treated water that are carcinogens.

Magnetic Nanoparticles

Magnetic nanoparticles act as adsorbents and nanocatalysts in water treatment. The separation efficiency of this method is comparable to that of the reverse osmosis process, but it uses less energy than the latter. It can also desalinate brine and seawater. Furthermore, the method is invaluable for the removal of oil spills from coastal waters. A commercial product has been developed at Rice University in the United States for the removal of arsenic from drinking water. After decontamination, these particles are easily removed from water with a magnet. The low production cost of these nanoparticles make this an appropriate technology for the developing world (Meridian Institute, 2006; Grinshaw, 2009).

Nanodetectors

Finally, sensitive, minute, and portable nanodetectors have been developed to detect single cells of chemical and biochemical species in water (Grinshaw, 2009; Hillie *et al.*, 2006).

Mitigating Some Barriers to Nanotechnology

The uses of nanotechnology have just recently begun, and it is both natural and prudent to contemplate the potential risks of such a powerful and unfamiliar new technology. There is not sufficient space here to address this topic in detail, but a brief summary of at least three general topics is appropriate. These can be outlined under the headings of nanotoxicology, consumer engagement, and technology transfer.

Nanotoxicology

A consequence of the extremely small size of nanomaterials is that they are difficult to recover from the environment and have the potential to present health risks long after they are used for water treatment. There are several ways in which humans can be exposed to nanomaterials, including ingestion and diffusion through the skin.

However, there is still scant information about the effects of nanomaterials on humans and the environment, and this has led to widespread concerns that inadequate attention has been given to nanotoxicology. One concern is the small number of publications in this field, especially in areas of concern to developing countries (Grinshaw, 2009; Hillie *et al.*, 2006.) An investigation conducted on the toxic effects cytotoxicity of carbon nanotubes on living cells (CNTs) indicated that any health risk could be minimized by coating the surface of the nanotubewalls, but this observation was made only under controlled conditions. The benefits of nanotechnology can be fully realized only when extensive field studies of such topics have been conducted. These studies should be pursued in a collaborative manner and promote free access to current knowledge in many settings.

Also, considerable ambiguity exists in how much we actually know about nanotoxicology. For example, some researchers believe that valuable information about the effects of engineered nanomaterials on organisms, particularly humans, can be deduced from information on the interaction of natural nanomaterials with organisms. Studies on the latter have demonstrated that *natural* nanomaterials can diffuse into the blood and the lymphatic system and would eventually spread to sensitive organs, such as the heart and kidneys, with adverse effects. However, this finding is not necessarily true for *engineered* nanomaterials, underlining the urgency of pursuing additional research on nanotoxicology (Grinshaw, 2009; Hillie *et al.*, 2006) and to share all aspects of knowledge in this field.

Community Engagement

Full engagement in the water crisis as an MDG priority can be achieved only when it includes the consumers of water, technology partners, and key decision-makers. Just as water is a basic human need and right, those who need and use it must be involved in its sustainability (Mehta, 2007).

Both the providers and consumers should understand the complexities of providing safe water in sufficient quantities, including knowledge about an integrated structure for efficient and effective delivery. Nanotechnology is not yet widely used (particularly in South Africa and other developing countries) because of the high purchase and maintenance costs of the technology. There is also a lack of local expertise in membrane design, construction, operation, and troubleshooting. Understandably, people are reluctant to use such a new technology unless it can be sustainable in the long term (Hillie *et al.*, 2006; Pillay and Jacob, 2004; Pieterson, 2005; Hlophe and Hillie, 2008). This reluctance can be addressed by establishing a forum of all stakeholders to build and ensure transparency, accountability, information-sharing, and cooperation. These provisions can help reduce the likelihood of communication barriers between service providers and consumers.

Many studies show that adequate water quality and supply are most difficult to achieve in rural areas. Such areas are usually characterized by challenging geographical location, low economic status, fixed cultural norms, and high rates of illiteracy (Mehta, 2007). These social features are usually ignored by water planners and other decision-makers, even though they contribute significantly to the inhabitants' willingness to take ownership of new technologies and trust in their sustainability (Haysom, 2006; Mfangavo, 2005; O'fairheallaigh, 2009).

There are valid reasons why rural people are reluctant to buy into new technologies. They are traditionally disempowered as consumers through lack of knowledge and skills, and consequently take little part in decision-making. They participate only passively in planning processes, relying on information given them by the technology experts. Some researchers (Hlophe and Hillie, 2008; Mfangavo, 2005; O'fairheallaigh, 2009) have demonstrated that rural consumers are generally not familiar with procedures for participating in decision-making or for making known their concerns and expectations. The result is that the consumers begin to appreciate the merits and demerits of the technology service only after the project is complete and the service provider has left. All too often, the service itself is subsequently rejected or left unused (Mfangavo, 2005; Funke *et al.*, 2007; Netshinswinzhe, 1999).

Recent case studies on water technologies conducted in Kenya, Uganda, Tanzania, Nepal, India, Bangladesh, and the Philippines provided the following lessons: (1) stakeholders have different perspectives of water service provision, so that joint efforts are required to build strong linkages and create mobilization; (2) working with poor communities requires specific knowledge, attitudes and skills; (3) local communities, after exposure to information, need a chance to think about these new ideas and make their own decisions; and (4) public awareness and community participation are critical aspects to sustainability and ownership of any development intervention (Mfangavo, 2005; Wellman, 1999; Jansky and Uitto, 2005).

Technology Transfer

Proper technology transfer includes ownership, adoption, and adaptation of technology in ways that meet end-users' needs. Adoption and adaptation of existing nanotechnologies requires local technical know-how to service and maintain. The level of this technical know-how depends on the complexity of the technology. It is imperative that local academic institutions be included in this process to provide proper training to the practitioners. According to Kolanisi, water technology programs should be designed in such a way that the people (users) become the focal area. This can be achieved through adopting the following points:

- The technology required for providing water service to a community must be in line with its water governance structure.
- Water should not be seen only as a human right, but also as a critical contributor to the economic status, public health, and cultural development of the country.
- The socioeconomic needs of the targeted population must to be clearly understood in order to determine their needs, preferences, expectations, and willingness to pay for services or maintenance, if required.
- Geographical and environmental conditions have to carefully researched, because they affect the costs of installing water technologies.
- Consumers must be prepared through outreach and communication to actively participate in transparent decision-making and implementation processes.

• Water technology providers must find a holistic and integrated approach that encourages active participation of communities, including a debate and discussion on how to advanced the technology locally. A holistic and integrated approach offers a the greatest opportunity for engagement, communication, and better understanding of stakeholders' perceptions and needs.

Conclusion

Nanotechnology is sufficiently advanced to help provide potable water and water for general consumption in developing countries. The technology to be implemented will depend on the available infrastructure, and in most remote rural areas in developing countries where potable water is required, these include such rudimentary basics as electricity and accessibility.

The risks of nanotechnology can be mitigated through sharing, training, and access to knowledge from both developed and developing countries. A number of studies in nanotoxicology have been successfully conducted, and wider dissemination of this information can facilitate the implementation of nanotechnology for potable water in poor developing countries.

It is critically important to involve the whole community as stakeholders from the beginning of the planning process. Water is essential to all livelihoods, and the poor should have more control of this basic element of their lives.

Finally, local capacity development is vital for the implementation of nanotechnology for water quality improvement. Local know-how is crucial in adopting and maintaining the technology, and providing for expansion. The participation of academia, the custodians of nanotechnology, is crucial as they can also take part in communicating their knowledge to the community and receiving essential feedback.

11.
SOLID-STATE LIGHTING
A Market-Based Approach to Escaping the "Poverty Trap"
Dave Irvine Halliday

Introduction

In 1997 Light Up the World, a Canadian non-profit organization I created and direct, set out to try and bring light to the more than one quarter of humanity (1.6 billion people) who had no access to electrical lighting. The guiding principles from the outset were that the form of electrical lighting to be offered to the poor would be safe, healthy, reliable, bright, energy-efficient, and affordable. To the extent possible it would use renewable energy, since the majority of people at the "Bottom of the Pyramid" (Prahalad, 2005) were not serviced by an electrical grid.

Light Up the World initially developed its own primitive form of solid-state lighting using multicolored light-emitting diodes (LEDs), but it was Shuji Nakamura and his Nichia white LED that provided the eureka moment and the foundation from which the non-profit would truly start to provide low-cost lighting in many countries. By 1999, Light Up the World had field tested its first solid-state lighting systems in Nepal. This effort was so successful that in 2000 it established permanent lighting in four Nepali villages—a world first. In 2001, additional villages were also lit in Nepal, India, and Sri Lanka, while Light Up the World partners were simultaneously lighting villages in Guatemala, Irian Jaya, and Bolivia. Since then, working with local partners and international industry leaders around the globe, it has demonstrated the economic feasibility of using solid-state lighting for "off-grid" populations, with over 30,000 systems installed in 50 countries (Irvine Halliday *et al.*, 2008). These systems are safe, healthy, bright, efficient, and affordable ways to assist in promoting literacy, education, equality, and economic and human development.

Efficiency and Cost of Fuel-Based Lighting

A typical kerosene wick lamp with a consumption rate of about 0.05 liters/hour,[1] has a light output of approximately ten lumens (a typical incandescent 100 watt light bulb emits in the order of 1,200 lumens). This is only one five-hundredth the efficiency of an incandescent bulb, which has the lowest efficiency (Louineau *et al.*, 1994) of any electric lighting source. A few years ago, researchers estimated that the global cost of fuel-based lighting was about US$38 billion/year, or US$77 per year per household (Mills, 2005). Light Up the World's own data—for example, in Afghanistan, Costa Rica, Ghana, Pakistan, and South Africa—show that many families spend more than US $100 per year on kerosene, a figure that is unfortunately bound to increase in the coming years. Spending on lighting fuels can be as high as 25 percent of monthly household income (Irvine Halliday, 1999; Rudolfo Peon, Doluweera *et al.*, 2005). Kerosene is often heavily subsidized by as much as 50 percent. Fuel-based lighting is very poor in light quality, it is unhealthy and extremely hazardous, and as we all now know, very expensive.

Health Hazards and Environmental Impacts of Fuel-Based Lighting

The uses of fuel-based lighting brings other disadvantages. It causes severe health hazards in the form of burn accidents, indoor air pollution, and fires started by accidental breakage of kerosene lamps. Surveys conducted by Light Up the World in Nepal and Sri Lanka reported burn accidents of some degree once in every month due to kerosene lamps, and in most cases the victims were small children and women (Irvine Halliday, 1999; Leon and Graham, 2005). A great, but generally unacknowledged, health risk of kerosene lamps is the indoor air pollution caused by the emission of harmful gases, such as carbon monoxide, sulphur oxides, nitrogen oxides, as well as particulate matter (Fan and Zhang, 2001; Schare and Smith, 1995). The pollutant emission rates of typical kerosene lamp are shown in Figure 11.1. Of these pollutants, carbon monoxide is lethal to humans, and the others cause chronic respiratory illnesses. The risks are compounded by the fact that kerosene lamp users are continuously exposed to them. Kerosene lamps also emit greenhouse gases, mainly carbon dioxide; burning one liter of kerosene emits 2.5kg of CO_2. Thus a household that uses about five liters of kerosene per month for lighting emits a ton of carbon dioxide in about six and a half years, while a village of 100 houses emits 15 tons of carbon dioxide annually.

Solid-State Lighting Systems

Over the past decade the white light-emitting diode (LED) has undergone dramatic improvements in efficiency, lumen output, reliability, choice of color, and cost. Present off-the-shelf white LEDs have efficiencies in the range of 80 to 160 lumens per watt, and

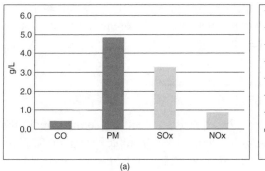
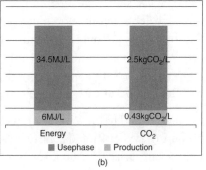

(a)   (b)

Figure 11.1 (a) Air Pollutants Emissions from a Kerosene Lamp; (b) Energy Requirements and CO2 Emission of Kerosene Lighting

the mean time to failure for a good quality, high power white LED can exceed 50,000 hours. A typical solid-state lighting system consists of white LED lamps, a renewable energy source, and an energy storage device. Due to its universal availability, very long life, minimum maintenance, and simplicity of use, the solar photovoltaic panel is the preferred option as the power source for most off-grid applications. For storing the energy, the 12-volt, 7 amp-hour sealed lead-acid battery is generally the best value for money (Rudolfo Peon, 2006). A typical rural household can be illuminated to a very acceptable level by using two or three single watt white LED lamps, each giving a light output in excess of 100 lumens. Sufficient energy to operate a system with two single watt lamps can normally be obtained using a five-watt photovoltaic panel, assuming four to five hours of average lamp usage every 24 hours and depending on available solar energy resources. As efficiencies for small white LEDs have already reached 200 lumens per watt, there is definitely a place for a solar home lighting system consisting of, for example, a single very bright lamp with onboard AA batteries and a two-watt, or even smaller, photovoltaic panel. This will enable solid-state lighting to penetrate affordably even deeper into the poorest communities. All of Light Up the World's lamps also have dimming features that can save energy, providing a highly desirable flexible lighting system (Rudolfo Peon *et al.*, 2005).

Compared to fuel-based lighting, solid-state lighting systems are emission-free in their use phase, and avoid the aforementioned health hazards of kerosene lighting. Furthermore, the avoided carbon dioxide emissions can be used as carbon credits and can be traded either in formal markets, such as the Clean Development Mechanism, or on growing voluntary carbon markets, such as those of Google, Nike, and Yahoo. Thus they could be used to finance solid-state lighting implementations in developing countries. It is also informative to appreciate both the initial energy required and carbon dioxide produced during the manufacturing of the kerosene, both of which are avoided by the use of solid-state lighting.

To further clarify the chasm between the lighting energy used by developing and "overdeveloped" worlds, the 2005 annual per-person light consumption in North America was nearly 13 times that of the developing world—the equivalent of somewhere between 30 and 40 100-watt incandescent bulbs burning for six hours, every day of the year, for each person in North America (Fan and Zhang, 2001; Schare and Smith, 1995). Stated somewhat differently, a single 100-watt incandescent bulb (for example, a driveway light) consumes as much power in ten hours as a kerosene lamp, burning for four hours a day, would in an entire year.

Light Up the World Activities in Africa: Rwanda, Uganda, and the Democratic Republic of Congo

In 2006, Light Up the World conducted a baseline assessment in a community in the bordering area of Rwanda, Uganda, and the Democratic Republic of Congo. Graham (2006) categorized the families into three income groups: low income: $0 to 40 per month ($480/year); moderate income: $40 to 100 per month ($480–$1,200/year); high income: greater than $100 per month ($1,200+/year).

Participants were asked to rank their opinions and experiences with various kinds of lighting.

Electricity

Electricity was valued highly by the majority of residents, ranking after only food in priority. Education was of great importance in nearly all households and it was very informative to learn that a majority of households (60 to 65 percent) with students indicated that kerosene lamps are used nightly for studying. Comments often reflected concern about the smoke emitted by conventional kerosene lamps, and a hope that electric lighting would relieve this source of pollution.

Source of Light

As is typical in the developing world, households used a variety of lighting sources, including open hearth fires, candles, kerosene wick lamps, lanterns, and flashlights. All households in all income groups used wick lamps, but the proportion using kerosene was lower in high income households, which favored lanterns.

Expenditures on Lighting

On average, 19 percent of all households used candles and 41 percent used flashlights. Households spent an average of $1.02 for candles and $1.44 for batteries each month. Not surprisingly, income level was a significant determinant of the amounts paid. A low-income household using a wick lamp or lantern spent on average $1.60 a month for kerosene; a middle-income household spent almost twice that ($3.00), while a high-income household spent nearly four times that amount ($6.00).

Kerosene Lighting

On average, about 90 percent of the houses in the study area used kerosene for lighting. Although houses had four to six rooms, only high-income houses generally had more than two lamps or lanterns per house. Lamps were used for an average of three hours a night. This is important, because the Light Up the World solid-state lighting system comes with two white LED lamps which will operate up to four to six hours. These would potentially replace all kerosene use in low- and moderate-income houses, resulting in monthly savings of $1.60 for low-income, $2.13 for moderate-income, and (assuming total kerosene replacement) $6.10 for high-income households. As a comparison it has been estimated that the average African household uses 55 or so liters of kerosene per year for lighting, at an approximate cost of $158 (Sireau, 2008).

Use of Lighting

Most of the families used light for household chores, especially in the kitchen and bedroom, and a majority of them also used light for socializing. Light was important particularly in high-income homes for studying, writing, and reading. Lighting appeared to have an important influence on income, since only 10 percent of low-income homes used light for income generation, whereas a significant 31 percent of high-income homes used light for income generation. This finding reinforces the intuitive belief that more disposable funds allow people to be more entrepreneurial. Lights are used in a variety of ways for income generation, including preparing lessons, writing reports, serving and making beer, selling goods, tending animals, keeping potatoes, cutting hair, and operating a health center. One household used a solar panel to charge cell phones for profit, apparently part of a growing trend in the region. The income generation potential of light has a greater impact in poorer houses.

Lighting Issues with Kerosene

Responses were similar across all income groups. In the main, people were concerned with, first, the cost, and second, the health and danger issues in using kerosene light. Poor luminosity and the lack of dependability were tertiary issues identified by around 50 percent of families.

Expectations of Electricity and Lighting

Respondents were asked to name three ways in which they would use electricity if it were available. The highest number of responses was for lighting, with more than 45 percent of responses indicating that lighting would be a primary use of electricity if it was available. As a means of putting this particular location in perspective economically, Table 11.1 shows the average kerosene lighting expenditures in a number of countries.

Papua New Guinea

The Light Up Papua New Guinea Project is taking place in honor of Nichola Goddard. A Canadian born in Papua New Guinea, Nichola was a captain in the 1st Regiment of the Royal Canadian Horse Artillery when she was killed in combat on May 17, 2006; she was serving with the Canadian military in Afghanistan. As part of her legacy, Light Up

Table 11.1 Annual Average Kerosene Lighting Expenditures in Various Countries ($US)

Country	Cost (USD)
Afghanistan	$240
Cambodia	$100
Costa Rica	$200
Ecuador	$200
Ghana	$120
Guatemala	$100
India	$30 (includes 50% subsidy)
Malawi	$120
Nepal	$70
Pakistan	$140
South Africa	$130
Tanzania	$200

the World is working with the Goddard family, school children, and people around the world to raise money to light up first aid posts and rural health centers in Papua New Guinea. The objective is to bring light to more than 1,100 of these facilities throughout the country by 2015.

Bringing light to aid posts and rural health care centers will improve the quality of health care provided to people in Papua New Guinea. To date, 194 solar systems have been installed in 137 health facilities that serve an estimated 770,000 people in eight of the 20 provinces. The rugged terrain in Papua New Guinea makes service delivery expensive and logistically challenging. However, Light Up the World project partner, AT Projects, is working to expand their reach into new target areas. Plans for 2010 include increasing the reach of the project with the installation of over 150 more solar systems. It is expected that one-quarter of the project will be completed by the end of its second year.

This project is a positive advancement for the health sector in Papua New Guinea, a country where 120,000 of 200,000 births per year occur without access to medical facilities. The solar lighting systems have resulted in vast improvements in the conditions for many birthing women, and an estimated 2,000,000 people will benefit when this project is completed. Displacement and Refugee Camps

In 2009, the United Nations High Commission for Refugees reported that nearly 43.3 million people worldwide were forcibly displaced due to conflict, persecution, and natural disasters (UN High Commissioner for Refugees). Refugee camps are often very poorly lit, using kerosene wick lamps, and there is typically no street lighting. This allows crimes such as robbery, assault, and rape to be committed under the cover of darkness. The direct lighting costs must be borne by the relief community, which includes the purchase of kerosene, electrical generators, lamps, batteries, and the associated transportation and distribution of these elements by air and road. A typical kerosene lamp operating for four hours per 24-hour period may consume around 60 liters of fuel per year, and as many refugee camps contain thousands, if not tens of thousands, of homes, supplying fuel-based lighting 12 months per year is an arduous and expensive task, given the high price of petroleum. Solid-state lighting provides an almost perfect lighting solution for refugee and displacement camps. It can be used for both homes and street lighting, and it is safe, healthy, bright, rugged, reliable, and cost effective. Table 11.2 shows a comprehensive list of lighting objectives and considerations for refugee and displacement camps and it shows how well solid-state lighting is suited to such environments.

In 2005 Light Up the World demonstrated the appropriateness of solid-state lighting for emergency situations when it supplied over 3,000 complete lighting systems to displacement camps in the coastal regions of Sri Lanka immediately after the tragic and devastating tsunami. In partnership with a local company, Crystal Electronics, every lighting system (named "Light in a Box") was manufactured in Colombo, thus keeping the majority of the funding in country and creating additional skilled employment. Considering the exceptional circumstances and the need to work quickly, it is estimated that the average cost of lighting each displacement camp home was around $140.

In 2006 Light Up the World's partnership with Kathmandu's Pico Power Nepal led to the lighting of a significant number of street junctions in the Damak ("Butanese") refugee camp on the eastern border of Nepal. This project significantly increased nighttime

Table 11.2 Lighting Objectives and Considerations for Refugee and Displacement Camps

Refugee and Displacement Camp Objective	SSL Lighting Considerations
Provide adequate and durable administrative, outdoor, common area services.	Administrative, outdoor, and common areas require illumination. Solid-State Lighting systems (using white LEDs) are longer-lived, more rugged, and less expensive to operate than traditional lighting solutions.
Minimize reliability on external resource imports.	Typical light sources require a steady stream of "imports" to the camp, including kerosene fuel, wicks, batteries, replacement bulbs, etc.
Sustain family and other social cohesion.	Social interaction typically requires lighting. Temporary family shelters often have no light.
Provide for schools, places of worship, and play areas for children.	Adequate illumination is essential for schools, places of worship, and safe play areas. Flame-based light is inadequate for reading and many other learning tasks.
Preserve individuals' dignity.	Individually controlled lighting provides control of privacy.
Ensure refugee safety, both inside and outside of shelters.	Lighting is a very important element of personal safety, especially for women and children. SSL systems eliminate fire-risks from kerosene lighting and are easily portable.
Support efforts at re-establishing livelihood.	The availability of lighting supports home based cottage industry after daylight hours.
Promote self-sufficiency.	PV-powered LED systems require a minimum of externally provided parts (batteries every second or third year) and no fuel.
Minimize vulnerability to disasters affecting camps.	PV-powered LED systems are not susceptible to disrupted kerosene or electricity supply lines.
Fortify occupants for future disasters.	If camp residents take the LED systems back to their permanent settlements, they will be better prepared for future disasters.
Minimize environmental impacts of establishing, operating, and decommissioning refugee camps.	Electric, fuel-based, and (non-rechargeable) battery-based lighting entail significant environmental impacts, including generator emissions and noise pollution, fuel spillage, and solid waste production/disposal.
Minimize vector and other disease risks.	Illumination in the yellow-red spectrum assists mosquito control, which is a need in many camps. LEDs can be "tuned" to virtually any wavelength and intensity of light output. WLED lighting tends to decrease the presence of insects, lizards etc. as it has virtually no UV and IR energy.
Provide culturally responsive conditions for burial.	Some cultures require a period of continual light on the graves of the deceased. SSL systems would provide a lower-cost alternative.
Place priority on sheltering disaster victims "in-place", with relocation to remote encampments as a last resort.	While not a panacea, pre-disaster distribution of SSL systems would support the shelter-in-place goals of disaster response.
Cost-efficiently provide essential relief services.	SSL systems eliminate the need for camp space dedicated to power production, storage and distribution of batteries, fuel, etc. They reduce the volume and weight of material requiring air and ground transport.
Mobile lighting at night.	White LED flashlights offer great costs savings, the bulbs are effectively unbreakable and the batteries last "ten" times longer.
Street lighting.	Solid-state lighting has many advantages over fluorescent and incandescent due to its lower energy usage, long life, low maintenance and continually increasing efficacy (brightness). It also enhances safety at night.
Fresh vegetables.	LEDs of various wavelengths may be used to grow vegetables in winter months at low energy cost.
Improved health.	Solid-state lighting is healthier than fuel based lighting since there is no exposed flame and smoking wick. Serious visual and breathing problems are endemic in countries where fuel based lighting is used.

safety in the camp, especially for women, and it was deemed a complete success by the United Nations High Commission for Refugees and Lutheran World Federation partners. The average installed cost of lighting each street junction was approximately $427.

In 2008 an in-house Light Up the World project showed that a photovoltaic powered solid-state lighting street lamp incorporating six Cree XLamp white LEDs would provide an acceptable lighting performance for use in rural areas in the developing world, and could be built and implemented at a total life cycle cost of approximately $570 (Kodisinghe, 2008).

In 2010 Light Up the World established in Peru its first regional office in a developing world country. With closer proximity to beneficiaries, the office will be able to increase the scale and scope of the projects to better address the needs of off-grid communities. The regional office will also act as a vehicle for expanding research and development; offer school and other education programs; and provide further opportunities for academic and technical partners to support more renewable energy and lighting projects in South America.

A significant feature of an appropriate solid-state lighting package for a refugee home is that it may be smaller than the classic "Light in a Box." For example, the total package may consist of one two-watt solar panel, one very bright one-watt white LED lamp, one 12V, 2 Ah SLA battery, and one white LED flashlight. In today's market the retail price of such a solid-state lighting system of good quality would probably be less than $20, if manufactured in reasonable numbers, and the retail price of the white LED flashlight would be approximately $3.

Socioeconomic Impact of Solid-State Lighting

To effectively evaluate the many effects of solid-state lighting on communities it is necessary to analyze its microeconomic impact, macroeconomic impact, and political economy.

- Evaluation of the microeconomic impact must be further disaggregated by exploring the household and community effects separately. One must understand how the entire household regards the impact of solid-state lighting on the family as a social unit. The community-level assessment attempts to aggregate the various household-level affects and thereby make inferences about how changes may affect the community as a whole. The community-level investigation also seeks to understand how solid-state lighting in the home may influence other institutions in the community.
- The macroeconomic impact needs to focus on how changes at the community level, especially in regard to consumption habits, may influence macroeconomic conditions in a country.
- The political economy of solid-state lighting explores how it effects other organizations, with other energy sources, that provide goods and services in the community. The impact of solar-powered LED lighting systems on a community depends, to a large extent, on the features of the source of lighting it is displacing.

The economic effects are based on households obtaining solid-state lighting systems through microcredit loans delivered by microfinance institutions. For households that purchase solid-state lighting systems with borrowed funds, repayment schedules for loans are designed to match kerosene expenditures that the household made prior to obtaining the system, since this is critical to understanding the range of its social and economic impacts. For instance, if solid-state lighting systems were donated to communities where the cash economy is less mature and households do not pay for lighting in the home, their adoption, by itself, would not generate the financial benefits realized by households that pay for lighting. For this reason, it is crucial to acknowledge the role of microcredit.

It is important to acknowledge that some community members will not benefit from solid-state lighting, at least in a commercial sense. Because households that have obtained solid-state lighting systems will no longer rely on kerosene for lighting in the home, business agents involved in the sale of kerosene (and other lighting sources) will experience lower income as a result of lower demand for their product.

It is also important to consider that the penetration of solid-state lighting into the community will depend on the development of services that facilitate the acquisition and maintenance of solid-state lighting systems. Therefore, the impact ultimately depends on the ability of solar LED systems to establish or converge with existing distribution networks. It should also be noted that the environmental impact of LED lighting is far lower than that of kerosene-based lighting (Parsons, 2007).

As an example of the ability of people to pay in different countries, Figure 11.2 illustrates the cumulative expenditures and savings when solid-state lighting replaces fuel-based lighting in the South African township of Tembisa, Johannesburg. In 2007 a number of families in Tembisa purchased Light Up the World solid-state lighting systems using microcredit. Within five years each family will have saved 80 percent of what they would have spent on kerosene; by way of comparison, the cost of a new fire-

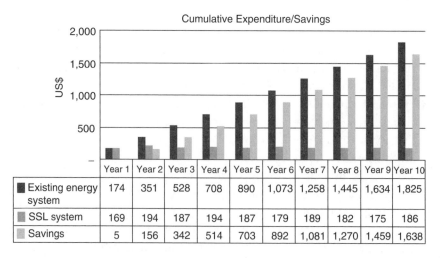

Cumulative Expenditure/Savings

	Year 1	Year 2	Year 3	Year 4	Year 5	Year 6	Year 7	Year 8	Year 9	Year 10
■ Existing energy system	174	351	528	708	890	1,073	1,258	1,445	1,634	1,825
■ SSL system	169	194	187	194	187	179	189	182	175	186
Savings	5	156	342	514	703	892	1,081	1,270	1,459	1,638

Figure 11.2 Shantytown Households in Tembisa, South Africa—Cumulative Expenditures (US$) of Existing Fuel Based Lighting System, the SSL system, and Cumulative Saving if SSL is Purchased through Micro-Credit

proof and weatherproof home is only the equivalent of three or four years of kerosene costs. The solid-state lighting system is also a real and valuable asset, unlike burning kerosene where their money literally goes up in smoke and is gone forever, so in a real emergency a family can always sell their solid-state lighting system. Figure 11.2 shows that the families of South Africa, some six million of which are not connected to the grid, could realize a total of approximately $1 billion per year in increased disposable income by changing to solid-state lighting systems.

Contributions of Solid-State Lighting to the Millennium Development Goals

Through promotion of solid-state lighting technology, Light Up the World is addressing serious socioeconomic and environmental problems in the developing world. The reported benefits of solid-state lighting technology as a development tool include improved living conditions, enhanced safety and health, improved physical environment, and the abilities to read and study after sunset as well as operate cottage industries by night. Given the potential impact of solid-state lighting technology on the well-being of the poor, there is no question that it will be an important tool in helping to achieve the Millennium Development Goals (UNDP, 2002).

Solid-State Lighting Hardware Suppliers for the Developing World

Solid-state lighting hardware for the developing world can be divided into two categories: lanterns and solar home systems. Lanterns are portable while the solar home system is permanently installed, normally lighting a number of rooms.

The companies which supply high-quality solar home systems include Barefoot Power, Duron, Philips, and Visionary Lighting & Energy. The number of lamps included varies from two to four; lamp output ranges from 70 lumens to 140 lumens, and system retail prices from $45 to $130.

Conclusions

The social and economic lives of people throughout the world are being rapidly transformed by solid-state lighting. Used as a development tool, solid-state lighting significantly improves living conditions of the poor by enhancing their safety and health, improving literacy, protecting the environment, and creating opportunities for income generation and enterprise development. With very low electricity requirements, solid-state lighting, especially when powered by renewable energy sources, is arguably the most appropriate lighting solution available to developing countries. The potential to eliminate the need for government subsidies for kerosene for lighting is another favorable aspect of the introduction of solid-state lighting, freeing up resources for other priority expenditures. Solid-state lighting can significantly advance the Millennium Development Goals and help to improve the Human Development Index of developing countries.

Fuel-based lighting in the developing world is the source of 200+ million tons of carbon dioxide emissions to the atmosphere each year, and 58 percent of the carbon dioxide emissions from global residential electric lighting (Mills, 2002). Solid-state lighting powered by renewable energy replaces fuel-based lighting, thus reducing green-house gas emissions contributing to climate change. Light Up the World estimates that replacing kerosene lamps with modern solid-state lighting technology reduces approximately 150kg of carbon dioxide per household per year. For these reasons, Light Up the World's solid-state lighting initiatives have demonstrated that such affordable lighting can be a significant and realistic exit strategy from the poverty trap.

12.
ENERGY FOR DEVELOPMENT
The Case of Bioenergy in Brazil
Carlos Henrique de Brito Cruz

In 2008, the use of ethanol made from sugarcane surpassed for the first time the use of gasoline in the transportation and other energy sectors of Brazil. In 2009, the gap widened as the nation used 6.0 billion gallons of sugarcane ethanol compared with 5.0 billion gallons of gasoline.

Sugarcane, in addition to producing fuel ethanol, is also burned to power the ethanol and sugar mills, and to generate electricity for sale to the electricity grid. The total energy generated from sugarcane in Brazil amounted in 2009 to 18.2 percent of the total energy produced in the country. This made sugarcane the second most important source of energy for Brazil, following oil and surpassing hydroelectricity.

A primary advantage of ethanol produced from sugarcane in Brazil is lower production costs, but it has important advantages in the area of emissions, especially in a regional framework. In south-central Brazil, for example, only one unit of fossil energy is used for each 8–9 units of energy produced by ethanol from sugarcane. Because carbon emissions from sugarcane ethanol are lower than those from gasoline, there is a saving of 2.1–2.4 tons of carbon dioxide not emitted to the atmosphere for each cubic meter of ethanol used as fuel. At the same time, no sulfur dioxide is emitted when using sugarcane ethanol as fuel.

Sugarcane was introduced to Brazil as long ago as 1532, so that the "Brazilian model" of producing sugar and ethanol together derived from long familiarity. In recent decades, it has brought important technical benefits and made possible an outstanding increase in Brazil's competitiveness in the international markets of both sugar and ethanol. Today about 50 percent of the sucrose of sugarcane produced in the country is used to produce sugar, while the other half is used to produce ethanol. Both industrial and academic research and development have led to a steady increase in the productivity of ethanol over the past 33 years, at a rate of 3.2 percent per year. This large gain in productivity has translated to a reduction in the total area planted by a factor of 2.6.

In 2008 the area devoted to sugarcane for ethanol production was estimated at roughly 19,200 square miles, amounting to 1.4 percent of the total land suitable for growing crops available in Brazil, and 0.6 percent of the land used for agriculture. In the same year, 61 percent of the ethanol produced in Brazil came from the state of São Paulo, where the productivity is the highest. Most of the recent expansion of harvest area is taking place in the center-west region of the country on degraded pasture lands.

Energy from Sugarcane in Brazil

World interest in biofuels, especially during the years after 2004 when oil prices rose to all-time highs, brought both opportunities and challenges for Brazil in this field. In 2008, 7.3 billion gallons of ethanol were produced in Brazil from sugarcane, an increase of 27 percent over the preceding year.[1]

Renewables are a sizable part of the Brazilian domestic energy equation, reaching nearly half (47.3 percent) of the total supply in 2009. This percentage is almost four times the world average for renewables (12.9 percent) and almost seven times the average in OECD countries (6.7 percent).

Energy and energy products generated from sugarcane include hydrated ethanol, which is added to gasoline; anhydrous ethanol which is used directly as fuel; and electricity generated by burning sugarcane bagasse. These products together account for 18.2 percent of the total energy used in the country (see Table 12.1). Sugarcane-based energy contributes the largest fraction of energy from renewable sources, greater than the 14.9 percent contributed by hydroelectricity.

Evolution of the Ethanol Program in Brazil

Ethanol in Brazil is produced by fermenting sugars extracted from sugarcane. Sugarcane is a semi-perennial grass which matures in 12 months, allowing, in Brazil, for five harvests in six years before it needs to be replanted.

Sugarcane was introduced to Brazil by Martim Afonso de Souza, a Portuguese colonizer who built the first sugar mill in the township of São Vicente, in the southern coastal region of what today is São Paulo state. Soon after its cultivation in São Paulo, sugarcane was introduced to the north-east, where it became the nation's first economic success story, driven by continuing large sugar demand in Europe.

After the 1929 financial crash, there was excess world production of sugar, and in Brazil and elsewhere, a shortage of liquid fuel. The first ethanol mill was installed around 1931, and in February 1931, President Getulio Vargas issued a decree which mandated that all gasoline sold in the country contain 5 percent ethanol.[2] To regulate production, the government created in 1933 the Sugar and Alcohol Institute (Instituto

Table 12.1 Composition of the Total Energy Supply in Brazil, 2009

Energy Sources, Brazil, 2009	%
Non-renewable sources	52.7%
Oil and its byproducts	37.9%
Natural gas	8.7%
Coal and its byproducts	4.7%
Uranium (U3O8) and byproducts	1.4%
Renewable sources	47.3%
Hydro	15.2%
Firewood	10.1%
Sugarcane	18.2%
Other renewable sources	3.8%
Total	100.0%

Source: Brazil, Ministry for Energy, "Brazilian Energy Balance."

do Açúcar e do Álcool, or IAA) with a mandate to establish production quotas, by mill and by state, as part of a nation-wide strategy to foster sugar and ethanol production.[3]

While having little immediate effect on ethanol production, these measures set the stage for the major changes to come, as shown in Figure 12.1.

In November, 1975, another presidential decree created the National Alcohol Program (ProAlcool in Portuguese). The immediate motivation was the global oil shock of the 1970s that caused Brazilian oil imports to jump fivefold during 1973 and 1974. This was the immediate cause of the steep increase seen in Figure 12.1, which began in 1975. In the following ten years, production increased 20-fold, reaching 3.1 billion gallons in 1985. Legislation mandated that gas stations offer ethanol, while at the same time the government ordered an increase in the proportion of ethanol in automobile fuel to 20 percent. The government further drove its strategy through subsidies to producers and tax incentives to consumers.

The automobile industry responded to the incentives by rapidly introducing ethanol-powered vehicles, beginning with the FIAT model 147 in 1978. Research and development to demonstrate the viability of ethanol engines and the conversion of gasoline engines to ethanol had been conducted for many years at the Aeronautics Technology Center (CTA), led by Professor Urbano Ernesto Stumpf. The evolution of ethanol-powered vehicle sales is shown in Figure 12.2, which indicates rapid acceptance of ethanol vehicles. Government policy forced gas stations to offer both gasoline (with added ethanol) and ethanol, and by 1984, 94 percent of the cars sold in Brazil were ethanol powered.

This quick rise in the number of ethanol-powered vehicles was followed by a plateau, from 1985 until 1989, and a sharp drop after that. For the next five years Brazil went through successive economic and political crises, characterized by high external debt, hyperinflation, and the impeachment of the president, in 1992. Throughout most of this period the world price of oil was kept low enough to discourage alternative fuels. In addition, the price of sugar had risen by the end of the 1980s in international markets. The combination of these factors brought the Brazilian government to change its

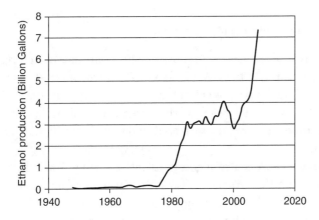

Figure 12.1 Yearly Production of Ethanol from Sugarcane in Brazil

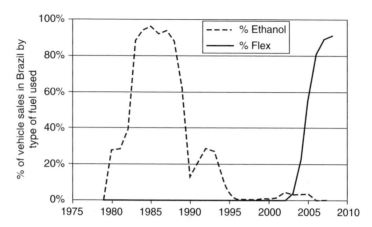

Figure 12.2 Percentage of Vehicle Sales in Brazil for Neat Ethanol-Powered Vehicles and Flex-Fuel
Vehicles, from 1979 to 2008

policy for ethanol in 1989, when it reduced state support for production. This resulted
in ethanol shortages, which caused the public to lose confidence. Sales and production of all-ethanol vehicles dropped steeply. From 1983 to 1989, 90 percent of cars sold
used only ethanol. This percentage dropped to 10 percent in 1990 and virtually zero in
1996 (see Figure 12.2). Full deregulation was achieved in 1998, when the government
announced the ending of price control for sugar and ethanol, effective February 1999.[4]

The economic and political stabilization that came after 1994 helped to create conditions for better planning by both government and industry. At the same time, deregulation gave producers the opportunity to build on their accumulated knowledge and
become more efficient and independent of government subsidies.

The next relevant event was the launching, in 2003, of flex-fuel vehicles that could
run on hydrated ethanol, gasoline, or a mixture of the two. Because oil prices were once
again high, these cars were well received by consumers, as shown in Figure 12.2. The
percentage of cars sold in Brazil that are flex-fuel rose to more than 80 percent in 2006
and 91 percent in 2008. By March 2009, 95 percent of the cars sold in Brazil were flex-
fuel vehicles.

Present and Future Land Area for Sugarcane

In 2008 Brazil used 34,440 square miles to plant sugarcane,[5] which represented an
increase of 60 percent over the area planted in 2004, which was 21,500 square miles
(see Figure 12.3). Roughly 61 percent of the cane was used to produce ethanol and 39
percent to produce sugar. Relevant questions regarding this trend are, "How much
further can this production area be increased, and to what extent does it compete with
food production?"

The most recent consolidated sugarcane planted areas for Brazil are shown in Table
12.2, using data from the agricultural census of 2006 and data on each of the main
crops published by the Ministry for Agriculture, Livestock and Food Supply. In 2006
the 11,600 square miles used for sugarcane for ethanol corresponded to 0.4 percent of

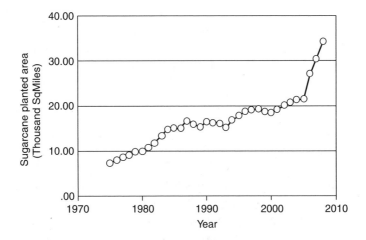

Figure 12.3 Growth of Area Planted to Sugarcane in Brazil, 1975–2008

the total land area of Brazil and to 0.8 percent of the roughly 1.4 million square miles listed as suitable for agriculture. The area used for ethanol production corresponds to one-seventh of the area used for soybeans and less than one-quarter of the area used for corn.

Data from the Brazilian agricultural censuses shown in Figure 12.4 demonstrate that the growth of land used for agriculture since 1970 happened at the expense of both non-tilled land and, most recently, pasture land. Land used as pasture has been reduced through the increase in the density of grazing herds, which doubled from 0.2 animals per acres in 1970 to 0.4 animals per acre in 2006, a density which is still far from what is considered intensive. This low density indicates that further expansion of sugarcane over pasture land is possible. In fact, one analysis (Cerqueira Leite *et al.*, 2008) found that allowing for an increase in cattle density from the present 0.4 animals

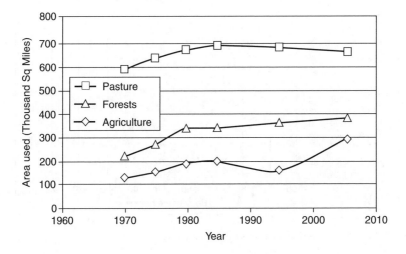

Figure 12.4 Variation of Area used in Brazil for Pasture, Forest, and Agriculture

per acre to 0.5–0.6 animals per acre in Brazil would make available 193,000 to 270,000 square miles of pasture without jeopardizing food production. Recent work points to additional gains from the integration of cane plantation with pasture, which produces additional feed for the cattle and accelerates the growth of cattle.

Contribution of Sugarcane Ethanol to the Reduction of Greenhouse Gas Emissions

Sugarcane ethanol as biofuel has the desirable quality of reducing greenhouse gas emissions (Figure 12.5). Early studies by Goldemberg,[6] using data from the period 1975 to 1977, found a ratio of 4.53 between the energy obtained from cane and the energy expended to produce the cane. A more detailed and recent study that includes the benefit of burning the bagasse (the fiber that is left over after sugarcane is crushed) to provide energy for the mill (Macedo *et al.*, 2008) found a ratio of 8.3–9.0. When they included the production of electricity at the mill by burning the bagasse at high pressure, they found

Table 12.2 Land Use Data for Brazil in 2006 (original data converted to square miles)

		Area (Th. Sq Miles)	%	
1	Total land area	3,280.61	100%	—
2	Land used	1,369.78	41,8%	100%
3	Pastures	665.21	20,3%	48,6%
4	Forests	385.56	11,8%	28,1%
5	Agriculture	296.05	9,0%	21,6%
6	Soybeans	84.76	2,6%	6,2%
7	Corn	48.70	1,5%	3,6%
8	Sugarcane	23.88	0,7%	1,7%
9	For sugar	46.08	0,4%	0,9%
10	For ethanol	45.16	0,4%	0,9%
11	Beans	15.49	0,5%	1,1%
12	Rice	10.41	0,3%	0,8%

Sources:
Lines 1–5: Brazilian Statistics Bureau, IBGE, "Agricultural Census 2006."
Lines 6–8 and 11, 12: Ministry of Agriculture, Livestock and Food Supply, "Statistics."
Lines 9, 10: Brazil, Ministry of Agriculture, "Balanço Nacional de Cana-de-Açúcar e Agroenergia 2007."

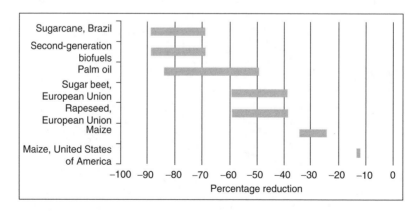

Figure 12.5 Reduction in GHG Emissions of Selected Biofuels
Sources: IEA, 2006, and FAO, 2008d.
Note: Excludes the effects of land-use change.

that the ratio can be expected to reach values as high as 11.6 by 2020. The value of the avoided emissions (in units of carbon dioxide equivalent) will depend on assumptions on the performance of the car engine, and in one study (Macedo *et al.*, 2008) ranged from 12.6 to 16.6 lbs. of carbon dioxide equivalent per square mile of ethanol used.

Figure 12.6 shows a comparison of the greenhouse gas emissions reduction obtained with sugarcane ethanol and other selected biofuels. It can be seen that the performance of sugarcane ethanol is as good as that expected for second generation biofuels.[7]

The similarity in greenhouse gas emissions reduction between sugarcane ethanol and second generation biofuels translates to a large advantage for sugarcane ethanol in terms of cost per unit of greenhouse gas emissions avoided, as shown in Figure 12.7.

The data above do not take into account the important issue of land use change that causes changes in the estimates for greenhouse gas reduction. Land use change effects modify the greenhouse gas balance because different kinds of land emit different amounts of carbon for the same crop. For example, if sugarcane is planted in an area that was previously used as degraded pasture, more carbon will be sequestered in the soil, thus causing a favorable greenhouse gas reduction. However when sugarcane is planted in land previously covered by rainforest, more carbon will be emitted. Considering the specifics of land use change in Brazil, one study (Nassar *et al.*, 2009[8]) demonstrated that the reduction in greenhouse gas emissions can be expected to be between 60 and 69 percent, thus meriting inclusion of sugarcane ethanol in the category of advanced biofuels as defined by the US Environmental Protection Agency.

Brazilian Sugarcane Ethanol Research and Development (R&D)

Since the start of the ProAlcool Program in 1975, industry, government, and academia in Brazil have pursued R&D activities aiming at increasing the productivity of both the industrial and the agricultural aspects of converting sugarcane to ethanol (see Figure 12.7).

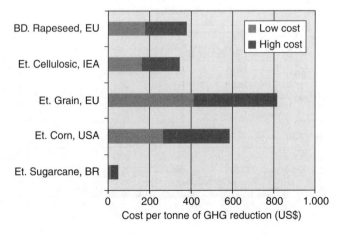

Figure 12.6 Cost Per Ton of GHG Reduction for the Case of Sugarcane Ethanol and Other Selected Biofuels

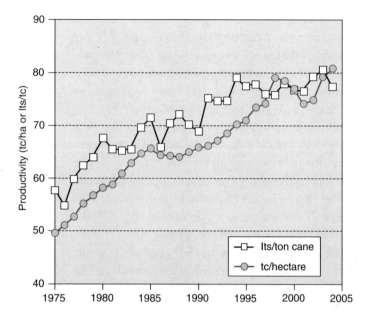

Figure 12.7 Evolution of Agricultural and Industrial Productivity for Sugarcane and Ethanol in Brazil, from 1975 to 2005

Overall, productivity more than doubled, from 299 gallons per acre in 1975 to 674 gallons per acre in 2004. This allowed for substantial savings on land use during this period, and reduction of most inputs, such as water, fertilizer, and energy.

One improvement brought about through the efforts of universities, private research organizations, and public research institutions was the development of several more efficient cane varieties that are well adapted to different regions of Brazil. Researchers also achieved advances in the agriculture of cane, fixation of nitrogen, reduction of fertilizer use, and soil conservation.

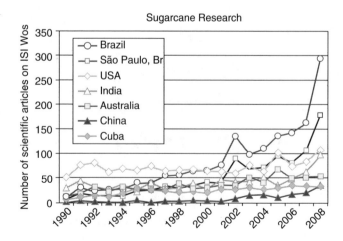

Figure 12.8 Number of Scientific Articles on Themes Related to Sugarcane Originating in Brazil, in the state of São Paulo, Brazil, and in the Main Countries That Publish in These Fields

As shown in Figure 12.8, the number of scientific papers originating in Brazil on themes related to sugarcane led the world after 2000, with a steep climb after 2006. The state of São Paulo alone, where most sugarcane research in Brazil is done, publishes more articles on sugarcane than any other *country*. This increase in Brazilian R&D was accelerated by the creation in 1999 of a special program for research in sugarcane genomics undertaken by the São Paulo Research Foundation (FAPESP). The program, called SUCEST, brought together almost 100 Brazilian scientists to study the genomics of sugarcane, creating basic and applied scientific results and, more importantly, training a new generation of scientists in the modern field of plant genomics.

This is an interesting case of how a developing country can create a strong indigenous scientific and technological capability by training personnel for many years and thereby assume world leadership in a field which can have substantial impact in world affairs.

Bioenergy and the Developing World

An important challenge for developed and developing countries alike is that of guaranteeing access to energy for their populations. While developed countries presently use most of the energy produced in the world, the International Energy Agency expects that by 2015, the now-developing countries will be using more energy than developed ones (Figure 12.9). This projected steep rise in consumption by developing countries poses serious challenges in the global effort to reduce greenhouse-gas emissions, and brings out the importance of developing more renewable energy sources.

Bioenergy, especially from first generation biofuels, is especially interesting for developing countries in Latin America and Africa, as we shall see. It is important to note first, however, that first generation biofuels, although based on simpler technology, can perform as well as advanced biofuels. It is common to associate advanced biofuels with second and third generation biofuels, but this would be a mistake, since the complexity in the production process does not directly relate to performance of the biofuels. The case of Brazilian sugarcane ethanol has demonstrated this distinction,

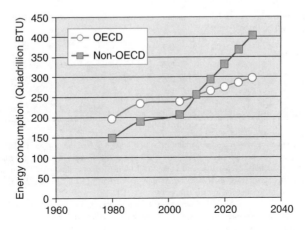

Figure 12.9 Realized and Predicted Energy Consumption by OECD and Non-OECD Countries

as noted by the Environmental Protection Agency's conclusion that it fulfills[9] all the requirements for advanced biofuels.

Table 12.3 shows an estimate for the land available for cultivation of biofuel crops by 2050, discounting from the available arable land the portions needed for food, forests, and infrastructure. From the data it can be seen that only South and Central America and Africa have positive estimates, respectively 965,300 and 700,000 square miles. If 20 percent of this area comes to be used for sugarcane at a productivity of roughly 641 gallons per acre (equal to the productivity in 2008 in Brazil), the expected production will be 136 billion gallons of ethanol. As a reference, the world consumption of gasoline in 2002 was 309 billion gallons, so that the estimated 136 billion gallons would be enough to substitute for 44 percent of the total world usage in that year. This volume of 136 billion gallons is 19 times larger than Brazilian production in 2008.

This back-of-the-envelope calculation, using conservative estimates of the available land and assuming an increase in productivity, serves to demonstrate that a sizable amount of energy can be generated in South/Central America and Africa by 2050 using sugarcane ethanol with technology used today in Brazil and many other countries.

Brazil's Future Leadership in Sugar and Ethanol Production

With the recent increase in interest in ethanol production in many countries, Brazil faces competition on many fronts to its current world leadership. In one arena, the ethanol sector is facing a paradigm change based on a new set of still pre-commercial

Table 12.3 Estimates for Available Land for Biofuels in 2050, According to Doornbosch and Steenblik

Land (in million sq miles)	North Am.	South & Centr. Am.	Europe & Russia	Africa	Asia	Oceania	World
Total land surface	8.11	7.72	8.88	11.58	11.97	3.47	51.72
1 Apt for rainfed cultivation	1.54	3.47	1.93	3.47	1.93	0.39	12.74
2 Apt and under forest	0.39	1.16	0.39	0.39	0.00	0.00	3.09
3 Apt, already in use	0.77	0.39	0.77	0.77	2.32	0.39	5.79
4 Necessary for food, housing and infrastructure until 2030/50	0.00	0.39	0.00	0.39	0.39	0.00	1.16
5 Available (Gross) [5=1–2–3–4]	0.00	0.97	0.31	1.70	–0.27	0.15	2.86
6 % for grassland	0%	0%	50%	60%	n/a	0%	
7 Additional land potentially available (7)=(5)x (1–% for grassland)	0.00	0.97	0.15	0.69	–0.27	0.15	1.70

Note: values recalculated to display units of square miles.

a. Most studies assume that only a small fraction of additional land is needed to feed the world's growing population—from 6.5 billion people at present to 9 billion people in 2050—and that most of the increase in food requirements will be met by an increase in agricultural productivity. Here it is assumed that 0.2 Gha is needed for additional food production (based on Fisher and Schrattenholzer, 2001 where a yearly increase in agricultural productivity of 1.1% is assumed); the remainder (roughly 0.1 Gha) is needed for additional housing and infrastructure.

b. A negative number is shown here as more land is cultivated than potentially available for rain-fed cultivation because of irrigation. The negative land available has not been rounded to zero because food imports are likely to be needed from other region with implications on their land use.

c. Numbers in this column don't add up due to rounding.

technologies, of which hydrolysis of cellulosic biomass is an important example. This situation suggests the necessity of a coordinated national effort, with the participation of the scientific and technological communities of both academia and industry, to guarantee Brazil's leadership role in sugar and ethanol production. Three recent initiatives have been designed to address this goal:

1. The FAPESP Program for Research on Bioenergy, BIOEN, aims at coordinating the R&D of both public and private laboratories to advance and apply knowledge in fields related to ethanol production in Brazil. The BIOEN includes five divisions:

   i   sugarcane plant technologies, including plant improvement and sugarcane farming;
   ii ethanol industrial technologies;
   iii bio-refinery technologies and alcohol chemistry;
   iv ethanol applications for motor vehicles (Otto cycle engines and fuel cells); and horizontal themes: social and economic impacts, environmental studies, land use, intellectual property.

2. The BIOEN Program has a solid core for supporting academic exploratory research related to these topics. It is expected that these exploratory activities will generate new knowledge and train scientists and professionals essential for advancing industrial capacity in ethanol-related technologies.

3. The FAPESP Program for Research on Bioenergy also establishes partnerships with industry for cooperative academic-industrial R&D activities which are to be co-funded by FAPESP and the private sector. For these collaborations, project details are specified according to the interests of the private partners and to FAPESP's commitment to fostering research in the state of São Paulo. Braskem, Dedini, and Oxiteno are the first three companies to join the program. Other research agencies from federal and state governments have been invited to participate in the program. The first 52 research projects, selected in 2009, received a total of US$35 million for periods averaging four years.

4. In 2009 the Brazilian Bioethanol Science and Technology Laboratory (CTBE) was created. CTBE has the mission of contributing to Brazilian leadership in the renewable energy sources and raw material production sectors, mainly by improving the sugarcane-bioethanol production chain through state-of-the-art research, development, and innovation. The facilities of CTBE are being built in Campinas, São Paulo. CTBE aims to be: (1) a research Institute that performs competitive RD&I to improve feedstock and conversion routes for bioethanol production from sugarcane; (2) a partner of other research organizations working in related areas, through a network of associated laboratories in universities and research institutes; and (3) a technology supplier for the industry, providing strategic information on issues of mutual concern.

   CTBE integrates the Brazilian Center of Research in Energy and Materials (CNPEM), a private not-for-profit organization. When completed, the 7,900 square meters of infrastructure will house up to 50 permanent researchers, a similar number of visitors (graduate students, PhD students, postdoctoral fellows, and other researchers) and 90 technical collaborators. CTBE received federal investments of almost US$35 million for infrastructure projects during the period 2008 to 2010.

5   The creation of the São Paulo Bioenergy Research Center, hosted by the three state universities of São Paulo (University of São Paulo-USP, University of Campinas-Unicamp, and University of the State of São Paulo-Unesp). The center will be funded by the state government (infrastructure), universities (personnel), and FAPESP (research grants). The estimated investment of US$80 million will support the first ten years of operation.

Conclusion

Today, one-third of the available energy in sugarcane, which is stored as sucrose, is used to advantage in the production of sugar and ethanol. The bagasse from the stalks—which contain approximately another third of the cane energy—is burned, with low energetic efficiency, to fuel the process of sugar or ethanol fabrication. Increasingly, mills are burning the bagasse to produce electricity, which is sold back to the grid. The last third of available energy, consisting of leaves, tops, and other cellulosic materials, is currently wasted because it is destroyed in the harvesting fire.

Emerging technologies, such as hydrolysis, will allow the fabrication of ethanol from cellulosic material, and gasification could lead to higher efficiency in electricity production or synthesis fuels. The production costs are not competitive today, but if researchers find ways to lower them, the use of two-thirds of the cellulosic material to generate ethanol might dramatically improve Brazilian ethanol production.

Considering existing biofuel opportunities, it makes sense to focus sugarcane R&D on optimizing not the sucrose content—which is relevant only to sugar production—but on optimizing the energy content. This strategy recognizes that there is energy both in the sucrose and in the cellulose that accounts for nearly two-thirds of the sugarcane plant. Such a plant, then, could be regarded as "energy-cane" instead of "sugar-cane."

In such a new ethanol paradigm, one would collect what is now regarded as trash by optimizing the harvesting process and elevating this "trash" into a useful component of "energy-cane." Developed hydrolysis and/or gasification processes could be applied to the residual bagasse and trash, transforming this cellulosic biomass into ethanol or other fuels, using fermentation of the generated sugar (hydrolysis) or the catalytic synthesis of the generated gas (gasification). The production of ethanol might increase from the current 640 to about 960 gallons per acre-year.

Rising oil costs will also push the petrochemical industry toward substituting ethanol for oil as an input for the manufacturing of certain petrochemical products as ethene.

The increase in world demand for ethanol will bring an increase in the area planted in sugarcane in Brazil, and more R&D will be necessary to evaluate and predict the environmental and social impacts.

Given these opportunities and challenges, it has been necessary for Brazil (and for the state of São Paulo) to intensify R&D activities related to the production of ethanol from sugarcane. Relevant themes are improvements in the sugarcane plant, improvements in the farming and harvesting of cane, industrial processes that produce ethanol from cane, the use of ethanol (alcohol) in the petrochemical industry, and the use of ethanol in automobile engines. Given recent advances in fuel cell technology, it might be relevant to study the uses of ethanol as hydrogen storage for fuel cells. Finally, considering the possible impacts of increased demand for ethanol in Brazil, it is important to foster research on social, environmental, and economic consequences of ethanol production.

13.
IMPLICATIONS OF NANOTECHNOLOGY FOR LABOR AND EMPLOYMENT
Assessing Nanotechnology Products in Brazil
Noela Invernizzi

Nanotechnology—defined as the understanding and control of matter at dimensions between approximately 1 and 100 nanometers, where unique phenomena enable novel applications (NTSC, 2007: 5) is considered as the basis for a new industrial revolution. Yonas and Picraux (2001) depict nanotechnology as a disruptive technology, meaning that its establishment as a dominant technological trajectory will render obsolete other existing technologies and products. Nanotechnology is also described as an enabling or platform technology, able to be incorporated into almost all production sectors (Harper, 2003; Bowman and Hodge, 2006). Treder (2004) predicts that its development will be faster than previous technological revolutions and that it will take place on a global scale from the outset.

Because of these characteristics, nanotechnology is expected to have deep economic and social implications. Indeed, a vivid academic and social debate on such implications started quite early, accompanying nanotechnology research and development (Crow and Sarewitz, 2001; Roco and Bainbridge, 2001; ETC Group, 2003; Meridian Institute, 2005; Invernizzi *et al.*, 2008; Allhoff and Lin, 2009, among others). However, the growing body of literature on the social implications of nanotechnology has barely begun to address work and employment issues, although these central aspects of society are subject to complex transformations during times of rapid technological change. The subject has garnered limited attention from policy-makers as well.[1] However, as has happened in previous industrial revolutions, workplaces, the labor process, and the labor market will encompass significant transformations. For a complete picture of nanotechnology's implications, researchers and policy-makers alike will have to address questions such as: what nanotechnology innovations may affect the labor processes and in which ways? What effects will the obsolescence of old technologies and products have on jobs? What new skills will be required for workers? Will there be changes in the distribution of jobs from one productive sector to another? Will the development of new materials affect jobs in natural raw material production worldwide? How will the combination of global-scale competition and rapid emergence of nanotechnology affect jobs?

Given that we are in the initial stage of nanotechnology development, researching how nanotechnology affects labor poses a number of methodological difficulties. According to Richardson (2008), at least in the short term, nanotechnology will not constitute whole new industries, but will gradually be absorbed into existing industrial processes, making its effects on work diffuse and difficult to evaluate. Available data is yet to be incorporated into employment statistics and definitions on nanotechnology jobs standards have barely been discussed.[2] In this context of the lack of data and scarce previous studies, and given the incipient character of the research object itself, this chapter is based on exploratory research.

I started analyzing the implications of nanotechnology for labor based on what is most concrete and visible today: a growing set of products, in diverse industry sectors, that incorporate nanotechnology-based innovations. Between June 2009 and March 2010 I compiled a database of Brazilian companies conducting R&D activities in nanotechnology, and focused on 96 products in advanced phases of development or already commercialized by Brazilian companies. While sufficient data do not yet exist to accurately measure the employment impacts of this as-yet early-stage technology in Brazil, drawing on this database it is possible to discern some likely prospects concerning both the quantity and quality of future jobs.

The chapter is divided into three sections. In the first, I review the scarce literature available on nanotechnology's implications for labor. In the second section, after a brief description of the Brazilian government policies to support nanotechnology, I present the landscape of the adoption of nanotechnology by Brazilian companies. In the third section, I examine these companies' nanotechnology-based products and analyze their potential implications on labor. I conclude by highlighting the main trends in nano-technology-driven labor changes suggested by the research.

Nanotechnology and Labor: What We Know

Nanotechnology innovations are capable of profoundly changing productive processes and products. In addition to reinforcing the trend of miniaturizing components and processes (top-down manufacturing), it offers the novelty of constructing materials from atoms, a bottom-up process (European Commission, 2004). The potentials of nanotechnology have only just begun to be explored. At the moment, passive nano-structures—those in which the nanomaterial or structure does not change its form or function—are predominant. These nanostructures are added to already existing products and materials to enhance them, configuring incremental innovations. Active nanomaterials, those that are able to change their form, function, or properties during operation will bring about major breakthroughs in the near future, having a more deci-sive impact on production processes (IRGC, 2007; Davies, 2008).[3]

Nanotechnology is moving quickly from the laboratory to the factories and the markets. Lux Research reported a nanotechnology market of US$240 billion in 2008, $254 billion in 2009 and estimates that the market will top the 2.5 trillion dollar mark in 2015 (Holman, 2009; Hwang and Bradley, 2010).[4] Since 2005, corporate R&D fund-ing is surpassing government investments worldwide (Cientifica, 2008). The number of nanotechnology companies is growing steadily around the world and, in addition to nanotechnology start-ups, many large corporations are adding nanotechnology to their operations (Baker and Aston, 2005; Hullman, 2006; Nanowerk, 2010). The number of consumer products with nanotechnology has been rising yearly, with over 1,000 by the end of 2009, according to the Woodrow Wilson Center's Project on Emerging Nano-technology inventory (PEN, 2009).

Projections on workforce demands to ensure the development of nanotechnology vary greatly. According to Roco (2003: 1248), two million nanotechnology workers will be required around the world in 2015, in addition to five million indirect jobs. Demand will be higher according to Lux Research, which foresees a need for ten million jobs in 2014, or 11 percent of jobs in manufacturing worldwide (Davies, 2008: 1). In 2006, 5,300 "white coat" nanotechnology developers were employed and this number was said to increase to 30,000 in the following two years (Lux Research, 2007). Zweck *et al.* (2008) reported between 20,000 and 114,000 jobs in nanotechnology in Germany in 2004. A prospective study by the US Department of Labor (USDL, 2006) estimated that 671,000 nanotechnology jobs would be available from 2006–2016 in the United States. The range of estimates and projections suggests both that the numbers are not well constrained, and that rapid growth is widely anticipated. These projections and studies, however, say little about the types of jobs that may be created and nothing about the jobs that may be lost, or undergo changes.

Some surveys and studies show that there is concern over the possible scarcity of qualified labor in nanotechnology (Pandya, 2001; Malsch and Oud, 2004; ENA, 2005; Abicht *et al.*, 2006; Singh, 2007). However, other studies suggest that current demands are still modest and concentrated in highly trained fields of R&D. Based on the analysis of job announcements over 2005–2006 Stephan *et al.* (2007) concluded that a market exists for those with skills in nanotechnology but it is relatively small at this time and most of the growth is centered at universities and government laboratories. In another study of job announcements from 2007 to 2008, and interviews with 80 companies, Freeman and Shukla (2008) found that job growth in nanotechnology is modest and that companies are not having any problems filling their hiring needs. Van Horn and Fichtner (2008) carried out interviews with more than 50 companies, educators and other stakeholders in Phoenix and Tucson, Arizona, to explore the workforce needs of companies and educational institutions engaged in nanotechnology research. They found out that while some employers are concerned about the supply of workers with necessary interdisciplinary skills, others believe that the shortage of skilled workers will be temporary as educational institutions adjust to industry needs. Another study by Van Horn *et al.* (2009) examined the workforce and skill needs of two large pharma-ceutical companies based in New Jersey. The companies reported employing few highly skilled nanotechnology workers. Instead, they hired workers with traditional degrees and provided most training on specialized nanotechnology skills, including interdisci-plinary skills, characterization, and knowledge of size and scale, on the job.

As nanotechnology increases its presence in production, more of the workforce will become involved. Abicht *et al.* (2006: 38) state that new demands in nanotechnology are beginning to emerge across a spectrum of jobs, including R&D, production and manu-facturing, quality assurance, documentation and marketing, and distribution, requiring new skills. The authors call attention to the need of general skills, based on interdiscipli-nary and cross-sectoral knowledge, as well as specific qualification regarding particular nanotechnology procedures. According to Gatchair (2010), since the products incorporating nanotechnology are at the early stage of the product life cycle, production workers are likely to require greater technical skills when compared to those involved with more mature products in which the processes have become routine. The risks of job displacement due to the obsolescence of technologies and skills, which will particularly affect workers in the most vulnerable positions, is highlighted in a report elaborated by CEST (2006). Other studies have focused on the need for education, especially university education, to prepare the workforce (Roco, 2003; Whitesides, 2005; Batterson, 2005).

Another dimension of nanotechnology implications for labor comes from the substitution of natural raw materials with new nanotechnology-based materials. A report prepared by the ETC Group for the South Centre (2005) alerts that a significant number of occupations could be at risk in a great number of developing world countries that are heavily dependent upon commodities. Case studies on rubber, textiles, platinum, and copper provide examples of how economies and workers in the global South could be affected by nanotechnology emerging R&D and products. However, at least for some countries, there is also an opportunity to add value to current commodities with nanotechnology. A study by the Meridian Institute (2007) reinforced the potentially far-reaching socioeconomic impact of commodities substitution in developing countries, as well as the opportunity opened by nanotechnology enhancement of certain materials. The possible impacts of a nanotechnology-induced shift in copper trade of two copper dependent countries, Chile and Zambia, are analyzed by Sarma and Chaudhury (2009). Considering current R&D that can cause substitution of this raw material, the authors conclude that those countries will likely experience several negative consequences, such as loss of employment.

As these studies show, it is still hard to assess changes in production processes and hiring practices as a result of nanotechnology adoption by companies, making it difficult to foresee nanotechnology implications for labor. However, it is possible to advance some implications of nanotechnology for labor, particularly those affecting employment, if we analyze nanotechnology products, where concrete nanotechnology innovations materialize in a more clear way at this stage of development. This research is based on products in the final development phase or already commercialized by Brazilian companies. Before turning to the product analysis it is necessary to examine the development of nanotechnology in Brazilian industry in order to show that even in a developing country, nanotechnology is being rapidly adopted by several industries and is likely to pose employment implications in the near future.

Nanotechnology in Brazil

The Brazilian Science and Technology Ministry (MCT) started to articulate efforts for the implementation of a national policy for nanotechnology in 2000. In 2001, the MCT funded four cooperative research networks in nanoscience and nanotechnology involving researchers from several universities, research centers and companies from different regions of the country (Toma, 2005). In 2004, a Program for the Development of Nanoscience and Nanotechnology was incorporated into the MCT's Multi-year Plan for 2004–2007 (MCT, 2004). The program had the purpose of fostering competitiveness and increasing the internationalization of Brazilian industry by advancing innovation in this emerging field. That first program was strengthened in 2005, giving way to a more comprehensive National Nanotechnology Program that was better aligned to the Industrial, Technological and Foreign Trade Policy started in 2004. Nanotechnology, described in the latter as "a gateway to the future," has been considered a strategic area to enhance the country's competitiveness. Moreover, the MCT's Plan of Action for 2007–2010 stated that the food, biotechnology, electrical/electronics, aerospace, textile, metal-mechanic, and energy sectors should be given priority for the development of the National Nanotechnology Program (MCT, 2007).

According to its focus on increasing competitiveness, Brazilian nanotechnology policy instruments were directed to train qualified human resources for R&D; develop research infrastructure; promote research projects oriented toward industrial application, involving cooperation between universities, research centers, and the productive sector; and fund R&D activities in companies as well as support new incubated nanotechnology firms. At least 74 R&D projects on nanotechnology proposed by Brazilian companies were funded up to 2009 by FINEP, an agency related to the MCT, the mission of which is to promote innovation in companies, universities, and research centers (Guimarães, 2010).

The database of Brazilian companies with activities in nanotechnology that I built from June 2009 to March 2010 shows that these policies are indeed promoting nanotechnology R&D in Brazil. Based on several sources,[5] I identified 155 companies that are carrying out nanotechnology R&D, or using nanotechnology in their products. Part of them are already commercializing products.[6] These companies are distributed among different productive sectors, the most important being the chemicals/petrochemical, pharmaceutical, cosmetic, medical supplies, textile, and nanostructured materials sectors (Figure 13.1).

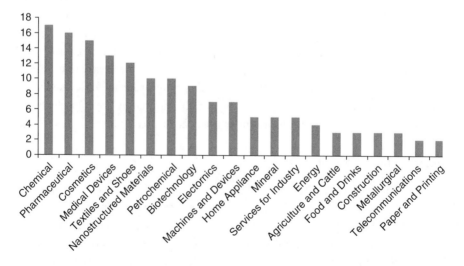

Figure 13.1 Number of Brazilian Companies with Activities in Nanotechnology, by Industrial Sector

These companies' activities in nanotechnology were classified into three stages: research, development, and commercialization of products.[7] One half or 78 companies are already commercializing products that incorporate some nanotechnology innovation; 23 firms are developing products, and 45 are in the research stage (Figure 13.2). In terms of the number of firms involved in commercialization, the chemical, textile, cosmetics, medical devices, petrochemical, and nanostructured materials are the most dynamic industrial sectors. Companies in sectors such as pharmaceutical, biotechnology and electronics have their activities more concentrated in the phases of research and development (Figure 13.3). In addition, five companies commercialize nanotechnology services for industry such as characterization, metrology, and testing.

These data suggest that several Brazilian companies are dynamically engaged in nanotechnology R&D, and a significant number of them are already commercializ-

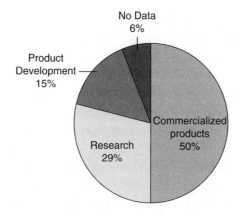

Figure 13.2 Stage of Development of Nanotechnology Activities Carried out by Brazilian Companies

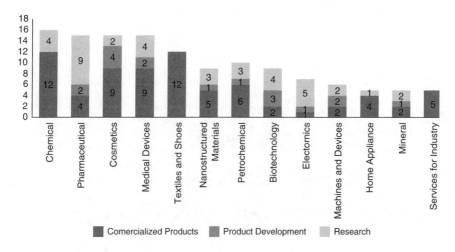

Figure 13.3 Brazilian Companies with Activities in Nanotechnology in Some Selected Industrial Sectors by Stage of Nanotechnology Activities

ing products. Moreover, nanotechnology is being diffused through several industrial sectors and in the different bonds of the production chains (materials, intermediate products, and consumer products). Although the labor force currently involved in nanotechnology production in these companies may be still reduced, this vigorous starting in nanotechnology adoption by a group of innovative firms suggest that, in the near future, more workers will be affected by changes produced by this new technology in the labor process and in the labor market.

Features of Nanotechnology Products and Implications for Labor

One can begin to anticipate the implications of nanotechnology for labor, mostly regarding employment, starting with the features and characteristics of products that are in the development stage and products that are already on the market.

The database for product analysis includes 96 companies selected from the total of 155. Companies whose activities in nanotechnology are in a primary research phase and companies that offer services to industry, such as tests, metrology, etc., were not considered. Other companies were excluded because the information about their products was insufficient. For each company, a representative product, or a family of similar products, was examined.

The specific features added by nanotechnology innovations to these products were grouped into four categories: (1) the products with nanotechnology are more efficient than their conventional competitors; (2) the products are multifunctional; (3) the products require fewer or/and different raw materials; and (4) the products have a longer market lifespan. Although these categories frequently overlap, their analytical distinction is relevant for the assessment of their implications for labor. Figure 13.4 shows a classification of Brazilian companies' products according to these four categories.

Let's consider each one of these product features and its implications for labor, looking at illustrative examples.

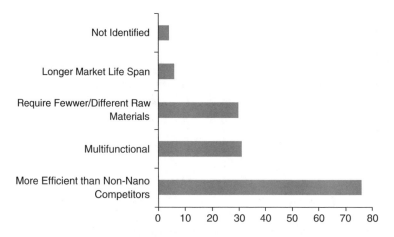

Figure 13.4 Characteristics of the Products with Nanotechnology

More Efficient Products

As Figure 13.4 shows, a pervasive characteristic of the products that incorporate nanotechnology is that they are (or are presented by manufacturers as) more efficient compared with their non-nanotechnology based counterparts. Consider, for instance, polypropylene with nanocomposites for engineering plastics developed by petrochemical Braskem.[8] This special polypropylene is four times more resistant to impacts, 30 percent more rigid and 30 percent lighter than other plastics. Additionally, it presents increased resistance to heat and better protection to sunlight and humidity. It can be used to build car parts, machines, and domestic appliances.[9] DEPT®, developed by the Solid State Chemical Department at the State University of Campinas, and manufactured by Contech Biodegradable Products, is a solid material with nanostructured synthetic clay for the remediation of effluents in the textile and paper industries. The clay eliminates 95 percent of the color of effluents, compared with the 50 percent achieved through traditional methods that use activated carbon. Moreover, it is recyclable and can be reused several times.[10] A new construction material, a light concrete block called InterBloco, was developed by the company Ecopore. A nanotechnology process made it possible to integrate non-toxic foam into the concrete, creating numerous micro-pores of air within the material. The blocks are extremely light, and adjust to one another without need of cement, allowing a reduction of 40 percent in the time and costs consumed in construction, compared to traditional methods and materials. In addition, it offers thermal and acoustic insulation.[11] The Brazilian oil company Petrobras developed an intelligent fluid for drilling in deep waters. The fluid is able to change its viscosity, responding to the water conditions, while the drill is working. When the water is agitated, the fluid turns into a lower viscosity, helping the drill to work better. When the operation is interrupted and the water becomes calm, the same fluid changes to a high viscosity, preventing the residues from perforation entering the oil well. The particles of the fluid were designed to separate in agitated environments and conglomerate in quiet environments. This innovation helps the company save US$150 million at each stop to change the drilling tools.[12]

Nanotechnology innovations enhanced these products' quality, making them more efficient. In addition, several of them would last longer or require fewer applications or be reused more times than the products they substitute. The new products thus can replace competing products on the market while at the same time reducing the demand for these products themselves. This means that manufacturing these products will require a smaller workforce as long as demand for them remains constant. Other products will directly increase production productivity, requiring less labor. It is important to note that these new products will change the competitive environment, and generate winners and losers among the existing companies which, in turn, will cause instability and shifts in the labor market.

Multifunctional Products

About one-third of the products examined are multifunctional. Nanotechnology is helping several products to add new function. We can differentiate two kinds of

multifunctionality. The first takes place when two or more products that were produced and sold separately merge into one product that performs different functions.
Other multifunctional products add new functions to their main purpose, such as
maintenance functions.

Some examples of the first kind of multifunctionality can be seen in the food
industry. Companies add vitamins, collagen, phyto extracts and other nanoencap-
sulated substances to food and drinks. Such combinations are called nutraceuticals,
or products that simultaneously serve feeding, esthetic and medicinal purposes that
were previously provided by different products. The company Funcional Mikron, for
instance, produces bio-active and functional ingredients, such as encapsulated Omega
3, collagen, probiotics, chitosan, iron phosphate, calcium, green tea extract, etc., that
are added to drinks, food, and cosmetics. In the textile industry, there have also been
advances in multifunctional products such as fibers or fabrics containing moisturizing
lotions, perfumes, vitamins, or medicines. CHT Brasil Química produces *Nouwell E,* a
textile fiber that performs cosmetic functions by transferring vitamin E to the skin and
releasing a perfume. Nanocapsules containing both vitamin E and perfume are distributed in the textile fibers and they open when the fibers touch the skin or are activated
by movement. Such a textile is presented as having anti-aging, anti-oxidant and anti-
free-radicals properties, in addition to moisturize and reduce odors.[13]

Multifunctional products demonstrate a trend toward greater interaction and even
the merger of branches of production, which may reconfigure current industrial sectors and the distribution of the labor force among them. Given the internationalization
of global production chains, these changes will exceed national borders. If there is a
merger of sectors, it is likely that there will be fewer jobs available and a demand for
broader, less sector-specific skills. The agglomeration of functions in one product also
leads to the centralization of transport, distribution, marketing and commercialization, which may possibly result in fewer jobs in these fields.

Products can also be considered multifunctional when they include ways of maintaining or preserving themselves that were previously the task of individuals. Nanum®
produces a glass coating with TiO2 nanoparticles that enable self-clean glass when
exposed to sunlight.[14] Textiles advertise their anti-wrinkle, anti-stain and other preserving properties. Cedro Textil, for instance, produces an intelligent textile, CEDROTECH,
based on the manipulation of the cotton molecule to change its properties. New properties such as fire retardant, chemical agents repellent, water repellent and anti-stain
are added to fabrics, creating new materials for the confection of protective work
uniforms.[15] Other textile companies are using nanotechnology to produce antibacterial and more absorbent towels and anti-wrinkle tablecloths and linens.[16] Nanox has
developed two nanostructured coatings, NANOX®BARRIER and NANOX®CLEAN.
The first can be applied to industrial equipment to protect surfaces against corrosion
and abrasion, particularly those produced by high temperatures, extending the equipment life and reducing maintenance. The second is a coating with biocide properties
that facilitates cleaning and sterilization processes when applied to any surface.

Many jobs, especially low-skill jobs, will be affected by the falling demand for
cleaning, washing and ironing and repairing activities, as well as the decrease in the

demand of the products used for these activities as a result of the new qualities and features being incorporated into nanotechnology products. Some other innovations may reduce more specialized maintenance activities of industrial facilities.

Products Requiring Fewer and/or Different Raw Materials

Another one-third of the products examined require fewer and/or different raw materials than do their counterparts that do not incorporate nanotechnology. The above cited company Funcional Mikron, which produces encapsulated active, bioactive, and functional ingredients, claims that a major advantage of nanotechnology is that it enables companies to use smaller quantities of raw materials, in some cases many times smaller, and achieve considerable enhancements in terms of flavor, aroma, bioavailability, and biocompatibility of ingredients.[17] Pharmaceutical companies also find the reduced amount of main ingredients, along with a faster-working and longer-lasting therapeutic action, appealing. That is the case of the first drug with nanotechnology produced in Brazil, a topical anesthetic developed by Incrementha PD&I (a research branch of the pharmaceutical companies Biolab and Europharma) and the Federal University of Rio Grande do Sul. In this medicine, a biodegradable capsule transports the drug to the nervous terminals of the skin, instead of to the blood stream, having a more rapid and longer therapeutic action and reducing collateral effects. It can be adjusted in size and composition to reach the target. All these enhanced effects are fulfilled with lower doses of the drug.[18] In these cases, there is less need for raw materials, thus directly affecting jobs in the sectors involved.

Other products exploit the advantages of new materials produced by nanotechnology to substitute for other raw materials. Carbon nanotubes have great potential in several production sectors due to their excellent conductivity, mechanical resistance that is 100 times higher than steel, and flexibility and pliability. The Physics Department at the Federal University of Minas Gerais produces carbon nanotubes in a semi-industrial scale that are commercialized though the university's foundation. A spin-off is in development to achieve greater production scale.[19] Similarly, state-of-the-art resins are replacing other materials. Nova Petroquimica (formerly Suzano, now merged with Braskem) produces a transparent polypropylene resin enriched with nanoparticles that substitutes glass in Suggar washing machines. The resin is lighter than glass and resistant to impacts.[20] Biphor, a white pigment for water-based paints manufactured from nanoparticles of aluminum phosphate, was developed by the Brazilian branch of the multinational company Bunge and the University of Campinas Chemistry Institute. Biphor may replace titanium dioxide, currently the only white pigment used in the industry for all types of paint, which is toxic. In five years, Bunge expects that Biphor will replace titanium dioxide in 10 percent of the market. The new pigment offers advantages when compared with titanium dioxide: its use makes possible the manufacture of more lasting paints, with better performance and at lower costs and it is non-toxic. In addition, the manufacturing process of Biphor, unlike the traditional pigment, leaves no residues.[21]

One special case is the change in the demand of natural raw materials. Nanotechnology innovations can both reduce the demand for natural raw material by its substitution for industrialized materials, and increase its demand by means of enhancement of natural materials with nanomaterials. This is well illustrated by innovations in the textile sector. Santista Textil is using nanotechnology to produce a 100 percent polyester fabric, Image, which imitates the fine touch and the appearance of wool and the quality of natural fibers textiles like absorbing perspiration. At the same time, it offers the advantages of synthetic fibers such as excellent hidrofility, fast drying and resistance to stains.[22] Conversely, other textile companies are directing their nanotechnology innovations to eliminate the difficulties that natural fibers present, adding characteristics such as faster drying, increasing absorbency, anti-odor, antibacterial, anti-stain and anti-wrinkle properties, which can expand the demand for these natural raw materials. This is the case of Renaux Blue Label, a company that produces different cotton fabrics with new properties.[23] In the next section, I will present other innovations that can reduce the demand for food production by means of spoilage reduction.

Overall, the industrialized materials subject to reduced demand and/or potential substitution by new materials with nanotechnology identified in the research were: steel and other metals, glass fiber, glass, different kinds of plastics, pharmaceutical active principles, natural fibers, and chemicals such as solvents and pigments. These changes in materials will alter the distribution of the workforce among different sectors. Given that the exploitation of materials is closely linked to natural resources, both at a national and international level, changes in demand can lead to a new regional and international distribution of labor.

Products with a Longer Market Shelf Life

The last characteristic, a longer market shelf life, hallmarks a small group of products, since it is mostly under the research phase. However, as it is an important trend in nanotechnology products innovation at the global level and affects particularly the food industry, one in which nanotechnology is developing fast, it is worth it to consider it here in spite of its low representation. These kinds of innovations are directed to help perishable products extend their market shelf life, increasing the time available for commercialization and consumption, and reducing the need for human check-up on the products' conditions for consumption. Embrapa (the Brazilian agribusiness company) has a nanotechnology research area on nanofilms, nanomembranes and biodegradable, bioactive, intelligent packages. One of the projects is developing organic barriers (edible films) with nanoparticles to cover macadamia nuts. These barriers block the entry of oxygen and water vapor, making the nut last longer.[24] Another project is developing films and edible and biodegradable coatings for fruits. Natural components are deconstructed and then restructured in the form of plastics. Some of them have biocide properties, and, in general, help block water losses and gas exchanges, which extends the shelf life of the fruit, which remains fresh up to 20 days.[25]

Other innovations are directed to create "active" and "intelligent" packaging. Suzano Petroquimica and Oxiteno are both developing special plastics with nanocomposites. This material can be used to manufacture food packages that allow the conservation of food for longer periods due to either better blocking capacity or capacity to kill bacteria that contaminates the food.[26] The adhesive labels with nanotechnology produced by Novel Print are able to identify if foods or drinks are suitable for consumption.[27] Embrapa is also developing packaging able to indicate food contamination or changes in conservation conditions. Moreover, packages can be designed to interact with the food content, releasing preservatives when the first signs of bacterial activity are detected.[28]

Using nanotechnology will allow companies to produce products that have a longer shelf life. This will generally be good for companies because it will reduce spoilage and waste. But, because these products can remain longer in storage and on supermarket shelves, activities involving the transport of goods, taking stock, checking on the state of products, and maintaining the products and sales will likely be reduced. That is, there will be fewer jobs as a result of this efficiency.

Conclusion

Nanotechnology is being absorbed into several industrial processes through incremental innovations. The effects of this emerging technology on labor are still difficult to evaluate and, to some extent, any attempt to do so is risky. Labor demands, in quantity and quality, although strongly related to technological changes, are not straightforward consequences of them. There are a number of complex economic and social factors, as well as political decisions at stake. In spite of these complexities, early evaluation of the directions of change in labor associated with nanotechnology is necessary and worthwhile to inform innovation, social, and employment policies.

Distilling Brazilian nanotechnology product innovations into particular features can help to anticipate some ways in which nanotechnology production may affect labor. Increased efficiency, multifunctionality, reduction and changes in raw materials, and extended shelf life are likely to change the nature of and need for labor over the coming years, giving rise to the following trends:

1. Labor force shifts between sectors of production, due to the increasing convergence of sectors and changes in the demand of raw and intermediate materials. Such shifts will redefine labor skills, making some skill profiles obsolete. When natural raw materials production is implicated, there could be changes in the geographical distribution of the labor force.

2. Reduced demand for labor in some production activities and services as a result of the increased efficiency and functionality of nanotechnology products. Job losses can be in absolute or relative terms depending on companies' and productive sectors' competitiveness and growth. The balance between local production and imports along the production chains will also determine whether jobs are retained or lost.

3. Labor creation in R&D and other specialized activities related to emergent nanotechnology skills, as well as in other manufacturing positions accompanying the creation of new nanotechnology-based companies. Since global nanotechnology development is clearly concentrated within northern countries and China

(Maclurcan, 2010), it is likely that a great part of nanotechnology potential for job creation is also concentrated in them.

4. Labor instability, because changes in competitive capabilities due to the introduction of nanotechnology will certainly provoke a deep industrial restructuring process, as a result of which many low competitive firms will fail, shedding jobs. The degree of instability caused by the change from one technological system to another will depend on the speed in which it takes place and the ways government intervenes in the process.

14.
SEEKING THE NON-DEVELOPMENTAL WITHIN THE DEVELOPMENTAL
Mobile Phones in the Globalized Migration Context[1]
Arul Chib and Rajiv G. Aricat

The meta-narrative of globalization has become embedded in the modern-day lexicon; and has permeated the key development discourses of the day. For the purposes of this examination, globalization has been defined along five major dimensions, supported by an advanced techno-sociological infrastructure: the internationalization of financial investment flows including FDIs (foreign direct investment); of increasingly networked cross-border trade comprising imports and exports; of an overarching media sky-scape of multinational organizations and services; of hitherto unimaginable labor movement and migration across nations; and finally, of information flows and communication connectivity on an unprecedented global scale (Robertson, 2004; Castles, 2003). The inter-relatedness of these dimensions makes it difficult to tease out any one dimension of this phenomenon while explaining a specific socio-cultural or economic scenario. Nonetheless, this chapter, focusing on the developmental impact of new communications technologies (specifically, of mobile phones) on international migrants, is situated mainly along the intersection of two dimensions of globalization mentioned: labor migration and the globalization of information and communication technologies (ICTs).

The underlying theme is one of development, in which the line of argumentation is arrived at from a perspective that borders on positivist; ICTs are pre-supposed to deliver significant improvements in critical measures of development, particularly for those that had until now been disenfranchised or marginalized.

A note on definitional boundaries prior to proceeding—the international migrants under examination are defined as marginalized within the developed host-country circumstances due to their limited legal, financial, and social status versus citizens; development objectives in this case could potentially run the gamut from health, education, poverty-eradication, human rights, etc., but are limited to livelihood advancement, and well-being in the adopted country; and finally, the ICTs in focus are limited to mobile phones, and to a certain extent, to the availability of advanced Internet-enabled services via mobile devices. Further, to avoid a techno-deterministic viewpoint, the discussion incorporates a critical perspective on the impact of technology adoption on low-income international migrants.

We begin with a discussion on how the notion of the information society has gained currency as the optimal model for the developing world in this era of globalization, moving on to literature that discusses how mobile phones have been helping various vulnerable and deprived sections to integrate into the emergent information network. We draw on the "blurring lives and livelihoods" framework developed by Jonathan Donner (2009), to distinguish between the complex inter-related contexts within which mobile phones find usefulness for migrants. Cross-border migrant movements warrant a situation in which information is sought by migrants not only from the home country alone, but also from the host country in which they work and reside. Although much of the communications involved is for the maintenance of relationships and dealing with loss and loneliness, information flows in local networks help migrants better adapt to the host society, improving professional careers and developing business networks. Empirical research elaborating on the mobile usage of migrants driven by these social and professional motivations is presented in the latter part of the chapter.

Information Society and Digital Divide

Although conceptualized differently by social theorists, the dictum "information is power" has remained unchallenged, or perhaps has gained more meaning, in recent times with the rapid and widespread diffusion of, and access to, modern information and communication technologies (Haftor, 2011; Webster, 2006). It suggests that the ramifications of modern ICTs extend far beyond the notion of economic power, into the domains of personal, social, professional, and political life. Castells (2000, 2001a, 2001b) delineates three important trends that lead to the formation of a network model in today's communication landscape. These trends pertain to the growing power and pervasiveness of modern ICTs, the emergence of a global economy and the increasing social value of free and open communication. According to Castells (2000), as the diffusion of communication technologies increases, traditional hierarchies have to be abandoned and a new information model needs to be conceptualized. Correspondingly, Bell (1999) observes how the services sector gains importance over industry-based manual labor in the information society. The emergent class structure in the information society favors education, even as theoretical knowledge supplants labor and capital in the new set up. For Bell, this would be the information society's point of departure with the preceding industrial societies. This notion becomes critical in the analysis of blue-collar migrants who offer up their labor in the pursuit of global capital. While this increasingly mobile labor-force has the ability to convert labor into capital, they remain laggards in the new global currency of information.

The capability of communication technology to make significant improvements in the critical development areas, like health, income, education, and other human rights, has been identified by leading transnational organizations. In *Target 8F* of the United Nations' Millennium Development Goals (MDGs) world leaders and the international community have been called upon to "make available the benefits of new technologies, specifically information and communication" to all the sections of the society (UNMDG, 2011). However, contingent on the infrastructure and social realities, the global diffusion of communication technology remains uneven. Some key statistics on the Internet present a picture of a widening information gap, termed the "digital divide" (Katz and

Rice, 2002; Lievrouw and Livingstone, 2002), resulting in differences in both access and usage. The number of Internet users per 100 inhabitants in Asia rose from six to 14 between 2002 and 2007, while the same number rose from 26 to 44 in Europe and 28 to 43 in the Americas (ITU, 2011). Along with insufficient or lack of access, the inability of various segments of the population to benefit from the technologies exacerbates the problem of the digital divide. Lack of ICT skills, widely seen among low-income, less-educated groups, presents one facet of the problem (Fink and Kenny, 2003). It has also been observed that other demographic variables like gender, race, caste, and age also determine one's access to, and benefits from, ICTs (Warschauer, 2002).

In the migration sector, which our study focuses on, clear divisions in terms of ICT access and benefits exist between blue-collar migrants, who provide replaceable and cheap labor for global capital, and white-collar information workers integrated into the privileged strata of any society. The digital divide thus acts as an outcome and a factor that leads to an issue more relevant to the development debate, i.e. the social opportunities divide amongst different strata of the population (Mendoza, 2001). Later we elaborate on how the information gap between these two sections of migrants can be bridged through advanced mobile technologies, in addition to strengthening the ICT skills of those engaged in blue-collar professions.

This study is situated in Singapore, where Chinese and Indian expatriates constitute a major share of the migrant population (Statistics Singapore, 2011). Internet penetration has been increasing rapidly in these migrants' host countries, with billion-plus populations, with urban regions enjoying greater access compared to the rural regions (Chib and Zhao, 2009). Although the rural masses constitute 56 percent of the total Chinese population, out of the 253 million Chinese people online as of June 2008, the rural users' share is only 25 percent (CNNIC, 1997, 2008). Rural Internet penetration increased from only 2.6 percent in 2004 to 12 percent by 2009 (CNNIC, 2010). Similarly, the urban population in India is just 5.3 percent of its total population, but among the 60 million Indians online, constituting 5–7 percent penetration, the majority are urban users (IAMAI, 2007; IWS, 2007; TRAI, 2009). For advanced technologies like the mobile broadband Internet, a similar gap in diffusion exists between developed and developing countries. While 38.7 percent penetration has been achieved in developed countries, in developing countries the rate stands at 3 percent (ITU, 2010).

This said, a notable reversal in the digital divide trend in some areas of technology diffusion is discernible. It is in the basic mobile phone subscriptions in developing countries that this reversal of trend is observed. Belying the diffusion trends followed by preceding information technologies such as the Internet, the growth of cellular subscriptions has accelerated remarkably in developing countries. Mobile subscriptions in developed countries were 27 times higher than developing countries in 1994, which was reduced to four times in 2004. In the year 2000, developing countries accounted for around 40 percent of total mobile subscriptions in the world, whereas their share rose to around 70 percent by 2009 (ITU, 2010). In China, cellular subscriptions stood at 859 million in 2010, up from 393 million in 2005, whereas during the same five-year period the total number of mobile subscriptions in India rose from 90 million to 752 million (ITU, 2011). In absolute numbers, subscriptions in developing countries stand at 3.2 billion in 2010, while the developed countries constitute just half of that, 1.4 billion. However, the mobile cellular subscription rate is an estimated 70.1 per 100 inhabitants by the end of 2009 in developing countries, whereas it is 114.2 percent in developed countries. This shows the growth potential of the mobile market in developing countries (ITU, 2010). Industry players have already begun to expand their business to the "bottom of the pyramid" (Prahalad, 2005), with universal access to telecom services already being an actively pursued agenda in developing countries like China and India (Zhang and Chib, 2011).

It is true that the data on mobile subscriptions present only part of the story about the developing world's transition toward information societies. On the ground, many social structures still need to be adjusted in order to facilitate the transition. An equally important aspect is the accessibility of Internet over mobile phones with the emergence of 3G and 4G technologies. Traditionally, the gap in the accessibility of the Internet had been the locus around which the debate on digital divide was formed. However, if we acknowledge that a "leapfrogging" has occurred through the convergence of the Internet with mobile technology and that the former can piggyback the latter in its attempt to diffuse, we should expect the disparities in Internet access observed to diminish in the future. Keeping this in perspective, our chapter argues that mobile phones have the potential to overcome the information obstacles of vulnerable populations in developing countries in general and for international migrants in particular. Our study investigates the role of mobile phones in helping the migrants to partake in the network model of the information society.

Mobile Phones and Development

Developmental efforts enabled by mobile technologies pertain to a wide variety of instrumental uses, which include buying and selling of products from farmers and fishermen, rural health services, small and medium entrepreneurial activities, to mention a few. Although the developmental outcomes are clear in the case of some targeted mobile interventions, nuanced interpretations have also been attempted using professional-social dichotomous perspectives. Donner (2009) suggests that mobile phone usage has both developmental and non-developmental uses and impacts, and that the complex nature of the mingled usage is not always distinguishable. He advances a dichotomy of the economic and social, suggesting an "intermingling of lives and livelihoods," which aims to account for a broad swath of mobile phone use. Our effort in this section is to introduce evidence of such mobile interventions and an interpretative reading of the outcomes.

From a developmental, or livelihood, perspective, researchers have focused on how the asymmetry and inefficiency of information flow prevalent in unorganized markets of developing countries become detrimental to their development agenda. In certain instances, mobile phones have been found to overcome this shortcoming, paving the way to a more level playing field for sellers, middlemen, and buyers. Mobile phones have taken up the mantle from the eighteenth-century telegraph in communicating price information, thereby bridging inter-market price differentials (Abraham, 2007;

Jensen, 2007). This is especially important in the case of perishable commodities, like fish, fruits, and vegetables, where the prices are volatile and short-term. In one case study (Abraham, 2007), conducted amongst the fishermen in the coastal villages of the south Indian state of Kerala, three segments in the fishing industry—merchants, agents, and transporters—had been regularly threatened by price fluctuations. However, when they began using mobile phones, price differentials reduced, whilst averting the possibility of glut in some markets and scarcity in another. They could also operate outside local markets thereby widening their business reach. In effect, consumers enjoyed reduced prices while the new communication facility ensured bringing higher prices for the producers. In the Jensen (2007) study, price dispersion was dramatically reduced, violations of the "Law of One Price" were almost nil, wastage was eliminated, fishermen's profit increased by 8 percent, consumer price decreased by 4 percent, and the consumer surplus in sardine—the fish variety focused in the study—consumption increased by 6 percent. On the fishermen's front, a reduction in the wastage of time and resources ensued as they began using mobiles. Time was saved on two fronts: time spent on searching for fish reduced, as also the fishermen's idling hours on shore—messages over mobile phones summoned them for work, when it was available, in nearby areas. The fishermen could enjoy "mobility" along with the other basic features of telephony. From a social perspective, these fishermen felt far more secure while venturing out in the sea with a mobile phone in hand. They could be alerted in times of an emergency, like a possible tsunami, and be in touch with their family while at sea.

In another instance, the Grameen Village Phone (VP), a GSM technology initiative to make available public telephone facilities in rural Bangladesh, allowed for leasing of talktime by rural women (Richardson *et al.*, 2000). The VP went hand-in-hand with the eponymous Grameen Bank's micro-credit services in rural regions. On average, the VP operators, who were mostly women, earned an income of 14,400 Taka (USD 300) per year providing telephone services to the villagers. The livelihood impact had a cascading social impact on women's lives. As the income from village phone was substantial, it was found to have elevated the operator's—the woman's—position in her own household, particularly in regards to decision-making. In addition, the village phone becomes a communication device that was shared by many women during their evening congregation. They used the phone to communicate with kith and kin at distant places, evading the watchful eyes and ears of their husbands. The financial agreement was made in such a way that the in-kind loan issued for the VP business could not be diverted to any other businesses, and hence the unnecessary intervention of the men folk in the transactions remained low (Bayes, 2001; Richardson *et al.*, 2000).

Similarly, a targeted healthcare-development project provides a glimpse into how issues like gender were successfully dealt with using communication technologies (Chib and Chen, 2011). A two-decades long civil conflict and, more recently, a tsunami disaster had broken the spine of the healthcare system in the Indonesian province of Aceh. An ICT for healthcare intervention utilized mobile phones distributed to front-line community health workers, specifically rural midwives (MWs). The project aimed at utilizing JAVA-based mobile applications to bring reproductive health services to rural communities back on track. MWs, coordinators, and doctors were linked via mobile phones, which transferred pregnancy-related data to a central Internet-based database. Mobile use addressed the constraints imposed by the shattered healthcare system, improving information flows amongst the various levels of the healthcare hierarchy, reducing critical response-ties, and speeding up information access in general (Chib, 2010). Beyond the developmental impact, the usage of mobiles made midwives aware of their capabilities, leading to a greater gender-consciousness (Chib and Chen, 2011), which then led to struggles in the male-dominated social hierarchy. Approaching the technology introduction from a benefit-constraints dialectic, the authors found that while the project healthcare objectives were met, a similarly profound impact was being created by the struggles of women in dealing with gender inequalities.

In sum, mobile phones have been adopted by various segments of developing societies to participate in the development process from a livelihood perspective, thus enabling negotiation with different stakeholders in the information society. However, in differing ways, depending on the socioeconomic spheres in which they work and live in, the beneficiaries of mobile technology also used it to advance their social lives. While a utilitarian framework could be used to explain how fishermen, healthcare workers, and village women elsewhere in developing countries use mobile phones to overcome traditional market barriers to improve livelihood options, a socio-structural approach could explain the social benefits of mobile phones as well. We do so by focusing on international migrants.

Mobile Phones and Migrants

Having established the facilitative role mobile phones play in development, i.e. livelihood, and non-development, or social, efforts, which ultimately help the beneficiaries to be part of the information society, we move on to examine the use of mobile phones from the perspective of migrants. Increasing job opportunities in cities have triggered the rural to urban domestic as well as international labor movements around the world (IOM, 2011). In large economies like China and India, domestic labor movements are in the millions, especially from depleted agricultural zones in the rural regions to the more lucrative non-agricultural labor zones in the cities. The estimated number of international migrants by mid-2010 in Asia was 61.3 million, an increase of 11 percent from the same period in 2005 (UN, 2009). In Singapore, migrant workers constitute 40.7 percent of the total population of 4.74 million (UNDESA, 2009), with a recent increased inflow (Forss, 2007), predominantly from South and Southeast Asian countries (Yeoh, 2007). Among the total migrants in Singapore, male migrants from South Asia constitute 30 percent (Rose, 2010). Male migrant workers are employed in blue-collar occupations, mainly in the construction and skilled tradesman sectors, landscaping services, and the shipyard business (Rahman and Lian, 2005).

International labor migrants suffer vulnerabilities at various levels, primary among them is the host-society attitude of discrimination, which often sees the out-group as society's "other" (Pedersen, 1995), leading to feelings of alienation and depression (Swagler and Ellis, 2003). Difficulties such as language barriers, non-availability of emotional support networks, vulnerability to exploitation, and limited personal resources are commonly faced by any migrant worker in the initial phase of adaptation (Ryan and Twibell, 2000; Vedder and Virta, 2005; Yeh and Inose, 2003). These challenges vary in different classes of migrants, considering that the labor migrants themselves are not a monolithic category within the host society. Thus, in their attempts to adapt (for short or long term) to the host society, different sections of migrants seek information of different kinds, while their communication needs remain diverse.

With increased access to ICTs such as mobile phones, migrants are increasingly using technological mediation for accessing social support, despite structural barriers encountered. Contextualizing the emergence of a network society of migrants in urban China in recent decades, Qiu (2009) observes how the informational needs of this burgeoning section of people fueled the growth of working-class ICTs in a short time-span. Low-cost mobile phones helped them negotiate with various agencies on a day-to-day basis. "Each of these many phone numbers [seen on the walls in Guangzhou or the back streets of Shanghai, advertising various services] represents a have-less individual or a group of them who do not have a stable job but can afford a mobile phone" (Qiu, 2009: 108). Wallis (2008) examined how rural female migrant workers (rural-to-urban) in China negotiated a hybrid rural–urban identity using mobile phones. Owing to limited literacy, financial resources, technical expertise, and their gender, the migrant women could be seen as on the losing side of the "digital divide." Nevertheless, for a female migrant worker from rural China a mobile phone could be interpreted as a means to shed her rural essence, establishing a unique identity in the adopted urban center.

In Singapore, foreign domestic workers (FDWs), such as maids, face restrictions from their employers in the use of mobile phones, which they overcome by covert communication techniques like short messaging service or SMS (Thompson, 2009; Lim and Thomas, 2010; Lin and Sun, 2011). Mobile phones help them ensure their presence in the network of friends, so as to make their social lives better. These scholars note how mobile phones can bring relief to maids from their repetitive daily chores. Calling and sending text messages to their family back home become private rituals using the phones, helping them escape the physical constraints faced within the four walls of the employer's house.

In this study, our investigations focused on: (1) What is the impact of mobile phones on Singaporean migrant workers' personal social lives? (2) What is the impact of mobile phones on Singaporean migrant workers' professional lives?

Methodology

Data for the study were collected through in-depth interviews with 23 migrant workers from Kerala, a southern state of India, over a period of four months (October 2010 to January 2011). The respondents, known as Malayalis, were between the ages of 20 and 34, with an average age of 29.3. As described in the next section, migrants' local networks in the host society are often formed and maintained around ethnic identities. Mobile communications can, thus, be a facilitator as well as an outcome of ethnic group formation. We therefore approached a few respondents for this study via a religious organization, the organization being one of the few available ethnic groupings for the migrant workers in the host country. Through snowball sampling, the rest of the respondents were selected. In effect, 13 of the respondents had some kind of affiliation with the religious organization and the rest belonged to either the same religion but with no organizational affiliation or a different religion altogether.

All participants were males who had been in Singapore for between one-and-a-half and six years, sometimes in several spells. The group comprised a variety of low-skilled and semi-skilled workers ranging from general technicians, riggers, fitters, and welders. All the interviews were conducted on a one-on-one basis. The lead researcher shared the same mother tongue—Malayalam—as that of the respondents, and hence the interviews were conducted in this language. Each interview lasted approximately 20 to 30 minutes. Global standards and norms for conducting ethical social science research were observed while conducting the study. Consent forms were administered, respondents were compensated SG$10 as an honorarium, and all names were ano- nymized for the sake of maintaining confidentiality.

Participants were asked questions under three main categories that relate to issues of accessing information and communicating to host and home cultures: (1) mobile use in general, especially the cost involved; (2) social uses of the phone; and (3) pro- fessional uses of the phone. In the first category, questions included experience and frequency of mobile phone usage, for example, "how long have you been using mobile phones"; and listing typical feature use, for example, "what features, like Internet, FM radio/news, SMS, etc. do you generally use," etc. In the second category on social uses, respondents were prompted to explain how they acculturated with the new host-soci- ety. Questions included, "are you a member of any ethnic group," "how do you get the updates from the group," "has the group helped you in any way to develop new skills related to ICTs and networking," etc. In the third category on professional uses, they were asked "do you think mobile phones can help you acquire professionally useful information," "what role does the mobile phone play in easing your current work," "how does the phone help you advance in your career," etc.

Findings and Discussion

The in-depth interviews revealed the pattern of mobile phone use among the Malayali migrants, their maintenance of home-country support networks, their communication exchanges with co-ethnic networks, and the pattern of their mobile phone usage in pro- fessional life. All of the respondents had between two and seven dependents back in India with whom they were regularly in touch, increasingly so due to lowered airtime tariffs. Interestingly, international call-time expanded local call-time opportunities, which were then used to bolster both social networks, enhancing participation in partic- ular local institutions, which offered emotional support and socialization opportunities, and professional networks, improving productivity. The increased ease over the years in communicating with all social networks, local and international, driven by decreasing airtime charges, was a change widely cited by senior respondents in the sample. Con- versely, for mobile phones pulling double-duty in social and professional settings, in this respondent group, compared to other instances in the literature (Chib, 2010; Donner, 2009; Idowu et al., 2003), personal airtime was utilized to subsidize professional calls.

Mobile usage ranged from basic communication to advanced voice-plus applications, some of which were enabled by the Internet. This advanced use, despite being more expensive, delivered esteem and credibility amongst both personal social and professional networks. We observed that the blurring of lives and livelihoods, as suggested by Donner, did occur to a major extent; yet, there were instances, with determinate motivations, for respondents to maintain a strict dichotomy between their personal social and professional lives.

Personal Social Usage, Communication Patterns and Information Access

Social calls, particularly maintaining contact with distant relatives in the home country, were by far the most important reason for mobile connectivity. Low-end mobile phones, attractive prepaid packages, easily accessible Internet over mobile, etc. helped the workers navigate between home and host cultures easily. Most talked to their kith and kin back home—"discussions across a kitchen table" (Vertovec, 2004: 222)—as well as with their co-ethnic networks in Singapore, almost daily. Migrants' increased communication patterns mirror a global pattern of access driven by increased affordability of both handsets and airtime charges (Vertovec, 2004). Notably, access to mobile voice communication occurred at both ends of the chain—for migrants in the developed host country, as well as the family in the home country; a phenomenon that failed to occur for Internet access.

> I used to talk less to family when working in Dubai in 2007. The call rates where high ... I was also earning less those days ... I used to send letters. After coming here, I don't write letters. I call home everyday, sometimes even thrice a day. I may be talking for a short time, maybe for 3 minutes or 5 minutes ... When my daughter returns from school, she "missed calls" me immediately. Even if I return late at night from work, I have to call home; otherwise there will be a barrage of "missed calls" from her. It is a pleasure being constantly in touch with family.
>
> Calling home is cheap ... I spend 60 Sing Dollar every month, mainly to call home daily and my friends twice a week. But calling my brother is a problem, as the calls to Middle East are expensive.

The international airtime charges subsidize local airtime, leading to increased in-country communication. Implemented by the three main service providers in Singapore (Singtel, Starhub, and M1), the scheme allows topping up balance amounts for international talktime, while acquiring virtually free local call facilities for a limited period. In effect, airtime expenditure was around US$20, 2.5 percent of an average worker's monthly income.

> I remember the long queue in front of mobile retailers in Little India, when the "free local calls worth SGD 100" scheme was launched. It not only reduced the international call charges considerably, but facilitated local communication by allowing virtually free local calls.
>
> Increased local calling was exhibited in communication with co-ethnic networks in the workplace as well as in residential quarters. In the initial stage of settlement, migrants

reached out to familiar co-ethnic groups for information, affirmation, and emotional support. In all such interactions involving newcomers in our sample, the mobile phones played an important role. Further, connections with social institutions were facilitated by mobile usage. Specialized ethnic groupings like prayer or choir groups planned activities, disseminating time and venue details, via mobile phones. This was achieved via a centralized distribution list or through circulation of messages in a chain manner. Although many of the institutional members later joined social networking sites (SNS), mobile phones remained the immediate channel of contact.

I asked a senior member in our group how they managed to organize activities for the prayer group when mobile services were not available. He said they had to actually go to each member personally and intimate him about the event.

I realized the importance of text messages fully after coming here [to Singapore]. How many calls can we make to the members? There are many members ... For a message, it's easy, put all numbers in the distribution list and send.

Advanced voice-plus applications utilizing the Internet delivered social capital in the personal network. For example, news portals in vernacular languages were an attraction of the mobile Internet due to the speed of delivery, reduced costs, and water-cooler bragging rights. Vernacular newspapers from India arrive in Singapore with a delay of two days, and the prices are higher by a factor of eight. Discussion within co-ethnic networks revolved around regional politics and social issues in the home country, often at the local state level. Thus, an informed opinion could strengthen a worker's position in the peer-group.

If I have no local airtime balance in the mobile, I feel tense. There is no way to know news from Kerala, if I don't check Internet on mobile.

Accessing Internet was a problem once. Internet cafes are rare. If we want to access Internet in library, we have to take an account first. It's complicated ... Dormitories are like a prison ... you don't have contact with the world outside.

Shared usage of advanced Internet applications offered dual benefits, not only reducing individual expenditure, but allowing the development of advanced technological familiarity. The minority of respondents who did subscribe to mobile broadband shared the connection between a group of between three and four people. While these Internet connections were capable of making voice or video calls, this feature was unutilized due to the fact that families back in India did not have broadband access.

Internet connection is not available in our area; where there isn't a tower for mobile phones ... Signals are feeble ... Nevertheless, I have to call on the mobile phone since we don't have landline connection at home. After I came here I asked my sister in Kerala to teach our mother how to use mobile phone. Now she knows how to "missed call" me if something is urgent.

We could call home via Internet. But I have only my mother at home. She cannot operate this. We had Internet connection at home, but later we cancelled it as my brother and me, both moved out of the country for work. Nevertheless, mobile call charges are not that high.

Non-developmental uses of advanced features such as the Internet predominated. The majority of respondents were attracted only to the familiar cultural expressions associated with entertainment—checking cricket scores, listening to popular film-songs and downloading jingles with nostalgic appeals. Other non-instrumental uses included the need for deepening social connections, acquiring networking skills on the Internet, learning about SNS after their association with the religious organization. While the mobile phones help the migrant workers find social and emotional support in the new culture, their association with co-ethnics help them explore the benefits of SNS. If the mobile Internet can foster relationships among fellow migrants, it's through the latter's participation in co-ethnic groups that they learn skills to acquire information, which further strengthens the relationships.

> During weekends we friends sometimes go for an outing, to Universal Studio or St. John's Island. We take pictures … and this is important … before we return back home the photos will be on Facebook or Orkut. If the camera is with me, I upload the photos after returning. To see the photos … that's enjoyable.
>
> If mobile broadband is used in my laptop, I cannot make voice or video calls at night. It causes disturbance to the room mates. Nevertheless I make at least 10 calls to Middle East every week. This helps me connect with my friends, who were once my classmates and colleagues.

We found evidence that the exposure of first-time users of the mobile Internet is to these non-developmental, non-instrumental social uses for entertainment, social networking and self-expression (Donner, 2009: 97). On the other hand, the effort on the part of the religious organization to formally organize a course to impart computer skills did not bear fruit, with respondents citing a lack of time. This suggests that the mobile interface might be the first one for certain groups to develop their Internet usage patterns.

> We gave extensive coverage to the programme which was conducted on a weekend. But only four people turned up on the first day and the number dropped to two the second day. In Singapore nobody has time to spare.
>
> I have neither used a personal computer, nor internet on PC. One friend of mine taught me to use internet on mobile, then I began using it. In fact, he himself was not an expert … we learned it together. First time we tried entering the web address we saw in some advertisement. It worked. Now I do everything, read news, check mail, everything … I want to learn how to work on computer also.

The ability to develop a strong social network due to increasing affordability is counter-balanced by schemes that deprive the mobile user of a unique identity. Particular mobile schemes offer incentives, such as double value, for initial purchase to attract switchers. This benefit is not available for repeat purchasers. In practice, those who are not particular about retaining their number throw away their SIM card when discharged, losing their unique numeric identity as a result, and buy a new SIM to enjoy this double talktime benefit. Consequently, in one fell swoop, one's identity is wiped out on one's social network's mobile memories. In effect, those who have less people to talk to, but need more talktime, are likely to be unmindful about the identity of a number, but change numbers often to get maximum monetary benefit. Those with a wide network of not-so-close friends are reluctant to give up their numbers in exchange for more talktime.

> I have given my number to all my friends in India as well as in Singapore. If I change number, they'll lose touch with me. So, this scheme is not suitable for me. For those who are calling home most of the time, they can benefit from this scheme. Most of them are doing that, in fact.

Professional Usage, Communication Patterns and Information Access

Professional usage of the mobile phone indicated high instrumental value, leading to micro-coordination at work and aiding productivity. Most respondents woke up early at around 5 a.m., and needed to report at a distant worksite at 7 a.m. Micro-coordination using mobile calls and SMS enables several workers to organize breakfast, board their vehicle and begin their journey to the worksite at such early hours (Ling and Yttri, 2002).

Migrant workers in the construction and shipyard sector go to distant industrial islands. Sometimes, due to technical glitches, machinery at the security gates fails to recognize their passes. In such cases, the workers report to their bosses immediately and resolve the matter.

> We have confidence that if we get into any trouble anywhere, we can call our boss. His number is with us ... Similarly, going into remote islands, we may face difficulty in punching at the gate. So we have to call our supervisors.

The respondents who carried mobile phones to the worksites called their supervisors or colleagues in order to improve productivity. It should be noted that, however, these mobiles were neither provided, nor was the airtime subsidized, by the employers. Personal devices owned by the migrant worker were used with no element of reluctance to do so.

> There are stores in each worksite. We can go there directly and collect the material. But I have fed the storekeeper's number in my mobile. I just call him when material is required ... It takes 15 minutes walking from the store to my worksite ... I can avoid that. Now I can coordinate my work properly.

Despite being a personal phone, most workers willingly use it for work-related calls, suggesting the "double-duty hardware/airtime" concept is in effect (Donner, 2009). It is possible that due to the co-mingled nature of migrants' social and professional networks, a work call is also a chance to renew a friendship simultaneously. The exact professional value of such calls are potentially indefinable or immeasurable, since migrants add to social capital while doing so.

Advanced voice-plus applications utilizing the Internet have the potential to advance migrants' careers and credibility within their professional networks. Gaining proficiency in English language and learning computer skills were reportedly primary requisites for career advancement. While some listened to the English news over FM radio while commuting to and from work, others look forward to gaining access to online dictionaries via mobiles.

> I failed in the "welding inspector" exam last year. The American Welding Society, which conducts the exam, gave feedback about my problems in constructing grammatically correct sentences. My friend is using iPhone and it has these industrial terms and their meanings in it. His method is to sneakily note down any new English word spoken to him by someone and look for its meaning in his iPhone dictionary when he's alone. This is the only reason why I have kept iPhone in my [shopping] agenda, although I know it is going to be costly.

Some migrant workers were aware of the potential of the mobile phone to provide information related to their work specialization. Unlike white-collar workers who have simultaneous access to various sources of information during work and unlike low-skilled workers (maids and sales staff) who do not need much work-related information on the fly, semi-skilled workers in our study often needed to clarify technical doubts when on duty, but have no means to do so.

> What we have in our course-related books is only basic information. Anything beyond that can be accessed by going to the Welding Society's website ... It's really vast ... Suppose we want to know what "welding crack" is or, what "welding discontinuity" is, while doing our work ... But we cannot take our laptop to the worksite. So, isn't it amazing if we get information on the phone, on the spot?

Access to the Internet, in addition to helping migrant workers become self-learners, helps them become self-explorers too. Understanding the technicalities of the search function on the Internet is crucial in this endeavor. Since there is much self-learning involved in attempts to locate the right source of information on Internet, those with the right predisposition, knowledge and the technological familiarity, gain a competitive edge.

> When one becomes confident of searching knowledge on Internet, there is no need to worry that "I have only pre-university education." We can learn anything on our own ... move to places like Australia or even America.

Blurring of the Personal and the Professional, Or Not?

While the blurring of lives and livelihoods, as suggested by Donner (2009), was observed, particular instances occurred where migrants maintained a strict distinction between personal social and professional uses of mobile phones. First, Donner (2009) provides us with a critical framework, arguing that the intermixing of personal calls with the professional calls, and vice versa, prompts us to think of how mobile technology blurs lives and livelihoods. In certain cases, we found evidence of this intermixing of calls amongst respondents occurring when workers talk to colleagues at the worksite, who were also their close friends. Confined mainly to co-ethnic networks, a call related to work may be initiated or terminated by asking about personal matters; friendship may be renewed after a professional call.

However, the reverse, personal social calls that included professional contexts, was mainly absent. In the case of low-skilled migrants in our sample, hardly any matter related to work was discussed over the mobile phone once they had left the worksite for the day. We argue that the overlapping of these two dimensions in the usage of mobile phones is minimized in the case of international migrants in particular instances.

Even in the case of workers who could carry phone to their worksites and substantially benefit from its usage, barriers to co-mingle contexts were observed. Unlike in the case of domestic workers in Singapore, a blanket ban on mobile phones in workplaces was absent in the case of blue-collar male workers. However, for some, maintaining the strict dichotomy was desirable, wishing not to carry mobiles to the worksite. The underlying reasoning was that, if a call from home brought them disturbing news while at work, it affected their work for the whole day. They preferred to keep the phone in their dormitory room and catch up with personal matters after each day's work. It is possible that access to mobile phones, rather than being a source of emotional support, increased stress felt by migrants, as discovered by other research (Chib and Wilkin, 2011).

Conclusion

The remarkable growth in mobile telephony, and the resultant "leapfrogging" achieved by mobile technologies by skipping the infrastructural deficits of landline telephony, is a widely reported phenomenon in developing countries. Yet there is more to mobile phones than developmental advantages such as economic progress and career advancement. Personal social contexts do matter, and often more so than instrumental benefits. Mobile phones ensure better communication and information channels for international migrant workers, both within social personal and professional contexts. Strong bonding with family back home and co-ethnic networks in the host country has been caused by plummeting rates of international and local airtime. Mobile broadband offers opportunities for entertainment, social networking, and information gathering.

The personal social context of the mobile phone for migrants could be seen as a gateway for developmental impact. Social uses affect overall well-being of migrants; reducing stress, building credibility, increasing knowledge, and developing social support networks. Over time, these translate into instrumental uses; allowing micro-coordination, developing language and technological skills, garnering technical knowledge, and allowing for inter-organizational communication. The advanced ICT infrastructure prevalent in the developed host country provides good opportunities for the migrant workers to advance careers, and integrate into the information society. However, those who lack the knowledge and skill to access information on mobile phones will be left behind in the long-term advancement of the information society.

At times, financial constraints restrict the users from fully taking advantage of the advanced mobile services offered. However, shared-usage patterns, competitive pricing, targeted subsidies, and promotional policies on the part of mobile service providers, employers, and the government allows the workers to participate in the information revolution that is unraveling with the convergence of different mediums on mobile. A phenomenon that requires further investigation is the sacrifice of "mobile identity" that low-cost-seeking mobile users must make in order to avail of attractive airtime schemes.

Finally, there is sufficient evidence to suggest that there is a fair bit of the "blurring of lives and livelihoods" that occurs. However, we find that specific circumstances arise that motivate mobile users to erect distinct silos in their personal social and professional lives regarding mobile phone usage. While we celebrate the hegemony of the mobile phone in all facets of our lives, as researchers it is worth pondering as to when it is worthwhile to keep our life domains distinct and mobile-free.

15.
RESPONSIBLE INNOVATION, GLOBAL GOVERNANCE, AND EMERGING TECHNOLOGIES
Andrew D. Maynard, Antje Grobe, and Ortwin Renn

The dogma that emerging technologies are essential to economic growth and improvements in quality of life is so ingrained within society that it is almost a truism. Certainly, it is hard to deny the benefits that have arisen from previous "technological revolutions" from as far back as the agricultural revolution to the more recent advents of synthetic chemistry, silicon-based semiconductors and genetic engineering. Yet these and other science and technology-driven innovations have not come without a price (Winston, 2010). From the spread of pandemics to global growth in obesity, and transportation-related fatalities to climate change, many of the challenges facing society today have their roots in past and present social/technological innovations.

Nevertheless, science and technology continue to promise new solutions to tough issues, ranging from access to cheap energy, clean water, and nutritious food to disease treatment and safe housing. The challenge is, and always has been, how to take advantage of the opportunities presented by technology innovation without causing undue harm. This is a challenge that has not always been addressed well in the past— as the continuing consequences of the industrial revolution and other technological advancements attest. In the past, societies have had the advantage of being part of a world where the adverse consequences of technology innovation could be, to a certain extent, absorbed. However, in today's increasingly complex and interconnected world, the opportunities and risks presented by emerging technologies are greatly magnified, meaning that there is little room for making mistakes in their responsible development. And while the consequences of ill-considered or misinformed actions have the potential to impact on all economies, it is perhaps emerging economies that have the most to gain or lose through the responsible or irresponsible development of emerging technologies on the global stage. These are economies that are struggling to build an acceptable quality of life for their citizens. Developing in a sustainable way, and not focusing too narrowly on the logic of accelerating the economic wealth, is one of the key challenges being faced by these economies.

Yet in facing this challenge, emerging economies are often at the mercy of more developed economies. Potential commercial exploitation is always a possibility. But there is a more subtle danger, inherent in "dreams of technology innovation" that more developed economies promote; they can afford to go wrong, but emerging economies cannot. As the rate of technology innovation increases, the interconnectedness of global society evolves and pressures on increasingly limited global resources continue to mount, it will become increasingly important for emerging economies to make science-informed and socially responsive decisions on how technologies are developed and utilized. And this in turn will require critical new thinking on how emerging technologies are governed at the local and global level.

The Emerging Challenges of Risk Governance

At the heart of the governance challenges presented by emerging technologies is the need to develop new knowledge, tools, and frameworks that enable potential and emergent risks to be identified and addressed within a complex sociopolitical context. Traditionally, risk governance has been built around a linear process of risk identification, assessment, and management that has relied on expert input and science-driven decision-making. However, shifts in the global landscape are beginning to undermine the efficacy, responsiveness, and social relevance of this approach. Four factors in particular are coalescing to shake up the context and framework within which effective risk governance is undertaken: *control, coupling , communication ,* and *culture.* These four factors are accompanied by directly opposed processes such as fears or rejections and exorbitant expectations, fortification and nullification, acceleration and deceleration, global and local orientations.

Control

Over the past century, scientists and engineers have developed an unprecedented degree of control over the physical and biological world. Research nearly 100 years ago into how atoms form molecules and materials has gradually led to an increased ability to change the nature of matter through intentional intervention and manipulation at the nanometer scale. In recent years, the combined influences of accelerating knowledge-generation, cross-disciplinary fertilization and technology innovation have pushed back the boundaries of what is possible in terms of engineering matter at the nanometer scale to produce new or enhanced properties at the human scale. As a result, scientists and engineers now have greater control over the matter that surrounds us than ever before in the history of humanity, and this ability is growing at an exponential rate.

Areas such as nanotechnology epitomize this increasing control over matter. By engineering matter at near-atomic scales, scientists and technologists are finding new ways of tapping into nanoscale-mediated materials' properties as they develop new products. The results range from the banal—odor-resistant socks infused with antibacterial silver nanoparticles—to the life-changing—a new generation of cancer treatments that selectively seek out and destroy tumors, for instance. Proponents of nanotechnology claim that we have barely begun to scratch the surface of what can be done using this technology to address challenges like energy generation, water purification, and food production. Yet nanotechnology is only one of a number of emerging technologies that are characterized by increased control over matter. Another is synthetic biology—the synthesis of new genetic codes on computers, followed by their construction and insertion into living organisms in the lab. Synthetic biology concerns increasingly detailed control over an organism's DNA, and holds the promise of being able to program organisms to perform a wide range of functions, from generating biofuels to helping combat disease.

Nanotechnology and synthetic biology are just two of an increasing range of technology platforms that are based on controlling matter over a range of length scales. Individually, these present new risk governance challenges. For instance, as will be discussed below, the potential new health risks presented by nanotechnologies have received substantial attention in recent years. And in the ethical and societal debate in some European countries, fears over citizens losing control over the things that affect their lives, and concerns over scientists "playing God" have been played out around these platforms. However, it is the technology innovations that emerge from the interactions between these emerging platforms and existing technology platforms that will stretch risk governance most fully (see Figure 15.1). The innovations arising from the interface between technology platforms will lead to complex and sophisticated materials, processes, and products that not only present new challenges to understanding and addressing the potential harm they might cause, but also offer new ways to address pressing social and economic issues. Charting a responsible course between these emerging risks and benefits will require a deeply integrated framework for risk governance.

Coupling

The continuing threat of anthropogenic climate change is a stark reminder that humanity's actions are intimately coupled to environmental re-actions. This dynamic relationship between our actions and our environment has epitomized the history of technology

Global Trends	
Climate change, environment, and sustainability	Increasing scarcity and unequal distribution of water
Rapidly growing demand for energy	Corporate global citizenship Limited resources
Limited resources	Social life in a technological world
Shifting centers of economic activity	Demographics, including shifting populations and mobility
Growing demand for food, nutrition, and health	

Technology Innovations			
Vaccines	Carbon sequestration	Smart grids	Better health diagnostics
Advanced sensors	Soil management	Smart materials	High conductivity materials
Next generation electronics	Efficient resources use	Bottom-up manufacturing	Safer nuclear power
Point of use energy generation	Climate control	Renewable energy sources	Substitute materials
Better food preservation	Resilient crops	Immersive communications	Targeted pesticides
Smart drugs	Increased land productivity	High value crops	Biofuels
Water desalination	Thermal insulators	Efficient resource extraction	Water separation
Strong, lightweight materials	Irrigation	Disease management	Sustainable production processes
Automated traffic management	Better batteries	Advanced prosthetics	At-source water purification

Technology Platforms			
Nanotechnology	Synthetic Biology	Information technology	Bio-interfaces
Geoengineering	Robotics	Biotechnology	Web 2.0
Cognitive technology	Computational chemistry	Artificial Intelligence	Data interfaces

Figure 15.1 Relating Technology Platforms to Global Trends through Technology Innovation

innovation. Today's world has been molded by a long series of technology-driven social changes that stretch back to the agricultural revolution, and possibly further. In the past this coupling between technology, society, and environment has been characterized by relatively small perturbations to the system and deep resource reservoirs, which together have had a damping influence on the rate and magnitude of change and have allowed for adaptation. Yet we are entering an era in which the situation is reversed: nearly seven billion people are placing greater than ever demands on rapidly dwindling global resources—a situation that is only exacerbated by technology innovation. As a result, the coupling between society and the global environment is shifting from a quasi-stable state typified by small/slow changes and near-limitless resources to a highly unstable one dominated by large/rapid changes and limited resources. This is leading to a better understanding of the effects of global factors at the local level and has resulted in greater awareness of the importance of sustainability. But it has also increased the instability of economic, social, and environmental systems, and fueled fears over possible results of actions. One of the consequences of this shift will be an increasingly non-linear coupling between societal actions and environmental re-actions, where the impacts of technology-driven change become increasingly hard to predict and control.

Communication

The early years of the twenty-first century have been dominated by a revolution in communication that has redefined social, political, and geographical boundaries. Through increasingly sophisticated web-based tools and other information technologies, people have begun to connect with each other and exert influence within society in new ways. This is illustrated by the extent to which global information flow across blogs and within social media communities such as Twitter and Facebook has begun to change the way geographically distributed groups can influence ideas, behavior, and decisions around the globe. But the communication revolution is also impacting directly on the relationship between business, government and the media, opening up both new opportunities for governance and new challenges (Friedman, 2005; Hajer, 2009).

This changing face of global communications is affecting science and technology in three ways, each of which will have an impact on how emerging technologies are governed. First, advances in modern communication are revolutionizing "peer–peer" and "peer–lay" information exchange. Twenty years ago, seeking out and assimilating scientific information was a physical process. Today, the latest research, together with its associated analysis and interpretation, is no further away than the click of a mouse. And with the increase in open access peer review articles and science blogs, more people have more access to more science and technology-related information than ever before. Researchers have access to vast arrays of new information in their own field, as well as new findings in other disciplines, and this cross-fertilization of ideas and knowledge is driving the generation of new scientific knowledge and technology innovation at an unprecedented rate. Much of this information is also available to non-experts—"lay publics"—and is not, by and large, restricted by geographical boundaries. This democratization and globalization of science is leveling intellectual and decision-making hierarchies. Non-experts can now interact and engage with scientists in new ways. But they can also act on information and influence decisions based on their own assessment and that of their peers—irrespective of whether their evaluations align with those of experts or not.

Second, advances in modern communication are revolutionizing the evolution of ideas. Ideas propagate along lines of communication and influence individuals and groups who come into contact with them. In the past, geographical and technological barriers have limited the growth and impact of new ideas around the world. But with the advent of interactive web-based communication, traditional barriers to the propagation of ideas are being eroded. This emerging interconnectedness is likely to have a profound impact on global society, and specifically on the development and governance of emerging technologies. In effect, the conventional intellectual "command and control" model of technology innovation and governance is disappearing, which means that the debate over how science is done, what areas of science are pursued, and which new technologies are developed (and how) is becoming increasingly public, and increasingly global.

Third, this new global exchange of ideas is leading to decentralization. Advancing communication capabilities are empowering citizens to influence the course of science and technology in ways that transcend traditional boundaries. This was seen to a clear extent with resistance to genetically modified organisms in Europe. This development became more visible in the global dialogues on emerging technologies such as nanotechnology, where civil society groups such as Friends of the Earth Australia and the Canadian-based ETC group have had a global reach, for example on the identification of risk-related issues and regulation, or in the current debate on climate change. The development of decentralized decision-influencing communities presents a growing challenge to traditional hierarchical models of governance. Yet it also empowers previously marginalized groups to participate on the global stage in ensuring the responsible and beneficial development of new technologies.

On the flip side, these three changing areas of communication are fostering a divergence between easy access to virtual information and the desire for clear and unambiguous information in decision-making at the national, local, and personal level. Additional uncertainties and issues arise around the concentration of power and privacy issues associated with the social network companies, the trustworthiness of sources and manipulation of data. These simultaneously diverse and opposing processes and social debates strengthen the need for rethinking risk governance processes at the global level.

Culture

As science and technology advance, global issues become more immediate and awareness of the consequences of technological missteps grows, global expectations of responsible development are changing. This is a shift that spans corporations, governments, small businesses, and individuals, and is being influenced by a complex and interrelated array of social drivers. At the corporate level, there is growing awareness that conventional business models that place profits and shareholders first and foremost are not sustainable in today's changing world. This message was forcibly brought home in the global economic collapse of 2008, but has been reinforced by emerging global challenges and attitudes toward big business. As a result, there is a move toward values-based business models that are increasingly responsive to stakeholders—including citizens. At the same time, citizen expectations of safety— or protection from risk— are growing. These trends, combined with rapid advances in increasingly complex technologies, are leading to a global culture of proactive, integrated, and participatory risk management. Rather than manage the impacts of technology innovation as they arise, businesses, governments, and citizens are increasingly looking to proactive risk assessment and management as tools that support responsible innovation and prevent harm from occurring. As a result, major technology research and development pushes in areas such as nanotechnology, synthetic biology, and geoengineering are increasingly combining developmental research with research into potential health, environmental, and societal impacts. This culture of proactive approaches to risk management and mitigation can also be seen in industry-focused initiatives to support the responsible development of new technologies (DuPont and Environmental Defense, 2007).

On the other hand, companies still have to balance stakeholder demands with shareholder values, and the need to get new products to market in a timely manner competes with the time constraints of engaging in stakeholder dialogue, societal risk appraisal, and the development of regulatory frames. Here again, new approaches to governance processes are needed to balance conflicting needs and pressures.

These four factors—control, coupling, communication, and culture—are profoundly changing the global landscape in which emerging technologies are developed effectively, responsibly, and sustainably. The shift in global dynamic they represent is sufficiently large to require new thinking on global governance of emergent risks; conventional governance frameworks that are built on assumptions of small technological perturbations in large systems and rigid top-down decision-making structures are looking increasingly outdated and ineffective in today's interconnected society. This flattening of the environment within which technology innovation is governed is both good news and bad news for emerging economies. The bad news is that local technology innovation is highly dependent on global factors, and this in turn raises new possibilities for global movements adversely affecting local decisions. The good news is that, with appropriate governance structures, there is an effective flattening of the playing field between emerging and well-developed economies. The challenge will be to develop new governance frameworks that ensure responsible, beneficial, and sustainable technology innovation at the local level, within a global context.

Rethinking Risk Governance for the Twenty-First Century

Complexity, uncertainty, and ambiguity lie at the core of systemic risks that tend to preoccupy modern societies (OECD, 2003). This is particularly true for emerging technologies. In this respect, society is faced with a paradox: on the one hand, innovative cross-disciplinary technologies lead to increasingly complex, uncertain, and ambiguous risk issues, while on the other hand there is the need to make collectively acceptable and binding decisions for a sustainable embedding of these technologies into a societal context. Unfortunately there is no alternative but to address this challenge. It is impossible *not* to make a decision regarding the regulation of new technologies, for instance. Even a moratorium on a given technology constitutes a decision. It is also impossible to avoid complexity, uncertainty, or ambiguity by ignoring evidence or doing nothing. Even silence will be interpreted as an indication of a "message" that will affect and possibly polarize the communication; in Paul Watzlawick *et al.*'s words: "You cannot not communicate" (Watzlawick *et al.*, 1967).

It is no surprise therefore that models, guidelines, and frameworks that might help govern these complex processes are in the focus of academic and public interest. Among them, the Risk Governance Framework developed by the International Risk Governance Council (IRGC, 2005) provides a useful perspective from which to address the governance of emerging technologies in the context of an increasingly interconnected global society. Here, we focus on the IRGC's work on nanotechnologies as an example of emerging technologies risk governance (IRGC, 2005, 2006, 2008, 2009) and its recommendations for an integrated Risk Governance Framework.

The IRGC's work was one of the first risk governance frameworks explicitly applied to nanotechnologies. Intended as a matrix for reflection, the Risk Governance Framework outlines key areas for governing risks; it brings together ideas from a range of disciplines and it articulates some of the major cross-disciplinary tasks inherent in the governance challenges of complexity, uncertainty, and ambiguity. In essence, it provides a model of emerging technologies' risk governance that is applicable both to emerging and established economies in a globalized world dominated by the four factors of control, coupling, communication, and culture.

Premises of the IRGC Risk Governance Framework

By defining *risk* as an uncertain consequence of an event or an activity with respect to something that people value (such as health, safety, or environment; Kates *et al.*, 1985), risk is always a social construct—implying that it is influenced by a mixture of overlapping factors affecting uncertainty. Therefore, a wider understanding of the interconnectedness of the different risk issues is needed for the implementation of appropriate risk management measures. In the development of the IRGC's Framework, a pre-study investigated more than 50 approaches to public problem-solving models and condensed the survey of core criteria to the three premises and four major consecutive stages of the framework model (IRGC, 2005).

The Risk Governance Framework is built on three value-based premises: functional integration, inclusiveness of actors, and normative principles of "good governance" (IRGC, 2005). A key component of the Framework is the consequent integration of the social and communicational factors into the risk assessment and risk management process. "Factual" and "socio-cultural" dimensions are deliberately included in the framework in order to achieve adequate science-based, economically, ecologically, and ethically reasoned decisions. The necessity for an integration of the sociocultural dimension is closely connected to the question of how to create a broader inclusiveness. Here the term *inclusiveness* denotes an early and meaningful involvement of organized, issue-related stakeholders and, in particular, of civil society. Communication among and between the different actors constitutes the core function of the IRGC Risk Governance model. It enables the growth of a shared knowledge base as the foundation for the different phases of pre-assessment, appraisal, characterization and evaluation, and risk management. Communication stands at the core of each of the assessment or evaluation processes because it constitutes the engine that generates substantial results. It also reflects the growing importance of communication in influencing decision-making at the local and global scale within society. Importantly, it is not an "add-on" for defending and announcing findings and decisions. Communication among and between stakeholders is crucial for the success of the framework as a whole (Renn, 2008).

This leads to the third major premise—the "good governance" criteria—as a guiding principle for developing more appropriate risk assessment and management instruments and for initiating more trustful relationships between industry, civil society, and the regulators. The criteria for good governance are transparency, effectiveness and efficiency, accountability, strategic focus, sustainability, equity and fairness, respect for the rules of law, and the need for the chosen solution to be politically and legally realizable as well as ethically and publicly acceptable (IRGC, 2005).

In addition to the normative premises, the IRGC Risk Governance Framework includes two major structural innovations compared with other taxonomies or frameworks.

1.   Inclusion of the societal context. Besides the generic elements of pre-assessment, risk appraisal, risk characterization and evaluation, risk management and risk communication, the framework gives equal importance to contextual aspects. These include the structure and interplay of the different actors dealing with risks; how these actors may differently perceive the risks; and what concerns they have regarding their likely consequences. Linking the context with risk governance, the Framework reflects the role of risk–benefit evaluation and the need for resolving risk–risk trade-offs.
2.   Categorization of risk-related knowledge. The Framework also proposes a categorization of risk which is based on the different states of knowledge about each particular risk, distinguishing between "simple," "complex," "uncertain," and "ambiguous" risk problems. The characterization of a particular risk depends on the degree of difficulty of establishing the cause–effect relationship between an agent of risk and its potential consequences (complexity), the reliability of this relationship (uncertainty), and the degree of controversy with regard to both what a risk actually means for those affected and the values to be applied when judging whether or not something needs to be done about it (ambiguity).

Before applying these normative and analytic criteria to the emerging technologies arena, it is worth describing the different stages of the risk governance framework in more detail and to show their importance to the debate on emerging technologies generally, and nanotechnologies in particular. Here, it should be noted that nanotechnologies are representative of a new way of approaching and engaging in technology-driven societal debate that introduces issues such as complexity, uncertainty, and ambiguity. However, the lessons learned from the development and introduction of nanotechnologies-enabled products hold important messages for the development of increasingly complex technologies within developing and developed economies.

The Risk Governance Framework and Its Application to Nanotechnologies

The IRGC's Framework presents an integrative approach to risk governance that includes four consecutive stages and one continuous activity. The process starts with pre-assessment and problem framing, continues with appraisal—the assessment of risks and concerns—which leads to characterization and evaluation and, finally, to the management phase, which includes implementation (Renn and Grobe, 2010).

Pre-assessment

The purpose of the pre-assessment phase is to capture the variety of mental frames that are associated with a certain risk. This includes indicators, routines, and conventions or value patterns from different stakeholders, their attitudes and associations (IRGC, 2005). This phase should be used as a tool for framing the problem, for designing early warning systems, for screening the knowledge base, and for determining the methods and research protocols for risk and concern assessment—the next stage in the process.

Risk Appraisal

Risk appraisal produces scientific knowledge on the seriousness of a given risk and describes the probable distribution of harmful effects that one might expect if exposed to a material or product (for example) arising from emerging technologies. In this respect, the IRGC Framework (IRGC, 2009) incorporates two dimension (Figure 15.2):

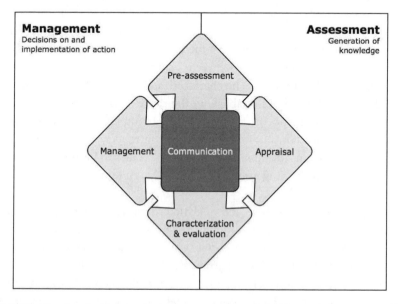

Figure 15.2 The Five Stages of Integrative Risk Governance Proposed by the International Risk Governance Council

1. Risk assessment of measurable physical, chemical, or biological properties (hazard identification and estimation) and the probability of exposure (exposure and vulnerability assessment).
2. Concern assessment of associations and perceived consequences of organized stakeholders and the broader public (risk perception, social concerns, and socioeconomic impacts).

In the context of engineered nanomaterials, most discussions on risk assessment recommendations to date recommend a "case-by-case" approach (Federal Office for Public Health, 2008; German NanoKommission, 2009; NIOSH, 2009; SCENIHR, 2009). A case-by-case approach for the many potential forms of engineered nanomaterials is, of course, cumbersome, and requires major resources and commitments by companies and regulators in terms of testing facilities and time allocation for conducting such tests. In addition, conventional testing strategies and dose-response models are not always adequate for testing the impacts of engineered nanomaterials. Although organizations such as the OECD are working on appropriate measurement protocols and necessary amendments (OECD, 2009), it remains unclear how the complex array of materials permutations potentially presented by engineered nanomaterials will be resolved. This is a challenge that will only increase with the advent of increasingly complex materials at the interfaces between different emerging technology platforms

With respect to concern assessment, nanotechnologies (and by extension, other emerging technologies) reflect the three major risk characteristics that the IRGC model highlights: high complexity, high uncertainty, and high ambiguity. When summarizing the results of the numerous surveys of risk perception regarding nanotechnologies in the United States (Hart, 2007; Kahan *et al.*, 2007), Europe (European Commission, 2006; Federal Institute of Risk Assessment, 2008), Australia (Department of Innovation, 2008) and Japan (Sekiya *et al.*, 2007; Sekiya, 2008), it is clear that the knowledge base and the level of awareness is still low in most industrialized countries. At the same time, most people show positive expectations when asked about the future of nanotechnologies and a majority of people expect that the benefits will outweigh the risks. The majority of the survey participants—independent from their cultural background—do not appraise nanotechnologies based on information or a reasoned risk–benefit-ratio decision. The reasons supporting their attitudes differ, however, from country to country and from study to study. Some authors indicate a general positive attitude toward technology innovation that are extended to nanotechnologies (Grobe *et al.*, 2008); others stress the importance of trust in the actors who advocate nanotechnologies (Macoubrie, 2005), as well as affective or emotional responses and value patterns (Kahan *et al.*, 2008) and long-term religious patterns and short-term media influences (Scheufele *et al.*, 2008). However, all of these interpretations should be treated with caution, due to the different methodologies and questions used (Grobe and Kreinberger, 2010; Renn and Grobe, 2010).

Perceptions surrounding nanotechnologies are also complex and ambiguous as a result of the diverse range of products and applications these technologies can result in. In some surveys, participants had the opportunity to make clear distinctions between desired and undesired fields of application. Other surveys limited their questionnaires to cover general attitudes only. Opposition to nanotechnologies was strongest when military applications were mentioned, followed by the use of nanomaterials in food. The use of nanomaterials in paint and other consumer products were seen as much more benign (Macoubrie, 2005; Department of Innovation, 2008; IRGC, 2008). It is still unclear how attitudes on a single application influence the appraisal of nanotechnologies in their general application. Depending on personal priorities with respect to each application (for example, persons who are particularly sensitive to food risks may generalize their negative attitude toward nanoparticles in food to an overall negative attitude) or the short-term media influences focusing on one application at the time of the survey, the responses to general questions vary from survey to survey.

Given these fluctuations, attitudes appear to be fragile and volatile because they are not founded in solid knowledge but on premature intuition, and because they represent a wide variety of responses as a function of application and wording of the questions. As long as the knowledge base tends to be insufficient and, subsequently, public attitudes remain volatile, the only viable approach to risk appraisal is one of continuous involvement, participation, and dialogue. With nanotechnologies specifically and emerging technologies more generally, we are still at the beginning of a long-lasting process of generating more reliable knowledge. The need to fill the knowledge gaps and to consolidate methods and routines requires more, not less, stakeholder involvement. Such involvement can help to collect and integrate knowledge of all stakeholders and support the search for precautionary but also progressive ways to enable the development of sustainable applications.

Characterization and Evaluation

The stage of characterization and evaluation in the Risk Governance Framework addresses the process of delineating a judgment about the acceptability and tolerability of a risk (IRGC, 2005). A risk is deemed "acceptable" if risk reduction is considered unnecessary, and "tolerable" if it is pursued because of its benefits and if it is subject to appropriate risk-reduction measures (IRGC, 2009). The process of judging includes both a scientific (evidence-based) "risk profile" focused on risk assessment and concern assessment, and a societal (value-based) balancing of benefits and risks.

Considering the uncertainties and ambiguities surrounding emerging technologies such as nanotechnologies (including the lack of appropriate methods and systems to quantify exposures and effects), a systematic process of balancing all the pros and cons would seem far away. However, in spite of these uncertainties and ambiguities, acceptable decisions have to be made. This is at the crux of the dilemma presented by the risk governance of emerging technologies. Again, deliberative methods can play an important role in addressing such difficult evaluation tasks, and they can provide one of the best approaches to balance the interests of those at risk with those who may gain most of the benefits. In the context of nanotechnologies, evaluations of risk have been performed within a number of stakeholder dialogues. One example is the German NanoKommission's preliminary assessment tool that structures nanomaterials in three categories, the so-called "levels of concerns":

- Group 1: probably hazardous—concern level high 1;
- Group 2: possibly hazardous—concern level medium 2; and
- Group 3: probably not hazardous—concern level low 3).

(German NanoKommission, 2009)

Another example is the Swiss Precautionary Matrix for Synthetic Nanomaterials, which uses criteria of relevance; life cycle; potential effects; physical surroundings; and exposure of human beings and the environment (Hoeck *et al.*, 2008). Swiss retailers have strongly recommended that their suppliers use this precautionary matrix if they want to sell products enabled by or produced with nanomaterials. In spite of the vagueness of some of these criteria, the mere attempt to use them and the willingness of the actors involved to monitor effects have certainly increased the awareness of industry to pay more attention to risk-related questions.

Risk Management

Risk management strategies and methodologies aim to reduce or avoid unintended and unacceptable consequences of activities and decisions. Depending on the outcomes of the tolerability and acceptability judgment, measures can be more or less severe. In the context of nanotechnologies, they range from labeling to mandatory insurance to exposure control to potential bans. The risk management phase of the IRGC Framework includes the generation and selection of options and their implementation, together with monitoring outcomes and collecting feedback from stakeholders. In the case of the use of nanotechnologies and nanomaterials in Europe, two major challenges are linked to risk management. First, companies have to follow the precautionary principle if not enough reliable data are available for quantitative risk assessment (the so-called "no data—no market" condition). The majority of companies interpret the precautionary principle as a request to minimize exposure and to apply process and personal exposure protection measures. This is accomplished by the use of a Material Safety Data Sheet for informing customers along the value chain about the characteristics and risks of the material. However, this practice has raised concerns within some stakeholder groups (Friends of the Earth, 2008; Which?, 2008; Friends of the Earth Australia, 2009) as to whether this may be sufficient to ensure human health and environmental safety over the entire life cycle of a material and its related products. Adequate and effective stakeholder inclusion is therefore a significant challenge during the risk management phase of the Risk Governance Framework.

The central question of "how safe is safe enough" is further complicated by a lack of transparency and limited stakeholder involvement. This leads to a second challenge: on the one hand, highly ambiguous risks require adequate stakeholder involvement in order to create tolerable and acceptable solutions, while on the other hand, intellectual property rights of a company set limitations for transparency. The question of how risk management can be evaluated and monitored without providing all the necessary information to regulators and stakeholders while at the same time ensuring that proprietary knowledge is preserved has not yet been adequately resolved. Recent attempts to deal with this challenge with engineered nanomaterials have not been very successful (German Chemical Industry Association and the German Federal Institute for Occupational Safety and Health, 2007; DEFRA, 2008). Several initiatives have been launched to implement monitoring systems (European Commission, 2008a; German NanoKommission, 2009). However, these systems need to be based on reliable and comparable data, and this is exactly where problems arise of first having access to good data and second comparing data that are available—especially where non-comparable definitions and test methods have been used. At this point we are back to the stage of pre-assessment, as this is the phase where knowledge gaps are being identified and where the status quo of the current scientific and societal debate on the definition, on the assessment of risks and concerns, the rationale for judgments and application of management measures of emerging technologies have to be re-evaluated.

Communication

The IRGC Framework places communication—or better, two-way communication (Renn, 2008)—at the center of the risk governance cycle. Communication should enable stakeholders and civil society to understand the rationality (or different rationalities of the stakeholders involved) of the process and the results of the risk and benefit appraisal—even if they have not been directly involved. It is the key to supporting informed choice—not only for consumers and decision-influencers, but also for decision-makers, who are obliged to include "soft issues" such as citizen hopes and concerns in the decision-making process. The two major challenges presented by communication in the context of the IRGC Framework can be described by two antinomies: "the contemporary of the non-contemporary" and "the win and the loss of identity."

The antinomy of "contemporary of the non-contemporary" (Renn and Grobe, 2010) characterizes the challenge of different timeframes associated with technology development, stakeholder awareness/engagement, and public debate. There is an unavoidable time delay between the professional, the stakeholder, and the public due to informational gaps between the three groups. Risk governance specifically addresses this challenge of time integration and inclusiveness. Problems can occur if representatives of civil society call for more transparency and information and this demand cannot be met because scientific results remain preliminary, contested, and uncertain among professionals, or if data are protected by Confidential Business Information laws. Without transparent communication on the reasons why information is withheld, stakeholders will develop a feeling of mistrust and an impression that they are participating in a game of "hide-and-seek" (European Commission, 2007). It should be emphasized that this loss of trust is not the fault of any of the actors in the process but rather is a product of insufficient and ineffective communication arrangements among the actors and between the actors and publics at large. The more obvious knowledge gaps become to stakeholders and members of the public, the more they are likely to demand better information. At the same time, the providers of such knowledge are likely to get increasingly nervous as they face the same problems of uncertainty and ambiguity. However, instead of sharing their doubts and questions with a wider audience, there is a tendency for developers to hide behind either legal provisions (proprietary knowledge) or communication stereotypes such as proclaiming "we will never market unsafe products." Both approaches have the potential to generate even more distrust and suspicion among civil society stakeholders and members of the public. In the case of nanotechnologies, several early dialogues have been organized with the goals of sharing as much information as possible and addressing both the risk assessment results and public concerns at an early stage of the debate. In addition, the call for more deliberative methods and for an integration of scientific analysis and risk perceptions has been echoed in a number of suggestions for codes of conduct on nanotechnologies research and development (European Commission, 2008b; IRGC, 2008). However no parties will be immune from "backlashes," which raises the danger of falling back into old patterns, such as attempting to influence and accelerate decision-making processes behind closed doors, withholding information that may pose challenges with respect to uncertainty and ambiguity—or falling back into traditional lobbying behavior after being armed with more knowledge from dialogue partners, in order to push through a predetermined agenda.

The second antinomy refers to "the win and loss of identities" (Renn and Grobe, 2010), which could similarly lead to disappointments and backlashes. A more successful two-way communication approach occurs when more stakeholders include the patterns and concerns of the other stakeholders in their own considerations, enabling them to reach a common understanding. But this approach increases the risk of each organization losing its identity. However, this danger of an accommodation of identities is true for all stakeholder groups: ensuring a balance between reaching a compromise across various stakeholders and saving one's face if confronted with the expectations of one's own group members is not easy. Yet retaining a strong identity is an important mechanism for helping reduce complexity and ensuring predictable behavior. It is therefore important for stakeholders to keep their identity in a dialogue. There are guidelines available that outline how to facilitate consensus or common agreements without compromising the identity of each group (OECD, 2002; National Research Council of the National Academies, 2008). One of the main requirements is that the whole group is given the opportunity to follow the same learning sequence as the spokespersons in the dialogue process. Constant feedback and transparent processes within dialogues are two major conditions for assuring a parallel learning process between spokespeople and their constituents. Innovative forms of dialogue and public communication are therefore essential in the emerging technologies arena. The call for sustainable innovation with emerging technologies needs to be accompanied by an equally urgent call for innovative communication strategies that bridge the gap between reaching a joint conclusion and saving each partner's identity.

Application of the Risk Governance Philosophy to Stakeholder Involvement

In 2005, the development of the Risk Governance Framework was not targeted toward nanotechnologies in particular, but as shown above, the framework seems to fit right into the present debate on emerging technologies—with nanotechnologies as a specific example—and their risks and opportunities. In this section we return to the three normative assumptions behind the risk governance framework; that is, integration, inclusion, and good governance principles; and discuss how these three premises can be used to analyze and design better stakeholder involvement processes in the area of emerging technologies.

Integration

Starting with the issue of integration, it can be stated that the necessity of taking public perception, value patterns, and social concerns into account is widely recognized at this time— driven largely by experiences in the debate over genetically modified organisms (GMOs). In the context of nanotechnologies, different communications from NGOs (Friends of the Earth (FoE), 2006, 2008; European Association for the Co-ordination of Consumer Representation in Standardization and European Consumers' Organization, 2009; Miller and Scrinis, 2010), companies (L'Oreal, 2008; BASF, 2009) and their associations (European Chemical Industry Council (Cefic), 2008; VCI, 2008; European Cosmetics Association, 2009), public authorities (European Commission, 2007, 2008a), and research programs (European Commission, 2008b) support the conclusion that the concerns of organized stakeholders and the broader public have to be taken into account. Most of these publications stress two sides of integration: the integration of an appropriate scientific knowledge base into risk assessment and evaluation, and the integration of stakeholder values and interests onto risk management and decision-making. Both elements are commonly identified as criteria for societal acceptability of nanotechnologies and, by extension, emerging technologies in general. There is, however, little consensus amongst actors of how best to accomplish this integration. This leads the second issue of inclusiveness.

Inclusion

A growing group of companies, associations, and public authorities are taking part in stakeholder involvement exercises. But it would be much too idealistic to presume that all actors share this proactive attitude. For instance, many chemical or cosmetics companies are much more cautious in the nanotechnology debate and have adopted a policy of "wait and see." Other sectors such as those covering paints, sport equipment, household products, electronic equipment, and the automotive industry are focused more on the benefits of nanotechnologies. Bolstered by the broad acceptance of their products by consumers, they are barely a part of the societal risk debate. This does not mean that the issues they raise are not relevant, just that they are influenced by a different socio-economic dynamic. Nevertheless, recent surveys suggest that the assumption of wide social acceptance is based on optimistic interpretations of potential innovations. However, the majority of interviewed people have not formed persistent attitudes towards nanotechnologies. People at this time tend to estimate that the benefits of nanotechnologies will outweigh the risks. But this could change dramatically if people are exposed to more information about potential adverse impacts. Under these circumstances, attitudes could rapidly move from one extreme to the other. In effect, attitudes to nanotechnologies at this stage in opinion formation are very fragile (Grobe *et al.*, 2008).

In addition, greater stakeholder inclusion is demanded by the stakeholders themselves in areas of prominent emerging technologies development. If this demand is not met, there is the chance that affected groups may mobilize their followers and generate organized opposition to emerging technologies. In this respect, it is in the best interest of all sides to invest in inclusion. There is some evidence for a successful inclusion of critical stakeholders in dialogue exercises regarding nanotechnologies. These exercises were directed toward aligning the strategies for innovative products with defined criteria of acceptability through the entire life cycle (COmparative Challenge of NANOmaterials, 2007; DuPont and Environmental Defense, 2007).

At this time, three challenges of inclusion have to be met: first, the extension of risk assessment dialogues toward including those industries that are using emerging technologies in their products, with the goal to gather consumer-relevant product safety information (European Commission, 2009; German NanoKommission, 2009); second, the early inclusion of political decision-makers in stakeholder dialogues on risk-related questions to avoid different levels of knowledge in the debate on regulation (European Parliament, 2009); and finally, the involvement of experts on ethical questions and societal concerns. Currently, the necessary ethical discourse on nanotechnologies is confined to an encircled group of scientists and very few projects take this issue into the open discourse (NanoObservatory, 2009). This is unlikely to be a productive model for emerging technologies more generally.

Since stakeholder dialogues need a focus of application due to the broad and complex field of emerging technologies, the challenge of integration and the limited resources of all stakeholders generate a need for more coordinated and focused activities directed toward an international (and cross-economy) comprehensive dialogue setting that brings the various actors together to consider the major findings of scientific research, review innovative product developments, and address health, safety, and environmental impacts as well as societal and ethical questions. As described above, the diversity of emerging technologies leads to a higher specification of the working groups, which run the risk of excluding relevant stakeholders. Unfortunately the broader dialogues are targeted to the same community of experts and are therefore often seen as repetitious. Yet it is better to condense forces into a few powerful, broad, and inclusive discourse activities—including political decision-makers—supported by well-coordinated small and effective working groups.

Criteria of Good Governance

The third group of premises are the "criteria of good governance." These criteria are central to successful communication. This section will deal with each criterion individually and relate it to the debate on nanotechnologies specifically and emerging technologies more generally.

"Transparency" is one of the most controversial items in stakeholder dialogues, mostly demanded by NGOs (ETC Group, 2005; Which?, 2008; Friends of the Earth

Australia, 2009) or governmental bodies (FDA, 2007; European Commission, 2008b). It consists of three dimensions. First, it includes reliable market surveillance on what kind of products are produced or enabled by which kind of emerging technology. This creates transparency for public authorities and, in a further step, for consumers and their organizations. Second, it includes "information" about the status of scientific knowledge with respect to potential benefits and risks regarding health, safety, and environment of these technologies and their associated products. Third, "transparent information" about product ingredients is required—especially where a new functional material based on an emerging technology is incorporated into a product. In the case of nanotechnologies, consumers want to know whether products contain, or have been enabled by, engineered nanomaterials, or if they demonstrate novel behavior through the use of nanotechnology. They want to know about the properties, the functionalities, and the effects on health and the environment (Grobe *et al.*, 2008). The overall aim is to enable consumers, regulators, and insurers to make informed choices.

The call for "effectiveness and efficiency" of risk governance processes and especially for a better coordination of dialogues and the information exchange is typical for advanced phases of an inclusive risk debate (OECD, 2009; SCENIHR, 2009). In the first phase of risk governance the focus lies on the establishment of a working dialogue and on the recruitment of the relevant stakeholders. When this is done, the call to be more effective and efficient will immediately arise since some stakeholders are already advanced in knowledge and risk evaluation, while others need more time and expertise to get prepared for the exchange of arguments. Sometimes it is in the interest of one or the other stakeholder to delay the process and demand more time and resources in order to buy time. This situation calls for an experienced and skilled mediator who has experience in dealing with diverse stakeholder groups, understands their needs and strategies, and finds ways to keep the process efficiently moving ahead without losing or offending one of the stakeholders. It is always important to explore the delicate balance between efficiency on the one hand and fairness toward each actor on the other hand. Therefore, effectiveness, efficiency, and fairness have to be seen as belonging to the same package right from the beginning of the risk governance process.

The next criterion is *accountability*, enabling trustful relations between actors and providing a foundation for monitoring and controlling the impacts of risk management outcomes. Accountability implies that claims posed by stakeholders can be substantiated and that scientific results that are brought into the discourse can be validated. The need for accountable facts is mentioned in several codes of conduct addressing nanotechnologies (DuPont and Environmental Defense, 2007; European Commission, 2008b; IRGC, 2008; Responsible Care, 2008; ResponsibleNanoCode, 2008; Bowman and Hodge, 2009; Meili and Widmer, 2010). However, accountability is often limited if the delegates in a dialogue are required to represent a diversity of actors. This may be true for many industrial sector associations, umbrella organizations of the NGOs, or citizen interest groups. It is always possible that, even where consultation processes have been carefully designed and completed, there will be no agreement on the facts, let alone the actions necessary for risk reduction. Furthermore, due to complexity, uncertainty, and ambiguity, the dialogue participants are often confronted with competing truth claims. It is then difficult to decide which of these claims can be taken as valid evidence and which can or should be dismissed. Joint fact-finding is frequently employed in these situations, which may or may not lead to "isles of consensus." This is difficult to predict. One can be sure that it is in the interest of at least one actor to either exaggerate or to underestimate degrees of uncertainty in any situation. What counts as evidence is therefore a subject of intense debate, and often compromises are needed to find an agreement or at least an arrangement of how to deal with competing truth claims.

Due to the unavoidable diversity of interests in addressing the risk governance of emerging technologies, a "shared strategic focus" of the risk governance process is another key criterion for good governance. Similar to effectiveness and efficiency, a shared strategic focus is one of the possible structuring and simplifying elements that are essential for handling complexity, uncertainty, and ambiguity. The term *shared* points to the difference between a societal, dialogue-driven communication approach and a conventional public relations or information strategy. Unfortunately, this conventional strategy is often the preferred route of some stakeholders. Many dialogues have failed because there was no way to find an agreement about the shared strategic focus. For risk governance processes one of the fundamental conditions for success is the task of exploring the common denominator that may link diverse strategic angles and to prepare the ground for finding or constructing a shared strategic focus. Being strategic is not per se a problem for a successful dialogue if it is possible to integrate sometimes-conflicting interests into a superior aim or context that is accepted by all stakeholders. Problems occur though if the strategic perspectives are guided by hidden agendas and only inspired by the goal of speeding up the process of innovation. Another focus should be on an agreement on the procedures and methods for conducting risk assessments, including public concerns, making trade-offs, and identifying the most appropriate risk management options.

Turning to "sustainability," or in general the responsible and sustainable development and use of emerging technologies, one could claim that this could serve as the lead criterion for a shared strategic focus. The overall aim here is to promote innovation in a socially acceptable and legitimate manner so that the technological progress is served and public and ethical acceptability is enhanced. The reason why sustainability as a concept is so attractive to all stakeholders is the inclusion of the three dimensions of ecology, economy, and social aspects (Strange and Bayley, 2008). Therefore, the term *sustainability* has become a main criterion in most of the currently discussed codes of conduct for nanotechnologies, for instance (DuPont and Environmental Defense, 2007; European Commission, 2008b; IRGC, 2008; Responsible Care, 2008; ResponsibleNanoCode, 2008).

Last, but not least, personal relations and the nature of interactions among and between different stakeholders shape the risk governance processes. Deliberating about acceptable risk and appropriate risk management measures relies on a communication style that is characterized by mutual trust and individual accountability of all actors involved in the process. The (IRGC, 2005) Framework mentions the following criteria for characterizing the quality of the decision-making processes: "equity and fairness," "respect for the rules of law," "politically and legally realizable," and "ethically and publicly acceptable."

All the criteria above are important to designing and evaluating dialogues on emerging technologies. The IRGC Framework is inspired by the need for a combination of analytic rigor and deliberative argumentation. This combination has been called an analytic-deliberative style in the literature (Stern and Fineberg, 1996; National Academy of Science, 2008). It presents a framework that can help risk managers to improve the conditions for risk assessments, to include the knowledge and values of the major stakeholders, and to gain public trust in demonstrating accountability and consideration for public concerns.

Risk Governance and Emerging Economies

Without a doubt, the accelerating pace of technology innovation is presenting society with new opportunities to address pressing challenges. Yet as we have discussed, in today's rapidly changing global landscape, the potential benefits of emerging technologies will only be realized through parallel innovations in how they are developed, implemented, and governed responsibly. The confluence of increasing control over matter; unprecedented coupling between human actions and environmental reactions; rapidly evolving communications; and shifting cultural norms and values is demanding a rethink of how new technologies are developed responsibly and sustainably within a global social, political, and economic context. This is a challenge that is being faced by established and emerging economies alike. And because of this, it perhaps provides less developed economies a window of opportunity to leapfrog more developed ones in governance innovation, as they look to exploit both new technologies and the new landscape within which they are arising.

From the perspective of emerging economies, the potential rewards promised by emerging technologies are immense—renewable energy, clean water, nutritious food, revitalized economies, jobs. Yet these economies face many challenges as new technologies emerge, including maintaining control over local resources, ensuring the equitable distribution of benefits and risks, and avoiding getting caught up in the hype surrounding emerging technologies being generated by economies that can afford to get it wrong. Realizing the benefits these new technologies have to offer is a high-risk endeavor, where the dangers of inaction are potentially as significant as those from inappropriate action—for all economies. But the greatest risks are potentially those faced by the poor and the marginalized—those who stand to gain the most from effective governance, and to lose the most through poor governance. Conventional approaches to risk governance have long favored developed economies, placing sometimes severe constraints on the ability of less developed economies to participate effectively on the global stage. Yet the need for innovation in risk governance is creating opportunities to change this dynamic.

Certainly, there is room at the table for new actors as the rules are being rewritten on how the risks of emerging technologies are avoided and the benefits exploited. This is a small but significant opportunity for emerging economies to contribute to new frameworks that support more equitable approaches to risk governance. The challenge remains though of developing new global frameworks that are built on a philosophical foundation that does not discriminate against emerging economies. In this, the risk governance framework developed by the IRGC offers some hope.

The IRGC Risk Governance Framework explored here is one of the first attempts to consider risk governance in the face of increasing complexity, uncertainty, and ambiguity, driven by a technologically advanced, resource-constrained, and interconnected society. While the framework is not specific to any particular stage of economic development or technology, it is highly relevant to responding to the challenges being faced by emerging economies in a globalized world. Perhaps most importantly, the framework's inclusion of the social context within which risk is governed, and its distinction between "simple," "complex," "uncertain," and "ambiguous" risk problems help to establish a model for addressing new risks in emerging economies within a changing social, economic, and political context. In particular, its emphasis on stakeholder inclusion and dialogue sets the stage for effective risk governance in a future that will be increasingly influenced by the confluence of the four factors of control, coupling, communication, and culture. And underpinning the framework, its three philosophical premises—integration, inclusion, and criteria of good governance—support a governance approach that reduces disparities between participants, and lowers the chances of minority voices being lost in the noise.

Looking to the future, the accelerating rate of technology innovation and socioeconomic change is demanding new approaches to risk governance. Irrespective of whether the IRGC approach is followed or alternatives are adopted, sustainable and responsible development will depend on innovation in how risks and benefits are handled in a technologically uncertain and socially complex environment. This shifting landscape favors emerging economies as innovators and early adopters of effective governance frameworks that are more responsive to modern challenges. The degree to which this advantage will be exploited remains uncertain. But given the potential opportunities and challenges being presented by emerging technologies, it is an advantage that is unlikely to be passed over.

16.
RISK PERCEPTION, PUBLIC PARTICIPATION, AND SUSTAINABLE GLOBAL DEVELOPMENT OF NANOTECHNOLOGIES

Barbara Herr Harthorn, Christine Shearer, and
Jennifer Rogers[1,2]

This chapter examines some of the barriers that are likely to limit the promised benefits of emerging technologies aimed at the poor, with a particular focus on the risks (and the public perception of risks) that such technologies might pose. These risks are not just physical: a fully realized "responsible development" of these technologies requires not only equitable access to their benefits, but also assessment and equitable control of their risks and potential harm. Thus in addition to technical risk assessment, which is essential, a key component is establishing genuine two-way communication and mutual understanding between technology experts and publics about the potential "social risks" posed by seemingly beneficial technologies. *Social risks* refer to situated social and cultural meanings of promised new technologies, and hence go beyond the technical, physical characteristics of the new materials and technologies. This chapter reports on a project that is intended to shed light on such social risks through combining publics' perceptions and beliefs about the use of nanotechnologies with those of experts. The basic premise of this chapter is that eliciting the views of the broader public reveals hopes and concerns often unconsidered by experts, which can help elucidate the various social risks posed by new technologies like nanotechnologies. Understanding, assessing, and minimizing these social risks, in turn, are important steps toward building up public trust and acceptability, key elements for responsible and successful development.

We draw on environmental, health, and social risk perception research conducted by the risk perception research groups led by the lead author at the Center for Nanotechnology in Society at UCSB (CNS-UCSB) and the UC Center for Environmental Implications of Nanotechnology (UC CEIN) on global industry environmental health and safety (EH&S) practices, public deliberations in the United States and UK, and public risk perception research in the United States and comparative other countries. This chapter draws in particular on the public deliberations conducted in the United States/UK in 2007 and in the United States in 2009; both sets focused on nanotechnologies for health, human enhancement, energy, and the environment. An emerging theme from these studies is the central importance of understanding cultural values about fairness and equitability that underlie technological risk perceptions and beliefs. Aspects discussed by participants and in this chapter include the need for information and education (of both publics *and* experts); desires for regulation by industry, government, and various publics; trust enhancing and trust diminishing factors important to the process of equitable development, and the degree to which public deliberation and participation can effectively contribute to safe and responsible technological development.

This chapter is based primarily on research that is comparative and international but not yet global in scope; nonetheless, these findings regarding issues of multicultural diversity and risk governance in the global North have implications for the South. Understanding and addressing publics' diverse views are essential to regulating risk and addressing ethical concerns. The upstream context for research on publics' views, wherein the majority of US, European, Japanese, and really, global publics continue to know little or nothing about nanotechnologies, makes this particularly challenging social research, but also allows for anticipation and addressing of emerging public hopes and concerns.

In the research discussed in this chapter, qualitative and quantitative social science methods are used to inform one another in developing knowledge about the range and prevalence of cultural beliefs, views, attitudes, feelings, perceptions, and ideas held by different populations. Thus, qualitative research in the form of expert interviews, mental models interviews, and deliberative workshops enables the exploration of cultural knowledge systems of scientists, regulators, and publics about technologies, risks, and forms of anticipated benefits, as well as ideas about regulation and responsibility. Quantitative research uses experimental phone, mail, and web-based surveys of specifically defined and wider representative samples to generate a picture of both particular and broader distributions of risk beliefs and attitudes across populations of US publics, global nanomaterials industries, and North American scientists and regulators.

Benefit Perceptions versus Risk Perceptions

While nanotechnology risk perception and attitudes are being studied by a range of scholars (Cobb and Macoubrie, 2004; Kahan, 2009; Lee *et al.*, 2005; Macoubrie, 2006; Scheufele *et al.*, 2007; Siegrist *et al.*, 2007b), the work in the CNS-UCSB has shown that benefit perceptions, in particular, have not been given adequate critical attention. Most important, it is clear in the nanotech case that technological advances that experts assume will be seen as "benefits" are not necessarily what different sectors of the public want or need. This is not only the case for nanotechnology. In one stark example about biotechnology's acceptability in Europe, Gaskell argues that, contrary to widespread views about risk aversion in Europe, it was not necessarily biotech risks that impaired biotechnologies' acceptability in the public's eyes in Europe, but rather the lack of perceived benefits of such technologies over existing food technologies (Gaskell *et al.*, 2004). Similarly, a survey of nano food applications found lack of perceived benefits was a significant factor in public hesitation to buying food and food packaging enhanced with nanotechnology (Siegrist *et al.*, 2007a; Siegrist, 2008). Early warnings from research about nanotechnology food applications (ours and others') indicate US and European publics see benefits of nanotechnologies for food accruing primarily upstream in the value chain, e.g. grocers benefit by longer product shelf life, while the publics assume the risks downstream (Satterfield *et al.*, 2011).

From research on risk and blame (Douglas, 1992; Harthorn and Oaks, 2003), and analysis of past risk controversies such as amplified public perceptions of the risks of nuclear power, genetically modified food, BSE, and foot-and-mouth disease, to name just a few (Pidgeon *et al.*, 2003), it is well documented that a social context highly likely to produce risk controversies is when the risk makers (e.g. decision-makers, science, and industry) are *not* the same as the risk takers or risk exposed (e.g. workers in technology production industries, members of the communities where industry is sited, downstream consumers, and those exposed to related environmental risks such as waste treatment processes; Bennett and Calman, 2007). One example of this is when a government decides a product is "safe" (enough) and hence does not regulate risk, as in the case of BSE in the UK; later evidence indicated that consumers (or workers or the environment) were actually harmed (economically, health-wise, and/or socially), and, even worse, lied to about the risks (Bennett and Calman, 2007; Leiss and Powell, 2004). This scenario of *involuntary exposures* has played out over and over in the history of technological developments (Slovic, 2000), and the most likely outcome is extensive public backlash, with accompanying stigmatization of the technology. This discrepancy between the risk and benefit views of technology beneficiaries and risk recipients is particularly acute under conditions of great inequality, for example when benefits are presumed by those in the global North without reference to differences that matter in situ, such as access, cost, added value, availability of existing and effective technologies (particularly locally produced ones), where such technologies stand in people's hierarchy of needs, and whether the industries producing them create or deplete local jobs, environmental quality, and community infrastructure. To address this discrepancy, experts and policy-makers need to engage with, listen to, and incorporate views of the risk exposed, particularly those with little agency or choice, as a structured aspect of responsible development. However, this simple prescriptive statement belies the complexity of fully realized public engagement and participation.

It is also important to note that perceived risk and perceived benefit are *not* mutually exclusive views. Research demonstrates that views can be (and often are) highly ambivalent, and one form ambivalence takes is of strong perceived benefit mixed with significant levels of fear and anxiety about possible negative consequences (Corner and Pidgeon, 2010). For example, in a survey of the UK public about genetically modified foods, Pidgeon *et al.* (Pidgeon and Poortinga, 2006; Pidgeon *et al.*, 2005) found concurrent high levels of both perceived benefit and perceived risk, indicating that cognitive assessments of the value of GM food were highly positive, but were accompanied by comparably high levels of fear about their potential for harm. In this case, potential for harm included perceived likelihood of government mismanagement. Thus, although important, benefit judgments alone are also not sufficient for assessing the range of public views about the implications of new technologies.

Broader surveys on public views concerning nanotechnology also suggest mixed views. In a meta-analysis of the full body of published nanotech quantitative survey research in the United States, Canada, Europe, and Japan, familiarity with nanotechnology across these nations was low (65 percent knew little or nothing). The study shows a benefit frame dominating over a risk frame. In the case of new nanotechnologies, the conditions of low awareness among the public about the technologies also produce confusion and uncertainty about what is happening and who will be most affected (on both benefit and risk issues), as evidenced by a large minority (44.1 percent) of respondents who say they are "unsure" about whether the risks will exceed the benefits or the benefits exceed the risks (Satterfield *et al.*, 2009). This large group that strongly resists expressing a judgment is undecided, awaiting more information, and more knowledge. This seems eminently reasonable, given shortfalls in both EH&S knowledge and regulation and other risk analyses, as demonstrated by the cases of involuntary exposure discussed earlier.

The Media and Public Perception

To what degree are these public views being shaped by the media? Social scientists look to media news coverage about risks to understand what messages the public are receiving about new technologies and to assess what impact these have on public views and perceptions (Leiss and Powell, 2004). With nanotechnology, the media contribute to the unfamiliarity and uncertainty effects cited above because, over the past decade, coverage has continued to be relatively low in volume (in the United States and abroad) and has lacked a dominant framing to provide clarity (Friedman and Egolf, 2005; Weaver *et al.*, 2009). In addition, there is evidence of some diminished attention to risks concerning emerging nanomaterials and technologies. For example, although an increasing number of scholarly scientific toxicological articles discuss the potential risks that specific engineering nanomaterials such as carbon nanotubes (CNTs), cerium oxide, or quantum dots may pose to environment or health (Ostrowski *et al.*, 2008), there is not necessarily rising concern about risks evident in media coverage of nanotechnologies. Research by CNS colleague Bruce Bimber and his students has tracked the pattern of print media coverage in the United States and the frames deployed (Weaver and Bimber, 2008; Weaver *et al.*, 2009). They have identified four main frames or explanatory themes used by elite newspapers to talk about nanotechnology, with the early days after the 2000 announcement of the US National Nanotechnology Initiative dominated by a Progress Frame, and to a lesser extent by Generic Risk, nonspecific mention of risk that does not focus on social risks. Generic Risk was found to be most common over all the time period studies, but with emergent Regulation and Conflict frames driving down the Progress Frame from 2004 to 2006, and decline in the amount of print media news coverage from 2007 to 2008 (Weaver *et al.*, 2009), which has continued, including into 2009–10 in the United States and UK (Friedman, personal communication). Compared with media coverage of the early days of nuclear power, the early years of nanotech coverage have somewhat more cautiously framed the benefits of nanotechnologies, showing a certain degree of prudence about hyping the technologies and a more realistic risk communication strategy (Freudenburg and Collins, 2010). The overall picture indicates that different media actors, much like many members of the public, are still assessing the information on nanotechnology, without committing wholly to a progress or risk framework. This upstream moment provides a unique opportunity for policy-makers to assess and address emerging public concerns, since the media has not yet put forward a strong, persistent frame.

Public Perceptions of Nanotechnologies

What are some emerging public views concerning nanotechnologies? There are three main areas that the work of the CNS-UCSB and UC CEIN have demonstrated, two of them with direct connection to fairness issues and the third indirectly linked. First, *inequality and discrimination* are fundamental issues in acceptability judgments. Second, closely related to social inequality and injustice, *trust* is a vital issue in people's judgments about risks and benefits. And finally, the particular *applications* of nanotechnologies (e.g. nanotechnologies for energy, environment, health, or food) are critical contextual features. Taken together, these social factors in public judgment production can often override the more narrowly defined technological advancement issues that form the basis for many experts' assumptions about public benefit perception (Engeman *et al.*, 2010; Harthorn *et al.*, 2006).

Perceptions of Inequality and Discrimination

CNS-UCSB US nanotechnology public perception survey research (2008, $n = 1,100$) revealed considerable sensitivity on the part of the US public to global fairness issues. In experimental framings, equitable global distribution of benefits is consistently associated with higher acceptability ratings. Similarly, distribution of benefits specifically to the world's poor also increases acceptance ratings among US respondents; and, asymmetrically, distribution of harm inequitably (by class or race or by location in the developing world) can lead to unacceptability (Satterfield *et al.*, 2011). Gender and race differences produce significant differences in risk judgments, with women and people of color demonstrating consistently higher perceived risk (Conti *et al.*, 2011). This finding reproduces past research on gender and vulnerability (Satterfield *et al.*, 2004) and has been correlated to experiences of injustice and perceived vulnerability (Conti *et al.*, 2011).

Issues related to social justice and inequality also permeate the research findings of the CNS public deliberation workshops held in both the United States and in the UK. Fairness and social justice, rather than physical risk governance, appear to be the most important issues to many members of the public. Indeed, it is not too strong a statement to assert that structural inequalities and structural violence (Farmer, 2003), which refers to institutionalized social orders that expose people to danger or prevent them from meeting their basic needs and then compound this injustice by failing to provide access to remedies such as health care or due process, could be the largest threat to public acceptability of new nanotechnologies in the global North. Distributional justice issues include concerns about who will benefit and who will have access to desired enhanced technological capabilities and anxiety over who will be excluded from access, as well as risk concerns about who will be directly or indirectly harmed—by unanticipated problems, by purely profit-motivated industrial practices, by pricing and targeting. Procedural justice concerns about fairness over how people will be treated is less evident a concern in this upstream context, although it will almost certainly rise as the technology moves downstream, controversies arise, and decision-making becomes more evident (Dietz and Stern, 2008). In any case, cultural ideals and values about inequality and discrimination in the technological realm signal significant potential concerns.

In qualitative small group deliberation research conducted in 2007, comparative US/UK workshops on energy and health applications found far more unmitigated enthusiasm for energy applications in both countries, while health and enhancement technologies aroused considerable concerns about distributive justice and potential government and industry mismanagement (Pidgeon *et al.*, 2009). In the energy application workshops, researchers found that the global North was seen by the overwhelming majority of participants as wasteful and self-indulgent; the global South was seen by these same participants as completely justified in wanting to have a comparable share of global resources and the ability to industrialize. This situation represents a kind of *equitability conundrum*, whereby global North participants viewed more and more abundant energy as the only acceptable solution, since virtually all participants rejected both conservation and global redistribution of energy resources as outside the realm of possibility, either politically or culturally. Health applications such as molecular targeted drug delivery for cancer treatment or inexpensive, low energy diagnostic sensors suitable for use in remote developing world contexts evoked ambivalent views—the technologies themselves were seen as beneficial, and the latter were seen as socially just, while complex nanoscale medical devices for internal drug delivery were seen as likely too expensive to benefit everyday people in either the United States or the UK (Pidgeon *et al.*, 2009). For some, new health application nanotechnologies even raised concerns about exacerbating existing social inequality: "If we do not get this readily available to everyone, we are liable to create a society made up of two races, the wealthy nanoprotected and then those that are not are not able to access the possibilities" (CNS-UCSB, US Health deliberation workshop, October 2009, female respondent).

In survey research, generic nanotechnology is seen as most acceptable, but when any specifications are added, even benefit features, acceptability declines. Contextual factors such as nanotechnology application or deeper cultural attitudes about domains within which applications are viewed (e.g. environment or health) have profound effects on judgments about risks and benefits of technologies designed to deploy in those domains, and need to be part of the discussion about any technological "solutions" formulated by the global North for dissemination (and consumption) in the global South. Indeed, in 2006 Zimbabwean residents participated in focus groups held by Demos, Practical Action, and the University of Lancaster, to discuss nanotechnology for cleaning water with scientists from around the world. Rather than just focus on the science of the new water cleansing applications, the residents raised distributive justice concerns around access and accessibility, issues that might not have been as thoroughly addressed with input from just scientists or participants in the global North (Grimshaw *et al.*, 2006).

As indicated above, gender (and race) differences are an enduring but often ignored aspect of technological risk perception, and nanotechnology is no different. This oversight is an area of particular concern around social risks, given the mismatch between the risk makers and risk exposed discussed earlier. Different social locations are highly predictive of different relative acceptability, and gender in particular has a strong persistent effect (Conti *et al.*, 2011; Satterfield *et al.*, 2011). Technological development can contribute to and exacerbate existing inequalities such as gender discrimination. For example, a recent comparative study of community organizing in Sweden and India found somewhat unsurprisingly that in India gender discrimination was endemic but that community organizations by women activists are providing both support and strategic inroads. However, the study also argued that things were far from equitable in Sweden as well, and that women were consistently impeded from participation in gender-based community organizations because the latter flew in the face of Swedish ideals of "equity" (Arora-Jonsson, 2009). The comparative study shows the importance of location and historical context to understanding gender equality and discrimination. Additionally, because discrimination operates differently in each social context, it is important to address the relationship between technological development and existing inequalities.

Risk and Trust

Trust is closely related to fairness, vulnerability, and risk perception regarding technologies. In particular, CNS-UCSB research has found that trust (about distributive justice for benefits and for risks, procedural justice, and science and technology development more broadly) is diminished by perceived recreancy, or the inability of organizations to live up to public expectations (Freudenburg, 1993), and enhanced by scenarios about adequate regulation and citizen involvement (Corner and Pidgeon, 2010; Satterfield *et al.*, 2011). In 2007 US–UK comparative deliberations, both US and UK publics indicated a trust vacuum (also called by some a "trust deficit"), with UK publics signaling significant mistrust of their government to handle risks safely and honestly, citing cases of being directly lied to by government in the handling of the BSE crisis, and US publics proving highly skeptical about the likelihood of corporate management of risks for the benefit of society:

> Humans should not be used as guinea pigs, and sure these are new technologies have got fabulous possibilities, but it's not fair or reasonable to just hoist them on us without our knowing and having the opportunity to say yes or no. I don't want that as part of my world.
>
> (CNS-UCSB, US Energy deliberation workshop, September 2009, female respondent)

Cross-cultural differences in trust narratives emerged in the CNS-UCSB study of US–UK nanotech deliberation. Distrust was found in the United States to be more general and diffused, while it was more focused with recent historical anchors for the UK. Recreancy is closely related to trust and similarly problematic; it is in many respects the other face of responsibility. UK participants were much more concerned about scientists' and government's failings, while the US discussion about recreancy and lack of trust focused more intensely on corporations, but both were seen as problematic organizations/institutions through either incompetence, unforeseen consequences, or intentional misuse (e.g. many US respondents think government is manipulated and controlled by corporations, hence not serving the public; UK respondents cited cases like BSE where government had information indicating serious potential risks to the public and lied). Nanoscience and technology development (and technological progress more generally) were pictured vividly as a large, runaway car, in need of regulation and control:

> When it comes to nanotechnology, I would trust a system that has, using the car as an analogy, a brake as well as an accelerator ... The accelerator works just great now as far as I can tell from reading things that you brought, from talking with the experts, *I'm much less convinced that there's a braking mechanism.*
>
> (CNS-UCSB US Health deliberation workshop, February 2007,
> male respondent; italics added)

Some US participants in the 2009 deliberations were skeptical of the motivations behind technological development:

> I think that developing new technologies is great. I think one of the things that are missing the most is the motivation in terms of what are you going to do with it? Are we going to exploit small countries? Is it for profit? Are we concerned about the waste matter later on?
>
> (CNS-UCSB US Energy deliberation workshop, September 2009,
> male respondent)

The issue of trust, however, can be addressed. In a 2008 CNS-UCSB US public perception survey, the public indicated their trust will decrease (by larger increments) if industry refuses to voluntarily report engineered nanomaterials' (ENMs) toxicity and if the government declares there is no need for nano regulations. Trust will increase (by smaller increments) if an environmental group calls for a ban on selling nano products, a program is established to provide consumer health guidelines for nano products, industry mostly complies with new regulations to register nano products, or if an independent watchdog organization promises to investigate public complaints against nanotech companies (Satterfield *et al.*, 2011). Thus, the implications are that in the United States industry and government are both currently seen as untrustworthy to manage technological risks wisely and safely, that NGOs and independent citizen organizations are seen as more trustworthy actors in these domains, and that trust increases if industry is compliant with regulations and responsive to public concerns.

Building trust enhancing technological development into regulatory and multistakeholder organizations may be essential—the work on the cultural contexts of the many different parts of the world represented in this volume has really not yet begun.

These findings are therefore suggestive but should absolutely not be taken to be universal. Some critics point out that much of the current focus on public engagement and deliberation is aimed as an intervention to deal with the "trust deficit" and hence gain (engineer) public acceptance of nanotechnologies, rather than motivated by a genuine desire to engage in two-way communication (Kearnes and Wynne, 2007). The politics of public engagement is much in discussion in Europe, and the research there on debating new technologies strongly suggests that genuinely addressing public concerns can begin to build up public trust, and that trying to coerce public acceptance without actually addressing public concerns will only lead to further distrust.

Another matter of importance to participants in deliberative research was fairness management, or what others have called "distributive justice" and "procedural justice" (McComas *et al.*, 2008). Research on social and cultural values ("ethics") about inequality should underpin our knowledge production about risk, perception, and responsibility because they so profoundly affect the way people make sense of these aspects of technological development. In this research, ideas about social risk were robust even in the absence of specific technical knowledge, even when people (especially women and people of color) *underestimated* their preparedness to deliberate. That is, a majority of participants in 2007 and 2009 workshops consistently valued the idea of public deliberation and participation in technological decision-making, while nonetheless consistently devaluing their own capacities to do this, which they assumed to require extensive scientific knowledge and training. The US public participants in our deliberative research have not had a clear idea about processes for public participation (what Gastil has noted as lacking "deliberative habits" (Gastil, 2008)), and hence the mechanisms and cultural knowledge for "collective consent" are lacking. This is an essential issue from an ethical standpoint. In the 2009 workshops, participants almost universally disclaimed trust in the public (in general, not themselves) to deliberate effectively about science and technology. Comments like "I don't think I know enough [to deliberate nano], and I don't think the general society just in the United States knows enough, let alone the world" (CNS-UCSB US Energy deliberation workshop, September 2009, female respondent) were common, yet participants offered important feedback in the workshops, including views that are often overlooked or neglected. Thus, their own expertise as social risk evaluators was opaque to them, even as they produced meaningful, experientially based judgments and interpretations of likely effects of particular nanotechnologies on them, their families, their society, and the larger global world. This effect of what the authors call *deliberative doubt* would likely be amplified in the developing world and signals an array of issues about how participation and perceptions might be sought and incorporated into global responsible technological development. Indigenous and local knowledge is often ignored in democratic, sustainable science:

> Global knowledge about environmental degradation has to be coupled with local knowledge to produce sustainable solutions. In the quest for sustainability, "universal" knowledge must be connected to "place-based" knowledge. As a corollary, indigenous or traditional knowledge is recognized as a cumulative body of knowledge that can provide alternative,

local perspectives. Science and traditional knowledge should be coupled in order to realize a more equitable partnership as well as mutual learning.

(Bäckstrand 2003a, 2003b)

Thus, public participation is vital, but the processes for achieving this are murky, even in a deliberative democracy. UK participants were more savvy about deliberation, which is primarily a northern European practice, but they were if anything more skeptical than those in the United States about public deliberation as a pathway to political change.

Another key justice issue concerns public participation as a form of *collective consenting* (Harthorn *et al.*, 2011). As seen above, this process needs to engage and address the diverse voices that historically have been overwhelmed by dominant "white male biased" techno-enthusiasts, particularly those of women and other minorities. These processes, which have only recently been studied in the global North, are essential to the project of sustainable (i.e. socially sustainable, or responsible) technological development. If you accept that consenting by "risk takers" is part of responsible development (especially, as above, when the "risk takers" are different from the "risk makers"), then it is all the more imperative that diverse voices need to be part of this process. Consensus processes may suppress difference (and the innovative problem solving different points of view can contribute), and researchers in the global North, even in a large multicultural nation like the United States that has a long history of struggle with such issues, have not begun to understand and propose adequate methods for engaging fully with the pronounced differences in risk perceptions and attitudes, for example by gender (and race/ethnicity)—those comprising much of the 44 percent of the survey populations who are "unsure" about risks versus benefits (Satterfield *et al.*, 2009).

To briefly recap, this chapter has argued for the importance of cultural values that underlie risk perceptions and beliefs, the need for information and education (by experts and publics), including information about modes of deliberation, and public deliberation and participation as a critical pathway to safe and responsible technological development. Fairness, justice, and attention to perceived social risks are arguably the foundation for socially sustainable development, whether in the global North or the global South.

How far can these findings, based on research in the global North, extend to the global South? Globalization has certainly increased transnational migration and the reproduction of working and living conditions that may have more parallels associated with the South than the North, for example among Mexican-origin farmworkers in rural California (Harthorn, 2003). Gathering a diversity of views in the North, therefore, may better gauge responses in the South as well as the North. This work, however, is framed with the understanding derived from cross-cultural studies, and thus *anticipates* the challenges of addressing the politics of difference and working across significant economic and cultural divides. In numerous respects, engaging publics, addressing diverse cultural and political values, and *fully* understanding perceived benefit and risk related to nanotechnology development in the global South will entail new research and hybrid approaches, led by or fully partnered with researchers and groups in those countries, and ongoing commitment to dialogue between North and South. This volume represents a needed first step in that direction.

17.
GLOBAL GOVERNANCE OF EMERGING TECHNOLOGIES
From Science Networking to Coordinated Oversight
Mihail C. Roco

The accelerated development of novel products and services through new technologies and their large scale applications in industry, medicine, and environment is a major trend at the beginning of this century. Developing countries have a primary interest participating in this endeavor while there are risks to under-realize the opportunities because of immediate economic challenges and limited institutional capacity, infrastructure and access to information. This chapter suggests a call for action for better taking advantage of this outstanding opportunity by the developing economies in the global context. One of the most dynamic areas—nanotechnology—will be used for several illustrations.

Emerging and Converging Science and Technology: A Source of General Wealth

The history of humanity is closely related to introduction of advanced tools for production, health, and safety. Science and technology currently is the main and increasingly powerful source of tool improvement. Typically, the introduction of new tools affects at the beginning a small fraction of potential users. However, when successful, such new tools reach the masses in the longer term. New technologies may create differences among potential users at the beginning. However, such differences may be diminished in time and even become sources of general wealth as they progress and become ubiquitous if proper governance is in place. For illustration, the use of the Internet—a high concern for inequalities in the 1980s—is now an essential tool for democratization of society. In the long term, the intrinsic progress of all countries is correlated to science and technology and the most added value tools are created by emerging technologies. National and global governance (Roco, 2008; Roco and Bainbridge, 2003; Varmus *et al.*, 2003) determines the speed of introducing emerging technologies and how the distributions of benefits are made. Both developing and developed countries have a strong interest in advancing emerging technologies even if the selected topics, time scales, and other aspects may receive a different emphasis. For example, the two long-term visions for nanotechnology (Nanotechnology Research Direction, 1999, for 2000–2010 (Roco *et al.*, 1999), and Nanotechnology Research Directions, 2010, for

2010–2020 (Roco *et al.*, 2010)) include equally developing and developed countries, and more than half of the countries with national programs established since 2001 are in developing or transitioning countries. Specific issues for developing countries and concerns of possible increase of differences between countries have been formulated in several reports since 2001 (Roco, 2001; NSF, 2004; Salamanca-Buentello *et al.*, 2005; Barker *et al.*, 2005; Bürgi and Pradeep, 2006; Renn and Roco, 2006; Bello, 2007; Kay and Shapira, 2009).

Scientific knowledge is growing exponentially and coherence of various multidisciplinary areas leads to emerging and converging technologies. Technology integration is a key trend and main source of added value in the first part of the twenty-first century. One may identify three main poles of technology integration based on the relative size of human dimension to specific tools. First, there is the convergence from the material nanoscale of the synergistic combination of nanotechnology, biotechnology, information technology, and cognitive sciences (NBIC) (Roco and Bainbridge, 2003). Second, there is technology integration about human dimensions including physical-virtual systems interactions, human-environment and human-machine interfaces. Third, technology integration applies for very large systems as compared to the human dimension, with many interactive components, is best characterized by complex behavior where the available tools have only limited measuring and transformative capabilities. Examples are geoengineering, space exploration, and integration of large infrastructure.

Functions of Global Governance

Governance approach of emerging technologies has several particularities. Four functions need to be implemented simultaneously (Roco, 2008):

- The holistic and long-term, upstream, sustained view is needed in planning (visionary function). New models are required for organization and business. The disturbance of the self-regulating ecosystem may have both positive and negative effects in the short term.
- Developing partnerships across disciplines and sectors of activity are based on a global view (inclusiveness function). Participation and collaborative governance of multiple stakeholders, producing/using/or bystanders of new technologies, is required more than ever before.
- Results in the short and long term are needed (transformative function). This is realized through investment policies; support for science and innovation policies; earlier transdisciplinary and global education and workforce training; and supporting the transformational tools and organizations
- Addressing societal needs and nanotechnology EHS and ELSI, including preparing regulations and oversight (responsible function). Risk governance has to be done earlier, and with larger uncertainty, and by considering unexpected and even irreversible implications. Regulation may be an enabling or constraint of technological innovation—these are two sides of the same coin (Renn and Roco, 2006). Innovation in emerging technologies has higher perceived uncertainties

and risks. There is a need of specific nomenclature, standard setting, informatics and regulations to be coordinated among disciplines, sectors of the economy and countries.

Several strategies for improving outcomes identified for nanotechnology for R&D investments (Roco, 2001) are true for other emerging and converging technologies:

- Countries are encouraged to adopt R&D focus areas, programs, and approaches as a function of country-specific or regional conditions.
- Education and training of people should start earlier and are primary conditions for long-term success.
- The common scientific and technical challenges and priorities addressing broad humanity goals should be a priority for emerging technologies; international collaboration is essential.
- Without manufacturing or other productive outcomes, emerging technologies are not sustainable in the long term.
- Broad partnerships and platforms enabling complementary activities, multi-disciplinarity and integrative activities are important factors for successful outcomes.

Several possibilities for improving the governance/organizations of converging technologies in the global self-regulating ecosystem are recommended:

- Using open-source and incentive-based implementation mechanisms.
- Establishing corresponding science and engineering platforms with multiple applications.
- Empowering the stakeholders and promoting partnerships among them.
- Developing methods and institutional capacity to address unexpected consequences.
- Institute voluntary, science-based and data-based measures for risk management, as well as risk assessment of revolutionary discoveries.
- Coordination of standardization, patent policies, regulation, and oversight among countries using bilateral agreement (as are now in development between the United States and the EU) or international organizations (such as the National Science Foundation International Dialogue 2004). The representation of developing countries needs to increase.
- Support an international co-funding mechanism for maintaining databases, nomenclature, standards, and patents.
- Implementing long-term planning that includes international perspective.
- Integrate the principles of good governance applied to four governance levels: adapting existing organizations and regulations; establishing new programs, organizations, and regulations specifically to handle converging technologies; building capacity for addressing these issues into national policies and institutions; international agreements and partnerships.

Opportunity for Developing Countries

There is a need for recognizing emerging technologies as a priority in developing countries in both their short- and long-term planning for using their natural, human, intellectual, and infrastructure opportunities in the respective country or region. Seeking complementary, collaborative projects and platforms with other developed centers may compensate limited institutional capacity, infrastructure, and access to information. Lower industry support and local private foundations' participation is a main challenge that may be compensated by leveraging with international organizations and industry, programs sponsored or coordinated by national governments, access to multidisciplinary information systems, and specific innovation pathways. One of the most under-evaluated aspects is stimulating creativity and innovation mechanisms in the conditions of non-competing classical infrastructure and availability of local workforce.

The leading advantages of emerging technologies in developing countries are perceived to be in healthcare, communication and information exchange, sustainable development of natural resources (clean water, food, energy), and nanomanufacturing with lower level of infrastructure (such as in mineral processing and nanobiology processing.) For example, Fabio Salamanca-Buentello *et al.* (2005) provide a detailed survey on application areas affected by nanotechnology. The authors conclude that nanotechnology can help eradicating poverty, improve maternal health and reduce child mortality, combat AIDS and malaria, and ensure environmental sustainability. There is a significant delay between identifying the applications as a function of local and global governance.

Looking Globally Forward

Explosion in communications, expansion of trade, people movement, and other factors push toward globalization. Overall, global introduction of emerging technologies is a source of wealth and the governance approach has to ensure social and transboundary equity. Technical and economic vision, societal values, cultural aspects, and higher human development purpose must be included in any longer term analysis of introduction of emerging technologies. The global development of nanotechnology suggests, for example, the power of an integrative concept and long-term vision for 2000–20 (Roco *et al.*, 1999; Roco *et al.*, 2010). Understanding the global self-regulating ecosystems and long-term perspective in the introduction of emerging technologies are essential because of broad societal implications possibilities and their effective testing and of the respective socioeconomic projects in various countries. Global governance of emerging technologies is needed particularly in developing countries to guide and facilitate various activities from science networking and standard settings to building capacity in organizations, coordinated regulatory systems and oversight.

This volume is timely in raising the attention, providing implementation ideas and looking for the future of emerging technologies and their governance for global societal benefit.

NOTES

1. Introduction

1 As of 2010, the United States was giving only 0.19 percent of its GDP for development assistance purposes (Huffington Post, 2010).
2 The Directory of Development Organizations (2010) alone lists some 65,000 organizations.
3 Remarks by the President at the University of Indonesia in Jakarta, Indonesia, November 10, 2010. Available online at www.whitehouse.gov/the-press-office/2010/11/10/remarks-president-university-indonesia-jakarta-indonesia.
4 Plan International recently released a report: "ICT: Enabled Development: Using ICT Strategically to Support Plan's Work," which provides further support for the concept of ICT-enabled development. It provides illustrations and examples as to why such efforts are not only important to the organization, but to the larger development community more broadly. See www.plan.fi/File/313852dc-874f-444c-b810-c9e13a98f767/ICT+Enabled+Development+%28Plan+2010%29.pdf for the full report.
5 A nanometer is a billionth of a meter, roughly equal to 3–6 atoms side-by-side. A human hair is roughly 80,000 nanometers wide.
6 The Woodrow Wilson International Center for Scholars Project on Emerging Nanotechnologies website provides an inventory of more than 800 products, produced around the world, that currently incorporate nanotechnology (see www.nanotechproject.org/inventories/consumer, accessed 1/2/11).
7 Conference presentations can be found on the conference website: www.nanoequity2009.cns.ucsb.edu.
8 Luc Soete (1985) coined the term technological leapfrogging with reference to the international diffusion of technology and the industrial development and economic growth associated with the microelectronics industry. Leapfrogging requires state investment in areas where the private sector is unable or unwilling to invest, and where typical commercialization remains several years (sometimes decades) out.
9 See http://opensourcenano.net/projects/project1/ for complete "recipe" for potential arsenic water filtration, and to learn more about the Open Source Nano project.
10 This approach is sometimes referred to as "participatory rural appraisal" (PRA). While it can be traced to the ideas of Brazilian activist and educator Paulo Freire, the phrase entered contemporary NGO literature in the early 1980s, with the writings of Robert Chambers, a fellow at the Institute for Development Studies (see, e.g., Chambers, 1995; Mukherjee, 2004).
11 According to one estimate, some three billion people across the globe still cook and heat with wood, charcoal, kerosene, and other non-renewable (and polluting) sources. It remains an open question, of course, whether it is more efficient and cost-effective to produce and maintain a large solar project that reaches millions of homes, or millions of off-the-grid individual projects spread throughout rural areas (Rosenthal, 2010). Where public investment is lacking, however, individual projects may be the best solution.
12 To take one example, China's largely unregulated factories are currently production sites for carbon nanotubes for export, a stage in the production of nano-enabled products where the greatest harm is likely to occur.

4. Achieving Equitable Outcomes Through Emerging Technologies

1 See, for example, the database of the Nanotechnology Citizen Engagement Organization www.
  nanoceo.net.

5. Emerging Technologies and Inequalities

1 This chapter draws in particular on case studies on Argentina, Costa Rica, Jamaica, and Mozambique, by Isabel Bortagaray, Lidia Brito, Roland Brouwer, Mario Falcao, Sonia Gatchair, and
  Dhanaraj Thakur. I wish to thank these authors also for thoughtful comments and corrections on
  a draft of this chapter. The Mozambican case studies were done as Work Package Four of ResIST, a
  project funded by the European Commission (see www.resist-research.net/home.aspx). The case
  studies in the Americas were funded as part of Project Resultar by the US National Science Foundation under Grant SES 072-6919. All opinions, findings, conclusions and recommendations are
  those of the author and do not necessarily reflect the view of the sponsors.
2 Any attempt to develop a crisply defined research agenda on inequality is challenged by the many
  dimensions of the phenomenon. At a very fundamental level, Sen (1992) points out that inequality
  is a multidimensional space, with different observers valuing different "focal inequalities," from
  abstract property rights through basic human needs. Empirically, there are income inequalities
  between and within countries; vertical and horizontal inequalities within countries; inequalities
  in other areas like computer access (the "Digital Divide"), health outcomes ("health disparities"),
  and environmental conditions ("environmental injustice"). Inequality and inequity are different
  concepts— one descriptive, one normative—although they are seldom carefully sorted out (see
  Cozzens, *et al.* 2007 for a discussion in S&T policy).
3 Project ResIST began with world regional consultations with policy-makers in Africa, Latin America, and Europe.
4 This review was done by Dhanaraj Thakur.
5 Approved Biotechnology Drugs—Biotechnology Industry Organization, www.bio.org/speeches/
  pubs/er/approveddrugs.asp (accessed 1/2/2007).
6 WHO Model List of Essential Medicines, http://whqlibdoc.who.int/hq/2005/a87017_eng.pdf.
  The WHO Essential Medicines list comprises the most efficacious, safe, cost-effective medicines
  for priority conditions.
7 This is an analogy to a concept in public health of the *epidemiological transition*: that one set of diseases characterizes countries with incomes up to a certain level, after which certain infrastructural
  conditions have been met and a different set of diseases emerges against the background of generally good public health. The first set is the "diseases of poverty" and the second set "the diseases
  of affluence." There may also be analogies with chemical processes. Geels (2002) also discusses
  technological transitions, but with a very different meaning.
8 Isabel Bortagaray, Resultar Argentina insulin case.
9 Isabel Bortagaray, Resultar Costa Rica banana case.
10 Sonia Gatchair, Resultar Jamaica plant tissue culture case.
11 See Gatchair *et al.* (2011) for some analysis of the national conditions that may be relevant.
12 Isabel Bortagaray, Resultar Argentina insulin case.
13 See www.sani.org.za.

6. The Progress of Nanotechnology in China

1 The analysis of scientific publications in this chapter is based on the MERIT Database of Worldwide Nanotechnology Scientific Publications. It is composed by scientific publications indexed by
  the Web of Science. The search strategy used to define nanotechnology publications is developed
  by the Georgia Institute of Technology and described in Porter *et al.* (2008). Huang *et al.* (2010)
  compared this search strategy and other popular strategies.
2 Throughout this chapter, a nanotechnology patent is defined as a patent with a Y01N classification. The classification code Y01N is attached to a patent application when the patent examiner at

the European Patent Office considers it to be related to nanotechnology. A detailed introduction
of the Y01N classification is provided by Scheu *et al.* (2006).

7. Food Security

1 For more information, please refer to Brian Tokar's *Redesigning Life? The Worldwide Challenge to Genetic Engineering* (2001), which is an edited collection of authors arguing different sides to the genetic engineering debate.
2 In the first month of 2007, tens of thousands of protesters marched and rallied throughout Mexico to demand a reduction of the price of tortillas. Gathered in the Zócalo (a large historic town square) in Mexico City, the protesters demanded a social contract to protect their salaries, food supply, and employment (*La Jornada*, January 31, 2007).
3 Studies by nongovernmental organizations following the 2001 findings confirmed the presence of GM corn in Oaxaca, Puebla, and in other parts of Mexico, however, the first peer-reviewed follow-up, led by Allison Snow, did not find significant traces of GM maize in Oaxaca (Fitting, 2006; Ortiz-García *et al.*, 2005). Studies concerning the presence of GM maize in Oaxaca were controversial because of the previous moratorium on the growth of GM maize in Mexico and because of the lack of evidence that traces of GM genes in seeds may disappear over time.

10. Nanotechnology for Potable Water and General Consumption in Developing Countries

1 See, www.tutorvista.com/content/biology/biology-ii/environment-and-environmental.
2 Ibid.
3 See, International Panel on Climate Change: www.ipcc.ch.
4 See Millennium Development Goals: www.un.org/millenniumgoals.

11. Solid-State Lighting

1 Metric units were used because they are the global and scientific standard for reporting such values. For those interested in other common units we have supplied a few common conversion factors: 1kg = approx. 2.2lbs, there are approx. four liters in one gallon, and one square meter is approximately 11 square feet.

12. Energy for Development

1 Brazil, Ministry for Energy (n.d.).
2 Porto (2005).
3 Moraes (1999).
4 Moraes (1999).
5 Brazil, Ministry of Agriculture (2009).
6 da Silva *et al.* (1978); Macedo *et al.* (2008).
7 Second generation biofuels are those derived from lignocellulosic crops, manufactured from various types of biomass.
8 www.iconebrasil.org.br/arquivos/noticia/1873.pdf.
9 PRNewswire (n.d.).

13. Implications of Nanotechnology for Labor and Employment

1 Research on health risks posed by nanoparticles in the workplace is clearly an exception in this landscape. There is a growing body of literature on toxicology and risks for labor. Recently, the International Labor Organization (ILO, 2010) added nanotechnology risks to its recommendations for labor risk prevention.

2 In May 2009, the Texas Skill Standards Board (TSSB, 2009) was the first office of its kind to recognize a Nanotechnology Technician Skill Standard.
3 According to Subramanian *et al.* (2009) research is moving fast toward active nanostructures, given the increasing number of publications in this area.
4 Lux Research dropped the earlier estimates of the total revenues from products incorporating nanotechnology in 2015 by 21 percent, as a result of the world crisis (*Hwang and Bradley, 2010*).
5 The database was initiated by a group of companies that had received public funding for nanotechnology R&D. In addition to the Ministry of Science and Technology as the main source of data, other sources as industry publications and websites, business publications, companies' websites, newspapers and innovation magazines helped to identify companies with activities in nanotechnology and provided information on their research and products. The search was conducted on the Internet.
6 It is worth noticing that I am in no position to assess if the products that companies claim contain nanotechnology in fact do so. Thus, the information presented here relies on companies' declarations on their products. In the cases of companies with public funding for R&D on nanotechnology (about a half of the total), their projects were reviewed by experts in the field.
7 Each firm was classified according to the most advanced stage attained. A firm classified as "commercializing products" may have other projects in the research or development stages. In some cases, firms are using nanotechnology that is not the outcome of internal R&D.
8 By the time this research was done, the petrochemical sector was at the final stages of an impressive movement of capital centralization. Several companies, including Suzano, Quattor, Pretrobras, and Braskem, which in turn had incorporated other companies during the past years are in the process of merging into a huge company that will be able to monopolize the production of basic petrochemicals in the country. This new company will be controlled by Braskem (51 percent) and Petrobras (49 percent). I kept the names of the different companies when they had earned public funds for R&D with their former names.
9 Braskem lança a primeira resina termoplástica brasileira com nanotecnologia e confirma sua liderança em inovação. Braskem Imprensa. Available at: www.braskem.com.br/upload/portal_braskem/pt/sala_de_imprensa/Press%20release%20PP%20nano%20-%2006-11-06.pdf; A indústria do átomo, Revista Digital. Available at: www.revistadigital.com.br/tendencias.asp?NumEdicao=359&CodMateria=3058.
10 Alves, O. L. LQES/UNICAMP e CONTECH: Um caso de sucesso de transferência em nanotecnologia para o meio ambiente. Workshop Nanotecnologias para o Nordeste, 2009. Available at: www.cetene.gov.br/painel/downloads/publicacoes/apresentacao-oswaldo-luiz-alves.pdf; Realizada em São Paulo a Nanotec Expo 2008 e o 4º. Congresso Internacional de Nanotecnologia, Nano em Foco. Dec. 2008, Available at: www.abdi.com.br/?q=system/files/08+12+-+Nano+em+Foco+(2).pdf.
11 InterBloco—Bloco InterTravado em Concreto Celular. Available at: http://ecopore.net.
12 Petrobras usa nanotecnologia e economiza na perfuração. Administradores.com. 11 de setembro de 2008. Available at: www.administradores.com.br/informe-se/informativo/petrobras-usa-nanotecnologia-e-economiza-na-perfuracao/17155.
13 Herbold, Fritz. Nanotecnologia na Industria Têxtil: Onde Estamos e para Onde Vamos, Presentation at NANOTEC 2005. Available at:www.abtt.org.br/artigos/confrits.pdf; Iser, Peter M., CHT Brasil Quimica Marketing Presentation: Terminación Textilquímica, Aplicación y Tecnología 66. Available at: www.detextiles.com/files/ACABADO%20TEXTIL%20HOY.pdf.
14 Nanum Nanotecnologia SA, Tecnologias: Vernizes fotocataliticos—Nano Glass Coating. Available at: www.nanum.com.br/interna.php?area=tecnologia&idIdioma=1&escolha=16.
15 Cedro aposta na nanotecnologia. Cedro Notícias, Dec. 6, 2006. Available at: www.cedro.com.br/br/noticia/noticia.asp?codCategoria=&CodNoticia=180&Page=6.
16 Vestuário: Panos quentes. Folha de S. Paulo on line, March 30, 2007. Available at: www1.folha.uol.com.br/folha/especial/2007/morar2/rf3003200712.shtml; Diferenciação do produto: estratégia da indústria têxtil para enfrentar a concorrência estrangeira, interview with Silvio Napoli, Inovacao Uniemp 3, 3 May–June 2007. Available at: http://inovacao.scielo.br/scielo.php?script=sci_arttext&pid=S1808-23942007000300002&lng=es&nrm=iso.

17 Funcional Mikron, Products. Available at: www.funcionalmikron.com.br/aplicacao-PROD-
   -TODOS.html; Funcional Mikron: Nanotecnologia na Indústria de Alimentos, Presentation at
   UNICAMP (October 1, 2009). Available at: www.fea.unicamp.br/img/File/Mikron.pdf.
18 Primeiro medicamento brasileiro desenvolvido com nanotecnologia. Inova Brasil, April 24,
   2007. Available at: http://inovabrasil.blogspot.com/2007/04/primeiro-medicamento-brasileiro.
   html; Press Release, Incrementha PD&I, Incrementha Lança Primeiro Fármaco Brasileiro Desenvolvido com Nanotecnologia, April 25, 2007. Available at: www.tramaweb.com.br/cliente_ver.
   aspx?ClienteID=75&NoticiaID=4029.
19 Rodrigues, W., Pequenas e Médias Empresas: Oportunidades de Desenvolvimento Vinculadas
   à Nanotecnologia. Presentation at NanoMercosur 2007. Available at: www2.mecon.gov.ar/fan/
   nano2007/presentaciones/wagner.pdf; Oliveira, Marcos. Nanotubos no mercado. Pesquisa Fapesp
   118. Available at: http://revistapesquisa.fapesp.br/?art=2770&bd=1&pg=1&lg=.
20 Nova Petroquimica e Sugar lançam mais uma inovação para o mercado de eletrodomésticos de
   linha branca. 7/02/2008. Available at: www.guiaconstruirereformar.com.br/noticia_335-.htm.
21 Gallembeck, F. *et al.* Nanotechnology for Waterborne Paint Improvement. Paints and Coatings
      Industry, January 18, 2006. Available at: www.pcimag.com/Articles/Feature_Article/
   257408c7830e8010VgnVCM100000f932a8c0; Bueno, R. Bunge Develops with Unicamp Special
   Pigment for Paints Based on Nanoparticles; Potential Market may Reach US$ 5 billion. Unicamp
   Innovation, May 2, 2006. Available at: www.inovacao.unicamp.br/english/report/news-universi-
   tybusiness.shtml.
22 Santista Textil entra na era da nanotecnologia. Available at: www.emprefour.com.br/novidades01.
   asp.
23 Renaux Blue Label. Available at: www.renaux.com.br/conteudo/index.aspx?t=colecaorele
   ase&categoriaid=5; Tecidos tecnologicos. Available at: http://floripa.sociesc.org.br/fgv-sc/
   _br/?secao=Noticias&noticia=150&tipo=E.
24 Assis, O. and L. Forato, Embrapa Desenvolve Coberturas Comestíveis para Minimizar Ranci-
   ficação de Nozes Macadamia, Toda Fruta, August 13, 2009. Available at: www.todafruta.com.
   br/todafruta/mostra_conteudo.asp?conteudo=19733.
25 Embrapa desenvolve películas a base de frutas, 22 January, 2010. Available at:: www.cib.org.br/
   midia.php?ID=49856.
26 MCT/FINEP/FNDCT—01/2007 Subvenção econômica Suzano Petroquímica S.A. Nanocom-
   pósitos de polipropileno para desenvolvimento de embalagens ativas e inteligentes. Available at::
   www.mdic.gov.br/portalmdic//arquivos/dwnl_1283373738.pdf; Forum de Competitividade em
   Nanotecnologia, Grupo de Trabalho em Mercado, June 2010. Available at: www.mdic.gov.br/
   portalmdic//arquivos/dwnl_1283373738.pdf; ABDI. Panorama da Nanotecnologia no Mundo e no
   Brasil. Available at: www.abdi.com.br/?q=system/files/Panorama_INI_Nanotecnologia_0.pdf.
27 Finep libera R$ 2,8 milhões para aplicação de nanotecnologia. Available at: www.cimm.com.
   br/portal/noticia/exibir_noticia/857-finep-libera-r-28-milhes-para-aplicao-de-nanotecnologia.
28 Embrapa. Nanotecnologia, o poder do quase invisível. Available at: www.embrapa.br/
   publicacoes/institucionais/pesquisa-em-rede/folhetos/Nanotecnologia.pdf; Mattoso, L. *et al.*,
   Nanotecnologia aplicada ao agronegocio: as acoes da Embrapa. Available at: www.sbiagro2007.
   cnptia.embrapa.br/apresentacoes/palestras/PalestraNaime_MR2.pdf.

14. Seeking the Non-Developmental within the Developmental

1 This study was funded by the Strengthening ICTD Research Capacity in Asia (SIRCA) program,
   sponsored by Singapore Internet Research Centre.

16. Risk Perception, Public Participation, and Sustainable Global Development of Nanotechnologies

1 This work is funded by NSF through cooperative agreement # SES- 0531184 to the Center for
   Nanotechnology in Society at UCSB; and grant # SES-0824024 to PI Harthorn. Also funded by

NSF & EPA through cooperative agreement #DBI- 0830117 to the UC Center for Environmental Implications of Nanotechnology. Any opinions, findings, and conclusions or recommendations expressed in this material are those of the author(s) and do not necessarily reflect the views of the National Science Foundation or the Environmental Protection Agency. This work has not been subjected to EPA review and no official endorsement should be inferred.

2 This chapter is based on work co-produced with numerous colleagues and students: expert studies: Karl Bryant (SUNY New Paltz), Hillary Haldane (Quinnipiac Univ), and Terre Satterfield, Milind Kandlikar and Christian Beaudrie (all Univ of British Columbia); US–UK deliberation research: Nick Pidgeon (Cardiff Univ, Wales, UK), Tee Rogers-Hayden (Univ of East Anglia, UK), Karl Bryant (SUNY New Paltz), and Joseph Summers (MIT); risk perception survey research and meta-analysis: Terre Satterfield, Milind Kandlikar, Christian Beaudrie, (all Univ of British Columbia), Joseph Conti (Univ of Wisconsin), and Nick Pidgeon and Adam Corner (both Cardiff Univ, UK); US deliberation on gender and equity: Jennifer Rogers (Univ of Long Island), Christine Shearer, Tyronne Martin, Indy Hurt, and Julie Whirlow (all UCSB); 2009–2010 international industry survey: Cassandra Engeman, Lynn Baumgartner, Benjamin Carr, Allison Fish, John Meyerhofer, and Patricia Holden (all UCSB). Our thanks to them all.

REFERENCES

1. Introduction

Bill & Melinda Gates Foundation (2010) "Foundation Fact Sheet: Funding from 1994 to Present." Available at: www.gatesfoundation.org/about/Pages/foundation-fact-sheet.aspx (accessed 1/1/2011).

BRAC (2010) "BRAC At a Glance." Available at: www.brac.net/content/stay-informed-key-statistics (accessed 1/1/2011).

Bürgi, Birgit R. and T. Pradeep (2006) "Societal Implications of Nanoscience and Nanotechnology in Developing Countries," *Current Science* 90 (5): 645–58.

CGI (2011a) "Clinton Global Initiative: About Us." Available at: www.clintonglobalinitiative.org/aboutus/default.asp?Section=AboutUs&PageTitle=About%20Us (accessed 1/1/2011).

CGI (2011b) "CHAI—What We Do." Available at: www.clintonfoundation.org/what-we-do/clinton-health-access-initiative (accessed 2/1/2011).

Chambers, Robert (1995; orig. 1983) *Rural Development: Putting the Last First.* New York: Prentice-Hall.

Conway, Gordon and Jeff Waage (2010) *Science and Innovation for Development.* London: UK Collaborative on Development Sciences (August). Available at: www.ukcds.org.uk/_assets/file/book/science_innovation_book_lowres.pdf (accessed 1/4/11).

Directory of Development Organizations (2010) "Directory of Development Organizations, 2010." Available at: www.devdir.org (accessed 1/1/2011).

Easterly, William (2007) *The White Man's Burden: Why the West's Efforts to Aid the Rest Have Done So Much Ill and So Little Good.* New York: Penguin.

Easterly, William (2009) "Can the West Save Africa?" *Journal of Economic Literature* 47 (2): 373–447. Available at: http://netdrive.montclair.edu/~lebelp/EasterlyWestToAfricaJEL2009.pdf.

Easterly, William (2010) "Reinventing the Wheel: Why No-Tech Ancient Civilizations Still Can't Catch Up," *Foreign Policy* (November): 44–5.

Harris, Eva (2004) "Building Scientific Capacity in Developing Countries," *European Molecular Biology Organization Reports* 5 (1): 7–11.

Huffington Post (2010) "Rich Countries' Foreign Aid Generosity," *Huffington Post* (February 6). Available at: www.huffingtonpost.com/2010/02/06/rich-countries-foreign-ai_n_446616.html?view=print (accessed 1/1/2011).

Invernizzi, Noela and Guillermo Foladori (2005) "Nanotechnology and the Developing World: Will Nanotechnology Overcome Poverty or Widen Disparities?" *Nanotechnology Law & Business* 2 (3): 101–10.

Lancaster, Carol (1999) *Aid to Africa: So Much to Do So Little Done.* Chicago: University of Chicago Press.

Lane, Neal and Thomas Kalil (2005) "The National Nanotechnology Initiative: Present at the Creation," *Issues in Science and Technology* (summer). Available at: www.issues.org/21.4/lane.html.

Lounsbury, M., C. Kelty, C.T. Yavuz, and V. Colvin (2009) "Towards Open Source Nano: Arsenic Removal and Alternative Models of Technology Transfer," *JAI Advances in the Study of Entrepreneurship, Innovation, and Economic Growth* 19: 51–78. Available at: http://kelty.org/or/papers/Kelty_Lounsbury_OSNano_2009.pdf.

MCC (2011) "Millennium Challenge Corporation: About MCC." Available at: www.mcc.gov/pages/about (accessed 2/1/2011).

McCray, W. Patrick (2009) "From Lab to iPod: A Story of Discovery and Commercialization in the Post-Cold War Era," *Technology and Culture* 50 (1): 58–81.

McNeill, R., J. Lowe, T. Mastroianni, J. Cronin and D. Ferk (2007) "Barriers to Nanotechnology Commercialization: Final Report prepared for the U.S. Department of Commerce Office of Technology Assessment," College of Business and Management, University of Illinois: Springfield, Illinois.

Moyo, Dembisa (2009) *Dead Aid: Why Aid Is Not Working and How There Is a Better Way for Africa.* New York: Farrar, Straus and Giroux.

Mukherjee, Amitava (ed.) (2004) *Participatory Rural Appraisal—Methods & Applications in Rural Planning: Essays in Honor of Robert Chambers.* Rev. Edn. Delhi: Concept Publishing Company.

NNI (2006) *The National Nanotechnology Initiative: Research and Development Leading to a Revolution in Technology and Industry. Supplement to the President's FY 2007 Budget.* Washington, DC: NSET (July). Available at: www.nano.gov/NNI_07Budget.pdf (accessed 1/2/11).

Renn, Ortwin and Mihail C. Roco (2006) "Nanotechnology and the Need for Risk Governance," *Journal of Nanoparticle Research* 8 (2): 153–91.

Roco, Mihail C. (2003) "Converging Science and Technology at the Nanoscale: Opportunities for Education and Training," *Nature Biotechnology* 21 (10): 1247–9.

Roco, Mihail C. (2009) "Global Development and Governance of Nanotechnology." Powerpoint presentation prepared for UCSB-CNS *Emerging Technologies/Emerging Economies Conference*, Woodrow Wilson International Center for Scholars, Washington, DC (November 4–6).

Roco, Mihail C. and William Simms Bainbridge (2003) "Nanotechnology: Societal Implications, Maximizing Benefits for Humanity," US NNI: Report of the NNI Workshop (December 3–5). Available at: www.nanowerk.com/nanotechnology/reports/reportpdf/report38.pdf.

Rosenthal, Elisabeth (2010) "African Huts Far From the Grid Glow With Renewable Power," *The New York Times* (December 24).

Salamanca-Buentello, Fabio, Deepa L. Persad, Erin B. Court, Douglas K. Martin, Abdallah S. Daar, and Peter A. Singer (2005) "Nanotechnology and the Developing World," *PLoS Medicine* 2 (5): 383–6.

Sastry, Kalpana, H.B. Rashmi, N.H. Rao, and S.M. Ilyas (2009) *Nanotechnology and Agriculture in India: The Second Green Revolution? OECD Conference on Potential Environmental Benefits of Nanotechnology: Fostering Safe Innovation-Led Growth.* Paris, France: OECD Conference Center (July 15–17). Available at: www.oecd.org/dataoecd/4/45/43289415.pdf (accessed 1/1/2011).

Shapira, Philip and Jue Wang (2010) "Follow the Money," *Nature* 468 (December 2): 627–8.

Singer, Peter A., Fabio Salamanca-Buentello, and Abdallah S. Daar (2005) "Harnessing Nanotechnology to Improve Global Equity," *Issues in Science and Technology.* Available at: www.issues.org/21.4/singer.html.

Singer, Peter A., Abdallah S. Daar, Sara Al-Bader, Ronak Shah, Ken Simiyu, Ryan E. Wiley, Pamela Kanellis, Menaka Pulandrian, and Marilyn Heymann (2008) "Commercializing

African Health Research: Building Life Science Convergence Platforms," *Global Forum Update on Research for Health*, Volume 5, pp. 143–50.

Soete, Luc (1985) "International Diffusion of Technology, Industrial Development and Technological Leapfrogging," *World Development* 13 (3): 409–22.

United National Commission on Science and Technology for Development (UNCTAD) (2008) "Report on the Eleventh Session" (May 26–30). Economic and Social Council. Official Records, 2008: Supplement 11. Available at: www.unctad.org/en/docs/ecn162008d5_en.pdf.

UN Millennium Project (2005) *Investing in Development: A Practical Plan to Achieve the Millennium Development Goals.* London: Earthscan. Available at: http://www.google.com/url?sa=t&source=web&cd=1&ved=0CB0QFjAA&url=http%3A%2F%2Fwww.unmillenniumproject.org%2Fdocuments%2FMainReportComplete-lowres.pdf&rct=j&q=investing%20in%20development%20a%20practical%20plan&ei=MbkfTaGtGImesQO9t6mICg&usg=AFQjCNEQX36xBm7wJFTm6noGOC1zLThp4w&sig2=aQJv7GhN-HTeya27SVS95Q.

Wagner, Caroline (2008) *The New Invisible College: Science for Development.* Washington, DC: Brookings Institution Press.

Wagner, Caroline S., Irene Brahmakulam, Brian Jackson, Anny Wong, and Tatsuro Yoda (2001) *Science and Technology Collaboration: Building Capacity in Developing Countries?* Santa Monica, CA (March).

World Bank (2010) "Poverty: At a Glance." World Bank website: http://web.worldbank.org/WBSITE/EXTERNAL/NEWS /0,,contentMDK:20040961~menuPK:34480~pagePK:64257043~piPK:437376~theSitePK:4607,00.html (accessed 1/1/2011).

2. Creating the Future

Arunchalam, V.S. and E.L. Fleischer (April 2008) "The Global Energy Landscape and Materials Innovation," *MRS Bulletin*, p. 264.

Auerswald, P. (Spring 2009) "Creating Social Value," *Stanford Social Innovation Review*, p. 51.

Avlonitis, S.A., K. Kouroumbas, and N. Vlachakis (2003) "Energy Consumption and Membrane Replacement Cost for Seawater RO Desalination Plants.," *Desalination*, p. 151.

Bement, A.L. Jr. (June 22, 2005) "Global Connections: National Science Foundation International Programs and Activities," *Global Conference on Environment, Science, Technology and Health Officers*, Washington, DC.

Benn, H. (May 14, 2009) *Confronting the Crisis of Sustainability and Resource Scarcity.* Washington, DC: Woodrow Wilson International Center for Scholars.

Braudel, F. (1981) *Les Structures du quotidien: le possible et l'impossible.*Paris: Librarie Armand Colin (English Translation: Braudel, F. (1981) *The Structures of Everyday Life.* New York: Harper & Row Publishers, Inc.).

CNN Presents Classroom (November 20, 2006) "We Were Warned: Tomorrow's Oil Crisis," Atlanta: CNN. Available at: www.cnn.com/CNN/Programs/presents.

European Commission Project 212492 (October 10, 2008) *CLARIS LPB Project: A Europe-South America Network for Climate Change Assessment and Impact Studies in La Plata Basin.*

Evans-Pritchard, A. (June 5, 2008) *Water Crisis to be Biggest World Risk.* UK: Telegraph Co.

Feynman R.P. (1960) "There's Plenty of Room at the Bottom: An Invitation to Enter a New Field of Physics," *Engineering Science* 23: 22.

Friedman, T.L. (2005) *The World Is Flat: A Brief History of the Twenty-First Century.* New York: Farrar, Straus and Giroux.

Ginley, D., M.A. Green, and R. Collins (April 2008) "Solar Energy Conversion Toward 1 Terawatt," *MRS Bulletin*, p. 355.

Green, M.A. (2004) *Third Generation Photovoltaics: Advanced Solar Energy Conversion.* Berlin: Springer-Verlag.

Hayman, B., J. Wedel-Heinen, and P. Brondsted (April 2008) "Materials Challenges in Present and Future Wind Energy," *MRS Bulletin*, p. 343.

Human Development Report (2006) *Beyond Scarcity: Power, Poverty and the Global Water Crisis.* New York: United Nations Development Programme.

Humphreys, C.J. (April 2008) "Solid-State Lighting," *MRS Bulletin*, p. 459.

Johansson, F. (2004) *The Medici Effect: Breakthrough Insights from the Intersection of Ideas, Concepts and Cultures.* Cambridge, MA: Harvard Business School Publishing.

Joint Science Academies Statement on Growth and Responsibility: Sustainability, Energy Efficiency and Climate Protection (May 2007) Available at: www.nationalacademies.org/includes/G8Statement_Energy_07_May.pdf.

Juma, C. and L. Yee-Cheong (2005) *Innovation: Applying Knowledge in Development, Millennium Project Task Force on Science, Technology and Innovation.* Sterling, VA: Earthscan.

Kaur, S., R. Gopal, W.J. Ng, S. Ramakrishna, and T. Matsuura (January 2008) "Next-Generation Fibrous Media for Water Treatment," *MRS Bulletin*, p. 21.

Kirby, A. (June 2, 2000) "Dawn of a Thirsty Century," *BBC News Online.* Available at: http://news.bbc.co.uk/2/hi/science/nature/755497.stm (accessed 10/12/2010).

Mayell, H. (June 5, 2003) *UN Highlights World Water Crisis, National Geographic News.*

Meinzen-Dick, R., M. Adato, L. Haddad, and P. Hazell (2004) *Science and Poverty: An Interdisciplinary Assessment of the Impact of Agricultural Research.* Washington, DC: International Food Policy Research Institute.

Millennium Project Task Force on Education and Gender Equity (2005) *Toward Universal Primary Education: Investments, Incentives, and Institutions.* Sterling, VA: Earthscan.

Millennium Project Task Force Press Release (a) (January 17, 2005) *Poor Countries Must Invest in Science and Technology.*

Millennium Project Task Force Press Release (b) (January 17, 2005) *Environmental Sustainability is a Critical Foundation for Ending Poverty.*

Moskowitz, S.K. (2009) *The Advanced Materials Revolution: Technology and Economic Change in the Age of Globalization.* New York: John Wiley and Sons, Inc.

National Academy of Engineering (US) (2008) *Grand Challenges for Engineering.* Washington, DC.

The Nobel Foundation (2007) The Nobel Prize. Available at: http://nobelprize.org/nobel_prizes/peace/laureates/2007/press.html (accessed 10/12/2010).

NSF Enables Pakistan to Connect to Global Research Community through New High Speed Link (October 28, 2008). *NSF Press Release 08–191*, Washington, DC. Available at: www.nsf.gov/news/news_summ.jsp?cntn_id=112503&org=OISE&from=news.

Osman, T.M. (January 2008) "The Nuclear Renaissance: A Challenge for the Materials Community," *Journal of the Minerals, Metals, and Materials Society* 60 (1): 10.

Pacey, A. (1974) *The Maze of Ingenuity: Ideas and Idealism in the Development of Technology.* Cambridge, MA: MIT Press.

Powell, C.A. and B.D. Morreale (April 2008) "Materials Challenges in Advanced Coal Conversion Technologies," *MRS Bulletin*, p. 309.

Rav, B., M. Vijayalakshmi, P.R. Vasudeva Rao, and K.B.S. Rao (April 2008) "Challenges in Materials Research for Sustainable Nuclear Energy," *MRS Bulletin*, p. 327.

Richards, D.J. (Spring 1999) "Harnessing Ingenuity for Sustainable Outcomes," *The Bridge (NAE)*, p. 16.

Scientific American.Special Issue: "Energy's Future: Beyond Carbon" 295 (3) (2006). Available at: www.sciam.com/issue.cfm?issueDate=Sep-06 (accessed 10/12/2010).

Shannon, M.A. and R. Semiant (January 2008) "Advancing Materials and Technologies for Water Purification," *MRS Bulletin*, p. 9.

Stanford Social Innovation Review (Spring 2009) "Turn on the TV, Class," p. 60.

Stockdale, A.M. (July 2009) "'2050 Challenge' Introduces College Students to Hands-On Technology Projects in Mali," *MRS Bulletin*, p. 482.

"Top Five Risks: Critical Perspectives on the Global Economy," *Global Investment Research Conference* (June 4, 2008) London.

Vainrot, N., M.S. Eisen, and R. Semiat (January 2008) "Membranes in Desalintation and Water Treatment," *MRS Bulletin*, p. 16.

Whittingham, M.S. (April 2008) "Materials Challenges Facing Electrical Storage," *MRS Bulletin*, p. 411.

3. Rural Development, Technology, and "Policy Memory"

Adnan, Shapan (1991) *Floods, People and the Environment: Institutional Aspects of Flood Protection Programmes in Bangladesh, 1990.* Dhaka: Research and Advisory Services.

Adnan, Shapan (2009) "Intellectual Critiques, People's Resistance and Inter-Riperian Contestations: Constraints to the Power of the State Regarding Flood Water Control and Water Management in the Ganges-Brahmaputra-Meghna Delta of Bangladesh," in *Water, Sovereignty and Borders in Asia and Oceania*, edited by Devleena Ghosh, Heather Goodall and Stephanie Hemelryk Donald, pp. 104–24. London: Routledge.

Bayes, Abdul (2001) "Infrastructure and Rural Development: Insights from a Grameen Bank Village Phone Initiative in Bangladesh," *Agricultural Economics* 25 (2–3): 261–72.

Biggs, Stephen, Scott Justice, and David Lewis (2011) "Patterns of Rural Mechanisation, Energy and Employment in South Asia: Reopening the Debate," *Economic and Political Weekly* XLVI (9): 78–82.

Bradnock, Robert W. and Patricia Saunders (2002) "Rising Waters, Sinking Land? Environmental Change and Development in Bangladesh," in *South Asia in a Globalizing World: A Reconstructed Regional Geography*, edited by Robert W. Bradnock and Glyn Williams, pp. 51–77. Harlow: Pearson Education.

Connerton, Paul (2009) *How Modernity Forgets.* Cambridge: Cambridge University Press.

Conway, Gardon and Jeff Waage (2010) *Science and Innovation for Development.* London: UK Collaborative on Development Sciences (UKCDS).

Cornwall, Andrea and Karen Brock (2005) "What do Buzzwords do for Development Policy? A Critical Look at 'Participation', 'Empowerment' and 'Poverty Reduction'," *Third World Quarterly* 26 (7): 1043–60.

Custers, Peter (1993) "Bangladesh's Flood Action Plan: A Critique," *Economic and Political Weekly* 28 (29/30): 1501–3.

Farrington, John and David Lewis (eds.) (1993) *Non-Governmental Organizations and the State in Asia: Rethinking Roles in Sustainable Agricultural Development.* London: Routledge.

Hari, Johann (2008) "Bangladesh is Set to Disappear under the Waves by the End of the Century," *Independent*, June 20. Available at: www.independent.co.uk/news/world/asia/

bangladesh-is-set-to-disappear-under-the-waves-by-the-end-of-the-century--a-special-report-by-johann-hari-850938.html (accessed 10/10/2011).

Hartmann, Betsy (2010) "Rethinking Climate Refugees and Climate Conflict: Rhetoric, Reality and the Politics of Policy Discourse," *Journal of International Development* 22: 233–46.

Hossain, M., D. Lewis, D., M.L. Bose, and A. Chowdhury (2006) "Rice Research, Technological Progress and Impact on the Poor: The Bangladesh Case," in *Agricultural Research, Livelihoods and Poverty: Studies on Economic and Social Impact*, edited by M. Adato and R. Meinzen-Dick, pp. 56–102. Baltimore: Johns Hopkins University Press.

Lewis, David (1991) *Technologies and Transactions: A Study of the Interaction between New Technology and Agrarian Structure in Bangladesh.* Dhaka: Centre for Social Studies, Dhaka University.

Lewis, David (1996) "'Appropriating' Technology? Tractor Owners, Brokers, Artisans and Farmers in Rural Bangladesh," *Journal of International Development* 8 (1): 21–38.

Lewis, David (2009) "International Development and the 'Perpetual Present': Anthropological Approaches to the Rehistoricisation of Policy," *European Journal of Development Research* 21 (1): 32–46.

Lewis, David (2011) *Bangladesh: Politics, Economy and Civil Society.* Cambridge: Cambridge University Press.

MoEF (2009) *Bangladesh Climate Change Strategy and Action Plan 2009.* Ministry of Environment and Forests, Government of the People's Republic of Bangladesh, Dhaka, Bangladesh.

Roberts, S.M., J.P. Jones, and O. Frohling (2005) "NGOs and the Globalization of Managerialism," *World Development* 33 (11): 1845–64.

Shiva, Vandana (1991) *The Violence of the Green Revolution.* London: Zed Books.

Sillitoe, Paul (2001) "The State of Indigenous Knowledge in Bangladesh," in *Indigenous Knowledge Development in Bangladesh: Present and Future*, pp. 1–22. Dhaka: University Press Limited.

Sogge, David (1996) "Settings and Choices," in *Compassion and Calculation: The Business of Private Foreign Aid*, edited by David Sogge with Kees Biekart and John Saxby, pp. 1–23. London: Pluto Press.

Wedel, Janine R., Cris Shore, Gregory Feldman, and Stacy Lathrop (2005) "Toward an Anthropology of Public Policy," *Annals of the American Academy of Political and Social Sciences*, 600: 30–45.

Willoughby, Kelvin (1990) *Technology Choice: A Critique of the Appropriate Technology Movement.* Boulder: Westview Press.

Yunus, Muhammad (2010) *Building Social Business: The New Kind of Capitalism That Serves Humanity's Most Pressing Needs.* New York: Public Affairs.

4. Achieving Equitable Outcomes Through Emerging Technologies

Australian Council of Trade Unions (ACTU) (2005) "Submission to a Senate Inquiry into Workplace Exposure to Toxic Dust, including Silica Dust and Nanoparticles," in *Anna Salleh Unions say Nano-loopholes may Hurt Workers.* ABC Science online: www.abc.net.au/cgi-bin/common/printfriendly.pl?/science/news/stories/s1451929.htm (accessed 7/28/2008).

Científica (2008) *The Nanotechnology Opportunity Report.* 3rd Edn.

CONACYT (Consejo Nacional de Ciencia y Tecnología) (2008) *Programa Especial de Ciencia, Tecnología e Innovación 2008–2012.* México: CONACYT. Available at: www.siicyt.gob.mx/siicyt/docs/contenido/PECiTI.pdf (accessed 10/31/2009).

CONACYT (Consejo Nacional de Ciencia y Tecnología) (n.d.) *Red Temática de Nanociencias y Nanotecnología*. Dirección de Redes. DAIC. México: CONACYT. Available at: www. conacyt.mx/Redes/Redes-Tematicas/Red-Nanociencias-y-Nanotecnologia.pdf (accessed 2/10/2010).

Decreto Presidencial 380/2005. República Argentina (2005) "Autorízase al Ministerio de Economía y Producción a constituir la Fundación Argentina de Nanotecnología." Available at: www.fan.org.ar/acerca_estatuto.htm (accessed 10/31/2009).

Delgado Wise, Raúl and Noela Invernizzi (2002) "México y Corea del Sur: Claroscuros del crecimiento exportador en el contexto del globalismo neoliberal," *Aportes, Revista Mexicana de Estudios sobre la Cuenca del Pacífico*, II, 2, 4: 63–86.

ETC group (2003) "The Big Down: Atomtech – Technologies Converging at the Nano-scale." Available at: www.etcgroup.org/article.asp?newsid=375 (accessed 7/27/2006).

ETUC (European Trade Unions Council) (2008) "ETUC Resolution on Nanotechnology and Nanomateriales." Available at: www.etuc.org/IMG/pdf_ETUC_resolution_on_nano_EN_25_June_08.pdf (accessed 6/26/2008).

FoE – Australia (Friends of the Earth – Australia) (2006) "Nanomaterials, Sunscreens and Cosmetics: Small Ingredients Big Risks." FoE. Available at: http://nano.foe.org.au/node/125 (accessed 3/20/2008).

Foladori, G. (2009) "La gobernanza de las nanotecnologías," *Sociológica* 24 (71): 125–53.

Foladori, G. and N. Invernizzi (2006) "La próxima revolución industrial comienza por lo suntuario," *Revista Paranaense de Desenvolvimento* 110: 127–34. Curitiba.

Foladori, G. and N. Invernizzi (2008) *Nanotecnologias en América Latina*. México D.F.: Miguel Angel Porrúa.

GT Nanotecnologia (Grupo de Trabalho em nanociência e nanotecnologia). Ministério da Ciência e Tecnologia. Brasil. Nanotecnologia (2003) Desenvolvimento da nanociência e da nanotecnologia. Proposta do Grupo de Trabalho criado pela Portaria MCT nº 252 como subsídio ao Programa de Desenvolvimento da Nanociência e da Nanotecnologia do PPA 2004–2007. Available at: www.mct.gov.br/upd_blob/0002/2361.pdf (accessed 10/31/2009).

Invernizzi, Noela (2010) "Science Policy and Social Inclusion: Advances and Limits of Brazilian Nanotechnology Policy," in *The Yearbook of Nanotechnology in Society. Volume 3: The Challenge of Equity and Equality*, edited by Susan Cozzens and Jameson Wetmore. New York: Springer.

ICTA (International Center for Technology Assessment) (2007) "Broad International Coalition Issues Principles for Strong Oversight of Nanotechnology," July 31. Available at: www.icta. org/press/release.cfm?news_id=26 (accessed 3/20/2008).

Juma, Calestous and Lee Yee-Cheong (coord.) (2005) *Innovation: Applying Knowledge in Development*. London and Sterling, VA: Earthscan, Millennium Project. Available at: www. unmillenniumproject.org/documents/Science-complete.pdf (accessed 9/13/2005).

Meridian Institute (2005) *Nanotechnology and the Poor: Opportunities and Risks*. Washington, DC: Meridian Institute.

Nanowerk Database (n.d.) Nanotechnology Nanomaterial Suppliers. Database. Available at: www.nanowerk.com/nanotechnology/nanomaterial/nanomatmatrix.php (accessed 3/5/2009).

NS&TC (National Science and Technology Council. Committee on Technology. Subcommittee on Nanoscale Science, Engineering and Technology) (2000, July) *National Nanotechnology Initiative. The Initiative and its Implementation Plan*. Washington, DC. Available at: www. nano.gov/html/res/nni2.pdf (accessed 10/31/2009).

OEI (Organización de Estados Iberoamericanos para la Educación, la Ciencia y la Cultura) (February 2, 2009) La nanotecnología en Iberoamérica. Situación actual y tendencias. Informe del Observatorio Iberoamericano de Ciencia, Tecnología e Innovación del Centro de Altos Estudios Universitarios de la OEI. Available at: www.oei.es/salactsi/nano.pdf (accessed 3/10/2009).

Salamanca-Buentello, F., D.L. Persad, E.B. Court, D.K. Martin, A.S. Daar and P. Singer (2005) "Nanotechnology and the Developing World," *PLoS Medicine* 2 (5). Available at: http://medicine.plosjournals.org/perlserv/?request=get-document&doi=10.1371/journal.pmed.0020097 (accessed 7/27/2006).

Trouiller, P., E. Torreele, P. Olliaro, N. White, S. Foster, D. Wirth and B. Pécoul (2001) "Drugs for Neglected Diseases: A Failure of the Market and a Public Health Failure?" *Tropical Medicine & International Health* 6 (11): 945–51.

UITA (2006–7) The IUF Resolution. Available at: www.rel-uita.org/nanotecnologia/resolucion_uita_nano_eng.htm (accessed 3/20/2007).

WWICS (Woodrow Wilson International Center for Scholars) (2009) "A Nanotechnology Consumers Product Inventory," Project on Emerging Nanotechnologies. Available at: www.nanotechproject.org/inventories/consumer/analysis_draft (accessed 10/31/2009).

Zumla, A. (2002) "Reflexion & Reaction – correspondence," *The Lancet*, July 2.

5. Emerging Technologies and Inequalities

Baghadi, G. (2005) "Gender and Medicines: An International Public Health Experience," *Journal of Women's Health* 14: 82–6.

Bisang, R., C. Cogliati, S. Groisman, and J. Katz (1986) "Insulina y Economía: El difícil arte de la política publica," *Desarollo Económico* 26: 1–25.

Brito, L. and R. Brouwer, R. (2010) "Para além dos limites da perversidade: como as politicas afectam a adaptação de tecnologia Estudo de caso de Moçambique," in *Proceedings of Dinâmicas da Pobreza e Padrões de Acumulação Económica em Moçambique*. Available at: www.iese.ac.mz/lib/publication/II_conf/CP10_2009_Brito.pdf (accessed 10/10/2011).

Brouwer, R. (2010) "Mobile Phones in Mozambique: The Street Trade in Airtime in Maputo City," *S cience Technology & Society* 15: 135–54.

Cozzens, S.E. (2010) "Building Equity and Equality into Nanotechnology," in *Yearbook of Nanotechnology in Society, Volume II*, edited by Susan Cozzens and Jameson Wetmore. New York: Springer.

Cozzens, S.E., E. Kallerud, L. Ackers, B. Gill, J. Harper, T.S. Pereira, and N. Zarb-Adami (2007) "Problems of Inequality in Science, Technology, and Innovation Policy," James Martin Institute Working Paper 5. Oxford, UK.

Cozzens, Susan E., Isabel Bortagaray, Sonia Gatchair, and Dhanaraj Thakur (2008) "Emerging Technologies and Social Cohesion," presented at PRIME Latin America Conference, Mexico City, September. Available at: http://prime_mexico2008.xoc.uam.mx/papers/Susan_Cozzens_Emerging_Technologies_a_social_Cohesion.pdf.

Cozzens, S.E., S. Gatchair, J. Kang, K. Kim, H.J. Lee, G. Ordóñez, and A. Porter (2010) "Emerging Technologies: Quantitative Identification and Measurement," *Technology Analysis and Strategic Management* 22: 361–76.

Dodier, N. (2005) "Transnational Medicine in Public Arenas: AIDS Treatments in the South," *Culture, Medicine, and Psychiatry* 29: 285–307.

Gagliardino, J.J. (2000) "An Overview of Argentine Contributions to Diabetes Research in the Decade of the 1990s," *Diabetes/Metabolism Research and Reviews* 16: 43–60.

Galvao, J. (2005) "Brazil and Access to HIV/AIDS Drugs: A Question of Human Rights and Public Health," *American Journal of Public Health* 95: 1110–16.

Gatchair, S., I. Bortagaray, and S. Cozzens (2011) "Biotechnology Paths in Developing Countries: Analyzing GM in Costa Rica and Jamaica and Learning from Plant Tissue Culture." Forthcoming in the *African Journal of Science, Technology, Innovation, and Development.*

Geels, F.W. (2002) "Technological Transitions as Evolutionary Reconfiguration Processes: A Multi-level Perspective and a Case-Study," *Research Policy* 31 (8/9): 1257–74.

Homedes, N. and A. Ugalde (2006) "Improving Access to Pharmaceuticals in Brazil and Argentina," *Health Policy and Planning* 21: 123–31.

James, C. (2005) "Global Status of Commercialized Biotech/GM Crops: 2005." Ithaca, NY: International Service for the Acquisition of Agri-Biotech Applications.

Juma, C. and Y.-C. Lee (2005) *Innovation: Applying Knowledge in Development.* London: Earthscan.

Sen, A. (1992) *Inequality Reexamined.* Cambridge, MA: Harvard University Press.

Thurston, Richard (2007) "European Commission Report Endorses Open Source," ZDNet, January 16. Available at: www.zdnet.co.uk/misc/print/0,1000000169,39285468-39001068c,00.htm (accessed 2/12/2007).

Von Hippel, Eric (2005) *Democratizing Innovation.* Cambridge, MA: MIT Press.

Walsh, G. (2005) "Therapeutic Insulins and their Large-Scale Manufacture," *Appl Microbiol Biotechnol* 67 (2): 151–9.

World Health Organization (2003) "Diabetes Cases could Double in Developing Countries in Next 30 Years." Available at: www.who.int/mediacentre/news/releases/2003/pr86/en/print.html (accessed 2/12/2007).

6. The Progress of Nanotechnology in China

Bai, C.L. (2001) "Progress of Nanoscience and Nanotechnology in China," *Journal of Nanoparticle Research* 3 (4): 251–6.

Bai, C.L. (2005) "Ascent of Nanoscience in China," *Science* 309 (5731): 61–3.

Economic Daily (2005) 国家科技计划支持纳米科技发展 (National Science and Technology Programs Support Nanotechnology Development). Available at: www.ce.cn/xwzx/gnsz/gdxw/200509/30/t20050930_4845537.shtml (accessed 5/28/2009).

Huang, C., A. Notten, and N. Rasters (2010) "Nanoscience and Technology Publications and Patents: A Review of Social Science Studies and Search Strategies," *Journal of Technology Transfer,* DOI 10.1007/s10961-009-9149-8.

Huang, C., C. Amorim, M. Spinoglio, B. Gouveia, and A. Medina (2004) "Organization, Programme and Structure: An Analysis of the Chinese Innovation Policy Framework," *R & D Management* 34 (4): 367–87.

Liu, Weizhen, Feng Huang, Yiqun Liao, Jing Zhang, Guoqiang Ren, Zangyong Zhuang, Jinsheng Zhen, Zhang Lin, and Chen Wang (2008) "Angew," *Chem. Int. Ed.* 47 (5619).

Liang, X.J. *et al.* (2010) Metallofullerene Nanoparticles Circumvent Tumor Resistance to Cisplatin by Reactivating Endocytosis. *Proceedings of the National Academy of Sciences* 107 (16): 7449–7454.

Lux Research (2008) *Nanomaterials State of the Market Q3 2008: Stealth Success, Broad Impact, 2008.* New York: Lux Research Inc.

National Center for Nanoscience and Technology (2009) 国家纳米科学中心简介 (Introduction to National Center for Nanoscienec and Technology). Available at: www.nanoctr.cn/intro/2.html (accessed 5/28/2009).

Porter, A., J. Youtie, P. Shapira, and D. Schoeneck (2008) "Refining Search Terms for Nanotechnology," *Journal of Nanoparticle Research* 10 (5): 715–28.

Scheu, M., V. Veefkind, Y. Verbandt, E. Molina Galan, R. Absalom, and W. Forster (2006) "Mapping Nanotechnology Patents: The EPO Approach," *World Patent Information* 28 (3): 204–11.

Tang, N., G.J. Du, N. Wang, C.C. Liu, H.Y. Hang, and W. Liang (2007) "Improving Penetration in Tumors with Nanoassemblies of Phospholipids and Doxorubicin," *Journal of the National Cancer Institute* 99 (13): 1004–15.

7. Food Security

Burrows, Beth (2001) "Patents, Ethics and Spin," *Redesigning Life? The Worldwide Challenge to Genetic Engineering*, edited by B. Tokar. New York and London: Zed Books.

Charles, D. (2010) "Genetically Modified Corn Helps Common Kind, too," *NPR*, October 7. Available at: www.npr.org/templates/story/story.php?storyId=130405227.

Cummings, C.H. (2002) "Risking Corn Risking Culture," *World Watch*, pp. 8–19.

Esteva, G. and C. Marielle (eds.) (2003) *Sin Maíz no Hay País*. Mexico, D.F.: Direccion General de Culturas Populares e Indigenas.

Fitting, E. (2006) "Importing Corn, Exporting Labor: The Neoliberal Corn Regime, GMOs, and the Erosion of Mexican Biodiversity," *Agriculture & Human Values* 23 (1): 15–26.

Food and Water Europe (December 2009) "Unseen Hazards: From Nanotechnology to Nanotoxicity."

Huang, J., R. Hu, S. Rozelle, and C. Prey (2005) "Insect-Resistant GM Rice in Farmers' Fields: Assessing Productivity and Health Effects in China," *Science* 308: 688–90.

Huang, J., S. Rozelle, C. Prey, and Q. Wang (2002) "Plant Biotechnology in China," *Science* 295: 674–6.

Jalonick, M.C. (2010) "Fish or Frankenfish? FDA Weighs Altered Salmon," *Yahoo News*, September 20. Available at: http://news.yahoo.com/s/ap/20100920/ap_on_bi_ge/us_modified_ salmon.

Joseph, T. and M. Morrison (2006) "Nanotechnology in Agriculture and Food," *Nanoforum Report. Institute of Nanotechnology. Reino Unido.*

Keeley, J. (2006) "Balancing Technological Innovation and Environmental Regulation: An Analysis of Chinese Agricultural Biotechnological Governance," *Environmental Politics* 15 (2): 293–309.

Kuzma, J. (2007) "Moving Forward Responsibly: Oversight for the Nanotechnology-Biology Interface," *Journal of Nanoparticle Research* 9: 165–82.

La Jornada On Line (January 31, 2007) *Llaman a crear nuevo pacto de defensa social*. Available at: www.jornada.unam.mx/ultimas/2007/01/31/constuir-un-pacto-social-incluyente-demanda-central-en-marcha (accessed 1/31/2007).

Lee, J. and R. Kigali (2006) Comparing NGO Influence in the EU and the US. Programme on NGOs and Civil Society. Geneva, Switzerland: Centre for Applied Studies in International Negotiation.

Miller, D.D. (2010) "New Leverage against Iron Deficiency," *Nature Nanotechnology* 5.

Nadal, A. (2006) "Mexico's Corn-producing Sector: A Commentary," *Agriculture & Human Values* 23 (1): 33–6.

Ortiz-García, S., E. Ezcurra, B. Schoel, F. Acevedo, J. Soberón, and A.A. Snow (2005) "Absence of Detectable Transgenes in Local Landraces of Maize in Oaxaca, Mexico (2003–2004)."

Proceedings of the National Academy of Sciences. Available at: www.pnas.org/cgi/doi/10.1073/pnas.0503356102 (accessed 7/3/2008).

Parker, R., C. Ridge, C. Cao, and R. Appelbaum (2009) "China's Nanotechnology Patent Landscape: An Analysis of Invention Patents Filed with the State Intellectual Property Office," *Nanotechnology Law and Business* 6: 524–39.

Pidgeon, N., B.H. Harthorn, K. Bryant, and T. Rogers-Hayden (2009) "Deliberating the Risks of Nanotechnologies for Energy and Health Applications in the United States and United Kingdom," *Nature Nanotechnology* 4 (2): 95–8.

Quist, D., and Ignacio H. Chapala (2001) "Transgenic DNA Introgressed into Traditional Maize Landraces in Oaxaca, Mexico," *Nature* 414: 541–3.

Rogers, J.B. (2008) *The Ma(i)ze of Globalization: Free Trade, Gender, and Resistance in Oaxaca.* Dissertation. University of California, Santa Barbara.

Sastry, R. Kalpana, N.H. Rao, R. Cahoon, and T. Tucker (2007) "Can Nanotechnology Provide the Innovations for a Second Green Revolution in Indian Agriculture," *NSF Nanoscale Science and Engineering Grantees Conference*, December 3–6. Available at: www.nseresearch.org/2007/overviews/Sastry_speaker.doc.

Satterfield, Terre, Milind Kandlikar, Christian Beaudrie, Joseph Conti, and Barbara Herr Harthorn (2009) "Anticipating the Perceived Risk of Nanotechnologies," *Nature Nanotechnology* 4 (11): 752–8.

Scott, N.R. (2007) "Nanoscience in Veterinary Medicine," *Veterinary Research Communications* 31 (Suppl.): 139–44.

Shand, H. (2001) "Gene Giants: Understanding the 'Life Industry'," in *Redesigning Life? The Worldwide Challenge to Genetic Engineering*, edited by B. Tokar, pp. 222–37. London and New York: Zed Books.

Shiva, V. (1991a) "The Failure of the Green Revolution; A Case Study of the Punjab," *The Ecologist* 21 (2): 57–60.

Shiva, V. (1991b) *The Violence of the Green Revolution: Third World Agriculture, Ecology and Politics.* London and New York: Zed Books.

Soleri, D., D.A. Cleveland, and F.A. Cuevas (2006) "Transgenic Crops and Crop Varietal Diversity: The Case of Maize in Mexico," *Bioscience* 56 (6): 503–13.

Stilgoe, J. (2007) *Nanodialogues: Experiments in Public Engagement with Science.* London: Demos.

Tauli-Corpuz, V. (2001) "Biotechnology and Indigenous Peoples," in *Redesigning Life? The Worldwide Challenge to Genetic Engineering*, edited by B. Tokar, pp. 252–70. New York and London: Zed Books.

Tokar, B. (ed.) (2001) *Redesigning Life: The Worldwide Challenge to Genetic Engineering.* New York and London: Zed Books.

8. (Nano)technology and Food Security

Berry, W. (1986) *The Unsettling of America: Culture and Agriculture.* San Francisco: Sierra Club

Buttel, F.H., M. Kenney, and J. Kloppenburg, Jr. (1985) "From Green Revolution to Biorevolution: Some Observations on the Changing Technological Bases of Economic Transformation in the Third World," *Economic Development and Cultural Change* 34 (1): 31–55.

Barlett, Peggy (1993) *American Dreams, Rural Realities: Family Farms in Crisis.* Chapel Hill: University of North Carolina Press.

Ceccarelli, S. and S. Grando (2007) "Decentralized-Participatory Plant Breeding: An Example of Demand Driven Research," *Euphytica* 155 (3): 349–60.

Das, R.J. (2002) "The Green Revolution and Poverty: A Theoretical and Empirical Examination of the Relation between Technology and Society," *Geoforum* 33 (1): 55–72.

FAO (Food and Agriculture Organization of the United Nations) (2009) *The State of Food Insecurity in the World 2009: Economic Crises—Impacts and Lessons Learned.* Rome: Economic and Social Development Department (FAO). Available at: www.fao.org/docrep/012/i0876e/i0876e00.htm.

Kloppenburg, J.R. (1988) *First the Seed: The Political Economy of Plant Biotechnology.* Cambridge: Cambridge University Press.

Lacy, S. (2004) *One Finger Cannot Lift a Stone: Family Farmers and Household Sorghum Production in Southern Mali.* Dissertation, Department of Anthropology. Santa Barbara: University of California.

Lacy, S., D. Cleveland, and D. Soleri (2006) "Farmer Choice of Sorghum Varieties in Southern Mali: Managing Unpredictable Growing Environments and Resources," *Human Ecology* 34 (2): 331–53.

Lacy, S. (forthcoming) *Follow the Seed: Understanding Plant Variety Protection and Intellectual Property Rights through Farmer Seed Systems in Southern Mali.*

Latour, B. and S. Woolgar (1986) *Laboratory Life: The Social Construction of Scientific Facts.* Princeton: Princeton University Press.

Lipton, M. and R. Longhurst (1989) *New Seeds and Poor People.* London: Unwin Hyman.

McNaughton, P.R. (1993) *The Mande Blacksmiths: Knowledge, Power, and Art in West Africa.* Bloomington: Indiana University Press.

NCHS (National Center for Health Statistics) (2010) Obesity and Overweight. Centers for Disease Control and Prevention. Available at: www.cdc.gov/nchs.fastats/overwt.htm (accessed 12/20/2010).

Paddock, W. (1970) "How Green is the Green Revolution?" *Bioscience* 20: 897–902.

PCAST (President's Council of Advisors on Science and Technology) 2010 "Report to the President and Congress on the Third Assessment of the National Nanotechnology Initiative." Washington, DC: Office of Science and Technology Policy, Executive Office of the President. Available at: www.whitehouse.gov/sites/default/files/microsites/ostp/pcast-nano-report.pdf.

Pearce, C., S. Fourmy, and H. Kovach (2009) "Delivering Education for all in Mali," *Oxfam International Research Report.* London: Oxfam International. Available at: www.oxfam.org.uk/resources/policy/education/downloads/delivering_education_for_all_mali_report.pdf.

Peterson, B. (2005) *Transforming the Village: Migration, Islam and Colonialism in French Southern Mali (West Africa), 1880–1960.* Dissertation, Department of History. New Haven: Yale University.

Richards, P. (1985) *Indigenous Agricultural Revolution: Ecology and Food Crops in West Africa.* Boulder: Westview Press.

Shiva, V. (1991) *The Violence of the Green Revolution: Third World Agriculture, Ecology, and Politics.* London: Zed Books.

USDA (United States Department of Agriculture) (2010) Extension: National Institute of Food and Agriculture. Available at: www.csrees.usdsa.gov/qlinks/extension.html (accessed 12/20/2010).

Weltzien, E. and V. Hoffmann (2005) *Setting Breeding Objectives and Developing Seed Systems with Farmers. A Handbook for Practical Use in Participatory Plant Breeding Projects.* Weikersheim: Margraf Publishers.

Weltzien, E., S. Lacy, A. Christinck, A. Touré, F. Rattunde, M. Diarra, S. Siart, A. Sangare, and M. Coulibaly (2008) "Farmers' Access to Sorghum Varieties and Benefit Sharing form Participatory Plant Breeding in Mali, West Africa," in *Whose Varieties are they? Clarifying Questions of Recognition, Access, and Benefit Sharing Related to the Development of New Varieties through Participatory Plant Breeding*, edited by Y. Song and R. Vernooy. Ottowa: International Development Research Centre (IRDC). IRDC File 102803-02.

World Bank (2008) *World Development Indicators 2008.* Washington, DC: World Bank.

World Bank (2010) *World Development Indicators 2010.* Washington, DC: World Bank.

10. Nanotechnology for Potable Water and General Consumption in Developing Countries

Arriens, Wouter Lincklaen (2007) "Coping With Water Scarcity: A Challenge for the 21st Century." Asian Development Bank (March). Available at: www.adb.org/water/Articles/2007/WoW-Water-Scarcity.asp.

Chemicalprocessing.com (n.d.) (accessed 10/26/10)

DAI (Development Alternatives Inc.), *What is Surface Water?*Available at: http://imnh.isu.edu/DIGITALATLAS/hydr/concepts/surfhyd/srfwtr.html (accessed 2011).

Frost & Sullivan (2006) "Impact of Nanotechnology in Water and Wastewater Treatment." Available at: www.marketresearch.com/map/prod/1432625.html.

Funke, N., K. Norte and K. Findlater (2007) "Redressing Inequality: South Africa's New Water Policy. Environment: Science and Policy for Sustainable-Development.," *Environment Magazine.* Available at: www.environmentmagazine.org/Archives/Back%20Issues/April%202007/Funke-full.html (accessed 3/19/2008).

Grinshaw, D. (2009) "Nanotechnology for Clean Water: Facts and Figures." Available at: www.scider.net/en/features/nanotechnology-for-clean-water-facts-and-figures.

Haysom, A. (2006) "A Study of the Factors Affecting Sustainability of Rural Water-Supplies-in-Tanzania." Available at: www.wateraid.org.

Hillie, T. and M. Hlophe (2007) "Nanotechnology and the Challenge of Clean Water," *Nature Nano* 2: 663–4.

Hillie, T., M. Munasinghe, M. Hlophe, and Y. Deraniyagala (2006) "Nanotechnology, Water and Development." Washington, DC: Meridian Institute.

Historyofwaterfilters.com (n.d.) Available at: www.historyofwaterfilters.com/ground-surface-water.html (accessed 2011).

Hlophe, M. (2009) "Water Safety and Security Plan for RLM" (unpublished report).

Hlophe, M. and T. Hillie (2008) "The Challenges of the Implementation of Nanotechnology Solutions in Water Issues in Africa," in *Nanotechnology Applications for Clean Water*, edited by M. Diallo, J. Duncan, N. Savage, A. Street, and R. Sustich, pp. 551–60. Washington, DC: William Andrew Applied Science Publishers.

Hlophe, M. and M.D. Venter (2009) "The Testing of a Membrane Technology Unit for the Removal of Nitrate, Chloride, Fluoride, Sulphate, Calcium and Magnesium Pollutants from Groundwater, and the Monitoring of Rural Consumer Knowledge and Attitude to Water Purification," *Report to the Water Research Commission (WRC) of South Africa*, Report no. 1529/1/09.

Jansky, L. and J. Uitto (2005) *Enhancing Participation and Government in Water Resources Management: Conventional Approaches and Information Technology.* United States of America: United Nations University Press.

Krantz, D. and B. Kifferstein (2010) *Water Pollution and Society*. Available at: www.umich.edu/~gs265/society/waterpollution.htm (accessed 10/10/2011).

Makoni, M. (2009) "Nanosponges: South Africa's High Hopes for Clean Water." Available at: www.scider.high-hopes-for-clean-water.

Mehta, L. (2007) "Whose Scarcity? Whose Property? The Case of Water in Western India," *Land Policy* 24: 654–63.

Mfangavo, C. (2005) "Policy Overview: A Review of Policy and Practice in Relation to Water and HIV/Aids in Tanzania." Bradford Centre for International Development. Bradford: University of Bradford.

Modise, S.J. and H.M. Krieg (2004) "Evaluation of NF for the Treatment of Rural Groundwater for Potable Water Use," *Report to the Water Research Commission (WRC) of South Africa*, Report no.1230/1/04.

Netshinswinzhe, B. (1999) "Sustainability of Community Water Supply Projects in S Africa," paper presented in the 25th WEDC Conference. Ethiopia: Addis Ababa, pp. 104–7.

O'fairheallaigh, C. (2009) "Public Participation and Environmental Impact Assessment: Purposes, Implications, and Lessons for Public Policy Making," *Environmental Impact Assessment Review* 30: 19–27.

Philips, N. (2011) "Ground Water and Surface Water: Understanding the Interaction," *Conservation Technology Information Center (CTIC)*. Available at: http://ctic.org/media/files/Ground%20Water%20and%20Surface%20Water.pdf (accessed 2011).

Physorg (n.d.) *Engineers Develop Revolutionary Nanotech Water Desalination Membrane*. Available at: www.physorg.com/news.82047372.html.

Pieterson, K. (2005) "Groundwater Crucial to Rural Development," *WRC, Water Wheel* 4 (2): 26–7.

Pillay, V.L. and E.P. Jacob (2004) "The Development of Small-Scale Ultra-Filtration Systems for Potable Water Production," *Pretoria: Water Research Commission*. WRC report no. 1070/1/04.

Sonjica, B. (2009) Available at: www.ierm.org.za/ejournal/2009/11/5/sa-needs-about-r70billion-to-improve-water-infrastructure.html.

South African Weather Service. Available at: www.weathersa.co.za/References/Climchange.jsp.

United Nations (2006) *The 2nd UN World Water Development Report: Water, a Shared Responsibility*. Available at: www.unesco.org/water/wwap/wwdr/wwdr2/table_contents.shtml.

United Nations (2008) *The Millennium Development Goals Report*. Available at: www.un.org/millenniumgoals/pdf/The%20Millennium%20Development%20Goals%20Report%202008.pdf.

United Nations (n.d.) Millennium Developmental Goals. Available at: http://en.wikipedia.org/wiki/Millenium_Development_Goals.com.

Wellman, P. (1999) "Study Pin-points Weaknesses in Celebrated Water Delivery Programme." *African Eye News Service*. Available at: http://Africanwater.org/SAWASProblems.html (accessed 2/12/2007).

Winpenny, J. (2003) *Report of the World Panel on Financing Water Infrastructure*. ISBN no. 92-95017-01-3.

World Health Organization (2005) *Water Safety Plans*. WHO/SDE/WSH/05.06.

World Water Day (2007) "Coping with Water Scarcity: Challenge of the Twenty First Century."

11. Solid-State Lighting

Fan, C.W. and J. Zhang (2001) "Characterization of Emissions from Portable Household Combustion Devices: Particle Size Distributions, Emission Rates and Factors, and Potential Exposures," *Atmospheric Environment* 35 (7): 1281–90.

Graham, S. (2006) *Sustainable Lighting in Rural Africa for Community Based Development – Baseline Report of Communities in the Project Area.* Light Up the World.

Irvine Halliday, D. (1999) *Feasibility Study of WLED Lighting Systems in Nepal.* Calgary: Light Up the World.

Irvine Halliday, D., G. Doluweera, I. Platonova, and J. Irvine Halliday (2008) "SSL – A Big Step Out of the Poverty Trap for the BOP!" *Journal of Light and Visual Environment* 32 (2): 258–66.

Kodisinghe, A. (2008) *Solid State Street Lighting for the Developing World.* Unpublished MEng diss., University of Calgary, Calgary.

Leon, S. and S. Graham (2005) *Village Lighting in Sri Lanka: Socioeconomic Impact Evaluation of LUTW Solid State Lighting Technology.* Unpublished Social Impact Assessment. Light Up the World Foundation.

Louineau, J., M. Dicko, P. Fraenkel, R. Barlow, and V. Bokalders (1994) *Rural Lighting: A Guide for Development Workers.* London: Intermediate Technology Publications.

Mills, E. (2002) *The $230-billion Global Lighting Energy Bill.* Paper presented at the First European Conference on Energy-Efficient Lighting, International Association for Energy-Efficient Lighting.

Mills, E. (2005) "The Specter of Fuel-Based Lighting," *Science* 308 (5726): 1263–4.

Parsons, D. (2007) *A Life Cycle Comparison of Alternative Lighting Technologies for Remote Areas in Developing Countries: A Study Done for Light Up The World Foundation.* University of Southern Queensland.

Peon, R. (2006) *Solid State Home Lighting Systems: A Brighter Option for the Developing World.* Unpublished MSc thesis, University of Calgary, Calgary.

Peon, R., G. Doluweera, I. Platonova, D. Irvine Halliday, and G. Irvine Halliday (2005) *Solid State Lighting for the Developing World: The Only Solution.* Paper presented at the Fifth International Conference on Solid State Lighting, San Diego, CA.

Prahalad, C.K. (2005) *The Fortune at the Bottom of the Pyramid.* New Jersey: Wharton.

Schare, S. and K.R. Smith (1995) "Particulate Emission Rates of Simple Kerosene Lamps," *Energy for Sustainable Development* 2 (2): 32–5.

Sireau, N. (2008) "The Power of the Sun: Solar Lanterns Transform Lives in Malawi, Africa." *RenewableEnergyWorld.com.*

UNDP (2002) *Nepal Human Development Report 2001: Poverty Reduction and Governance.*

12. Energy for Development

Brazil, Brazilian Statistics Bureau, IBGE, "Agricultural Census 2006." Available at: ftp://ftp.ibge.gov.br/Censos/Censo_Agropecuario_2006 (accessed 5/24/2009).

Brazil, Ministry of Agriculture, "Anuário Estatístico da Bioenergia" (Brasilia, 2009). Available at: www.agricultura.gov.br/images/MAPA/arquivos_portal/anuario_cana.pdf (accessed 5/23/2010).

Brazil, Ministry for Energy, "Brazilian Energy Balance." Available at: https://ben.epe.gov.br/default.aspx (accessed 11/21/2010).

Cerqueira Leite, R.C. de, *et al.* (2008) "Can Brazil Replace 5% of the Gasoline World Demand with Ethanol?" *Energy.*

da Silva, J.G., G.E. Serra, J.R. Moreira, J.C. Gonçalves, and J. Goldemberg (1978) "Energy Balance for Ethyl Alcohol Production from Crops," *Science* 201: 903–6.

FAO (2008) "The State of Food and Agriculture 2008." Available at: www.fao.org/docrep/011/i0100e/i0100e00.htm (accessed 5/24/2009).

IEA, "International Energy Outlook 2009." Available at: www.eia.doe.gov/oiaf/ieo/index.html (accessed 11/21/2010).

IEA, "Technology Roadmap: Biofuels for Transport." Available at: www.iea.org/papers/2011/biofuels_roadmap.pdf (accessed 5/24/2009).

Macedo, I.C., J.E.A. Seabra, and J.E.A.R. Silva (2008) "Green House Gases Emissions in the Production and Use of Ethanol from Sugarcane in Brazil: The 2005/2006 Averages and a Prediction for 2020," *Biomass and Bioenergy.*

Moraes, Márcia Azanha Ferraz Dias de (1999) "A Desregulamentação Do Setor Sucroalcooleiro Brasileiro," Doctorate Thesis, ESALQ, USP.

Nassar, A., L. Harfuch, M. Moreira, L. Bachion, and L. Antoniazzi (2009) "Report to the U.S. Environmental Protection Agency regarding the Proposed Changes to the Renewable Fuel Standard Program Impacts on Land Use and GHG Emissions from a Shock on Brazilian Sugarcane Ethanol Exports to the United States using the Brazilian Land Use Model (BLUM)." Available at: www.iconebrasil.org.br/arquivos/noticia/1873.pdf (accessed 11/21/2010).

Porto, Lia de Mendonça, "Modelagem de Processo Industrial de Fermentação Alcoólica contínua com Reatores de Mistura Ligados em Série," Tese apresentada á Faculdade de Engenharia Química da Universidade Estadual de Campinas para obtenção do título de Doutor em Engenharia Química. Dezembro 2005. Available at: http://libdigi.unicamp.br/document/?code=vtls000381157 (acessed 6/12/2009).

PRNewswire, "EPA Reaffirms Sugarcane Biofuel is Advanced Renewable Fuel with 61% Less Emissions than Gasoline." Available at: www.prnewswire.com/news-releases/epa-reaffirms-sugarcane-biofuel-is-advanced-renewable-fuel-with-61-less-emissions-than-gasoline-83483922.html (accessed 11/21/2010).

13. Implications of Nanotechnology for Labor and Employment

Abicht, L., H. Freikamp, and U. Schumann (2006) "Identification of Skill Needs in Nanotechnology." European Centre for the Development of Vocational Training, Cedefop Panorama Series 120. Available at: www2.trainingvillage.gr/etv/publication/download/panorama/5170_en.pdf.

Allhoff, F. and P. Lin (2009) *Nanotechnology & Society: Current and Emerging Ethical Issues.* New York: Springer.

Baker, S. and A. Aston (2005) "The Business of Nanotech." *Business Week.* February 14, 2005. Available at: www.businessweek.com/magazine/content/05_07/b3920001_mz001.htm.

Batterson, J. (2005) "Education and Human Resource Development," in *Nanotechnology: Societal Implications. Maximizing Benefits for Humanity,* edited by M. Roco and W.S. Bainbridge. Arlington: National Science Foundation. Available at: www.nano.gov/nni_societal_implications.pdf.

Bowman, D. and G. Hodge (2006) "Nanotechnology: Mapping the Wild Regulatory Frontier," *Futures* 38 (9): 1060–73.

CEST (Commission de l'Ethique de la science et de la technologie. Gouvernement du Québec)

(2006) "Ethics and Nanotechnology: A Basis for Action." Position Statement. Available at: www.nanowerk.com/nanotechnology/reports/reportpdf/report121.pdf.

Cientifica (2008) "The Nanotechnology Opportunity Report 2008." Available at: http://cientifica.eu/blog/research/nor.

Crow, M. and D. Sarewitz (2001) "Nanotechnology and Societal Transformation," in *Societal Implications of Nanoscience and Nanotechnology,* edited by M. Roco and W.S. Bainbridge, pp. 55–66. Dordrecht:: Kluwer Academic Publishers.

Davies, C. (2008) "Nanotechnology Oversight: An Agenda for the New Administration." Washington, DC: The Woodrow Wilson International Center for Scholars. Project on Emerging Nanotechnologies. Available at: www.nanotechproject.org/process/assets/files/6709/pen13.pdf.

ENA—European NanoBusiness Association (2005) "The 2005 European NanoBusiness." Available at: www.nanoeurope.org/survey.htm.

ETC Group (2003) *The Big Down: Atomtech—Technologies Converging at the Nano-Scale.* Available at: www.etcgroup.org/upload/publication/171/01/thebigdown.pdf.

ETC Group (2005) "The Potential Impacts of Nano-scale Technologies on Commodity Markets: The Implications for Commodity Dependent Developing Countries." South Centre Trade Research Papers, 4. Available at: www.etcgroup.org/upload/publication/45/01/southcentre.commodities.pdf.

European Commission (2004) *Towards a European Strategy for Nanotechnology.* Luxembourg: EUR-OP. Available at: ftp://ftp.cordis.europa.eu/pub/nanotechnology/docs/nano_com_en_new.pdf.

Freeman R. and K. Shukla (2008) "Science and Engineering Workforce Project Digest: Jobs in Nanotech? Creating a Measure of Job Growth." National Bureau of Economic Research. Available at: www.nber.org/~sewp/SEWPDigestJun2008.pdf.

Freeman, R. and K. Shukla (September, 2010) "Jobs in Nanotech—Creating a Measure of Job Growth." Science and Engineering Workforce Project Digest. Available at: www.nber.org/~sewp/SEWPDigestJun2008.pdf.

Gatchair, S. (2011) "Potential Implications for Equity in the Nanotechnology Workforce in the US," in *Yearbook of Nanotechnology and Society,* Vol. III: *Nanotechnology, Equity and Equality,* edited by S. Cozzens and J. Wetmore. New York: Springer.

Guimarães, C. (2010) "Desenvolvimento da nanotecnologia em empresas brasileiras e suas potenciais implicações para o emprego." Master Disssertation on Technology. Universidade Tecnológica Federal do Paraná, Curitiba, Brazil.

Harper, T. (2003) "What is Nanotechnology?" *Nanotechnology* 14 (1). Available at: http://iopscience.iop.org/0957-4484/14/1/001.

Holman, M. (2009) Nanotechnology: State of the Markets in 2009. Presentation. Euro Nano-Forum. Plenary Session: Nanotechnology for Sustainable Economy. June 2. Available at: www.czech-in.org/enf2009/ppt/Plenary_1_Holman_Y.pdf.

Hullman, A. (2006) "The Economic Development of Nanotechnology—An Indicators Based Analysis." European Commission DG Research. Available at: ftp://ftp.cordis.europa.eu/pub/nanotechnology/docs/nanoarticle_hullmann_nov2006.pdf.

Hwang, D. and J. Bradley (September, 2010) "The Recession's Ripple Effect on Nanotech." Available at: www.electroiq.com/index/display/nanotech-article-display/5049629279/articles/small-times/nanotechmems/materials/general/2010/april/the-recession_s_ripple.html.

ILO (September, 2010) "Focus on New Emerging Hazards in a Changing World of Work."

Geneva: ILO. Available at: www.ilo.org/global/About_the_ILO/Media_and_public_information/Press_releases/lang--en/WCMS_126383/index.htm.

Invernizzi, N., G. Foladori, D. Maclurcan (2008) "Nanotechnology's Controversial Role for the South," *Science, Technology and Society* 13 (1): 123–48.

IRGC (2007) "Nanotechnology Risk Governance Recommendations for a Global, Coordinated Approach to the Governance of Potential Risks." Policy Brief. International Risk Governance Council. Available at: www.irgc.org/IMG/pdf/PB_nanoFINAL2_2_.pdf.

Lux Research (2007) "Nanotechnology Moves from Discovery to Commercialization: $50 billion in 2006 product sales, $12 billion in Funding." Available at: www.luxresearchinc.com/press/2007-lux-research-nanotech-report-5.pdf.

Malsch, I. and M. Oud (2004) Outcome of the Open Consultation on the European Strategy for Nanotechnology, European Nanotechnology Gateway. Nanoforum.org. Available at: www.nanoforum.org/dateien/temp/nanosurvey6.pdf.

MCT (Ministério da Ciência e da Tecnologia) (2004) "Plano Estratégico do MCT 2004–2007." Brazil: Ministério da Ciência e da Tecnologia.

MCT (Ministério da Ciência e da Tecnologia) (2007) "Ciência, Tecnologia e Inovação para o Desenvolvimento Nacional. Plano de Ação 2007–2010." Available at: www.mct.gov.br/upd_blob/0021/21439.pdf.

Meridian Institute (2005) "Nanotechnology and the Poor: Opportunities and Risk: Closing the Gaps within and between Sectors of Society." Available at: www.meridian-nano.org/gdnp/NanoandPoor.pdf.

Meridian Institute (2007) "Nanotechnology, Commodities and Development." Background Paper for the International Workshop on Nanotechnology, Commodities and Development, Rio de Janeiro, May 29–31. Available at: www.merid.org/nano/commoditiesworkshop/files/Comm_Dev_and_Nano_FINAL.pdf.

Nanowerk (September, 2010) "Well over 2000 Companies Worldwide Already Involved in Nanotechnology." Available at: www.nanowerk.com/news/newsid=16967.php.

NTSC (2007) "The National Nanotechnology Initiative: Strategic Plan." Executive Office of the President, National Science and Technology Council, Nanoscale Science, Engineering and Technology Subcommittee. Available at: www.ostp.gov/galleries/default-file/NNI_Strategic_Plan_2007_Final.pdf.

Pandya, B.H. (2001) "Nanotechnology Workforce Pipeline Challenges: A Current Assessment and the Future Outlook." American Society of Mechanical Engineers. Available at: www.wise-intern.org/journal/2001/brianpandya2001.pdf.

PEN (2009). Consumer Products Inventory. Analysis. Project on Emerging Nanotechnology. Woodrow Wilson International Center for Scholars. Available at: www.nanotechproject.org/inventories/consumer/analysis_draft.

Richardson, C. (2008) "Uncovering the Social Impacts of Nano: The Hidden Effects of Hidden Technology." Working Document. University of Massachussets at Lowell Labor Extension Program.

Roco, M.C. (2003) "Broader Societal Issues of Nanotechnology," *Journal of Nanoparticle Research* 5: 181–9.

Roco M.C. and W. Bainbridge (eds) (2001) "Societal Implications of Nanoscience and Nanotechnology." National Science Foundation Report (also Kluwer Academic Publishers, Boston, 370pp.).

Sarma, S.D. and S. Chaudhury (2009) "Socioeconomic Implications of Nanotechnology Applications," *Nanotechnology, Law & Business* 6 (2): 278–310.

Singh, K.A. (2007) "Nanotechnology Skills and Training Survey. Summary of Outcomes." Institute of Nanotechnology UK. Available at: www.nanoforum.org/dateien/temp/Nanotechno logy%20Skills%20and%20Training%20Survey%20Results.pdf?15102010220616.

Stephan, P., G.C. Black and T. Chang (2007) "The Small Size of the Small Scale Market: The Early-stage Labor Market for Highly Skilled Nanotechnology Workers," *Research Policy* 36: 887–92.

Subramanian, V., J. Youtie, A. Porter, and P. Shapira (2009) "Is there a Shift to Active Nanostructures?" *Journal of Nanoparticle Research* 12 (1): 253–79.

Toma, H.E. (2005) "Interfaces e organização da pesquisa no Brasil: da Química à Nanotecnologia," *Química Nova* 28: 48–51. Available at: www.scielo.br/pdf/qn/v28s0/26775.pdf.

Treder, M. (2004) Nanotechnology and Society. Times of Change. Presentation. I International Seminar on Nanotechnology, Society and Environment, São Paulo, October 18. Available at: www.crnano.org/Speech%20-%20Times%20of%20Change.ppt.

TSSB (2009) "TSSB Recognizes Nanotechnology Technician Skill Standards. Texas Skill Standards." Available at: www.tssb.org/wwwpages/home/newsarchives/2009_nano.htm.

USDL (2006) Carrier Voyages. Nanotechnology. United States Department of Labor. Available at: www.careervoyages.gov/nanotechnology-main.cfm.

Van Horn, C. and A. Fichtner (2008) "The Workforce Needs of Companies Engaged in Nanotechnology Research in Arizona." The Center for Nanotechnology in Society, Arizona State University. Available at: cns.asu.edu/cns-library/year/?action=getfile&file=189&section= lib.

Van Horn, C., J. Cleary and A. Fichtner (2009) "The Workforce Needs of Pharmaceutical Companies in New Jersey that use Nanotechnology: Preliminary Findings." The Center for Nanotechnology in Society, Arizona State University. Available at: cns.asu. edu/cns-library/type/?action=getfile&file=109&section=lib.

Whitesides, G. (2005) "Science and Education for Nanoscience and Nanotechnology," in *Nanotechnology: Societal Implications: Maximizing Benefits for Humanity*, edited by M. Roco and W.S. Bainbridge. Arlington, VA: National Science Foundation. Available at: www.nano. gov/nni_societal_implications.pdf.

Yonas, G. and T. Picraux (2001) "National Needs Drivers for Nanotechnology," in *Societal Implications of Nanoscience and Nanotechnology*, edited by M.C. Roco and W.S. Bainbridge, pp. 37–44. Final Report from the Workshop held at the National Science Foundation, September 28–29, 2000. Available at: www.wtec.org/loyola/nano/NSET.Societal.Implications.

Zweck, A., G. Bachmann, W. Luther, and C. Ploetz (2008) "Nanotechnology in Germany: From Forecasting to Technological Assessment to Sustainability Studies," *Journal of Cleaner Production* 16: 977–87.

14. Seeking the Non-Developmental within the Developmental

Abraham, R. (2007) "Mobile Phones and Economic Development: Evidence from the Fishing Industry in India," *Information Technologies & International Development* 4 (1): 5–17.

Bayes, Abdul (2001) "Infrastructure and Rural Development: Insights from a Grameen Bank Village Phone Initiative in Bangladesh," *Agricultural Economics* 25 (2–3): 261–72.

Bell, Daniel (1999) *The Coming of Post-Industrial Society: A Venture in Social Forecasting*. New York: Basic Books.

Castells, M. (2000) *The Information Age: Economy Society and Culture, Vol. 1: The Rise of the Network Society*. Oxford: Blackwell.

Castells, M. (2001a) "Information Technology and Global Capitalism," in *Living with Global Capitalism*, edited by W.G. Hutton, pp. 52–74. London: Vintage.

Castells, M. (2001b) *The Internet Galaxy*. Oxford and New York: Oxford University Press.

Castles, Stephen (2003) "Migration and Community Formation under Conditions of Globalization," *Globalization and Society: Processes of Differentiation Examined*, edited by Raymond Breton and Jeffrey G. Reitz, pp. 219–32. London and Westport, CT: Praeger.

Chib, A. (2010) "The Aceh Besar Midwives with Mobile Phones Project: Design and Evaluation Perspectives Using the Information and Communication Technologies for Healthcare Development Model," *Journal of Computer-Mediated Communication* 15 (3): 500–25.

Chib, A. and V.H.H. Chen (2011) "Midwives with Mobiles: A Dialectical Perspective on Gender Arising from Technology Introduction in Rural Indonesia," *New Media & Society* 12 (3): 486–501.

Chib, A. and H. Wilkin (2011) "Singapore's Migrant Workers Use of Mobile Phones to Seek Social Support: An Investigation into Gender, Culture, and Livelihood." Presented at International Communication Association, Boston, MA, May 26–30, 2010.

Chib, A. and J. Zhao (2009) "Sustainability of ICT Interventions: Lessons from Rural Projects in China and India," in *Communicating for Social Impact: Engaging Communication Theory, Research, and Pedagogy*, edited by L. Harter, M.J. Dutta, and C.E. Cole, pp. 145–59. *ICA 2008 Conference Theme Book*. Creskill, NJ: Hampton Press.

China Internet Network Information Center (1997, October) *Statistical Report on the Development of Chinese Internet*. Available at: www.cnnic.net.cn/develst/9710/e-9710.shtml (accessed 4/14/2003).

China Internet Network Information Center (2008, July) *The 22nd Statistical Survey Report on the Internet Development in China*. Available at: www.cnnic.net.cn/uploadfiles/pdf/2008/7/23/170516.pdf (accessed 7/31/2008).

CNNIC (2010) "Report on Rural Internet Development 2009." Available at: www.cnnic.cn/research/bgxz/ncbg/201004/P020101230475751808990.pdf (accessed April 2011).

Donner, Jonathan (2009) "Blurring Livelihoods and Lives: The Social Uses of Mobile Phones and Socioeconomic Development," *Innovations: Technology, Governance, Globalization* 4 (1): 91–101.

Fink, C. and C.J. Kenny (2003) *W(h)ither the Digital Divide*. Washington, DC: World Bank.

Forss, P. (2007) "50,000 More Foreign Workers Needed in Construction Sector." Available at: www.channelnewsasia.com/stories/singaporelocalnews/view/254682/1/.html (accessed 1/23/2011).

Haftor, Darek M. (2011) *Information and Communication Technologies, Society and Human Beings: Theory and Framework*. Hershey, PA: Information Science Reference.

Idowu, B., E. Ogunbodede, and B. Idowu (2003) "Information and Communication Technology in Nigeria: The Health Sector Experience," *Journal of Information Technology Impact* 2.

International Organization for Migration (IOM) (2011) *Migration in Recent Times*. Available at: www.iom.int/jahia/Jahia/about-migration/migration-management-foundations/migration-history/migration-recent-times/cache/offonce (accessed 7/8/2011).

International Telecommunication Union (ITU) (2010) *Measuring the Information Society: Version 1.01*. Available at: www.itu.int/ITU-D/ict/publications/idi/2010/Material/MIS_2010_without_annex_4-e.pdf (accessed 6/23/2011).

International Telecommunication Union (ITU) (2011) *Information and Communication Technology (ICT) Statistics*. Available at: www.itu.int/ITU-D/ict/index.html (accessed 7/8/2011).

Internet and Mobile Association of India (IAMAI) (2007) *Internet in India: I-Cube 2007*. Available at: www.iamai.in/Upload/Research/I-Cube-2007-Summary-Report-final.pdf (accessed 6/23/2011).

Internet World Stats (IWS) (2007) *India Internet Usage Stats and Telecommunications Market Report*. Available at: www.internetworldstats.com/asia (accessed 7/30/2008).

Jensen, R. (2007) "The Digital Provide: Information (Technology), Market Performance, and Welfare in the South Indian Fisheries Sector," *Quarterly Journal of Economics* 122 (3): 879–924.

Katz, J.E. and R.E. Rice (2002) *Social Consequences of the Internet Use: Access, Involvement, and Interaction*. Cambridge, MA: The MIT Press.

Lievrouw, L.A. and S.M. Livingstone (2002) *The Handbook of New Media: Social Shaping and Consequences of ICTs*. London: Sage.

Lim, S.S. and M. Thomas (2010) "Walled-In, Reaching Out: Benefits and Challenges of Migrant Workers' Use of ICTs for Interpersonal Communication." *Conference Papers—International Communication Association*.

Lin, T.C. and H.L. Sun (2011) "Connection as a Form of Resisting Control: Foreign Domestic Workers' Mobile Phone Use in Singapore," *Media Asia* 3 (4): 183–214.

Ling, R. and B. Yttri (2002) "Hyper-Coordination Via Mobile Phones in Norway," in *Perpetual Contact: Mobile Communication, Private Talk, Public Performance*, edited by James E. Katz and Mark A. Aakhus, pp. 139–69. Cambridge: Cambridge University Press.

Mendoza, M.F.T. (2001) *The Global Digital Divide: Exploring the Relation between Core National Computing and National Capacity and Progress in Human Development over the Last Decade*. Unpublished doctoral dissertation, Tulane University, New Orleans. Available at: http://studentweb.tulane.edu/~mtruill/diss/Beginning.pdf (accessed 9/23/2008).

Pedersen, P.B. (1995) *The Five Stages of Culture Shock*. Westport, CT: Greenwood.

Prahalad, C.K. (2005) *The Fortune at the Bottom of the Pyramid*. New Jersey: Wharton.

Qiu, J.L. (2009) *Working-Class Network Society: Communication Technology and the Information Have-less in Urban China*. Cambridge, MA: MIT Press.

Rahman, M.M. and K.F. Lian (2005) "Bangladeshi Migrant Workers in Singapore: The View from the Inside," *Asia-Pacific Population Journal* 20: 63–88.

Richardson, D., R. Ramirez, and M. Haq (2000) *Grameen Telecom's Village Phone Programme in Rural Bangladesh: A Multi-Media Case Study*. Ontario: Canadian International Development Agency.

Robertson, R. (2004 [1992]) "Globalization as a Problem," in *The Globalization Reader*, 2nd edn, edited by F.J. Lechner and J. Bohli. Oxford: Blackwell.

Rose, C. (2010) "Singapore Must Keep Migrant Population Low," *Singapore Bureau; Dow Jones Newswires*. Available at: www.morningstar.co.uk/uk/markets/newsfeeditem.aspx?id=134292890323130.

Ryan, M.E. and R.S. Twibell (2000) "Concerns, Values, Stress, Coping, Health, and Educational Outcomes of College Students who Studied Abroad," *International Journal of Intercultural Relations* 24: 409–35.

Statistics Singapore (2011) "Theme on Population." Available at: www.singstat.gov.sg/pubn/reference/yos11/statsT-demography.pdf (accessed 7/8/2011).

Swagler, M.A. and M.V. Ellis (2003) "Crossing the Distance: Adjustment of Taiwanese Graduate Students in the United States," *Journal of Counseling Psychology* 50: 420–37.

Thompson, E.C. (2009) "Mobile Phones, Communities and Social Networks among Foreign Workers in Singapore," *Global Networks* 9 (3): 359–80.

TRAI (2009) "Annual Report 2009–10." Available at: www.trai.gov.in/annualreport/AnnualReport_09_10English.pdf (accessed April 2011).

United Nations, Department of Economic and Social Affairs, Population Division (2009) *Trends in International Migrant Stock: The 2008 Revision.* Available at: http://esa.un.org/migration/p2k0data.asp (accessed 3/31/2010).

UNDESA Population Division (2009). *Trends in International Migrant Stock: The 2008 Revision.* Available at: http://esa.un.org/migration/p2k0data.asp (accessed 3/31/2010).

United Nations Millennium Development Goals (UNMDG) (2011) Available at: www.un.org/millenniumgoals/global.shtml (accessed 7/8/2011).

Vedder, P. and E. Virta (2005) "Language, Ethnic Identity and the Adaptation of Turkish Immigrant Youth in the Netherlands and Sweden," *International Journal of Intercultural Relations* 29: 317–37.

Vertovec, S. (2004) "Cheap Calls: The Social Glue of Migrant Transnationalism," *Global Networks* 4 (2): 219–24.

Wallis, C. (2008) "Techno-Mobility and Translocal Migration: Mobile Phone Use among Female Migrant Workers in Beijing," in *Gender Digital Divide*, edited by Mannar Indira Srinivasan and V.V. Ramani. Hyderabad: Icfai University Press.

Warschauer, M. (2002) "Reconceptualizing the Digital Divide," *First Monday* 7 (7).

Webster, Frank (2006) *Theories of the Information Society*, (3rd edn. London and New York: Routledge.

Yeh, C.J. and M. Inose (2003) "International Students' Reported English Fluency, Social Support Satisfaction, and Social Connectedness as Predictors of Acculturative Stress," *Counseling Psychology Quarterly* 16: 15–28.

Yeoh, B. (2007) "Singapore: Hungry for Foreign Workers at all Skill Levels." Available at: www.migrationinformation.or (accessed 12/10/2009).

Zhang, W. and A. Chib (2011) "Internet Studies and Development: The Cases of China and India," paper presented at the 9th China Internet Research Conference, Washington, DC, May.

15. Responsible Innovation, Global Governance, and Emerging Technologies

BASF (2009) *Code of Conduct Nanotechnology.* Ludwigshafen, Germany: BASF.

Bowman, D.M. and G.A. Hodge (2009) "Counting on Codes: An Examination of Transnational Codes as a Regulatory Governance Mechanism for Nanotechnologies," *Regulation & Governance* 3 (2): 145–64.

COmparative Challenge of NANOmaterials (2007) "CONANO Endbericht—A Stakeholder Dialogue Project—Vergleichende Nutzen-Risiko-Analysen von abbaubaren und nicht abbaubaren Nano-Delivery-Systemen sowie konventionellen Mikro-Delivery-Systemen in pharmazeutischen und kosmetischen Anwendungen." Available at: www.ecology.at/files/berichte/E11.565.pdf (accessed 10/6/2010).

DEFRA (2008) T*he UK Voluntary Reporting Scheme for Engineered Nanoscale Materials: Seventh Quarterly Report.* London: Department for Environment Food and Rural Affairs.

Department of Innovation, Science and Research (2008) *Australian Community Attitudes Held About Nanotechnology—Trends 2005 to 2008.* Canberra: Market Attitude Research Services.

DuPont and Environmental Defense (2007) *Nano Risk Framework.* DuPont and Environmental Defense.

ETC Group (2005) *Down on the Farm: The Impact of Nano-scale Technologies on Food and Agriculture.* Ottawa: ETC Group.

European Association for the Co-ordination of Consumer Representation in Standardization and European Consumers' Organization (2009) *Nanotechnology: Small is Beautiful, But is it Safe?* Brussels: ANEC and BEUC.

European Chemical Industry Council (Cefic) (2008) Enabling Responsible Innovations of Nanotechnologies—Stakeholder Engagement Workshop. Brussels, Cefic.

European Commission (2006) "Europeans and Biotechnology in 2005: Patterns and Trends." Available at: http://ec.europa.eu/public_opinion/archives/ebs/ebs_244b_en.pdf.

European Commission (2007) First Annual Nanotechnology Safety for Success Dialogue. Brussels, DG Sanco.

European Commission (2008a) 2nd Annual Nanotechnology Safety for Success Dialogue Workshop. Brussels, DG Sanco.

European Commission (2008b) "Commission Recommendation on a Code of Conduct for Responsible Nanosciences and Nanotechnologies Research." Available at: http://ec.europa.eu/nanotechnology/pdf/nanocode-rec_pe0894c_en.pdf (accessed 10/6/2010).

European Commission (2009) Follow-up to the 2nd Nanotechnology Safety for Success Dialogue: Top Ten Actions To Launch by Eastern 2009. Brussels, DG Sanco.

European Cosmetics Association (2009) "Nanotechnology." Available at: http://www.colipa.eu/safety-a-science-colipa-the-european-cosmetic-cosmetics-association/products-and-ingredients/nanotechnology.html (accessed 10/6/2010).

European Parliament (2009) *Report on Regulatory Aspects of Nanomaterials (2008/2208(INI)).* Brussels: Commission Committee on the Environment, Public Health and Food Safety Commission.

FDA (2007) *Nanotechnology. A Report of the U.S. Food and Drug Administration Nanotechnology Task Force.* Washington, DC: Food and Drug Administration.

Federal Institute of Risk Assessment (2008) "Public Perceptions about Nanotechnology. Representative Survey and Basic Morphological-Psychological Study." Available at: www.bfr.bund.de/cm/290/public_perceptions_about_nanotechnology.pdf.

Federal Office for Public Health (2008) "Precautionary Matrix for Synthetic Nanomaterials." Available at: www.bag.admin.ch/themen/chemikalien/00228/00510/05626/index.html?lang=en (accessed 10/6/2010).

Friedman, T.L. (2005) *The World is Flat. A Brief History of the Twenty-First Century.* New York: Farrar, Straus and Giroux.

Friends of the Earth (FoE) (2006) *Nanomaterials, Sunscreens and Cosmetics: Small Ingredients, Big Risks.* Melbourne: FoE Australia and FoE United States.

Friends of the Earth (2008) *Out of the Laboratory and On to Our Plates: Nanotechnology in Food and Agriculture.* Melbourne: FoEA, FoEE, and FoEUS.

Friends of the Earth Australia (2009) *Nano and Biocidal Silver—Extreme Germ Killers Present A Growing Threat to Public Health.* Melbourne: FoE Australia.

German Chemical Industry Association and the German Federal Institute for Occupational Safety and Health (2007) "Stakeholder Dialog on Industrial Health and Safety." Available at: www.vci.de/template_downloads/tmp_VCIInternet/121338WS_Nano_Arbeitssicherhiet_II_2007_englisch.pdf?DokNr=121338&p=101 (accessed 10/6/2010).

German NanoKommission (2009) "Responsible Use of Nanotechnologies, Report and Recommendations of the German Federal Government's NanoKommission for 2008." Available at: www.bmu.de/english/nanotechnology/general_information/doc/44143.php (accessed 10/6/2010).

Grobe, A. and N. Kreinberger (2010) *Public Perception of Nanotechnologies: Challenges and Recommendations for Communication Strategies and Dialogue Concepts. Nanotechnology and Energy—Science, Promises and its Limits.* Singapore: Pan Standfortd Publishing.

Grobe, A., C. Schneider, V. Schetula, M. Rekic, and S. Nawrath (2008) "Nanotechnologien: Was Verbraucher wissen wollen, Studie im Auftrag des Verbraucherzentrale Bundesverbandes e.V." Available at: from www.vzbv.de/mediapics/studie_nanotechnologien_vzbv.pdf (accessed 10/6/2010).

Hajer, M.A. (2009) *Authoritative Governance. Policy-Making in the Age of Mediatization.* Oxford: Oxford University Press.

Hart, P.D.R.A. (2007) *Awareness of and Attitude Toward Nanotechnology and Federal Regulatory Agencies. A Report of Findings Based on a National Survey Among Adults.* Washington, DC: Woodrow Wilson International Center for Scholars.

Hoeck, J., H. Hofmann, H. Krug, C. Lorenz, L. Kimbach, B. Nowach, M. Riediker, K. Schirmer, C. Som, W. Stark, C. Suder, N. von Gotz, S. Wengert, and P. Wick (2008) *Precautionary Matrix for Synthetic Nanomaterials.* Berne: Federal Office for Public Health and the Federal Office for the Environment.

IRGC (2005) *Risk Governance: Towards an Integrative Approach.* Geneva: International Risk Governance Council.

IRGC (2006) *Nanotechnology—Risk Governance* (White Paper). Geneva: International Risk Governance Council.

IRGC (2008) *Risk Governance of Nanotechnology Applications in Food and Cosmetics.* Geneva: International Risk Governance Council.

IRGC (2009) *Appropriate Risk Governance Strategies for Nanotechnology Applications in Food and Cosmetics.* Geneva: International Risk Governance Council.

Kahan, D., P. Slovic, *et al.* (2007) *Nanotechnology Risk Perceptions: The Influence of Affect and Values.* Washington, DC: Wilson Center Project on Emerging Nanotechnologies.

Kahan, D.M., D. Braman, *et al.* (2008) "Cultural Cognition of the Risks and Bene?ts of Nanotechnology," *Nature Nanotechnology,* DOI: 10.1038/NNANO.2008.341.

Kates, R.W., C. Hohenemser, and J.X. Kasperson (1985) *Perilous Progress: Managing the Hazards of Technology.* Boulder: Westminster Press.

L'Oreal (2008) *Sustainability Report 2008.* Paris: L'Oreal.

Macoubrie, J. (2005) *Perceptions of Nanotechnology and Trust in Government.* Washington, DC: Project on Emerging Nanotechnologies.

Meili, C. and M. Widmer (2010) "Voluntary Measures in Nanotechnology Risk Governance: The Difficulty of Holding the Wolf by the Ears," in *International Handbook on Regulating Nanotechnologies,* edited by G.A. Hodge, D.M. Bowman, and A.D. Maynard. Cheltenham: Edward Elgar.

Miller, G. and G. Scrinis (2010) "The Role of NGOs in Governing Nanotechnologies: Challenging the 'Benefits versus Risks' Framing of Nanotech Innovation," in *International Handbook on Regulating Nanotechnologies,* edited by G.A. Hodge, D.M. Bowman, and A.D. Maynard. Cheltenham: Edward Elgar.

NanoObservatory (2009) "Societal Issues." Available at: www.observatory-nano.eu/project/catalogue/4 (accessed 10/6/2010).

National Academy of Science (2008) *Science and Decisions. Advancing Risk Assessment.* Washington, DC: National Research Council Board on Environmental Studies and Toxicology.

National Research Council of the National Academies (2008) *Public Participation in Environmental Assessment and Decision Making*. Washington, DC: The National Academies Press.

NIOSH (2009) "Approaches to Safe Nanotechnology, Managing the Health and Safety Concerns Associated with Engineered Nanomaterials," NIOSH publication no. 2009-125. Washington DC: National Institute for Occupational Safety and Health.

OECD (2002) *Guidance Document on Risk Communication for Chemical Risk Management*. Paris: Organisation for Economic Co-operation and Development.

OECD (2003) *Emerging Systemic Risks: Final Report to the OECD Futures Project*. Paris: Organisation for Economic Co-operation and Development.

OECD (2009) *Preliminary Analysis of Exposure Measurement and Exposure Mitigation in Occupational Settings: Manufactured Nanomaterials*. Paris: Organisation for Economic Co-operation and Development.

Renn, O. (2008) *Risk Governance: Coping with Uncertainties in a Complex World*. London: Earthscan.

Renn, O. and A. Grobe (2010) "Risk Governance in the Field of Nanotechnologies: Core Challenges of an Integrative Approach," in *International Handbook on Regulating Nanotechnologies*, edited by G.A. Hodge, D.M. Bowman, and A.D. Maynard. Cheltenham: Edward Elgar.

Responsible Care (2008) "Responsible Care 2008." Available at: www.econsense.de/_CSR_MITGLIEDER/_CSR_NACHHALTIGKEITSBERICHTE/images/VCI/VCI_ResponsibleCare_2008.pdf (accessed 10/6/2010).

ResponsibleNanoCode (2008) Available at: www.responsiblenanocode.org.

SCENIHR (2009) *Risk Assessment of Products of Nanotechnologies*. Brussels: Scientific Committee on Emerging and Newly Identified Health Risks.

Scheufele, D.A., E.A. Corley, T.J. Shih, K.E. Dalrymple, and S.S. Ho (2008). "Religious Beliefs and Public Attitudes toward Nanotechnology in Europe and the United States," *Nature Nanotechnology*, DOI: 10.1038/NNANO.2008.361.

Sekiya, M. (2008) "Bridging the Gap between Nanotechnology R&D." *NSTI Conference*. Boston, June 1–5, 2008.

Sekiya, M., S. Ishizu, and M. Ata (2007) "Nanotechnology and Society. Our Approach." *3rd International Symposium on Nanotechnology, Occupational and Environmental Health*. Taipei, September 1, 2007.

Stern, P.C. and V. Fineberg (1996) *Understanding Risk: Informing Decisions in a Democratic Society*. Washington, DC: National Research Council, Committee on Risk Characterization, National Academy Press.

Strange, T. and A. Bayley (2008) *Sustainable Development: Linking Economy, Society, Environment*. Paris: OECD.

VCI (2008) *Responsible Production and Use of Nanomaterials*. Frankfurt: Verband der Chemischen Industrie e.V. (German Chemical Industry Association).

Watzlawick, P., J. Beavin-Bavelas, and D.D. Jackson (1967) *Pragmatics of Human Communication—A Study of Interactional Patterns, Pathologies and Paradoxes*. New York: W.W. Norton.

Which? (2008) *Research Highlights Nano Regulation Gaps*. London: Which?

Winston, R. (2010) *Bad Ideas? An Arresting History of Our Inventions*. London: Bantam Press.

16. Risk Perception, Public Participation, and Sustainable Global Development of Nanotechnologies

Arora-Jonsson, S. (2009) "Discordant Connections: Discourses on Gender and Grassroots Activism in Two Forest Communities in India and Sweden," *Signs* 35 (Autumn): 213–40.

Bäckstrand, Karin (2003a) "Civic Science for Sustainability. Reframing the Role of Experts, Policymakers and Citizens in Environmental Governance," *Global Environmental Politics* 3 (4): 24–41.

Bäckstrand, Karin (2003b) "Precaution, Scientisation or Deliberation? Prospects for Greening and Democratizing Science," in *Liberal Environmentalism*, edited by Marcel Wissenburg and Yoram Levy. London and New York: Routledge.

Bennett, Peter and Calman, Kenneth (eds.) (2007) *Risk Communication and Public Health.* Oxford: Oxford University Press.

Cobb, M.D. and J. Macoubrie (2004) "Public Perceptions about Nanotechnology: Risks, Benefits and Trust," *Journal of Nanoparticle Research* 6 (4): 395–405.

Conti, Joseph, Terre Satterfield, and Barbara Herr Harthorn (2011) "Vulnerability and Social Justice as Factors in Emergent US Nanotechnology Risk Perceptions." *Risk Analysis.*

Corner, Adam, and Nick Pidgeon (2010) "Not Yet a Hot Topic? Affective Ambivalence and Nanotechnologies." Under review.

Dietz, Thomas, and Paul C. Stern (eds.) (2008) *Public Participation in Environmental Assessment and Decision Making.* Washington, DC: National Academies Press.

Douglas, Mary (1992) *Risk and Blame: Essays in Cultural Theory.* London: Routledge.

Engeman, Cassandra, Lynn Baumgartner, Benjamin Carr, Allison Fish, John Meyerhofer, Patricia Holden, and Barbara Herr Harthorn (2010) "Reported Practices and Perceived Risks Related to Health, Safety and Environmental Stewardship in Nanomaterials Industries." Paper presented at International Sociological Association. Gothenburg, Sweden.

Farmer, Paul (2003) *Pathologies of Power: Health, Human Rights, and the New War on the Poor.* Berkeley: University of California Press.

Freudenburg, William (1993) "Risk and Recreancy: Weber, the Division of Labour, and the Rationality of Risk Perceptions," *Social Forces* 71 (4): 909–32.

Freudenburg, William, and Mary Collins (2010) "Temporal Myopia: A Case of Promising New Technologies, the Federal Government, and Inherent Conflicts of Interest (A Study of Public–Private Partnerships)." In preparation.

Friedman, S.M. and B.P. Egolf (2005) "Nanotechnology Risks and the Media." Ieee Technology and Society Magazine 24 (4): 5–11.

Gaskell, George, *et al.* (2004) "GM Foods and the Misperception of Risk Perception." *Risk Analysis* 24 (1): 9.

Gastil, John (2008) *Political Communication and Deliberation.* Thousand Oaks, CA: Sage.

Grimshaw, David J., Jack Stilgoe, and Lawrence Gudza (2006) The Role of New Technologies in Potable Water Provision: A Stakeholder Workshop Approach Report on the Nano-Dialogues held in Harare, Zimbabwe. Practical Action.

Harthorn, Barbara Herr (2003) "Safe Exposure? Perceptions of Risks from Agricultural Chemicals among California Farmworkers," in *Risk, Culture, and Health Inequality: Shifting Perceptions of Danger and Blame*, pp. 143–64. Westport, CT: Praeger Publishers.

Harthorn, Barbara Herr, and Laury Oaks (eds.) (2003) *Risk, Culture, and Health Inequality: Shifting Perceptions of Danger and Blame.* Westport, CT: Praeger Publishers.

Harthorn, Barbara Herr, Hillary Haldane, and Karl Bryant (2006) "Risk and Responsibility: How Nanoscientists and Engineers View the Nano-enterprise." Presentation at the annual meetings of 4S (the Society for the Social Study of Science). Vancouver, Canada.

Harthorn, Barbara Herr, Jennifer Rogers, Christine Shearer, and Tyronne Martin (2011) "Debating Nanoethics: US Public Perceptions of Nanotech Applications for Energy and Environment," in *Debating Science: Deliberation, Values and the Common Good, an Anthology*, 2nd edn, edited by Dane Scott and Blake Francis. New York: Prometheus Books. Forthcoming.

Kahan, D.M. (2009) "Nanotechnology and Society: The Evolution of Risk Perceptions," *Nature Nanotechnology* 4 (11): 705–6.

Kearnes, Matthew and Brian Wynne (2007) "On Nanotechnology and Ambivalence: The Politics of Enthusiasm," *NanoEthics* 1 (2): 131–42.

Lee, Chul-Joo, Dietram A. Scheufele, and Bruce V. Lewenstein (2005) "Public Attitudes toward Emerging Technologies: Examining the Interactive Effects of Cognitions and Effect on Public Attitudes toward Nanotechnology," *Science Communication* 27 (2): 240–67.

Leiss, William and Douglas Alan Powell (2004) *Mad Cows and Mother's Milk: The Perils of Poor Risk Communication*, 2nd edn. Montreal and Ithaca, NY: McGill-Queen's University Press.

McComas, K.A., J.C. Besley, and Z. Yang (2008) "Risky Business Perceived Behavior of Local Scientists and Community Support for their Research," *Risk Analysis* 28 (6): 1539–52.

Macoubrie, Jane (2006) "Nanotechnology: Public Concerns, Reasoning and Trust in Government," *Public Understanding of Science* 15 (2): 221–41.

Ostrowski, Alexis D., Tyronne Martin, Joseph Conti, Indy Hurt, and Barbara Herr Harthorn (2008) "Nanotoxicology: Characterizing the Scientific Literature, 2000–2007," *Journal of Nanoparticle Research* 11 (2): 251–7.

Pidgeon, Nick, and Wouter Poortinga (2006) "British Public Attitudes to Agricultural Biotechnology and the 2003 GMN Nation? Public Debate: Distrust, Ambivalence and Risk," in *New Genetics, New Social Formations*, edited by P. Glasner and P. Atkinson, pp. 10–36. London: Routledge.

Pidgeon, Nick, Roger Kasperson, and Paul Slovic (eds.) (2003) *Social Amplification of Risk*. Cambridge: Cambridge University Press.

Pidgeon, Nick, Barbara Herr Harthorn, Karl Bryant, and Tee Rogers-Hayden (2009) "Deliberating the Risks of Nanotechnologies for Energy and Health Applications in the United States and United Kingdom," *Nature Nanotechnology* 4 (4): 95–8.

Pidgeon, Nick, W. Poortinga, G. Rowe, T. Horlick-Jones, J. Walls, and T. O'Riordan (2005) "Using Surveys in Public Participation Processes for Risk Decision Making: The Case of the 2003 British GM Nation? Public Debate," *Risk Analysis* 25 (2): 467–79.

Satterfield, Terre A., C.K. Mertz, and Paul Slovic (2004) "Discrimination, Vulnerability, and Justice in the Face of Risk," *Risk Analysis* 24 (1): 115–29.

Satterfield, Terre, Joseph Conti, Anton Pitts, Barbara Herr Harthorn, and Nick Pidgeon (2011) "Early Warnings Across Malleable Perceptions of Nanotechnologies: Risk, Benefit, Betrayal and Trust." Under review.

Satterfield, T., Milind Kandlikar, Christian Beaudrie, Joseph Conti, and Barbara Herr Harthorn (2009) "Anticipating the Perceived Risk of Nanotechnologies," *Nature Nanotechnology* 4 (11): 752–8.

Scheufele, Dietram A., Elizabeth A. Corley, Sharon Dunwoody, Teung-Jen Shih, Elliott Hillback, and David H. Guston (2007) "Scientists Worry about some Risks more than the Public," *Nature Nanotechnology* 2 (12): 732–4.

Siegrist, Michael (2008) "Factors Influencing Public Acceptance of Innovative Food Technologies and Products," *Trends in Food Science and Technology* 19 (11): 5.

Siegrist, M., Marie-Eve Cousin, Hans Kastenholz, and Arnim Wiek (2007a) "Public Acceptance of Nanotechnology Foods and Food Packaging: The Influence of Affect and Trust," *Appetite* 49 (2): 459–66.

Siegrist, Michael, Arnim Wiek, Asgeir Helland, and Hans Kastenholz (2007b) "Risks and Nanotechnology: the Public is More Concerned than Experts and Industry," *Nature Nanotechnology* 2: 67.

Slovic, Paul (2000) *The Perception of Risk.* London: Earthscan.

Weaver, David, and Bruce Bimber (2008) "Finding News Stories: A Comparison of Searches using Lexis Nexis and Google News," *Journalism and Mass Communication Quarterly* 83 (3): 515–30.

Weaver, David, Erica Lively, and Bruce Bimber (2009) "Searching for a Frame: Media tell the Story of Technological Progress, Risk and Regulation in the Case of Nanotechnology," *Science Communication* 31 (2): 139–66.

17. Global Governance of Emerging Technologies

Barker, T., M.L. Lesnick, T. Mealey, R. Raimond, S. Walker, D. Rejeski, and L. Timberlake (2005) *Nanotechnology and the Poor: Opportunities and Risks—Closing the Gaps Within and Between Sectors of Society.* Washington, DC: Meridian Institute. Available at: www.docstoc.com/docs/1047276/NANOTECHNOLOGY-and-the-POOR.

Bello, Mark Summer (2007) "NanoFrontiers: Nanotechnology and Low-Income Nations," WWCS, Washington, DC.

Bürgi, Birgit R. and T. Pradeep (2006) "Societal Implications of Nanoscience and Nanotechnology in Developing Countries," *Current Science*, 90 (5).

Kay, L. and P. Shapira (2009) "Developing Nanotechnology in Latin America," *J. Nanopart. R es.* 11: 259–78.

National Science Foundation (NSF) (2004) *Report: International Dialogue on Responsible Research and Development of Nanotechnology.* Washington, DC: Meridian Institute. Available at: www.nsf.gov/crssprgm/nano/activities/dialog.jsp.

Renn, O. and M.C. Roco (2006) "White Paper on Nanotechnology Risk Governance." Geneva, Switzerland: International Risk Governance Council (IRGC). Available at: www.irgc.org/Publications.

Roco, M.C. (2001) "International Strategy for Nanotechnology Research," *J. Nanopart. Res.* 3 (5–6): 353–60.

Roco, M.C. (2008) "Possibilities for Global Governance of Converging Technologies," *J. Nanopart. Res.* 10 (1): 11–29.

Roco, M.C. and W.S. Bainbridge (eds) (2003) *Converging Technologies for Improving Human Performance.* Boston: Springer.

Roco, M.C. C.A. Mirkin, and M.C. Hersam (eds.) (2010) "Nanotechnology Research Directions for Societal Needs in 2020," NSF/WTEC report, Springer, 2010 (see Chapter 13) (called "Nano2").

Roco, M.C., R.S. Williams, and P. Alivisatos (eds.) (1999) *Nanotechnology Research D irections: Vision for Nanotechnology R&D in the Next Decade.* Washington, DC: NSTC; and Springer [2000]. Available at: www.nano.gov/html/res/pubs.html.

Salamanca-Buentello, Fabio, Deepa L. Persad, Erin B. Court, Douglas K. Martin, Abdallah S. Daar, and Peter A. Singer (2005) "Nanotechnology and the Developing World," *PLoS Medicine* 2 (5): e97.

Varmus, H., R. Klausner, E. Zerhouni, *et al.* (2003) "Grand Challenges in Global Health," *Science* 302: 398–9.

INDEX

Notes: The following abbreviations have been used – f = figure; n = note; t = table